PROFESSIONAL CROSS-PLATFORM MOBILE DEVELOPMENT IN C#

PROFESSIONAL

Cross-Platform Mobile Development in C#

Scott Olson
John Hunter
Ben Horgen
Kenny Goers

John Wiley & Sons, Inc.

Professional Cross-Platform Mobile Development in C#

Published by
John Wiley & Sons, Inc.
10475 Crosspoint Boulevard
Indianapolis, IN 46256
www.wiley.com

Published by John Wiley & Sons, Inc., Indianapolis, Indiana

Published simultaneously in Canada

ISBN: 978-1-118-15770-1
ISBN: 978-1-118-22603-2 (ebk)
ISBN: 978-1-118-23942-1 (ebk)
ISBN: 978-1-118-26400-3 (ebk)

Manufactured in the United States of America

10 9 8 7 6 5 4 3 2 1

Library of Congress Control Number: 2011945557

To my wife Michelle, for finding her way
to love a geek like me.

— Scott Olson

To my family and friends, for their support and dedication without which this wouldn't have been possible.

— John Hunter

This book is dedicated to my wife Alisha Horgen whose support through my career, and this writing process, has been instrumental in helping me reach success often and rebound faster after failures. To a best friend, Ben Meister, who early in life taught me how to crack open a computer and dive into how it works. To my father Paul Horgen for teaching me the value in making reading a priority; and to my mother Betty Horgen who introduced me to Jesus Christ.

— Ben Horgen

To my girlfriend Tricia, for putting up with late nights, offering encouragement and picking up my slack throughout the course of the book; to my parents, for giving me my work ethic and determination; and to my children for keeping me on my toes.

— Kenny Goers

ABOUT THE TECHNICAL EDITORS

ARIC AUNE has worked in the consumer packaged goods and retail industries for the past 14 years, focusing primarily on marketing, web applications, and mobile systems. In addition to his work on application architecture and design, Aric actively works to evangelize Agile development principles in the organizations he works for. He has an MBA from the Carlson School of Management and is a Certified Scrum Master (CSM) and Certified Scrum Developer (CSD). When not playing with technology, Aric enjoys playing with his three children. He lives in Minnetonka, MN.

PETER ERICKSEN has designed and developed enterprise systems in the education, communications, and healthcare industries for more than 16 years. When he is not developing mobile systems for Fortune 500 firms, he is a contributing writer for *iPhone Life* magazine and a consulting iOS and Android game developer. He lives in Saint Paul, MN, with his wife and two children.

ABOUT THE AUTHORS

SCOTT OLSON has spent the past 18 years building software and advising clients on the potential of software and mobility. He is a contributing writer for *iPhone Life* magazine and technical editor of *iPad in the Enterprise: Developing and Deploying Business Applications*. He leads the development team at ITR Mobility. Throughout his career, Scott has worked with many of the Fortune 500 companies including Best Buy, Target Corporation, Medtronic, and Prudential Financial. He believes that what is happening in the mobile software industry today will change the way people write and use software. He lives in Hudson, WI, with his wife Michelle and his three children: Samantha, Trevor, and Soren.

JOHN HUNTER has spent the past 23 years building software and advising clients on software architecture and capabilities. He is a lead consulting architect for the development team at ITR Mobility, and throughout his career has worked with many of the Fortune 500 companies including 3M, Allianz, CHS, Medtronic, and Best Buy. He believes that to plan for the future people must keep their heads in the clouds and their feet firmly on the ground, and with mobility, people can do both. He lives in Bloomington, MN, way too close to the Mall of America....

BEN HORGEN is the lead technical analyst for Mobile Applications at Ameriprise Financial. He has a decade of experience architecting software for a wide range of mobile platforms. A majority of his career has been spent writing firmware and SDK interfaces for emerging mobile devices. Ben has a passion for embedded hardware and the challenges that accompany software development for mobile computing platforms. You can contact him at ben@benhorgen.com.

KENNY GOERS has been working with mobile platforms since 1998; previous to that he worked on Cray supercomputer and mainframe operating system kernels. He has worked with Windows CE, Windows Mobile, Windows Phone, iPhones, iPads, and Android phones and tablets in both their native development languages and Mono extensively. He is a contributor to a few open source Mono projects. He is a mentor for Simley High School's robotics team and is also a marginal ice hockey player. Currently he is a mobile architect with ITR Mobility. He lives in West Saint Paul, MN, with his girlfriend Tricia Curry and five children: Kat, Joshua, Maggie, Sam, and Sarah.

CREDITS

ACQUISITIONS EDITOR
Mary James

PROJECT EDITOR
Linda Harrison

TECHNICAL EDITORS
Aric Aune
Peter Ericksen

PRODUCTION EDITOR
Rebecca Anderson

COPY EDITOR
Apostrophe Editing Services

EDITORIAL MANAGER
Mary Beth Wakefield

FREELANCER EDITORIAL MANAGER
Rosemarie Graham

ASSOCIATE DIRECTOR OF MARKETING
David Mayhew

MARKETING MANAGER
Ashley Zurcher

BUSINESS MANAGER
Amy Knies

PRODUCTION MANAGER
Tim Tate

VICE PRESIDENT AND EXECUTIVE GROUP PUBLISHER
Richard Swadley

VICE PRESIDENT AND EXECUTIVE PUBLISHER
Neil Edde

ASSOCIATE PUBLISHER
Jim Minatel

PROJECT COORDINATOR, COVER
Katie Crocker

PROOFREADER
Scott Klemp, Word One New York
James Saturnio, Word One New York

INDEXER
J&J Indexing

COVER DESIGNER
Ryan Sneed

COVER IMAGE
© maxuser / iStockPhoto

ACKNOWLEDGMENTS

THE KNOWLEDGE, CODE, AND INSIGHTS passed on in this book were developed and tested in an ecosystem composed of passionate developers from multiple locations and organizations. This book would not have been possible without the distinct and diverse talents of all those involved.

Special thanks to Peter Ericksen and Aric Aune for keeping us honest in our technical discussions. Your diligent attention to detail has made this book something of which we can all be extremely proud.

An extra special "thank you" to our families for their support and encouragement throughout the long nights and weekends while we were working on this project.

Thank you to the rest of the dedicated propeller heads who weren't afraid to dream and create with us; there are more of you than we can possibly thank individually, but you know who you are. To name just a few, in no particular order: Nathan Clevenger, Sam Lippert, Jonathan Bruns, Brian Koehler, Brian Porter, Boris Momtchev, Naveed Ahmed, Stuart Dahlberg, Joe Sauve, Garrett Woodford, and the rest of ITR Mobility's iFactr development team; Tim Gergen, Ben Butzer, Dan Lamppa, Dean Gahlon, Jessica Knutson, Kelli Swanson, Christian Antoine, Mike Long, Priya Kurra, Carrie Kuckler, Jeff Bipes, Andrew Mogren, Kevin Pecore, Tom Jones, Jim Mettling, and the rest of the Field Services Team at Medtronic; Bob Gilman, Carlos Eberhart, Ari Olson, Pat Galligan, and the rest of Target Corporation's Mobile Forward team. Each of you has been extremely generous in sharing your challenges, experiences, and expertise with us.

Finally, a huge thank you to Nat Friedman, Miguel de Icaza, the team at Xamarin, and the Mono open source community around the world for your vision, determination, and dedication creating the technology that makes it possible for us to write the best mobile apps on the planet using the technology we love!

CONTENTS

INTRODUCTION

PEOPLE TAKE UP MOBILE DEVELOPMENT these days for a lot of reasons. For some it is all about learning something new, but for many it comes out of necessity of a job or career. Perhaps you see mobile development as the next big thing, just like client-server development was in the 1990s, or web development became in the 2000s. Maybe you've been asked to learn more about mobile development techniques and technologies to make a recommendation to your boss for an approach to get your company started building mobile applications. Or you might be an independent software consultant who's feeling the demand for mobile software and is responding to the demand by learning the skills you need to stay ahead of the technology curve and deliver solutions to your customers.

Whatever your reason for picking up this book, thank you — and congratulations! Whether this is your first foray into mobile development or you've been writing mobile applications for years, you've just taken the first step on a journey that can be both technically challenging and tremendously rewarding. The technologies and techniques in this book can give you an edge over your competition. You then can speak authoritatively about mobile software best practices and proven enterprise mobility techniques wrought from years of experience. You can be confident recommending an approach for mobile development to your organization that can provide flexibility across mobile platforms and architectures. You can be the hero who puts your company on a path that is optimized for future changes in the marketplace — one that can result in savings of both time and money by leveraging your existing skills in .NET and C# development. This book gives you everything you need to catch the wave. Join us on the incredible ride that's only just beginning in mobile application development!

WHO THIS BOOK IS FOR

This book is written by professional developers for professional developers. It is not a book about technology for technology's sake. The approaches outlined in this book, whether around choosing a mobile architecture, designing your user experience, or coding for reuse across platforms, come out of our experiences as professional developers in an enterprise setting. Solving the real-world business and technical problems facing companies across industries is the primary purpose of the material in this book.

This book is for experienced developers who are proficient in the .NET Framework and the C# language. The concepts and examples provided in this book require a fundamental knowledge of object-oriented principles and software design patterns. You don't need to know anything about mobile development. A basic understanding of the principles of layered architectures and the Model-View-Controller pattern is all you need. If you've ever written a web application using ASP.NET, you probably have the knowledge necessary to succeed with this book. You learn how to translate that skill and knowledge to become proficient at mobile development. With a little study and determination, you can lead your organization into the world of mobile apps!

WHAT THIS BOOK COVERS

This book covers everything you need to know to build enterprise mobile applications in C# that can be delivered on all the major mobile platforms in the market today. You build applications that share code on native iPad, iPhone, Android, Windows Phone, and the mobile web. You learn about the chief technical considerations to take into account when building mobile applications, such as user experience, device access, and disconnected capabilities. Security and deployment needs are also considered, all with an eye toward helping you start coding. You learn what questions to ask when deciding whether to build for the mobile web and native platforms or to use a hybrid approach. You learn the design and prototyping techniques necessary to take advantage of the unique interfaces and form-factors available on modern mobile devices and how to translate that into working applications. You code real-world examples and deploy them across platforms, all from a single code base. Mobile data services design and consumption, data synchronization, device utilities, and accessing device functionality are all covered in depth, as are hybrid development techniques and ways to extend your application to the desktop using thick client, web, or cloud approaches. This book contains all the essentials of cross-platform mobile development.

HOW THIS BOOK IS STRUCTURED

Part I, "Mobile Development Overview," covers the architecture and design phases. Chapter 1, "Choosing the Right Architecture," covers the essentials of mobile application architecture and many of the considerations you need to discuss when settling on an approach for your application. Chapter 2, "Designing Your User Experience," covers designing your user experience using proven design and prototyping methods specifically geared toward mobile application usability and mobile device usage. The content included in this part is an essential component to succeed in mobile application development. You may be tempted to skip this section and get right to the code examples in Part II, but you should give Part I due attention. It can pay off when you get to the subsequent examples.

Part II, "Developing Cross-Platform Applications," covers the nuts and bolts of cross-platform development using C# and .NET following a logical progression. You learn everything you need to know to set up your development environment in Chapter 3, "Setting Up Your Development Environment." Chapter 4, "The MonoCross Pattern," introduces the MonoCross pattern and outlines the rationale behind the design of the framework to orient you for the following examples. In Chapter 5, "Building Shared Applications," you build your first cross-platform application. It's a simple example that illustrates all the key concepts you need to work with to be successful with the MonoCross pattern.

In Chapter 6, "Building MonoCross Containers," you build your user interfaces and deploy your application to multiple platforms, and you begin to see the power of the MonoCross pattern. Chapter 7, "Designing and Building Data Services," covers mobile data services design, and Chapter 8, "Consuming Data Services," shows you how to consume those services from your application on the device.

Chapter 9, "Accessing the Device," and Chapter 10, "Using MonoCross Utilities," cover accessing the resources and features on the device using the MonoCross Utilities and native device APIs. Chapter 11, "Hybrid Applications," brings it all together with advanced techniques to deliver hybrid applications taking advantage of both native and web-based techniques from a single application architecture. Finally, Chapter 12, "Delivering Applications to the Enterprise," shows you how you can take your application to the enterprise desktop and presents advanced techniques for extending your cross-platform development strategy using view abstraction and mixed view models.

WHAT YOU NEED TO USE THIS BOOK

If you're an experienced .NET/C# developer, most of the code in this book can be written, tested, and deployed using the tools and frameworks you're already familiar with. You can write all the code samples discussed in this book using Microsoft Visual Studio, and you can compile, test, and run all but the iOS samples using the Visual Studio IDE as well. The iOS samples require the MonoDevelop IDE (a free download) and a MacBook or other Apple computer to compile and run.

Beyond the latest version of the Microsoft .NET Framework, you need the latest iOS SDK from Apple, Android SDK from Google, and Windows Phone SDK from Microsoft. All are free downloads.

You also need to install MonoTouch and Mono for Android from Xamarin. Both products offer a free, fully functional trial version from the Xamarin website at `http://xamarin.com`. The only limitation on the trial versions is that they run only in the iOS simulator and Android emulator, respectively. You need to purchase a license if you want to deploy your application to a device.

Chapter 3 covers the details on everything you need to set up your development environment, so check out the details there as well.

CONVENTIONS

To help you get the most from the text and keep track of what's happening, this book uses a number of conventions.

- We *highlight* new terms and important words when we introduce them.
- We show keyboard strokes like this: Ctrl+A.
- We show filenames, URLs, and code within the text like so: `http://monocross.net`.

We present code in two different ways:

```
We use a Monofont type with no highlighting for most code examples.
We use Bold to emphasize code that is particularly important in the present context
or to show changes from a previous code snippet.
```

SOURCE CODE

As you work through the examples in this book, you may choose either to type in all the code manually or to use the source code files that accompany the book. All the source code used in this book is available for download at `www.wrox.com`. When at the site, simply locate the book's title (use the Search box or one of the title lists) and click the Download Code link on the book's detail page to obtain all the source code for the book. Code included on the website is highlighted by the following icon:

Available for download on Wrox.com

Listings include the filename in the title. This book provides a structure for storing the code that appears in a code note such as this:

Found in the MonoCross.Navigation/MXView.cs file of the download

Because many books have similar titles, you may find it easiest to search by ISBN; this book's ISBN is 978-1-118-15770-1.

After you download the code, just decompress it with your favorite compression tool. Alternatively, you can go to the main Wrox code download page at `www.wrox.com/dynamic/books/download.aspx` to see the code available for this book and all other Wrox books.

ERRATA

We make every effort to ensure that there are no errors in the text or in the code. However, no one is perfect, and mistakes do occur. If you find an error in one of our books, such as a spelling mistake or faulty piece of code, we would be grateful for your feedback. By sending in errata, you may save another reader hours of frustration, and at the same time, you can help provide even higher quality information.

To find the errata page for this book, go to `www.wrox.com` and locate the title using the Search box or selecting one of the title lists. Then, on the book details page, click the Book Errata link. On this page, you can view all errata that have been submitted for this book and posted by Wrox editors. A complete book list, including links to each book's errata, is also available at `www.wrox.com/misc-pages/booklist.shtml`.

If you don't spot "your" error on the Book Errata page, go to `www.wrox.com/contact/techsupport.shtml` and complete the form there to send us the error you have found. We'll check the information and, if appropriate, post a message to the book's errata page and fix the problem in subsequent editions of the book.

P2P.WROX.COM

For author and peer discussion, join the P2P forums at `p2p.wrox.com`. The forums are a web-based system for you to post messages relating to Wrox books and related technologies and interact with other readers and technology users. The forums offer a subscription feature to e-mail you topics of interest of your choosing when new posts are made to the forums. Wrox authors, editors, other industry experts, and your fellow readers are present on these forums.

At `p2p.wrox.com`, you can find a number of different forums to help you, not only as you read this book, but also as you develop your own applications. To join the forums, just follow these steps:

1. Go to `p2p.wrox.com` and click the Register link.
2. Read the terms of use and click Agree.
3. Complete the required information to join, as well as any optional information you want to provide, and click Submit.
4. You will receive an e-mail with information describing how to verify your account and complete the joining process.

You can read messages in the forums without joining P2P, but to post your own messages, you must join.

After you join, you can post new messages and respond to messages other users post. You can read messages at any time on the web. If you would like to have new messages from a particular forum e-mailed to you, click the Subscribe to this Forum icon by the forum name in the forum listing.

For more information about how to use the Wrox P2P, be sure to read the P2P FAQs for answers to questions about how the forum software works, as well as many common questions specific to P2P and Wrox books. To read the FAQs, click the FAQ link on any P2P page.

INTRODUCTION TO THE MOBILE DEVELOPMENT LANDSCAPE

IN JUNE 2007, APPLE INTRODUCED the iPhone. There was no SDK. There was no App Store. Mobile development, particularly in the enterprise, was done mostly on rugged Windows Mobile devices or Palm devices provided by the company to the users that needed them to do their jobs. The applications weren't glamorous, but they got the job done, and the centrally provisioned model of device and application distribution worked well. The iPhone hit the market with little notice in business circles. It was just another consumer device — a novelty more than anything.

In summer 2008, Apple launched the iPhone 3G and with it the App Store. On that first day you could download any of the 500 available apps using your iTunes account and your existing credit card. Within 3 days there were 800 apps available, with more than 10 million downloads! The iPhone quickly became *the device* to have, and "there's an app for that" entered our popular lexicon. But Apple wouldn't be the only game in town for long.

By August 2008, Google announced the Android Market. By summer 2010 there were 80,000 apps in the Market, with 1 billion downloads! But Apple wasn't ceding any ground; by then the App Store had 225,000 apps and 5 billion downloads. The mobile app wars were now in full force; and one more player wanted in.

Microsoft launched Windows Phone 7 in October 2010, including the Windows Phone Marketplace, and the Windows Phone SDK. By July 2011, Windows Phone users could choose from 26,000 apps available in the Marketplace.

Take a look at those names again: Apple, Google, and Microsoft — arguably the three biggest players in the software industry duking it out over the mobile device and application market. Surely they see an opportunity here. That opportunity was made clear in summer 2011, when Chetan Sharma Consulting released its Global Mobile Industry report, which stated the expected global revenue in the mobile industry would reach $1.3 trillion — that is a national debt-sized number.

To put that into perspective, The International Monetary Fund estimates the economy of Canada at $1.6 trillion in 2011. India comes in at $1.5, and at $1.3 trillion the global mobile industry is $100 billion larger than the economy of Australia. In July 2011, ReadWriteWeb estimated that the mobile industry now represents 2 percent of the world's gross domestic product. No wonder the three largest players in the software industry are making a play for the market.

In 1997, Harvard Business School professor Clayton Christiansen wrote *The Innovator's Dilemma*; in it he describes what he calls disruptive innovation. Disruptive innovation is the tendency for new technologies to be disruptive in the market, often in ways the market doesn't expect. He describes how this type of innovation creates disruption through technology displacement, where new technologies emerge to create a new market and value network that eventually displaces an existing market and value network.

For example, consider the personal photography industry. Eastman Kodak pioneered personal photography 100 years ago, which remained unchanged for most of its history. You would purchase a roll of film and load it into your camera. The film was relatively expensive, and you could use it only once. After you snapped your shots, you had to take the film to a photo processor, where you paid even more money to have your photos processed. Only when they came back from processing — in as little as 1 hour, but more often 1 to 2 days — did you know which shots turned out, and which didn't. It was often a disappointing exercise, and the whole process was rather inconvenient. But it was the available technology, and there were no forces in the market driving any innovation — until the first digital cameras hit the market. At first, digital cameras weren't good; the images were poor quality, and the memory was expensive. Despite these shortcomings, the cameras served a segment of the market just fine, and as the technology improved, this segment grew. Image quality improved, memory cards became less expensive, and people began to see the value in this new technology. No photo processing was required. Newer cameras included a small screen on the back that allowed you to see your photos immediately, and you could delete the ones you didn't like. When your memory card filled up, you could download the images to your computer, where you could print your own copies, or even share them online with friends and family. Plus you could reuse your memory to take more photos to add to your collection later. Software such as Adobe Photoshop enabled you to fix lighting and exposure problems that you would have been stuck with using film.

Digital photography put the full process into the consumer's hands and created a new convenience value network that overtook the old. Eastman Kodak had to fight for survival as people abandoned film photography in mass. Businesses that were built around photo processing disappeared as the disruption progressed, and the ones that did survive had to reinvent their value propositions to account for the paradigm shift to digital photography.

This same kind of disruption is happening today in the mobile industry. Smartphone and tablet devices are displacing PCs and laptops. Wireless networks are becoming more ubiquitous and accessible, with the competition between providers driving the cost of access down. People are buying and using these smaller devices and greater connectivity in ways never dreamed possible only a few years ago, and the disruption is all about the apps. You can find a restaurant nearby and get turn-by-turn directions from your smartphone. You can place a bid for an item on eBay and monitor the auction while you're on the go. You can track a FedEx package when you win the auction and have the item shipped. You can even make a claim on your auto insurance, complete with pictures of the damage and the precise location of the accident using the geo-location functions on your phone. There are mobile applications for just about anything you can dream of. The bar has been raised on consumer expectations, and consumers bring those expectations to work.

We live in a remarkable time in software development. The emergence of smartphones in recent years and the proliferation of mobile applications have had a profound effect on the way people write and use software. In the enterprise, this trend creates turmoil for the IT department, with more and more employees bringing their own devices to work and demanding support to do their jobs. The consumerization of IT is driving the adoption of multiple devices in the formerly homogenous world of enterprise mobility. IT can no longer dictate device choice, and the disruption caused by this shift is driving the need for cross-platform mobile development. Business leaders are responding to this disruption in unconventional ways. The barriers to entry into mobile development are low; it costs only $99 to join the Apple iOS developer program and $25 to sign up for the Android program. Cloud computing and the virtualization of IT as a commodity through services such as Amazon Elastic Cloud and Windows Azure enable rapid and inexpensive provisioning of infrastructure to support any online requirements of your mobile application. Using these technologies, corporate department heads can circumvent IT to develop their own applications to respond to consumer demand and competitive pressures. The demand for mobile applications continues to grow, and IT departments need to develop creative ways to support this demand. They need to support multiple device platforms and respond to new devices as they emerge in the marketplace. So how can you as C# developers take advantage of this disruption to help bring your organizations and your applications into this new world order?

The first opportunity is in technology standardization. Hundreds of large enterprises with thousands of developers have invested heavily in C# and .NET. Add the Mono technologies to the equation, and now these developers can bring their skills and talent to the mobile world with MonoTouch and Mono for Android. All your enterprise applications can be standardized on a single technology stack enabling organizations to deliver functionality efficiently to multiple platforms.

The second opportunity is code portability. By standardizing on C# and .NET, enterprises can leverage their existing investment in these technologies to bring existing functionality to these new platforms. Enterprise software modules that already exist and provide a cross-platform service, such as a single-sign-on, can be ported with little effort, saving development time and money. The business logic in existing applications can be reused, and moved into your mobile applications without the need to rewrite it in a different language. You can even port code from your client application to the server and back again if your application needs changes.

The third opportunity is cross-platform support. You can write your applications once and deploy them to multiple platforms with little or no modification. You can deploy a single application to an iPad and an Android smartphone. If you later decide you need to deliver that application via the Web, you can deploy it to the server. If a new device hits the market, you can bring your application to it with minimal effort. And, you can support the consumerization of IT by offering a version for your users that matches their device choice.

Now you may think this all sounds great, but do you wonder whether it is for real? It is. Scores of enterprise clients in dozens of industries have realized these benefits. The patterns and techniques in this book are currently in place at seven of the Fortune 500, including the largest iPad deployment of 2010, "The Year of the iPad."

The MonoCross pattern introduced in this book is the foundation of those implementations and is based on mobile and software industry best practices. You learn how to choose the right architecture for your application by considering the key areas of mobile enterprise development. You learn techniques to optimize your user experience design to maximize adoption of your application by your users. You learn how the MonoCross Model-View-Controller pattern enables you to share your business logic and data access code, while optimizing your presentation for the devices you target. You learn how to write and consume data services in a mobile application and how to handle synchronization of data from the device to the server, even when your device is disconnected. You learn techniques for building native applications, web applications, and applications across the web/native hybrid spectrum, including techniques for code portability. Finally, you learn how to take your application to the next level and deliver it to the enterprise using techniques such as view abstraction and the mixed view model.

So start coding now!

PART I
Mobile Development Overview

1

Choosing the Right Architecture

WHAT'S IN THIS CHAPTER?

- Recognizing mobile development challenges
- Evaluating mobile architectures
- Developing for multiple platforms

Enterprise development is changing. If you are like most of the developers we talk to at our corporate clients, you've probably been asked to evaluate one or more mobile development platforms. You may even have been asked to write an application — probably on short notice — to support some business unit or executive who decided your organization needs a mobile application — and needs it now.

Mobile development is different from other areas of enterprise development. You need to have a clear understanding of the challenges that are unique to mobile development, particularly cross-platform mobile development. In this chapter you explore some of the architectural considerations any enterprise developer should think about when making the transition to building mobile applications. You explore (at a high-level) the technical aspects of mobile development, including device connectivity, storage and processor limitations, application deployment, and more. The goal of the discussion is to help guide you down a path to implement a cross-platform mobile architecture that works best for your organization. Each environment is different, and yours is no exception. Making architecture decisions is always a game of trade-offs. This chapter helps you on that journey into mobility and mobile software.

UNDERSTANDING MOBILE ARCHITECTURE

For software developers, designing and implementing good application architecture is paramount to success. Enterprise software architecture activities must take into consideration myriad concerns when choosing an approach: everything from technology standards to deployment options, potential user profiles, expected user loads — and don't forget scalability, extendibility, and maintainability. Software application architecture is ultimately a game of trade-offs between all these considerations. You often must compromise in one area to accommodate another to arrive at a workable solution. Three considerations may be unfamiliar to most enterprise architects, which represent the most important points to evaluate when architecting mobile applications.

The first consideration is connectivity. Mobile applications are, by definition, mobile. When users carry a device with them wherever they go, there are times, sometimes frequently, when they have no connection. Wireless technologies have come a long way in recent years, but "always connected" is still not a reality. The best you can expect is "usually connected," meaning more often than not users have a network connection. However, your specific situation may vary greatly depending on the application and the profile of your users.

Mobile devices also exist largely outside of the corporate network, while many enterprise applications are maintained behind the corporate firewall. If you expect mobile users to access your application using their existing cellular service, you'll need to expose your application outside the Local Area Network. Although most enterprises have already addressed this requirement via enterprise web applications, it may present a challenge for mobile applications. If enterprise web applications are for internal use only, the infrastructure to support connectivity over the Internet may not exist, and will need to be procured and configured.

The second consideration is device access. Modern smartphones and tablets have some whiz-bang features that make mobile applications uniquely useful, and fun to write! Geo-location services enable "find near me" features or geo-fencing; accelerometers and gyroscopes enable you to create motion-sensitive applications. Still and video cameras, audio recording and playback, and interactive touch screens can make for fully-immersive multimedia experiences.

Finally, the third — and perhaps the most important consideration — is usability. The smaller form-factors and multitouch interfaces of modern mobile devices represent a shift in user interface design for most enterprise architects. User experience in traditional enterprise applications is often an afterthought — if it's even thought of at all. Mobile applications require a more thoughtful approach, and your design should reflect the best-of-breed applications available in the various mobile app stores.

You should keep these three considerations in mind when evaluating a mobile architecture on other dimensions. These three items represent the most critical points of any evaluation and should take precedence wherever possible to enable a workable mobile architecture. You may decide to compromise on one of these three items for a legitimate architectural reason, but you should be particularly thoughtful when making such a compromise. Understanding the implications of such a decision can mean the difference between success and failure.

Now that you have a better understanding of mobile application architecture, following are some additional considerations that can help you design a solid mobile architecture for your applications.

Connecting to the Network

As mentioned previously, network connectivity is one of the most important considerations when designing a mobile application. Most enterprises have wireless connection options while on premises and offer access to company information via isolated, secure WiFi hotspots. This approach offers a great option for mobile users while they're in the office and may be adequate for many internal applications. This scenario represents the closest achievable approximation of an "always connected" state and can offer great flexibility for your proprietary enterprise mobile applications.

However, more often than not, you face situations that require mobile users to access corporate information and run their applications from outside the tightly controlled and security-minded enterprise wireless network. Mobile users don't just want access to information from the office; they want it at home, in the car, or on the train. They want it when and where they want it; and they expect it to work on their terms. This often represents a significant challenge for any organization when mobilizing its workforce.

This "work from anywhere" attitude requires a mobile enterprise to provide functionality over less-than-reliable public networks. When you make the decision to support this capability, it prompts many more questions regarding what information you can or should provide on the device and what functionality you need in a disconnected state.

For applications that primarily deliver information (that is, executive dashboards, product catalogs, sales brochures), you can use data-caching schemes to maximize the amount of work that a user can complete while disconnected, but if your application requires any transaction processing (for example, field product sales or inventory management), providing disconnected capability is more complex. Users often need to queue transactions on the device for processing at a later time, which may or may not be an acceptable trade-off.

Recognizing Storage and Processor Limitations

The mobile devices of today have come a long way in terms of processing power and storage. Moore's Law remains in effect, and we all benefit from the incredible power available in the palm of our hands. But mobile devices are still resource-constrained when compared to the increasingly scalable cloud environments in place at most large companies.

This constraint becomes an especially important consideration when evaluating application data and data services. Most organizations take a decidedly "outside-in" perspective for enterprise data. Enterprise data services tend to package and present information in ways that closely mirror the back-end data store where the information resides. The ubiquity of relational database systems resulted in service-oriented architectures that deliver information in a highly normalized fashion. Multiple service calls piece together a clear representation of the data required for the application to function. This can result in placing an undue processing load on the device, which can severely impact performance and usability.

Another unfortunate side effect of the easy availability of storage on enterprise servers and desktops is the structure of the presented data. Most enterprise data services use XML, and a majority of those use SOAP to deliver information. XML is a notoriously verbose way to represent data, and many back-end systems use highly descriptive names for the presented data elements. Couple this verbosity with the additional overhead of a SOAP envelope, and storage resources on a mobile device can quickly become overwhelmed, especially when working with large data sets.

To mitigate this risk, you should be diligent about providing the correct amount of information to the device only at the time it is needed. Think carefully about what the user needs to see. Scrolling through a list of 5,000 customers is not a good mobile experience, so think of ways you can partition or filter this information to present it in smaller chunks. Setting up a workflow that organizes customers by country, region, state, and city may result in a few more touches than delivering the entire list at once, but the additional touches might also result in a more responsive application with a smaller resource footprint.

Securing Data on the Device

Consider three areas for data security in your mobile applications: authentication and authorization, data encryption, and data destruction if a device is compromised.

Authentication and Authorization

You can currently accomplish authentication and authorization in most large organizations using an implementation of the Lightweight Directory Access Protocol (LDAP), such as Active Directory. These mechanisms can provide seamless authentication services across applications, but most mobile development platforms lack integration with them, so you need to plan to develop your own authentication scheme to manage access to corporate information.

By taking advantage of unifying technologies, such as Mono, you can create cross-platform single-sign-on (SSO) modules to drop wholesale into your various mobile applications to provide this service. You can standardize authentication using traditional username/password, or RSA hard or soft tokens. You can then embed a token in the header of your service requests, where it is subject to SSL encryption over the wire. You can set these tokens to expire at various intervals to ensure appropriate security and require re-authorization on a periodic basis. Implementing a unified SSO approach in your applications and associated data services is a significant investment in your mobile application strategy, but when correctly done can pay dividends in future development efforts as your mobile application portfolio grows.

Data Encryption

Think of data encryption from two perspectives when designing a mobile architecture: communication encryption and encryption of data at-rest.

To enable communication encryption, various SSL and VPN options are available out-of-the-box with most commercial hosting vendors and services platforms, ensuring a level of encryption adequate for most situations. In addition, most enterprise development platforms, including .NET and Mono, offer flexible cryptography APIs that support the latest algorithms, such as AES256, enabling you to double-encrypt information shared between the device and server if you deem that level of security necessary.

You can use these same cryptography libraries to provide software-level encryption of any data to be cached or stored on the device. Some vendors offer additional encryption capabilities. Apple, for example, offers data protection services in iOS that use a combination of the device passcode and hardware-level encryption to provide a strong key. You should explore implementations that take advantage of these features wherever possible, while maintaining a balanced approach and common security API across applications and platforms.

Data Destruction

Traditionally, enterprises have managed data destruction using device-centric approaches. Mobile device management vendors provide the means to wipe all the data on a compromised device.

Unfortunately, in an increasingly consumer-centric IT environment, bring-your-own-device (BYOD) is becoming more prevalent. This BYOD approach results in a conundrum for many organizations with respect to mobile application security architecture.

The simplest way to handle security is to require the user to accept data destruction as a condition for using enterprise applications on a personal device. The user accepts any liability for loss of information due to a lost or stolen device and must sign a legal agreement to that effect before the application is available for use. This carrot-and-stick approach puts the onus on the users to decide what applications they want to use on their own devices.

Although the all-or-nothing approach is effective for some user profiles, it is not right for everyone. Your enterprise users have important personal information, and they may not be comfortable with an employer destroying that information at any time the organization deems it necessary. In this situation you can use a more judicious approach to data destruction by using an application sandbox.

In the application sandbox approach, you treat the device as "enemy territory" and put all controls necessary to protect sensitive information in place at the application level. You can create the sandbox for each application, or share it across applications and implement all the necessary encryption of information, access points, authorization, and authentication algorithms needed for your specific use case. By sandboxing your application data in this manner, you can include an algorithm or event hook to destroy the sandbox if a device is compromised.

Building Scalable Applications

Application scalability is an important consideration for any enterprise application — including mobile applications. Generally, you can scale your application in two ways: scaling up, or scaling out.

Scaling up involves upgrading storage and processing resources to accommodate additional load. Scaling up is not an option for mobile application capability due to the storage and processor limitations on mobile devices and the fact that most devices don't provide a mechanism for upgrade outside of replacing the device.

Scaling out involves adding additional nodes to a group or cluster of existing nodes to balance and share the load. This is the most common technique of scaling applications in the enterprise. But the news on the mobile front is not good here either because clustering mobile devices is not possible, nor would it make sense. A user has a single device, neither more, nor less.

You need to build scalability on the server-side as you've always done. You can upgrade server nodes and expand clusters easily to accommodate increased loads. With cloud services, such as Microsoft Azure and Amazon Elastic Cloud, you can configure virtual instances to scale in and out on demand to match application load at the moment in real-time.

Consider how you can take advantage of these technologies in your mobile application architecture, especially for applications with large user populations that may fluctuate greatly over time. Using hybrid application design techniques, you can deliver large portions of functionality from the cloud, but be aware of the sacrifices required in terms of connectivity, device access, and user experience before making this choice. The benefits of server-side scalability can be great, but the cost is not free. As with any architectural decision, it is a trade-off.

Planning for Deployment

One of the reasons web applications have become so popular in the enterprise is the ease of deployment. You can centrally deploy and manage a web application, and the only client-side application you need is a web browser. You can easily scale web applications as well, adding to their appeal, and cost of ownership is much lower whenever you use a web-based approach.

Deployment of mobile applications is often not as simple. Disconnected capability, device access, and user experience are all directly impacted by the decision to use a web-centric approach to application deployment. Because these are the three most important considerations in mobile architecture choice, you often land in a place where you need to manage and deploy native and native/web hybrid applications.

Most Mobile Device Management (MDM) vendors offer internal application stores as a part of their packages, which you can use to deliver applications to your enterprise with ease. Apple's over-the-air deployment model makes custom development of your internal application store simple and offers a lot of flexibility in app store design and deployment.

Device APIs, such as Apple's over-the-air provisioning and deployment, make custom-built app stores and device management solutions possible as well, if you discover the MDM vendors can't meet your specific needs.

Consider both web-based and native/hybrid approaches, but make sure you understand the implications of application deployment. Managing your mobile application deployment, whether you use MDM or choose to do it yourself, can have a big impact on the cost of ownership of your mobile application portfolio.

Writing Extendible Modules

When choosing a mobile architecture, it is valuable to take an approach that emphasizes reusable components. For example, security components, such as the SSO service mentioned previously, are among the most obvious and valuable components that you can design for reuse. Providing a shared library for functions such as authentication, authorization, and encryption enforce a consistent security model. This approach is an effective way to keep your applications extendable into the future.

Device and hardware abstraction layers can provide support for multiple functions and peripheral devices (for example, barcode scanners) and enable replacement of the peripherals as needed without re-engineering your entire application. Utilities for application configuration, logging, or analytics can provide valuable application services that enhance your deployment capability. Standardizing on basic functions can provide significant value, so you can spend less time resolving these common problems and more time building your mobile applications. Figure 1-1, reprinted with permission from Nathan Clevenger's book, *iPad in the Enterprise: Developing and Deploying Business Applications* (Wiley, 9781118022351, page 247), shows potential extendibility modules.

Data	Device	Security	Utility
• Entity Serialization • Entity Deserialization • RESTful Caching • RESTful Queuing	• Barcode Scanning • Barcode Generation • Calendar • Camera • Contacts • Geo-location • Signature Capture	• Authentication • Authorization • Communication Encryption • Storage Encryption • Remote Wipe • Self Destruct	• Alerting • Analytics • Configuration • Logging • Presence

FIGURE 1-1: Functional enterprise modules can enhance extendibility of your mobile applications.

Maintaining Application Code

Designing and writing maintainable object-oriented code often involves a strong focus on proper encapsulation of functionality and a logical organization of concerns within your application domain. Writing maintainable mobile application code also includes consideration of whether the code is meant to run on the device or in the cloud, and for cross-platform mobile applications, what platforms it is intended to execute on.

.NET and Mono provide a clear advantage for developing maintainable code at the architecture level due to the unification of language and APIs, but the implementations across platforms vary according to the lower-level capabilities of the targeted platform. MonoTouch, for example, cannot support certain C#/.NET conventions that require dynamic compilation and execution at runtime.

In addition, Windows Phone 7 uses the Silverlight concept of isolated storage in place of the traditional `System.IO.File` concept on other platforms. When accessing storage it is necessary to use a different approach for each platform. You should minimize the need to maintain multiple algorithms in common code by separating your platform-specific approaches in components compiled specifically for the platform in question.

CHOOSING AN ARCHITECTURE

Now that you identified and assessed your architectural options, you're ready to choose the approach that best fits your specific application use case. You can take several approaches, depending upon the decisions you make for your specific cross-platform requirements. You can divide the approaches into three high-level categories: native applications, web applications, and hybrid applications.

Building Native Applications

If you choose a purely native approach, chances are you determined an overwhelming need to satisfy requirements around disconnected functionality, device access, and/or a rich, immersive user experience. Native applications can uniquely meet these requirements, which is their biggest advantage. But there are also disadvantages.

Advantages

The first advantage of writing native mobile applications is full access to richness and flexibility of the native user interface APIs. Today, mobile devices are extremely personal devices, and the touch interface experience is unique. Users are attached to their devices and expect an exceptional experience that they cannot duplicate using technologies other than the native capabilities of the native device API. If your application requires sophisticated graphics or custom controls to deliver the experience, a native app is often the best choice.

Secondly, native applications provide full access to all the unique functions available on the device. Geo-location services, accelerometer and gyroscope, camera, video recording, audio recording, compass, and so on are all exposed via the native device API and platform. If you require one or more of these functions, a native application can deliver.

Finally, native applications offer the capability to work in a disconnected mode, either intermittently or constantly. You can cache and retrieve data from the device, execute business logic, and present information to the user without the need for a network connection. If you need to run your application when the device is in airplane mode, using a native application is your only choice.

Disadvantages

Taking a purely native approach has some disadvantages. First, the development of a native application requires some form of application management to facilitate deployment of your application, which means an internal app store, provided as a feature of MDM or built from scratch. It also requires some way to manage provisioning of new devices that users periodically add. Be sure to make updates to applications available to the user population, and refresh provisioning profiles. This generally leads to an increased cost of ownership surrounding the deployment and management of a native application portfolio.

Building Web Applications

Mobile web applications are centrally deployed and run on the server just like their enterprise counterparts, and many tools and frameworks specifically address the challenges of mobile web application development. The convenience of web applications, however, comes with a price of limited device access stronger connection dependence.

Advantages

The first advantage of adopting a web-based approach for your application is that existing web applications often work as-is on the newer tablet form-factors. Beyond that, you can easily port most web applications, if they are written with cleanly separated user interfaces, to the smaller form-factors of the various smartphones with relatively little effort. Web development skills are prevalent in most organizations, and the learning curve for a web developer to write mobile applications is short. So, developing new applications using this approach is often attractive.

Web application deployment is centrally managed and offers the second significant advantage over native applications. You do not need device provisioning and deployment strategies, and the questions of device management are much simpler when the application is in the cloud. When the application runs fully in the browser, there is little difference from a management and security perspective from a traditional desktop web application. Your organization likely already has a security policy and development best practices that support this approach.

The final advantage of taking a web-only approach is the cross-platform capabilities of HTML 5. Leveraging HTML 5 to deliver a satisfying user experience to multiple platforms offers great advantages. Capabilities such as hardware graphics-accelerated transitions supported in iOS and rich CSS support can create application experiences that can rival the native experience for out-of-the box, data-driven controls. HTML 5 even supports geo-location services to enable location-aware applications, and the HTML 5 cache manifest standard enables caching of application resources to support offline functionality.

Disadvantages

Lack of access to device functions can be a big drawback in using a web-only approach. If your application requires access to the device beyond geo-location, you must use a native or hybrid approach. Users expect features that take advantage of these services; they know what their devices can do and often demand that functionality. If your application needs these capabilities, a web application can't deliver.

Connection dependence is another drawback of web applications, especially if users need to manage offline transactions on the device. Although the HTML 5 cache manifest standard provides for offline access to web resources (for example, markup, images, multimedia, XML or JSON data), it is designed and optimized for resource consumption only. You cannot easily modify or create new resources for processing by a centralized system using HTML 5, and access the native API functions, such as storage and threading, are necessary to manage these items.

Finally the cross-platform HTML 5 standard does not support the rich, immersive user-experiences mobile users have come to expect. The mobile web framework space is currently immature, but it is evolving rapidly. More creative solutions using CSS and JavaScript emerge every day, but the native APIs evolve as well. Whether HTML 5 and the mobile frameworks that use it can catch up and deliver a user-experience that matches the native platforms remains to be seen, but for now, it is a significant drawback to a web-only approach to mobile development.

Building Hybrid Applications

A *hybrid application* is one that uses both native and web-based functionality to deliver a unified experience within a single application. Taking a hybrid approach can offer great flexibility in delivery of use cases that don't fit well into a purely native or purely web-based approach. Hybrid applications can offer best-of-both-worlds architecture, but they also carry with them the same disadvantages of native and web applications.

Advantages

By taking a hybrid approach, you can choose to deliver some portions of your application using web technologies and other portions using native controls and APIs. If you can easily deliver most of your application centrally via a web application, you can do that while building native custom views to deliver the few features that require native access or improved user experience. Conversely, if you have a small amount of information available on the web that you can style to fit your mobile application, you can deliver that content using web controls within an otherwise native application.

Hybrid applications also offer limited deployment choices. Because a hybrid app is essentially a native "wrapper" application that delivers some content via the web, the same deployment and provisioning requirements of native applications apply. But you can limit the amount of information delivered natively to mitigate some of the risk of deploying a fully native application. If, for example, there is a particularly sensitive class of information that requires an exception to data security policies to deliver at-rest in a native application, you can choose to offer that information only online via existing web security policies. You can natively deliver the rest of your application where data security is less of a concern.

Ultimately, the flexibility of a hybrid approach is its greatest advantage. By judiciously applying this architectural style, you can realize the advantages of both native and web applications, while minimizing the compromises necessary in taking either of those approaches independently.

Disadvantages

Hybrid applications require device deployment. All the deployment and provisioning requirements previously mentioned with regard to native applications are in play. There is no way around it. You must consider increased costs of management, whether via MDM vendor or internal IT departments.

Because hybrid applications need to navigate between native and web components, they can sometimes suffer from decreased performance. Device access through web pages requires a JavaScript abstraction to mitigate the mismatch between the native APIs, and content delivered via the web can suffer from bandwidth constraints. Carefully consider the need for application responsiveness and performance before taking a hybrid approach.

Finally, the web content delivered in a hybrid application cannot match the native user experience. Be careful when designing the transitions between approaches because an obvious degradation moving from native to web can severely impact your user experience in a negative way. Hybrid applications can be flexible, but you should carefully consider the user experience you deliver using this approach.

BUILDING FOR MULTIPLE PLATFORMS

The goal of cross-platform development is to maximize the amount of code shared while maintaining the native look and feel of each platform. Each native platform has its own unique flavor; you must consider a few things when choosing which platforms to support with your cross-platform applications.

Choosing iOS Applications

MonoTouch provides for C# compilation to the native functions and also includes the core Mono .NET assemblies compiled specifically for iOS. You can write C# code in the Integrated Development Environment (IDE) of your choice, but it must be compiled and deployed from a Mac using the MonoDevelop IDE. The resulting assemblies are compiled to static code, which results in limitations surrounding dynamic generation and execution. As a result, MonoTouch does not support .NET APIs that require dynamic code generation or execution. These include `Reflection.Emit()`, Generic Virtual Methods, and P/Invokes in generic types, among others. Full details are available from the Xamarin documentation site at `http://docs.xamarin.com/ios/about/limitations`.

You can also bind to native iOS libraries to take advantage of existing or third-party components written for iOS. Mono supports binding to native Objective-C libraries using the .NET P/Invoke framework (as long as the classes you bind to are not generics). You can find details at `http://ios.xamarin.com/Documentation/Binding_New_Objective-C_Types`.

If you prefer to statically link your Objective-C libraries, that option is also available. You can check it out at `http://ios.xamarin.com/Documentation/Linking_Native_Libraries`.

Choosing Android Applications

Mono for Android provides C# compilation to the native Android SDK, much like its iOS counterpart, MonoTouch. It also includes the core Mono .NET libraries, along with access to native Android APIs via the `Mono.Android` namespace. You can also write Mono for Android code in the IDE of your choice and compile it in both Microsoft Visual Studio and MonoDevelop on either a PC or a Mac. Mono for Android applications run in the Mono runtime environment and sit side-by-side with the native Android Dalvik virtual machine. Figure 1-2 shows a diagram of this architecture.

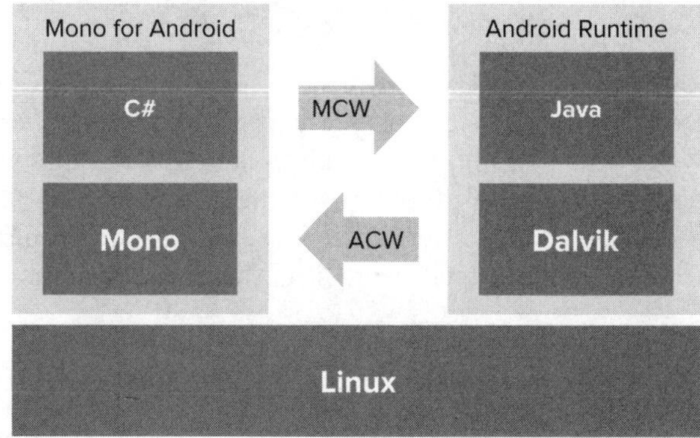

FIGURE 1-2: The Mono for Android runtime exists alongside the native Android runtime.

Whenever you need communication between the Mono and Dalvik runtimes, Mono for Android uses wrappers (represented by the arrows in Figure 1-2) to bridge the gap. Mono for Android generates Managed Callable Wrappers (MCWs) and uses them whenever managed code in the Mono runtime needs to invoke native Android code. All the APIs exposed via the `Mono.Android` namespace make use of MCWs. Conversely, Android Callable Wrappers (ACWs) are a native Java bridge used by the framework whenever native Android code needs to invoke managed code in the Mono runtime. You need ACWs to overcome the lack of dynamic class registration in Dalvik at runtime. You can find details of the Mono for Android architecture at `http://android.xamarin.com/Documentation/Architecture`.

Because Mono for Android must generate ACWs at compile time to support calls from Dalvik to Mono, you cannot use dynamic languages, such as IronPython or IronRuby, to subclass Android Java classes. The `Android.OS.IParcelable` and `Java.IO.ISerializable` interfaces are not implemented, and there is limited support for generics. You can review details on all Mono for Android limitations at `http://android.xamarin.com/Documentation/Limitations`.

Choosing Windows Phone Applications

The Windows Phone SDK is the only fully native .NET environment. It is built on top of both the Silverlight and XNA game platforms published by Microsoft. You must write Windows Phone applications using the Microsoft Visual Studio IDE. The free SDK download includes Visual Studio 2010 Express for Windows Phone. You can download the SDK at `http://create.msdn.com/en-us/home/getting_started`.

One of the most significant areas in which a Windows Phone application differs from other platforms is the use of isolated storage for IO operations. Because the foundation of Windows Phone is Silverlight, you must perform IO using the asynchronous isolated storage methods exposed there anytime you want to directly access storage on the device. Windows Phone also has support for structured data using the SQL Server Compact Engine. Access to the structured store is available via Language Integrated Query (LINQ), which greatly simplifies access to device storage. You can find full details of the Windows Phone SDK on MSDN at `http://msdn.microsoft.com/en-us/library/ff402535(v=VS.92).aspx`.

Choosing Web Applications

Writing cross-platform web applications is often the simplest way to provide support across a wide variety of platforms. Both the iOS and Android mobile browsers include support for HTML 5 via the Apple WebKit rendering engine; Windows Phone does not, so the examples in this book do not work in mobile Internet Explorer. Fortunately, many available rapidly evolving mobile web frameworks offer robust support across devices. The MonoCross pattern introduced in this book is ultimately framework-agnostic for web applications. You can experiment with other implementations as you become familiar with the concepts.

The examples in this book are based on the WebApp .NET micro-framework. You can find details on the framework at `http://webapp-net.com`. WebApp .NET offers a mobile optimized HTML user experience based on the Apple iOS paradigm. It makes extensive use of the styling elements available in WebKit and uses hardware graphics acceleration to simulate the sliding transitions of an iPhone application. The framework has robust AJAX support, which manages the navigation stack for you.

SUMMARY

In this chapter you learned about some of the basic tenants of mobile architecture. You now understand how network connectivity, device access, and user experience form the foundation of mobile architecture decisions. You explored the various mobile application considerations surrounding device limitations, security, scalability, and more. Then, you explored various architectural approaches including native, web, and hybrid applications discussing the pros and cons of each. Finally, you learned more about the four platforms explored in this book: iOS, Android, Windows Phone, and Web. You learned about the specific nuances of each platform with an eye toward choosing the right ones for your organization.

In the next chapter you learn how to design your mobile application user experience using proven prototyping techniques. This design is the foundation of the samples used throughout the book, and represents the first step into cross-platform mobile development.

2

Designing Your User Experience

WHAT'S IN THIS CHAPTER?

- Defining a functional scope for each screen
- Evaluating what data should be displayed
- Whiteboarding exercises to facilitate app design and identify discrete pieces of functionality
- Prototyping to get stakeholder and user feedback
- Using Agile to get software into the hands of beta testers

Almost as diverse as the development languages and mobile operating systems of the targeted devices, the User Interface (UI) controls that make up the user experience on today's mobile platforms vary greatly. A common thread is the complete abandonment of the DataGrid layout. Made famous in Windows Forms, the DataGrid quickly made the migration to the mobile platform when Microsoft ported the UI control to Windows CE. Although DataGrids performed reasonably well in desktop applications, the significantly reduced screen resolution of quarter VGA mobile devices forced the fonts used within DataGrids to be too small when rendered on the device.

When Apple launched the iPhone, it included some data-intensive workflows. The first killer app for iOS was iTunes. The application provides users with a rich experience while they browse a vast array of digital entertainment content. By implementing a linear application workflow, Apple enabled iTunes users to browse through the details of each song by drilling through lists. Using the linear paradigm enables developers to display information in a more readable fashion when it is displayed on mobile devices. Two primary advantages of this approach are larger font sizes and the lack of horizontal screen scrolling.

When Microsoft introduced the successor to Windows CE at the launch of Windows Phone 7, it was impossible to miss the use of extra large fonts. The mantra of the device, "Get it and get out," made it clear there was no time for putting on your reading glasses. The device is ready for use by all ages. The UI paradigm for Windows Phone 7 is a far cry from the DataGrid.

In the spirit of advancing mobile applications, Google brought its own version of innovation to the mobile application landscape. The Android platform gave the open source community a vast array of computing devices for which to develop software. Google harnessed the power of social coding and built a mobile operating system (OS) with future innovation in mind. The UI is not as polished as iOS or as dramatic as Window Phone 7; but the combination of a powerful UI API and XML gives UI designers and developers the ability to tag-team in creating almost any UI experience the pair can dream up.

As mobile devices have matured, users' expectations for the applications they use have heightened. Using mobile apps can be fun and convenient. However, the individual user's experience can be crushed if the app's navigation is clunky, its performance is poor, or it requires a user manual to master. Today's apps need to be sleek, perform seamlessly, and be optimized for the tasks at hand. The application design discussions in this chapter center around defining the app. Things to consider when designing the UI are data, process flow, and objectives. Carefully consider what data needs to be displayed and at which points of the workflow each piece of data becomes relevant. Verify each piece of data retrieved is necessary for the user to complete their core workflow objectives.

MAKING YOUR APPLICATIONS USABLE

The secret to creating usable apps is to keep the app simple. The initial design process is the starting point for identifying key parts of your application's functionality. Project managers and developers alike can start drawing initial conclusions around timeline and scope as teams start defining workflows and identifying the data those workflows rely on. In addition, the initial workflow design and mockup exercises often highlight unnecessary data or nice-to-have workflows that don't need to be included in the initial scope.

Remember the 80/20 rule and focus first on designing the app to handle 80% of the functionality; don't focus on the edge case functionality until after the application has a general flow.

Identifying the Scope of Each Screen

Historically, one of the biggest challenges to mobile software development was designing the UI for smaller screen resolutions. Although tablets are starting to bring larger resolutions to handheld devices, developers are still forced to limit the content and pieces of functionality contained in each screen.

When starting to design the application, you need to break the application into functional sections. With each section identified, an individual or small team can work to determine what each section's screens might look like.

In the enterprise, a majority of the applications are designed to deliver information for real-time business decisions. Identifying the data you want to display is a crucial step in the design process.

Failing to weed out the data that is not needed on the screen can, ultimately, result in wasting hours trying to provide and display useless information.

After you identify the data to be displayed, it is then best to designate information as either primary or secondary information. Primary information should be presented in larger fonts, without truncation, whereas secondary information can be presented in less distinguishing fonts and colors — or placed on a subscreen. A paradigm made popular by today's modern smartphones is making it possible to reveal secondary information by touching a portion of the primary information or its disclosure decorator.

A disclosure decorator is a visual cue on the screen that a user can touch to reveal more information about a specific piece for data. This is most commonly seen in List views, such as a contact list.

Conforming to Platform Standards

Perhaps one of the greatest cost-saving benefits of today's new mobile applications is the lack of training materials. In the cutting-edge book *iPad in the Enterprise* from Wrox, author Nathan Clevenger assembles a mass of enterprise application implementation use cases. In his research, Clevenger points out that an entire ecosystem of mobile applications was produced without training and documentation departments having to produce a single page of user documentation, quick reference sheets, or supporting wikis. Creating an app that harnesses the power of UI adoptability is the responsibility of those designing the UI. Using the controls and conventions native to each platform drastically cuts the time each user must spend learning the app. Applications that utilize the native controls and workflows of the platform help the user intuitively learn the app's functionality. Much as immersion is useful for teaching languages, creating an application the user can navigate intuitively should increase the adoption rate of your enterprise apps.

Apple is the undisputed leader in the realm of user experience on mobile devices. Its iOS interface has proven intuitive to everyone from toddlers to grandparents. This achievement did not come without causing some frustration among Apple's application development community. As the first apps made their way into the app store, Apple meticulously reviewed their conformity to a published set of UI standards. It was not uncommon for Apple to reject an app because the reviewer did not like how the user controllers were laid out. Although Apple has largely relaxed its rigid enforcement of UI guidelines, it did so only after the user base had gotten used to the "the right way to do things."

Google took a different approach. The Android Market is open, and apps are generally rejected only if basic functionality is failing. Even with the lack of UI convention enforcement, there is still a standard way to do things. If you have any confusion on how to implement specific functionality or workflows, it's best to review the apps that come loaded on every Android device. Those apps generally adhere to the best practices of the platform and can help jump start ideas on how to implement your own workflows.

Microsoft has never willingly been outdone by competitors. With Apple and Google encroaching on the mobile enterprise space, Microsoft released Windows Phone 7, which uses Silverlight under the hood. The result is a UI paradigm that relates well to web pages. This is convenient for cross-platform development because placement of navigation endpoints throughout a screen is one of the easiest ways to write portable code. Each navigation endpoint provides the controller (the shared business code) an opportunity to execute shared C# code before the rendering or re-rendering of a screen.

By far the most loosely standardized platform is the World Wide Web. There are a ton of advantages that come with web-based implementations. Ease of deployment is probably its greatest asset. With web-based deployments, the transition from one version of the UI to another is as simple as updating the web server. Updates to the web server immediately transition the entire user base to the new version. This is something that cannot be accomplished with applications deployed to individual devices. Writing and deploying apps to each user's device, by nature, introduces a migration period. Web-based deployments also bring the advantage of contained data access, where all data remains stored behind a firewall. No datasets are transferred off premise of the data center. Web applications can access data servers and retrieve information necessary for creating a view without exposing that traffic to public networks. With data securely retrieved, the web app can send only the data contained within the view to the mobile web client.

Webkit is a layout engine web browsers use under the covers. The standardized use of the engine provides a more reliable rendering of web pages across multiple browsers. While the Webkit standard is no substitute for developing a native app with native controls, it does allow developers to have reasonable confidence that their Webkit-compatible web pages will render nicely across several mobile platforms. The heavy adoption of the Webkit engine by mobile browsers opens the door for real cross-platform web-based implementations. With general standardization on the Webkit browser engine, mobile web applications have a de facto browser standard to target. This empowers developers and solution designers to develop full-featured web-based apps or to utilize embedded web controls in their native apps.

Each mobile platform has its own set of best practices. Apple, Google, and Microsoft have all published and revised their user interface guidelines. It can be beneficial to take a look through them before diving into designing an application. Each guideline document is published by its respective organization and placed on the organization's public-facing websites. The document names are different, but the content is all similar. Windows Phone 7 has User Experience Design Guidelines. Apple publishes the iOS Human Interface Guidelines. And Google publishes the more traditionally named User Interface Guidelines.

Each of the guidelines should be easy to find with a Google or Bing search for the document's name. At the time of publication the guidelines were available at the following URLs.

Microsoft:

```
http://msdn.microsoft.com/en-us/library/hh202915(v=vs.92).aspx
```

Apple:

```
http://developer.apple.com/library/ios/#documentation/user
experience/conceptual/mobilehig/Introduction/Introduction.html
```

Google:

```
http://developer.android.com/guide/practices/ui_guidelines/
index.html
```

SEPARATING PLATFORM FROM DESIGN

When targeting an application for cross-platform deployment, you need to separate function from implementation. You can accomplish the same objective using entirely different user interface implementations. At the most rudimentary level, there is the native control. On Android devices developers can work with a familiar UI control concept, the drop-down box. On iPhones you observe an entirely different implementation with the select list. Both implementations enable the user to select a single option from a list of choices. The drop-down box overlays the choices on the current screen. Apple's select list concept utilizes the entire screen real estate to display the list of options. A third paradigm common among Webkit implementations is the picker wheel. Much like the drop-down list, the picker wheel displays on the same screen, usually appearing docked to the bottom of the screen when the control is touched.

Before focusing on the controller, it is important to consider the workflow. Developers can choose many different approaches to collecting data. A traditional approach is the form. Take an address form, for example. To enter the last three fields in an address, the user would move between the City, State, and ZIP code fields. After entering data in all the fields, the user would locate the UI control for triggering a submission of that data. An entirely different approach is the step-through workflow. The users can select a single UI control that transitions them into a workflow that first selects a State, then a City, and finally a ZIP code. This kind of workflow provides new opportunities to improve usability. One opportunity for streamlining the workflow in this example might be to take advantage of the GPS technology in most smartphones and prepopulate the ZIP code field with a default value and then render a UI control for the user to confirm or correct the prepopulated value.

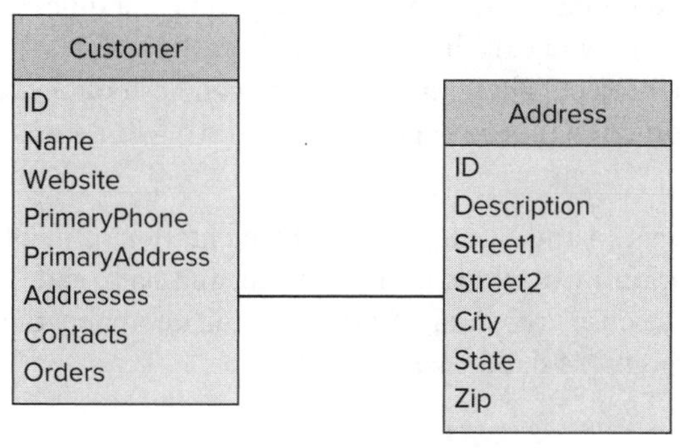

FIGURE 2-1: A customer management application can use a simple data model diagram.

Implementations vary drastically. What makes sense for one business group might not for another. When starting to design cross-platform applications, don't get bogged down in these types of details. The primary goal for the initial design sessions should focus around data and tasks. Identify what data the user must see to complete the tasks the application is being built to facilitate. Consider the example of a customer management application. The purpose of the application is to display company information. The data necessary to accomplish that are typical address book data and order history information (see Figure 2-1).

When the data elements are identified first, it can help declutter your UI. It is not only helpful, but also necessary to limit the information displayed at any given time; the smaller screen sizes demand such discipline.

Using the example of the application and the data defined in Figure 2-1, you can begin the workflow discussion. In this simple example the goal is to help the user locate and display information about a particular customer. The first design decisions encompass the workflow for selecting the customer. The user could drill through menus to locate a company or contact name. The user could be presented with a paginated list and click through it page by page while looking for the customer. Or the user could see the full list and use a search bar to filter it. These kinds of workflows are at the root of the MonoCross pattern. They affect the number of views you have to create as well as the opportunities for the shared code in the controller to execute. Such decisions are generally worked out among teams. To help facilitate decisions about shared code, most teams use the process of prototyping.

PROTOTYPING

Most development groups engage in some sort of prototyping exercises early in their development process. *Prototyping* is the process of developing less-than-complete implementations of software for the purpose of evaluating scope, functionality, and usability. This process can become invaluable when writing cross-platform applications.

It can be easy to assume, with today's object-oriented programming languages, that rapid application development means you can quickly modify your code if it doesn't meet user's needs, but the challenge in the enterprise is not so much to create something quickly as it is to create something solid. Creating applications that are efficient in workflow, intuitive in nature, and rock solid in execution can reap immeasurable benefits for your organization. Whiteboarding and prototyping exercises are worth the expenditure of time and effort, and when you are engaging in cross-platform development the rewards associated with those exercises are exponential.

The following prototype exercises should help you flesh out application experiences without getting caught up on individual platform differences.

Whiteboarding

In today's smartphone world, every whiteboard is a digital whiteboard. It's easy to take a quickly sketched mockup and capture it as a digital photo that you can share by e-mail, post on collaborative websites, and archive for reference later in the project. These initial designs can flesh out general business requirements and then be parlayed into functional prototypes as general workflows are pushed out.

There are many steps between the conception of an app and a completed implementation. One of the most vital is the up-front design of the application's workflow, user interface, and back-end data modeling. The root of most enterprise applications is the data. Whiteboarding an application's workflow is the first opportunity to size up the amount of data it will require.

Deciding What Data to Display

A primary step in mobile application development is distilling what data must display on each screen. One of the easiest ways to do this is to steal a subset of the relational database modeling language and model it out screen by screen. Using a simple diagramming paradigm, you can quickly identify and document the amount and type of data each screen needs to display.

As an example, continue using the customer management use case. You mapped out the important data about a customer, but now you must put the data to use by displaying it on pertinent screens. Figure 2-2 is an example of a two-screen workflow for a customer lookup workflow.

In the example you see two screens. On the left side is a repeating set of information for each customer in the list. The list just displays the primary pieces of information. Selecting an item transitions it to a screen (to the right) that includes more details about that particular customer. Neither of these screens is specific about platform UI control, or even the location of the control. The purpose of this diagramming exercise is to identify the data and where within the app it will display. Layout can be tackled in a different whiteboarding exercise.

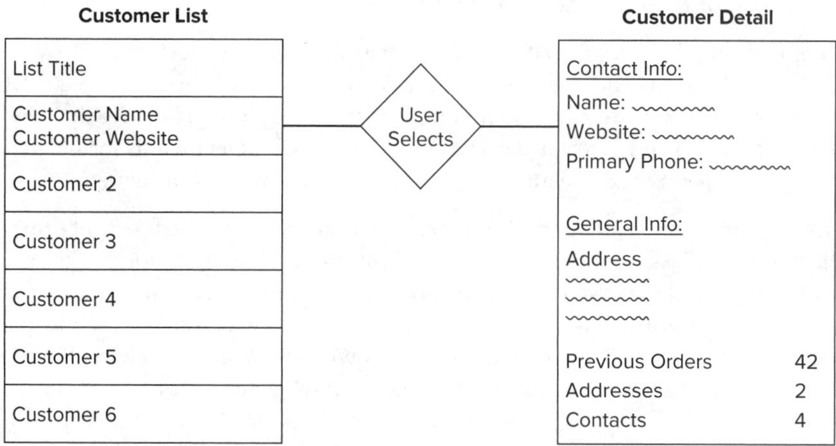

FIGURE 2-2: An activity diagram helps describe general functionality and required data.

Diagramming Activities

The first step in application workflow design is defining the exit points for each screen. One suggestion might be to start with an initial screen and work your way out. Here you explore how to diagram different tasks associated with a customer. A user sitting at the customer detail screen might have several tasks that can be performed on that customer. Possibilities include things such as editing the customer's profile or starting a transaction for that customer. Figure 2-3 is an example of what a rudimentary activity diagram might look like.

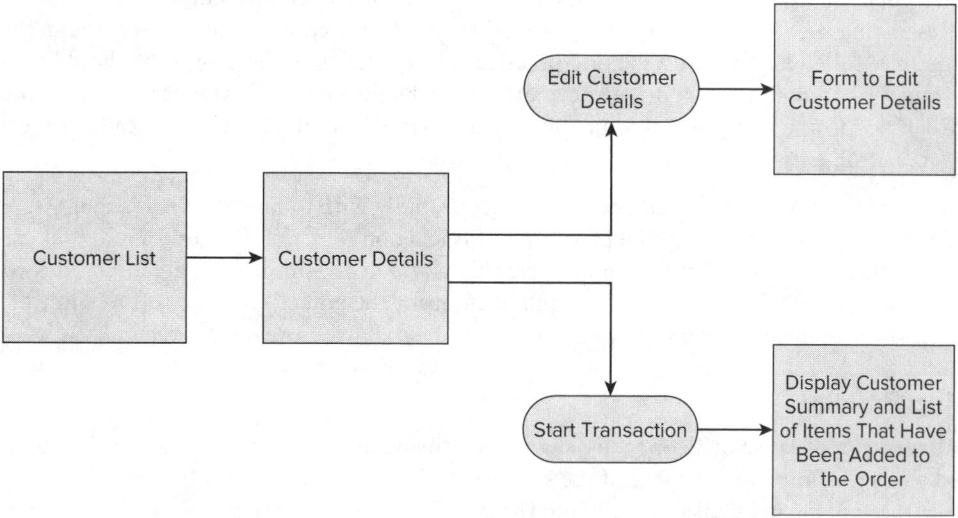

FIGURE 2-3: This activity diagram is useful for designing the Customer screen.

In the diagram in Figure 2-3, the ovals contain descriptions of actions that can be taken from the Customer detail screen, whereas the boxes identify screens and the data they display. Here you see three exit points from the Customer details screen. A user can choose to edit the customer, start a transaction for the customer, or return to the customer list screen.

So, how does this all fit into the MVC design pattern? Whiteboarding exercises such as an activity diagram can be directly translated to general development tasks. Each piece of data displayed on the screen must be retrieved by the Model. Each exit point on the screen must be coded to reach a new endpoint through the Controller. The whiteboard exercise can help development teams formulate what Views will contain while getting a feel for the amount of data and complexity of the exit points.

Whiteboard exercises can also serve as a good way to create UI interfaces for different platforms. Although object-oriented languages do facilitate rapid application development, nothing is as down and dirty as a whiteboard. Even the worst art class dropouts can usually draw a few shapes that can resemble native controls. After the data and actions are defined for each screen, the inevitable question is: How will they be displayed? Each platform comes with its own set of controls and its own UI best practices. Even with the variations, it's possible to draw general UI principals in a whiteboard mock up.

Using Functional Prototypes

Before investing in a team of database developers and software testers, you need to create a functional prototype. The prototype can display canned data and doesn't need to include every screen. It just needs to be sufficient to provide a solid walk-through of the primary tasks of the application. There is a lot that goes into a finished enterprise software application; a good functional prototype can help verify the complexity of the application will not outweigh the return on investment, and in so doing, save on the bottom line.

Functional prototyping, also referred to *wireframing*, is a development strategy that uses basic UI controls to construct application workflows. Each screen in the prototype needs only one valid navigation point, and the entire navigational structure of each screen does not need to be completed. Restricting the wireframed app's functionality to a few tried-and-true paths through the app, sometimes called happy paths, is good practice. The objective of the prototype should be to demonstrate the app with tried-and-true navigational paths through it. Developers should refrain from hardening the app to a point at which users can deviate from the happy path and expect the app to respond robustly.

Development of these applications can generally occur rapidly with today's modern languages. Leveraging C# and .NET across all the platforms adds icing on the cake. Building a minimal application with a skeleton look and feel with little graphic pizzazz can still provide great feedback to the project stakeholders. It can also serve as an indicator for the potential level of effort some of the application's development tasks might take.

Prototyping Pitfalls

There are plenty of pitfalls you need to avoid when venturing into wireframing your mobile project. You need to keep in mind the purpose of the exercise. If the goal is to create a functional walk-through of the app, it can be easy to walk into the pitfall of focusing only on the straightforward workflows. Using a prototype is an opportunity to work through the more difficult workflows and perhaps create multiple solutions to explore the differences in feasibility and user acceptance between them.

You do not need to add polish and shine to your functional prototype. Wireframing is not the time to get bogged down with fancy graphics or lengthy implementation tasks. If something is difficult to implement, take a few minutes to note the challenges, and then put a placeholder screen in that location. The placeholder screen could consist of nothing more than a single control that contains a screenshot from previous prototyping exercises in the application design process. The purpose of the functional prototyping exercise is to size up the task and put a basic application in the hands of the subject matter experts.

Creating Functional Prototypes

Consider a customer management theme. Let's look at what your prototype might look like. You addressed the customer and customer editing. From those workflows you can derive two workflow paths and three screens. When you start discussing screens, it immediately brings the platform back into the discussion. You cannot create a prototype without implementing it on more than one platform. For the purpose of this example, start with the console. Although the console is not likely a target platform for most implementations, it nicely illustrates how native UIs can translate down to the lowest common denominators on less capable platforms. In addition, the user experience can individually be raised to the level typical of each native platform.

The first screen to look at is the customer list screen (see Figure 2-4). In the console, the content is straightforward: a numbered list. Choosing a number can bring the user to the details of that customer. It's not likely this prototype can be improved, so its look and feel would likely stand as-is.

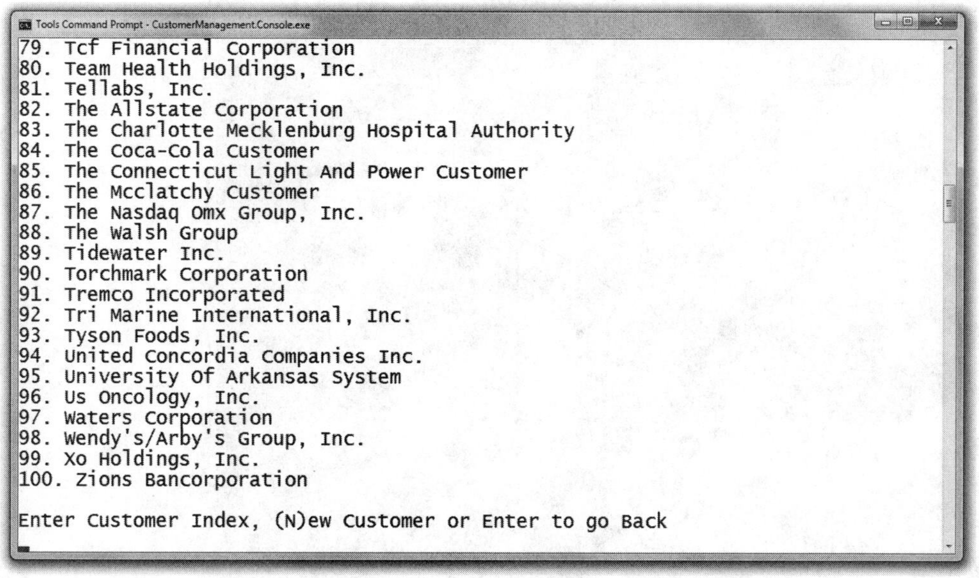

```
Tools Command Prompt - CustomerManagement.Console.exe
79. Tcf Financial Corporation
80. Team Health Holdings, Inc.
81. Tellabs, Inc.
82. The Allstate Corporation
83. The Charlotte Mecklenburg Hospital Authority
84. The Coca-Cola Customer
85. The Connecticut Light And Power Customer
86. The Mcclatchy Customer
87. The Nasdaq Omx Group, Inc.
88. The Walsh Group
89. Tidewater Inc.
90. Torchmark Corporation
91. Tremco Incorporated
92. Tri Marine International, Inc.
93. Tyson Foods, Inc.
94. United Concordia Companies Inc.
95. University Of Arkansas System
96. Us Oncology, Inc.
97. Waters Corporation
98. Wendy's/Arby's Group, Inc.
99. Xo Holdings, Inc.
100. Zions Bancorporation

Enter Customer Index, (N)ew Customer or Enter to go Back
_
```

FIGURE 2-4: A functional prototype can be created to display a customer list.

A little more work goes into wireframing the application on an iPhone (as shown in Figure 2-5), and there is usually a great discrepancy in the graphical sizzle in the prototype as compared to the final application.

The customer look-up screen on the iPhone can be improved in countless ways. The native UI controls available for today's smartphone and tablet devices include transparency, tint, shading, and color gradients. A developer with UI expertise or a strong graphical eye can spend painstaking hours tweaking those settings to achieve a beautiful application. A prototyped app is, of course, not the place to invest this kind of effort.

Similar to the iPhone's application, the Customer Management app on Android can be spruced up using countless graphical tricks and secrets (see Figure 2-6). With Android controls being laid out in XML, it's possible for coders to hand off styling tasks to those who are graphically inclined. For developers with both graphical and software development skill sets, application development for the Android platform will exercise both skill sets.

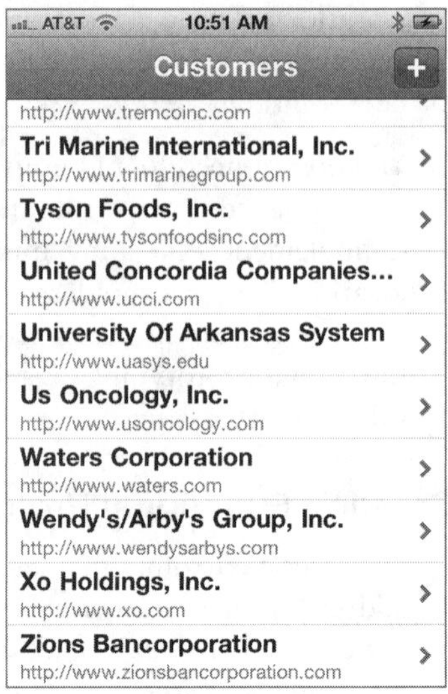

FIGURE 2-5: The customer list prototype looks different on an iPhone.

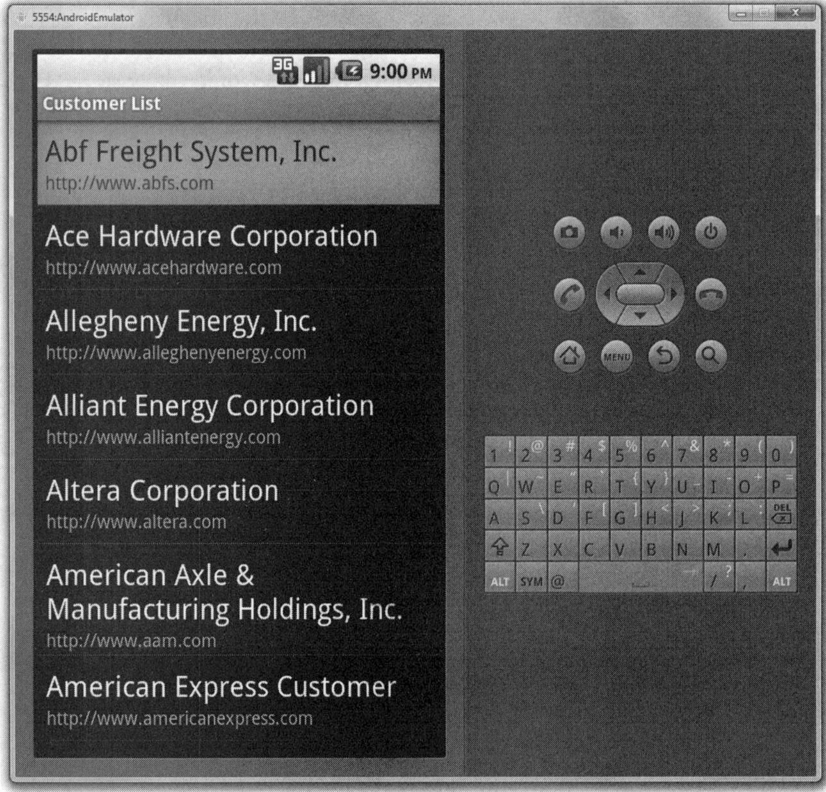

FIGURE 2-6: The Android Simulator displays the customer list prototype.

Web-based implementations can take advantage of those same graphical skill sets, because the HTML can be laid out in any tool the designer chooses (see Figure 2-7).

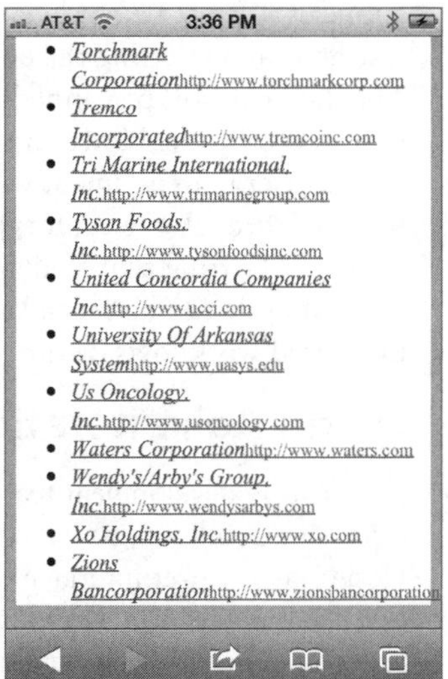

FIGURE 2-7: The customer list prototype displays on an iPhone.

Although the customer list on the prototype could be improved, there still isn't much to that screen. If you look at the customer details screen, you see there is more to display. Looking at the console screen in Figure 2-8 you see something that closely matches the Customer Detail screen whiteboarded in Figure 2-2. Because of the graphically limiting nature of the console, it's no surprise the elements on the screen closely match the properties from your Model.

As you move to the prototype on the iPhone, you can focus on the screen location of each piece of data. Although the general look and feel of the final software product is important, hard-coding information into native controls or HTML base views can speed up prototyping. HTML generally cannot provide all the functionality of standalone native applications, but it can be leveraged to provide reusable UI between devices. Figure 2-9 shows the iPhone version of the customer details screen.

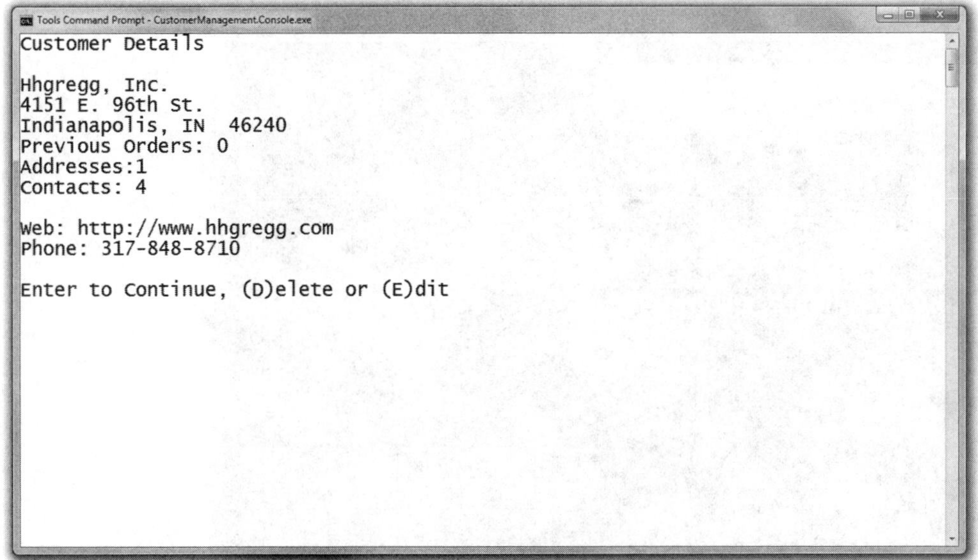

FIGURE 2-8: The customer detail prototype displays in the console with little or no graphics.

The Android UI, shown in Figure 2-10, is built using a few basic native controls to display the different pieces of information about the customer.

Obtaining User Feedback

One of the advantages of prototyping an application is that it provides a skeleton application that members of the targeted user base can test. To make the most of such an opportunity, the prototype application must be hardened a bit. Generally speaking, usability testing is about letting the end user work throughout the app. The data can still be canned from local XML files or hard-coded in to the C# code. However, workflows need to be robust enough for the user to experiment with the app. The user might not want to move through the prototyped workflow exactly as you envisioned it. Getting that feedback early in your application development cycle can be crucial in preventing the development of undesired workflows or functionality.

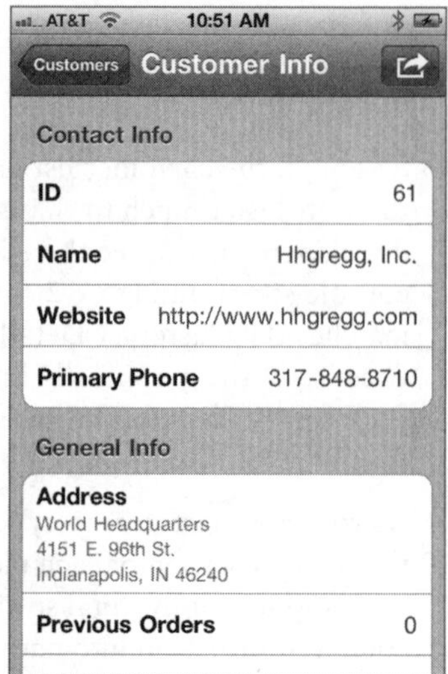

FIGURE 2-9: The iPhone displays the customer detail prototype.

Using Agile Iterations

Application development teams no longer need to pigeonhole their efforts into following a waterfall-style development approach. Designing the user interface is a great time in the development cycle to embrace Agile development practices. Such practices center around not being locked down to requirements for long periods of time. Although you need to keep a consistent requirement while developing a feature, the development cycle should never be so long that throwing away the work is too costly. Quick development cycles enable you to gather feedback in a timely manner.

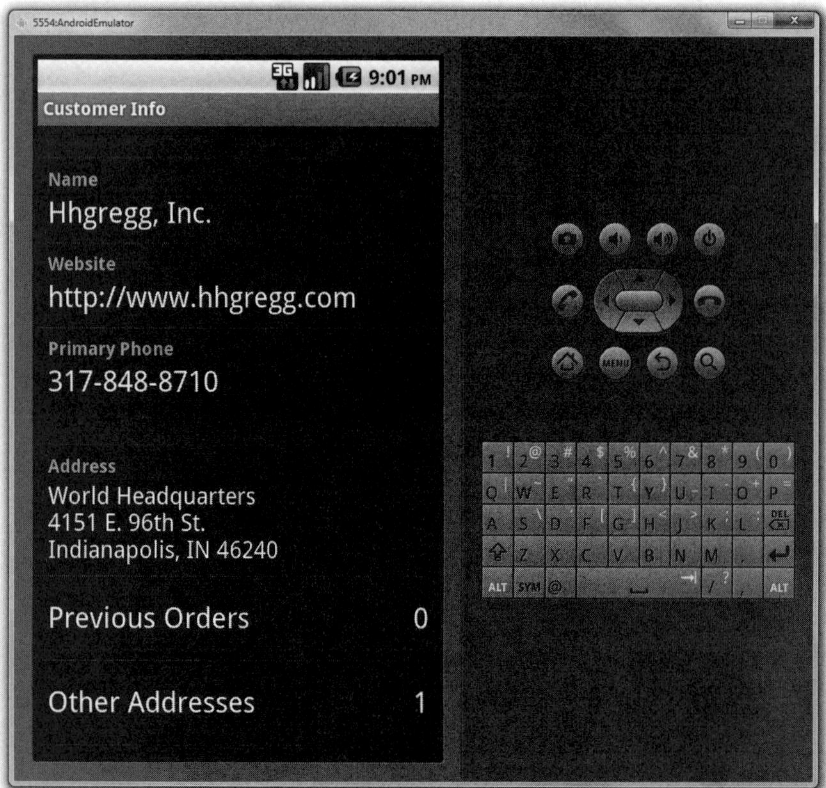

FIGURE 2-10: The Android Simulator displays the customer detail prototype.

The principles of Agile development rest firmly in achieving an outcome of functional software, not producing pristine documentation or dogmatically following processes. Agile practices generally start with chunking the development tasks into small pieces of functionality. When the application's functionality is compartmentalized to discrete pieces, it enables development groups to turn around working software in shorter time periods. The sooner pieces of functionality can be evaluated by the end user, the sooner the project stakeholders can be assured the investment is on the right track. Consequently, the same is true if functionality does not meet the end user's need. The ability to modify the development direction earlier in the development life cycle means more efficiency and happier end users.

One of the cruelest penalties in software development is creating applications that don't get used, or worse, are thrown away before they make it into production. The penalties feel the worst when you've gone through formal testing of code. Hot-off-the-press code usually includes a few bugs; that isn't anything new. Getting applications to enterprise grade takes a few more steps. You must take the time to get user feedback early and often. Users can ultimately judge whether the application is worthy of daily use.

For the investment to pay off, the application must be accessible, intuitively usable, and responsive. Individual user groups may vary in their determinations of whether an application meets those criteria; however, getting your software in front of them increases adoption. Agile development is a tool designed for that purpose.

Collaboration is at the heart of an Agile development process. It's the development team that is well-versed in the principles and best practices for creating software, but the user group is best qualified to envision the day-to-day use and function the application needs to fulfill. Demonstrating functioning software to users is, by far, the best way to communicate the development team's ideas and develop a shared vision with the project stakeholders.

SUMMARY

Developing carefully crafted designs for applications that will be deployed across several platforms requires a lot of groundwork. The code portability options provided by the Mono toolsets can increase productivity and maximize the deployability of each line. And just as with desktop development, over-engineering solutions can slow down your implementation schedule. Those same perils can exist in developing mobile applications, but they become amplified when the implementation is extended to multiple platforms. Keeping your design simple is imperative when managing scope, risk, and delivery of the software.

The exercises discussed in this chapter are not a set of sequential steps. The necessity of whiteboarding and prototyping varies with each application. The same can be true for diagramming data. The important thing to remember is that each requirement or implementation detail you flesh out in the design phase can prevent unnecessary code from finding its way into the development effort of multiple platforms.

In the next chapter you look at the development environment. You learn who makes the tools and where to find the software development kits.

PART II
Developing Cross-Platform Applications

3

Setting Up Your Development Environment

WHAT'S IN THIS CHAPTER?

- Understanding the development environments used in this book
- Installing the development tools
- Installing the platform SDKs
- Organizing multiplatform projects and code
- Navigating the sample code

In this chapter you are exposed to all the tools used throughout the book to build and run the sample code. Some information on organizing your multiple platform code bases is also presented.

In preparation for installing your development tools, you need to know in advance what platforms you are interested in supporting. Glance at Table 3-1 to ensure you have the proper hardware and operating systems available to you.

TABLE 3-1: Operating Environment Required for Target Platforms

DEVELOPMENT TARGET	MAC OSX	WINDOWS
iOS/MonoTouch	X	
Android/Mono for Android	X	X
WebKit/ASP.NET		X
Windows Phone		X

GETTING YOUR DEVELOPMENT TOOLS

All the samples in this book are provided in project files that require Microsoft Visual Studio for Windows or MonoDevelop for Mac OSX to build, deploy, and run. In some cases the code can be built in other ways, but these tools are the most commonly available to enterprise developers. You can explore alternative ways to build the samples as an exercise if you are interested in pursuing those avenues.

Because this book focuses on cross-platform development, little is said about the native platform tools except where they are needed.

Installing Microsoft Visual Studio

Visual Studio 2010, which runs only on a PC running Windows, is required to build, deploy, and run all the Windows Phone 7, Mobile Web (WebKit), and Console sample code referenced in this book. The Android samples can be built in Visual Studio or MonoDevelop (discussed later in this chapter), but Mono for Android support is most stable on the Windows platform with Visual Studio 2010.

1. Obtain a copy of the **Professional**, **Premium**, or **Ultimate** versions of **Visual Studio 2010**. Other versions do not include the tools needed to build these projects. See Microsoft's Visual Studio website at `www.microsoft.com/visualstudio` for answers to any questions you may have on hardware requirements or on the different versions available from Microsoft.
2. Locate and run the program setup from the DVD or other mounted media. You will be greeted by the window, as shown in Figure 3-1.

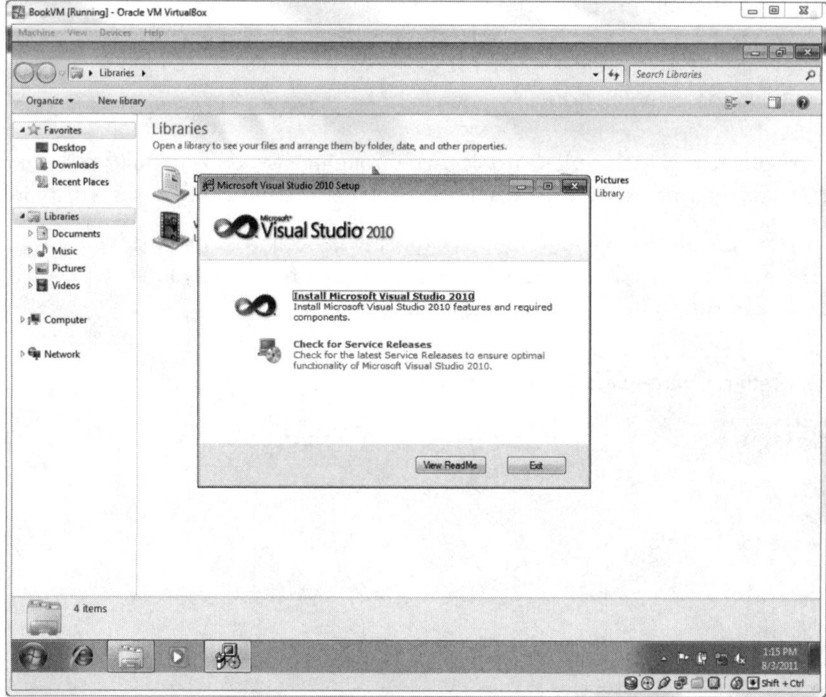

FIGURE 3-1: The Visual Studio Professional Installation Wizard helps you start.

3. Click the highlighted and underlined **Install Microsoft Visual Studio 2010** link. Upon starting, the Installation Wizard checks the Windows version you are using and the installed components, as shown in Figure 3-2. When it determines all is well, the wizard prompts you to begin, as illustrated in Figure 3-3.

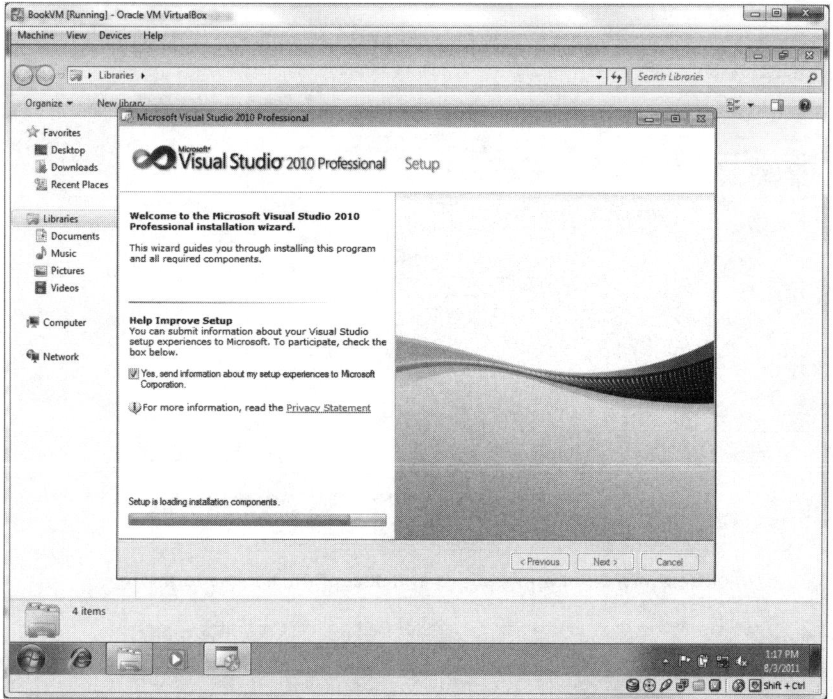

FIGURE 3-2: The Visual Studio Professional Installation Wizard checks your system in preparation for installation.

4. Read and accept the licensing terms; then click **Next**. You are now presented with options (see Figure 3-4) for what to install and where to install Visual Studio. The disk space requirements are also listed. You can also customize which languages and tools to install, but use the default installation settings. When initiated, the setup takes a fair amount of time.

5. Click **Next** and get comfortable. About halfway through the installation, you will be prompted to restart Windows. This is necessary to complete the installation of Visual Studio.

Occasionally, Visual Studio installation will not continue after restarting Windows. If this happens, locate the Setup application you started the installation from initially and restart the installation. After a few initial prompts, it will continue where it left off.

6. After Windows restarts, log in. Setup should continue. When Visual Studio 2010 setup is complete, the window shown in Figure 3-5 displays.

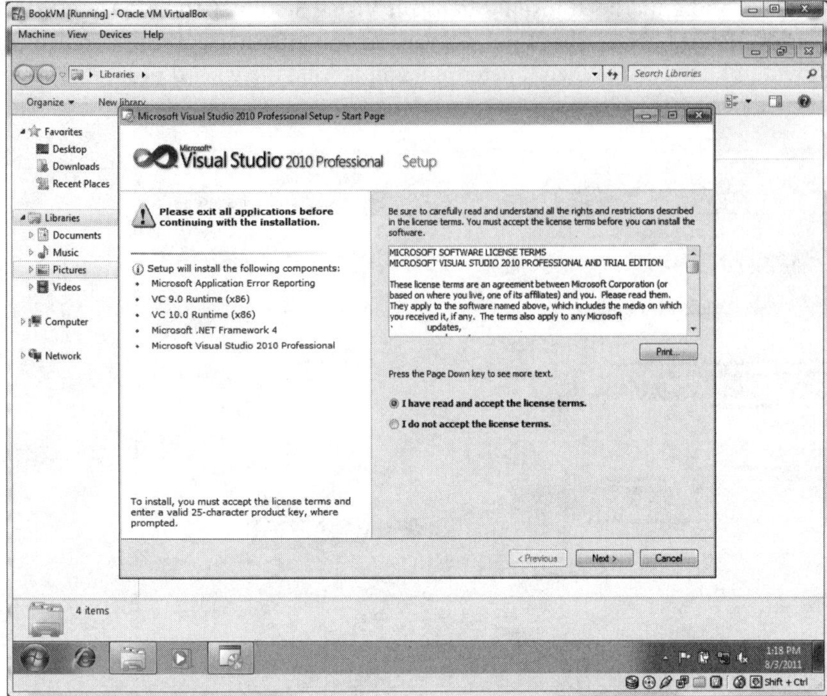

FIGURE 3-3: Be sure to close down other applications and accept the license terms.

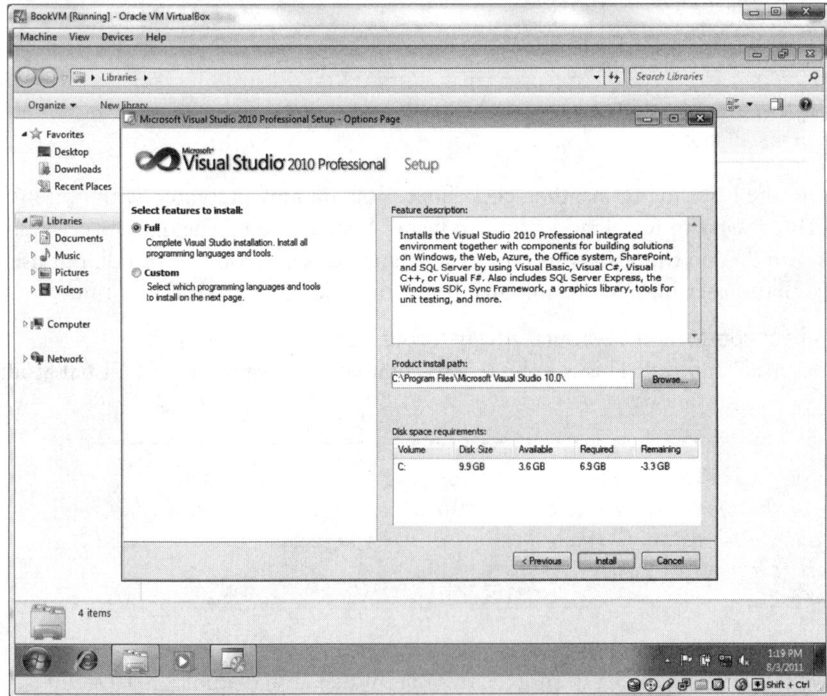

FIGURE 3-4: Stick with the default options whenever possible.

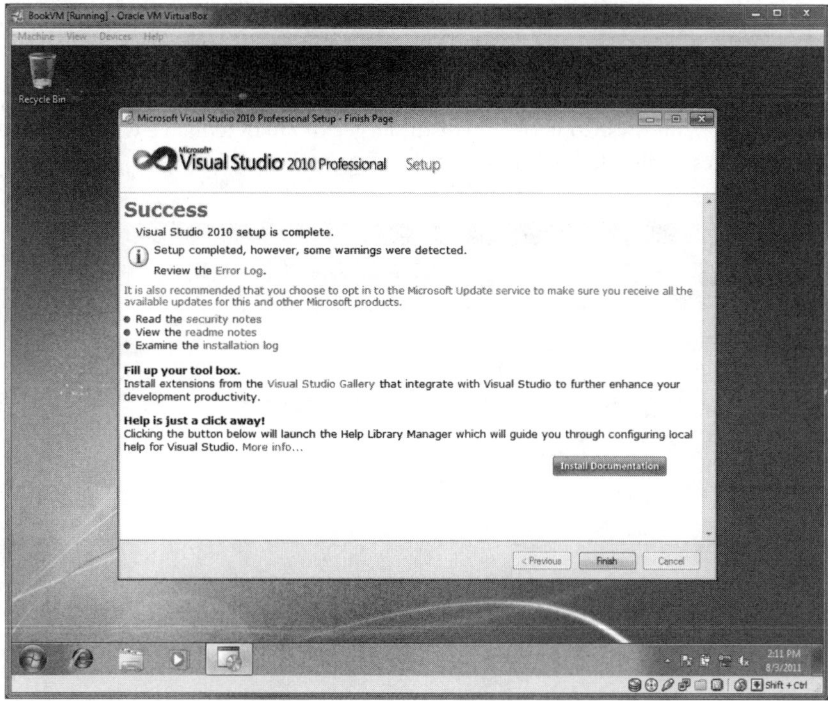

FIGURE 3-5: Visual Studio installation is now complete.

7. Now that you have Visual Studio 2010 installed, you need to find, download, and install the latest **Visual Studio 2010** Service Packs. You can find a link to the download from Microsoft's Visual Studio website at `www.microsoft.com/visualstudio` under the Products menu. After you have it downloaded, locate the downloaded file, and run it. The Service Pack is a small initial download, but expect the installation to take an hour or more.

The Windows Phone 7 SDK requires Visual Studio 2010 with the latest available service pack installed. As of this writing, Service Pack 1 is the latest available service pack.

Installing Internet Information Services (IIS)

After installing Visual Studio, you need to make certain to enable Internet Information Services (IIS) to build, deploy, and run the WebKit sample code. If you aren't interested in the WebKit samples and don't want to install IIS, you can get by without installing it, but you get an error when opening the solution files. You can safely ignore the error and remove the offending projects from the solution if you want to.

1. Click the **Windows Start** button, and then click the **Control Panel** item from the Windows Start menu.
2. If the Control Panel is in Category view, select the **Programs** item, then select **Programs and Features**. If the Windows Control Panel is in larger or small icons view, select **Programs and Features**. The result should be as illustrated in Figure 3-6.

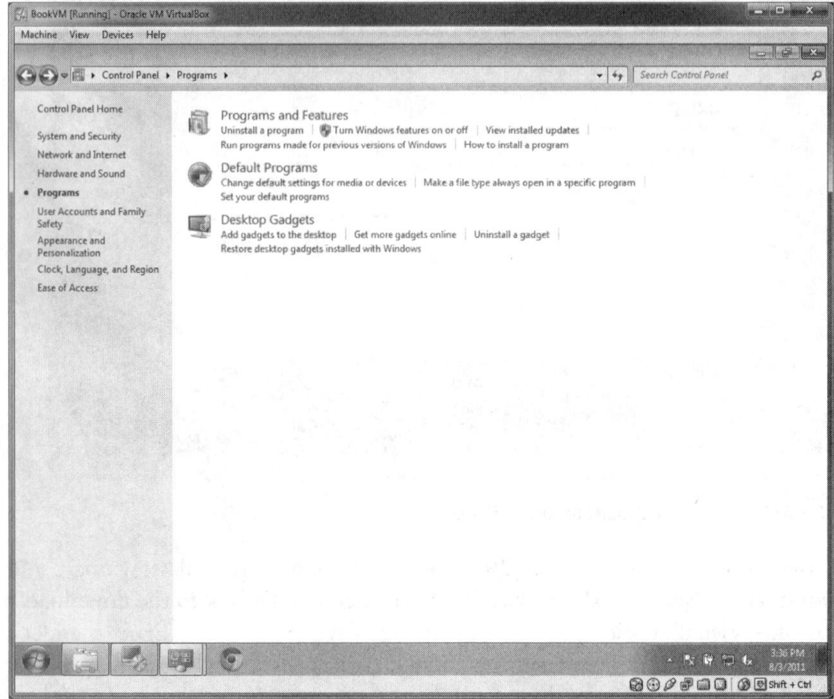

FIGURE 3-6: The Control Panel Programs and Features group provides the option you are looking for.

The page heading reads *Uninstall or Change a Program*, but the item you are looking for is on the left of the window and is titled *Turn Windows Features On or Off*. This option is highlighted in Figure 3-7.

3. Click **Turn Windows features on or off.** At this time a dialog window displays with a hierarchical list of Windows features in which checked items are already installed and unchecked are not. By default *Internet Information Services* will be unexpanded in the list and will *not* have a check mark or filled-in box in front of it.
4. Expand the **Internet Information Services** item and all items below it. Your list should look like the list in Figure 3-8, but with none of the items checked off.

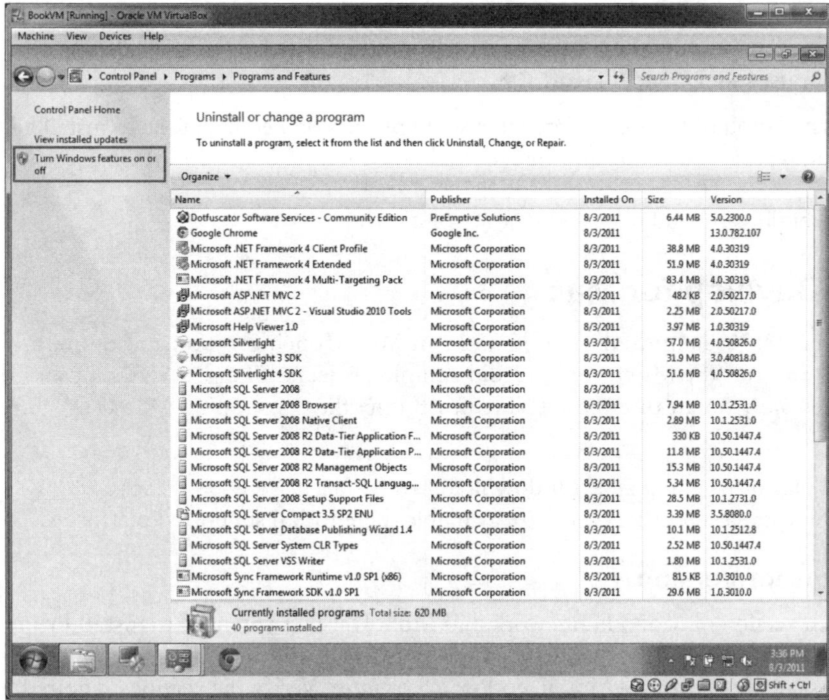

FIGURE 3-7: Turn on Windows features.

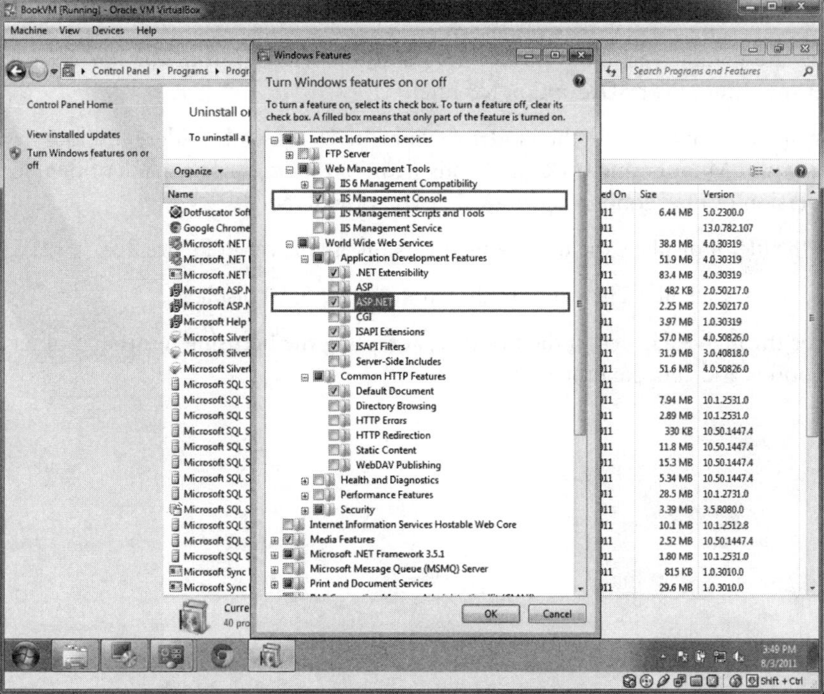

FIGURE 3-8: Select IIS Management Console and ASP.NET to continue the installation process.

5. Click the check boxes for **IIS Management Console** and **ASP.NET** to select them. As a result of checking these items, other items in the list will automatically be checked. After selecting the items, your list should match Figure 3-8.
6. Click **OK**. Installation of IIS is complete after Windows has had enough time to install additional files and services. A restart may be required.

At this point you can build, run, and debug ASP.NET solutions.

Installing MonoDevelop for Mac

MonoDevelop for Mac OSX is required to build and run MonoTouch projects and optionally can be used to build and run the Mono for Android sample projects. The iOS SDKs require that development be done *solely* on an Intel-based Macintosh (any flavor) running Mac OSX 10.6 or newer.

MonoDevelop for all platforms is available for download from `http://monodevelop.com/download`. Up-to-date installation instructions are available there for all supported platforms.

Determining the Correct Version

First, determine which version of Mono Framework and MonoDevelop you need to install by taking into account the platforms you are targeting. Currently MonoTouch and Mono for Android require you to install the latest stable version — MonoDevelop 2.8 or *later.* Verify the versions required by MonoTouch and Mono for Android before you proceed.

Installing the Mono Framework

1. Download the latest stable version of **Mono** (2.10.3 at this writing) from `www.go-mono.com`. Choose either the Runtime or SDK option for Intel.
2. After the download completes, use the Finder to view the Downloads folder, and look for a file that starts with "MonoFramework" and ends with ".x86.dmg". The name of the file also includes the version of the Mono framework that you downloaded.
3. Double-click the file. It displays the unpackaged version, as shown in Figure 3-9.
4. Double-click the package file. The window shown in Figure 3-10 displays.
5. Click **Continue** through each step in the installer, accepting the licensing terms and other installation options and choosing the defaults.

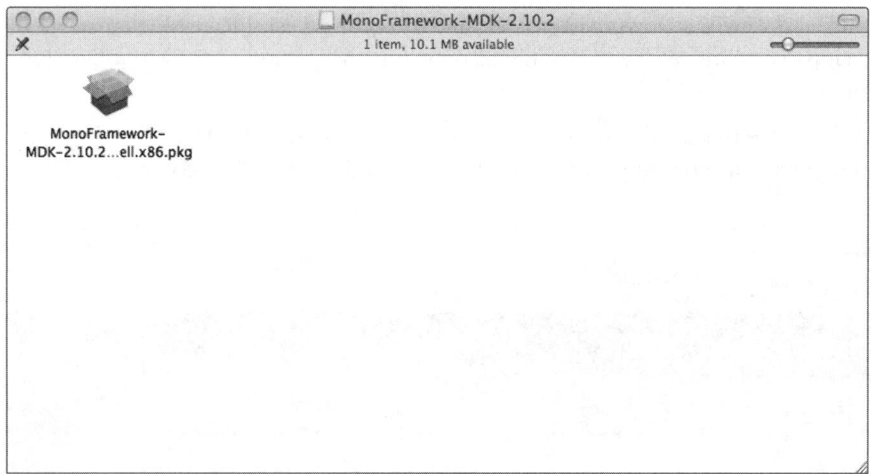

FIGURE 3-9: The icon represents the Mono Framework installation package.

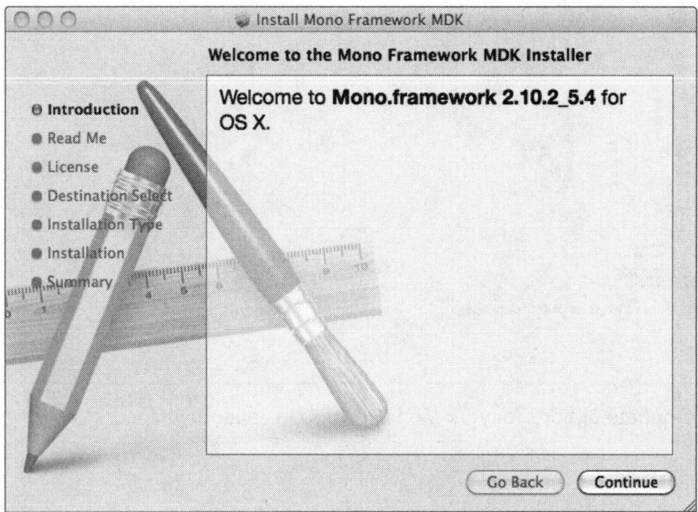

FIGURE 3-10: The Mono Framework Installer guides you through the installation process.

Installing MonoDevelop

Now that you have the Mono Framework installed, go to `http://monodevelop.com/download` to find and select the version of MonoDevelop you need for the mobile platforms you will work with (iOS and/or Android). Then select the Mac as discussed previously and download the installation package. Figure 3-11 shows the options as described for the latest version of MonoDevelop for Mac OSX.

1. Use the Finder to view the Downloads folder, and look for a Disk Image file that starts with MonoDevelop. The name of the file should also include the version of the MonoDevelop that you downloaded.
2. Double-click the file to start the installation, as shown in Figure 3-12. Drag and drop the **MonoDevelop icon** into the Applications folder and installation will be complete.

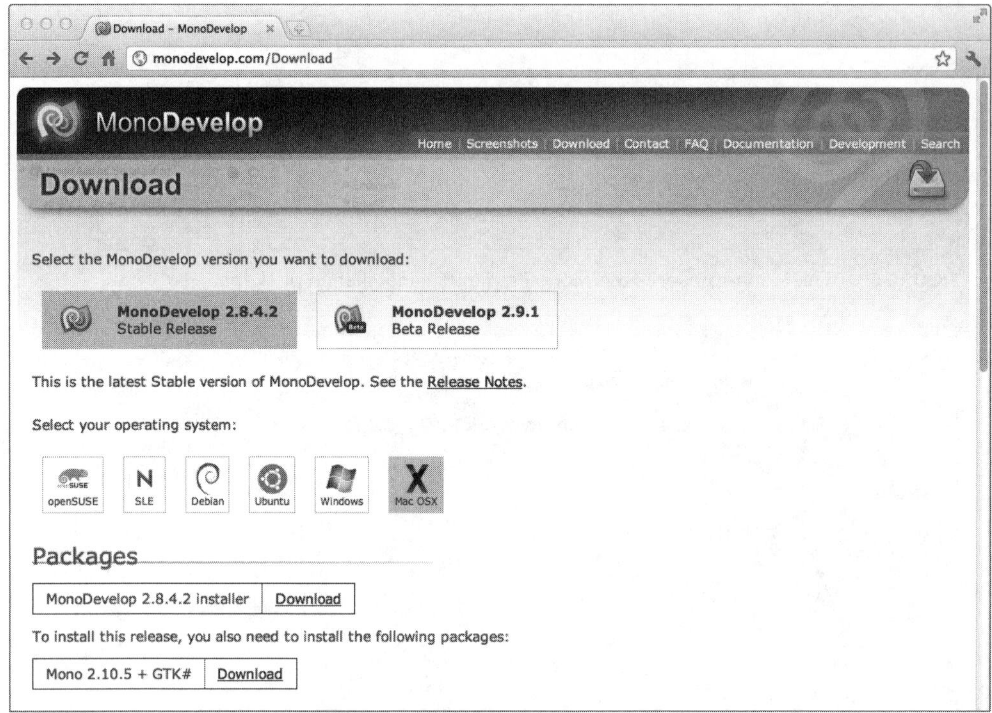

FIGURE 3-11: Select the appropriate options for your MonoDevelop Installer download.

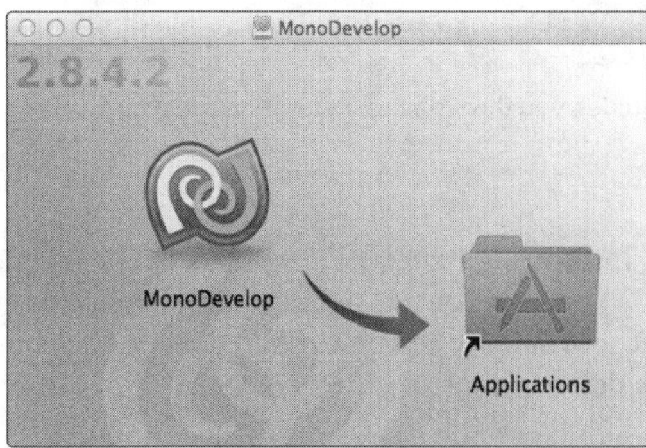

FIGURE 3-12: Copy MonoDevelop to Applications.

That completes the installation of the development tools; next you move on to installing the device frameworks.

You should not skip ahead to installing MonoTouch or Mono for Android because they are dependent on their respective SDKs. If you skip ahead, you may have to reinstall the framework from scratch or manually set up the paths to the SDKs manually.

INSTALLING DEVICE FRAMEWORKS

Now that you have the development environments installed for the platforms you are interested in developing for, you can install the SDKs for those environments. If you plan to support WebKit on any of the platforms discussed in this section, you should still install the SDKs because they include emulators and simulators for the target platforms. The emulators and simulators described here all have a web browser and can be used to test your mobile web implementation without using a device.

Installing the Windows Phone SDK

Visual Studio does not include Windows Phone support out-of-the-box. You must download and install the Windows Phone stack from Microsoft's MSDN site at `http://create.msdn.com`. In addition to the development stack downloads, the site houses links, articles, and documentation. This book and its samples were written using Windows Phone Developer Tools 7.1. All the features used in the book should be compatible with later versions; just find the latest version of the Windows Phone Developer tools and any provided updates from the site.

The Windows Phone Developers Tools contain the additional tools you need to build Windows Phone Applications. It contains code libraries, emulators, sample code, and much more. As a side note, you will notice the initial download is small, but the install pulls all its content from Microsoft's servers and can easily take an hour as the installed size of the update was nearly two gigabytes.

1. Go to `http:// create.msdn.com`, then click the **Download the Free Tools** image.
2. Click the **Download the SDK 7.1** link.
3. Select the appropriate language (defaults to English) and click the **Download** button, and the download will begin.
4. Run the downloaded file from your Downloads folder, or from wherever your web browser places download files by default. The installation process asks for your acceptance of the licensing terms. Once you accept, the installer downloads all the required components and then installs them.

5. When completed, start **Visual Studio** and select **File ➪ New ➪ Project.** Go down the list under C# projects, and you should find a section titled "Silverlight for Windows Phone." The project templates in Figure 3-13 should be available if installation was successful.

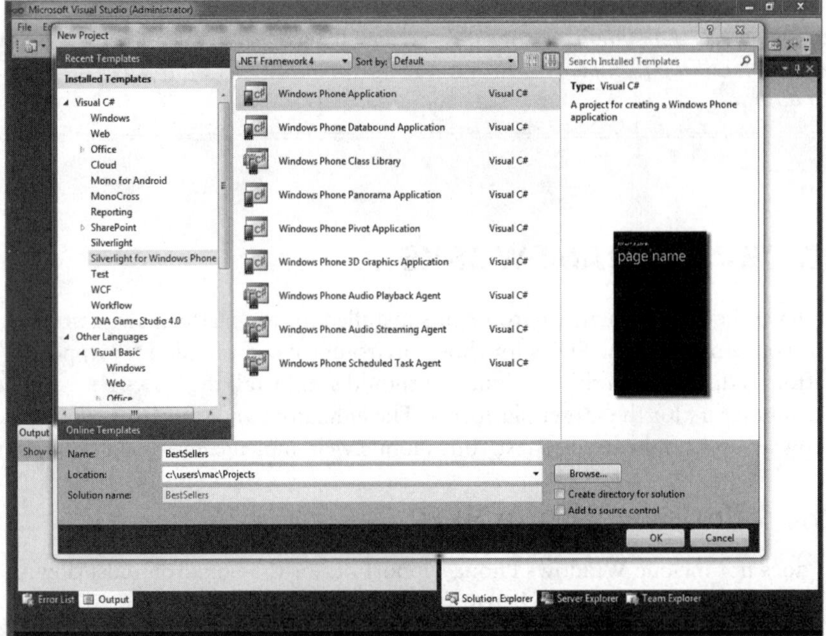

FIGURE 3-13: These templates for Windows Phone 7 project types should be available.

6. After installing the Windows Phone SDK, you can also start the Windows Phone Emulator for testing websites without starting Visual Studio 2010 or start a Windows Phone project. Simply go to the **Windows Start Button ➪ All Programs ➪ Windows Phone Developer Tools ➪ Windows Phone Emulator** and select it to run the emulator. Figure 3-14 shows an example of the emulator displaying a web page.

Preparing for iOS Development

To develop for iOS devices, you need the iOS SDK. MonoTouch uses the iOS SDK and its compiler to generate code from compiled .NET assemblies. This section goes over the installation of those components.

Be aware before you start that the Xcode developer tools require you to run Mac OSX 10.6 or newer.

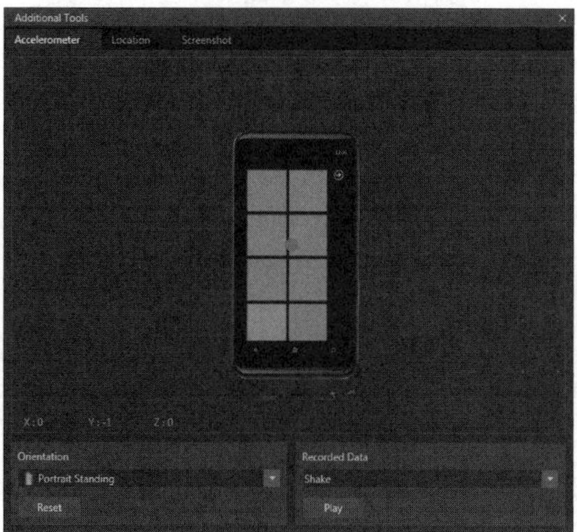

FIGURE 3-14: The Windows Phone Emulator can display a web page.

Installing the iOS SDK (iPod/iPhone/iPad)

Download and install Xcode and the iOS SDK as a single Disk Image file (.DMG) from `http://developer.apple.com/ios`. All versions of the iOS SDKs are bundled with Xcode, and you must have an Apple ID to download them. Select the latest version of the Xcode and iOS bundle that is available.

This is a single, large download (over 4.5GB). It contains the entire Xcode development environment and a version of iOS SDK. Like the Windows Phone 7 Developer tools, be prepared to wait. Included in the package are the developer's tools and iPad and iPhone simulators. Look for Xcode under the Applications directory, start it up, and make sure all installed properly. Figure 3-15 shows the Xcode development environment.

As with the Windows Phone emulator, you can test your code or your WebKit websites without using an actual device. Unlike the Windows Phone SDK, the iOS SDK provides a simulator instead of an emulator. The difference is that the code generated for a simulator is different from the code generated for an actual target device. For example, when installing an application to the Windows Phone emulator, you can install the identical code you would use on an actual phone, but with a simulator the code must be rebuilt to target an actual device. This is important in two ways. The first being that code you test against the simulator is significantly different than the code you would test against an actual device. Second, the simulator is much faster than an actual device because it's built against your development machine, uses your computer's hardware natively, and can give false expectations of how fast your application will run on an actual iPhone or iPad. This is significant in that it highlights why it is important to test the performance of your application on a real device to make certain it meets your user's expectations.

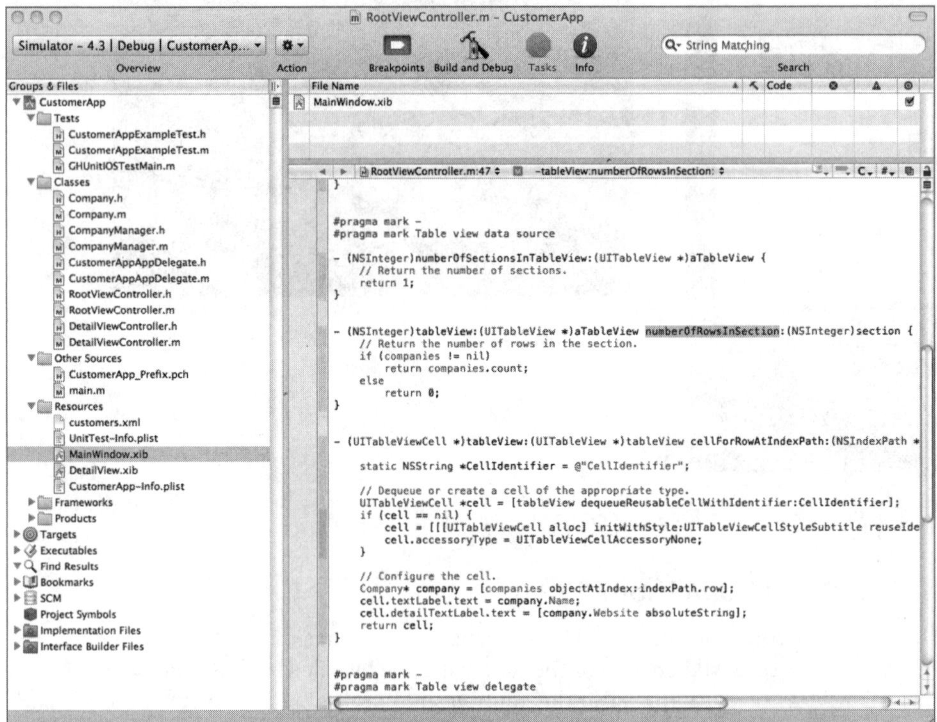

FIGURE 3-15: The Xcode development environment looks like this when it runs after installation.

To start the emulator without working in either Xcode or MonoDevelop, open **Finder**, and browse to **Developer ➪ Platforms ➪ iPhoneSimulator.platform ➪ Developer ➪ Applications ➪ iOS Simulator** where you can find the simulator application. Just double-click the application icon to start the simulator. Figure 3-16 shows Google running in the mobile Safari browser in the simulator.

FIGURE 3-16: The Google application is running in the iPhone simulator.

Installing MonoTouch

Download MonoTouch from `http://xamarin.com/trial` or if you purchased a licensed copy from `http://ios.xamarin.com/download`. The only difference between the trial and the licensed versions is that you need the licensed version to install to an actual device. The trial versions do not include the software needed to generate an app that can run on the physical device, so you must reinstall the software when you move from the trial version to the licensed version.

1. Start the installation by selecting the installer from the Downloads folder. You will be presented with a window containing a package install as you were when installing the Mono Framework. Double-click on the icon in the folder that comes up and you get the window shown in Figure 3-17.
2. After the installation finishes, start MonoDevelop from **Applications**, and select **File ⇨ New Solution.** You should see the MonoTouch templates, as shown in Figure 3-18. At this point your MonoTouch installation is complete; no further configuration is required to do iOS development with MonoTouch.

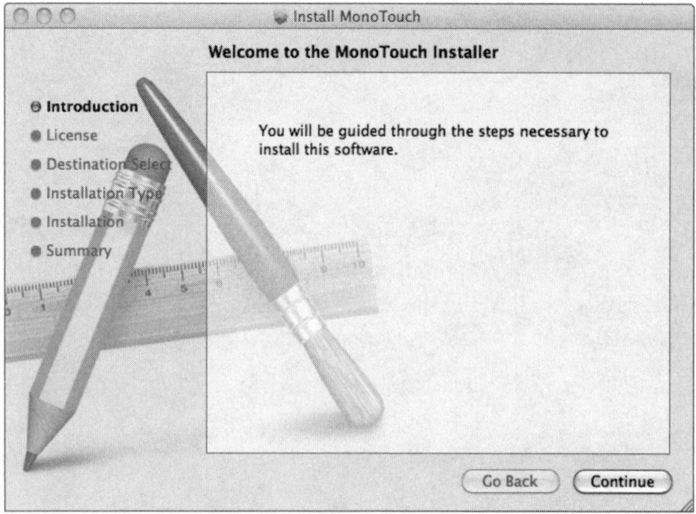

FIGURE 3-17: The MonoTouch installation application will provide steps to a successful installation.

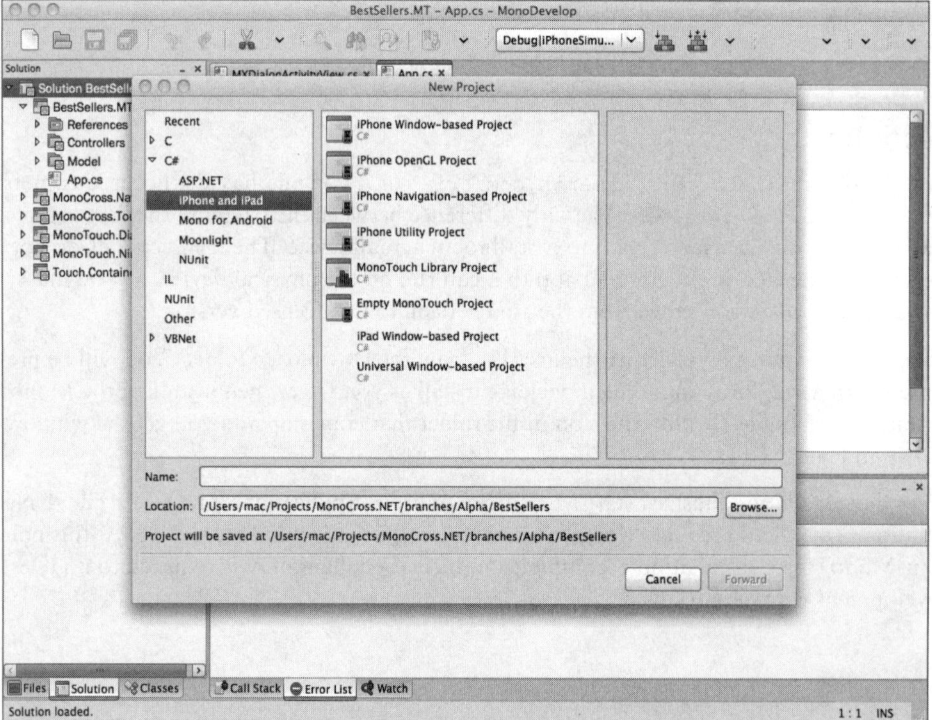

FIGURE 3-18: Your MonoTouch project templates are available in MonoDevelop.

Preparing for Android Development

Following is a quick walk-through of the installation of the Android development environment for both Windows and Mac OSX installation. The native tools for Android are all Java-based, and as such, the installation is largely the same for both Windows and Mac. Differences between the platforms are noted in the installation steps.

Installing the Java JDK

If you are running a version of Mac OSX prior to 10.7 Lion, you do not need to download and install the JDK because it is included natively in all Mac OSX installations. For versions 10.7 and beyond, find a Mac OSX version of the JDK that is available from the URL in step 1.

1. If you are installing to a Windows PC, download and install a 32-bit version of the Java JDK (Java Development Kit) from `www.oracle.com/technetwork/java/javase/downloads`.

   The download link of the version you need for development can be a bit hard to find; however, the download filename should be something like `jdk-6u26-windows-i586.exe`, where the `6u26` is the version number, as in Java version 6 update 26. Do *not* install the Version 7 Java JDK; it does not work for Android development at this time. See Figure 3-19 for a little help in selecting the correct version for Android development, because the Oracle download site can be a bit confusing for non-Java developers. You see the current version circled.

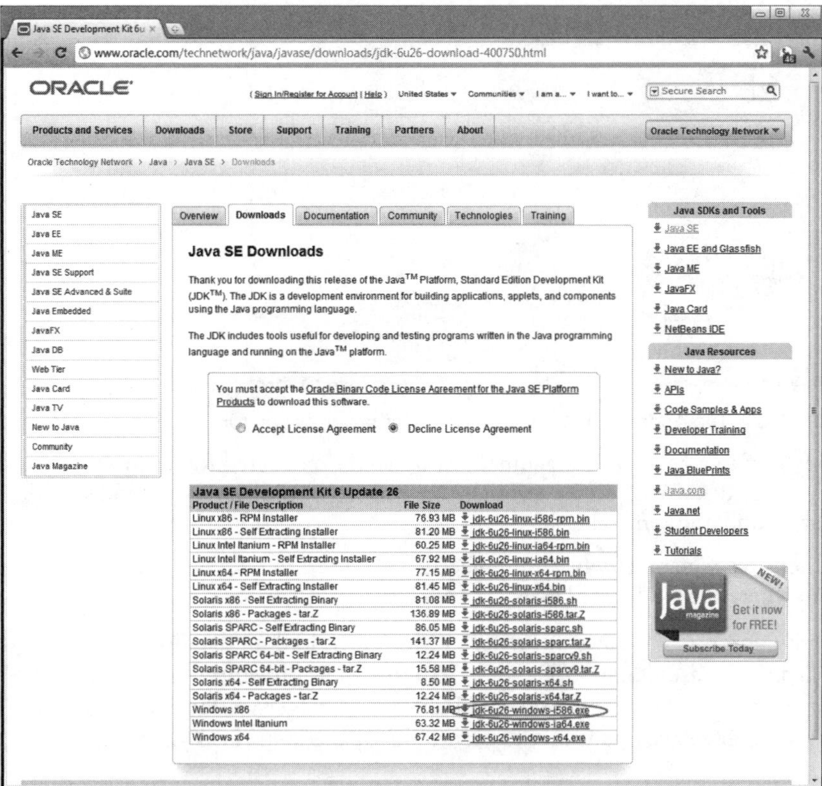

FIGURE 3-19: Select the correct version of the Java JDK.

2. Start the installation by running the installer. The normal Installation Wizard displays, where you must accept terms of service and installation location.

Installing the Android SDK

Google provides several installation options for the Android SDK; the simplest is to first install the starter kit it provides.

1. Download the Android Developer Starter Kit from `http://developer.android.com/sdk/index.html`.
2. If installing to a Windows PC, the native installer (.EXE) version is recommended because it sets up some of your environment for you, which can help later, and it makes it easier to uninstall in the future should that be needed. Also install it somewhere outside your Program Files directory because that can cause issues later with Windows security protections in some cases, particularly if you don't have admin rights to your PC. Figure 3-20 shows the install location changed to a directory named *Android* off the root of the primary hard drive.

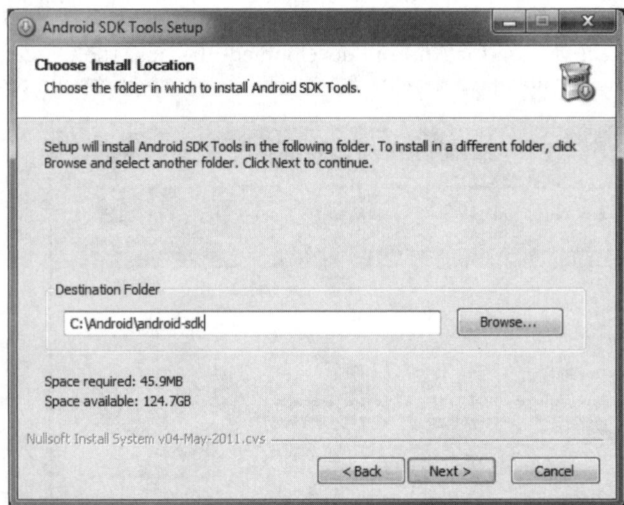

FIGURE 3-20: The Android SDK Windows installer prompts you for the installation location.

If installing to a Mac OSX machine, just move the extracted folder to a convenient location. A folder titled Android off the primary hard drive would also be a good selection because it is easy to find and remember.

In either case remember where you place it. You need to tell your MonoDevelop or Visual Studio where the Android SDK is located.

3. Using Explorer in Windows or Finder in Mac OSX, look in the directory where you just installed the Android Starter Kit, and go to the Tools directory; then run the `android` batch command file. This starts the Android Platform Manager via the command line terminal. Select **Available Packages** from the left window pane, and check off at least one Platform

from the list and any tool updates. See Figure 3-21 for an idea of what this looks like upon completion.

Looking at Figure 3-21, you might have noticed that there are several SDK platforms available and many other items in the available packages. The SDK packages are quite large, so choose only those that you need. If you don't know which version to select, note that SDK Platform 2.2 is the most prevalent on Android phones and SDK Platforms 3.X are meant only for tablets. Android 4.0 and beyond are combined. Additionally, add the latest version of the SDK Platform tools. Mono for Android uses them to package and deploy your solutions.

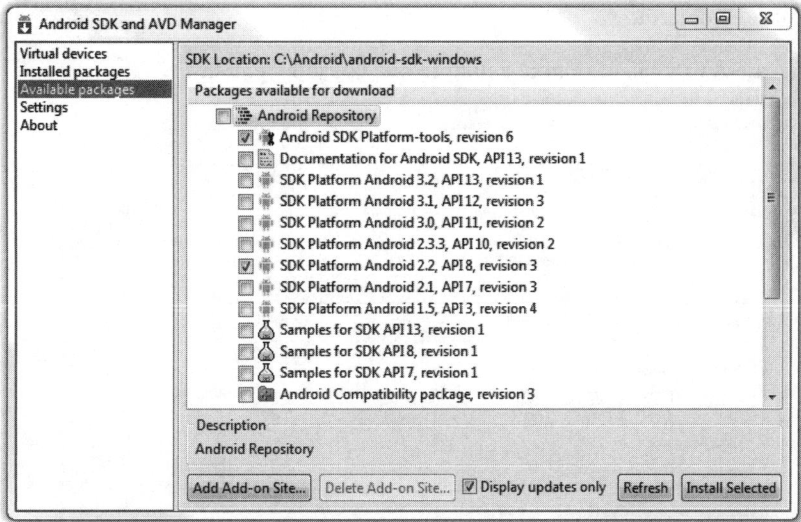

FIGURE 3-21: Select the appropriate downloads available from the AVD Manager.

4. You may be required to start the installation several times if there are dependencies among the platforms and the SDK tools. Carefully watch the progress because there is only minimal warning when the installation completes. You also need to return to the Android Platform Manager whenever you need to update or add new versions of the Android platform.

Now that you've installed the SDK platforms tools, you are done with the Android-specific installation. Now take a quick look at configuring and using the emulator.

Adding a Virtual Device

Unlike the Windows Phone emulator and iOS simulator, Android emulators must be created and configured. Although it requires a bit more work, it enables you to create emulators that more accurately depict actual devices for both testing and debugging purposes.

1. From the Andriod SDK and AVD Manager, select **Virtual Devices** from the left pane, as shown in Figure 3-22.

2. Click **New**.

3. Give this instance a name, then select an Android platform version from the dropdown list and an amount of memory for the external memory card. Add any other hardware attributes you'd like your emulator to have. In Figure 3-22 several are filled in to give you an idea.

   One particularly useful additional attribute is Device Ram Size; this enables you to specify the amount of memory Android and your program have to run in on the emulator. By default, the amount of memory allocated will be 256MB, far below your average device. Adding more memory can make debugging and running your program much faster. For additional resources, go to `http://developer.android.com` and look for the section on the Android emulator.

4. Click **Create AVD**. This can take a minute or two, so be patient.

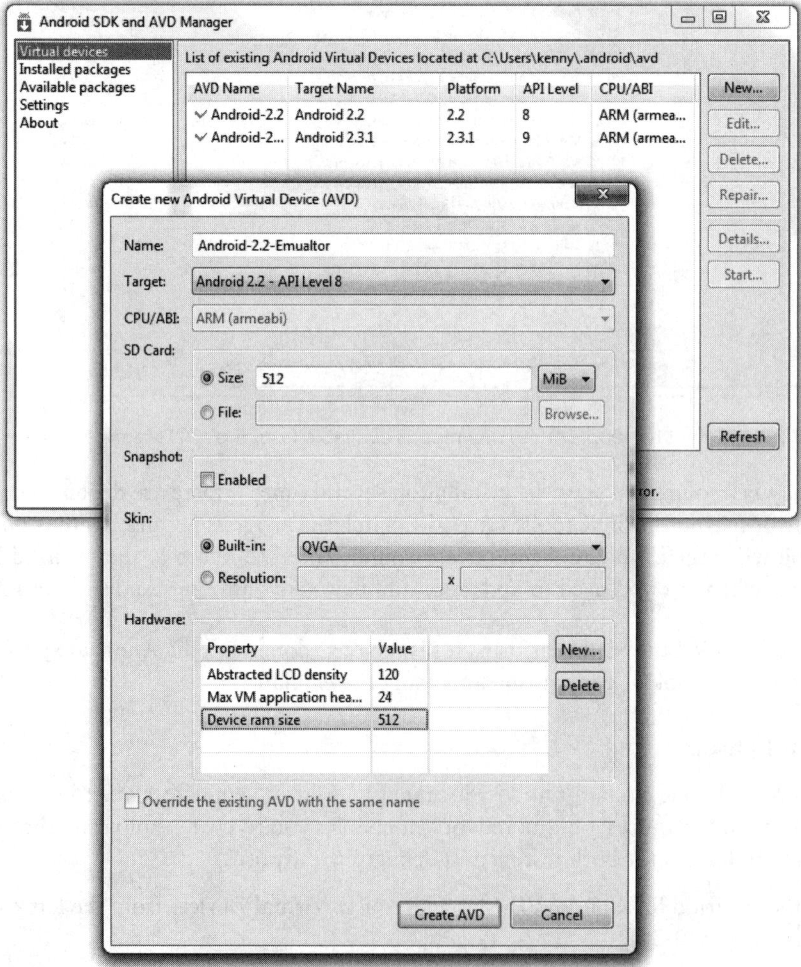

FIGURE 3-22: You can create an Emulator Image from the AVD Manager.

5. When complete you will be back to the AVD manager; select the emulator instance you just created, and click **Start**.
6. The emulator comes up and goes through its boot sequence and then is available for interaction. Figure 3-23 shows the emulator running its built-in browser.

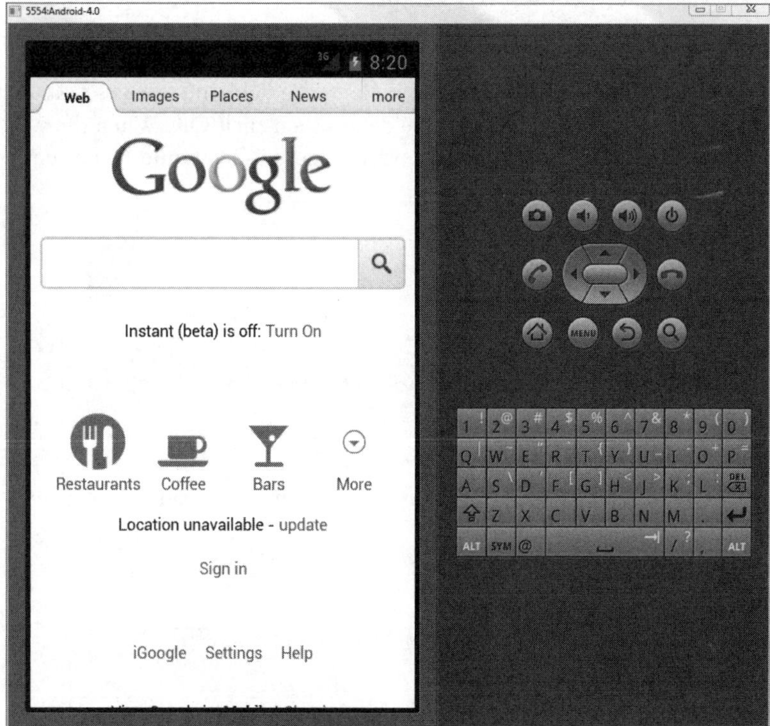

FIGURE 3-23: You can use the browser in the Android emulator to test your web solutions.

You now have an emulator instance to use for development and testing. You can add more instances that mimic different hardware configurations at any point.

Installing Eclipse

At this point you have enough of the Android SDK installed to run and build the samples; however, you should also install the Eclipse development environment and Android plug-ins for Eclipse. There is at least one good reason for this: the functionality of the Eclipse plug-ins for Android to visually edit and preview Android layout files. No external tool or Mono for Android, itself, has this capability. You can come back to this section at a later time because it has no effect on developing in Mono for Android.

Download and install the most recent version of Eclipse Classic from `www.eclipse.org/downloads`. Make certain you get the version labeled the 32-bit version because the Eclipse Plug-In for Android supports only the 32-bit version of Eclipse at this time. Eclipse is a self-contained environment in that it doesn't have or need an installer.

- On Windows you can just copy the extracted directory to the Program Files subdirectory and create a shortcut on the desktop.
- On Mac OSX you can just copy the extracted directory to the Applications folder.

Installing the Android Plug-In for Eclipse

To install the Android Plug-In for Eclipse, start Eclipse:

1. Select **Help ➪ Install New Software**. The Install window pictured in Figure 3-24 displays.
2. Click the **Add** button, put **`Android Plugin`** in the name field and **`https://dl-ssl.google.com/android/eclipse/`** in the Location field, and then click **OK**. When the window closes, the Developer Tools and the other items shown in Figure 3-24 should be present.

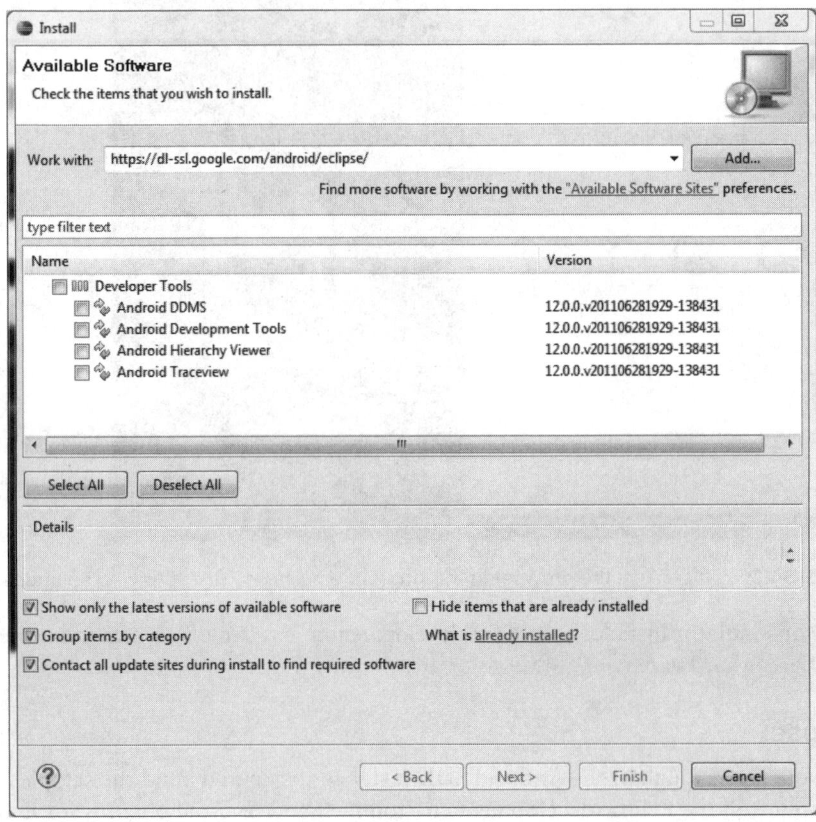

FIGURE 3-24: After you install the Eclipse Android plug-in, a number of developer tools are available.

3. Check the box in front of **Developer Tools**, and click **Next** through the next few pages and accept the licensing terms. Upon completion, the Finish button should be active.

4. Click **Finish**. The Android plug-in for Android installs.

Upon successful installation, you can create a new utility project and add a layout file to try out the various design tools that the Android plug-in provides. Figure 3-25 illustrates what the workspace is like. For more information on using the Android plug-in in Eclipse, see `http://developer.android.com`.

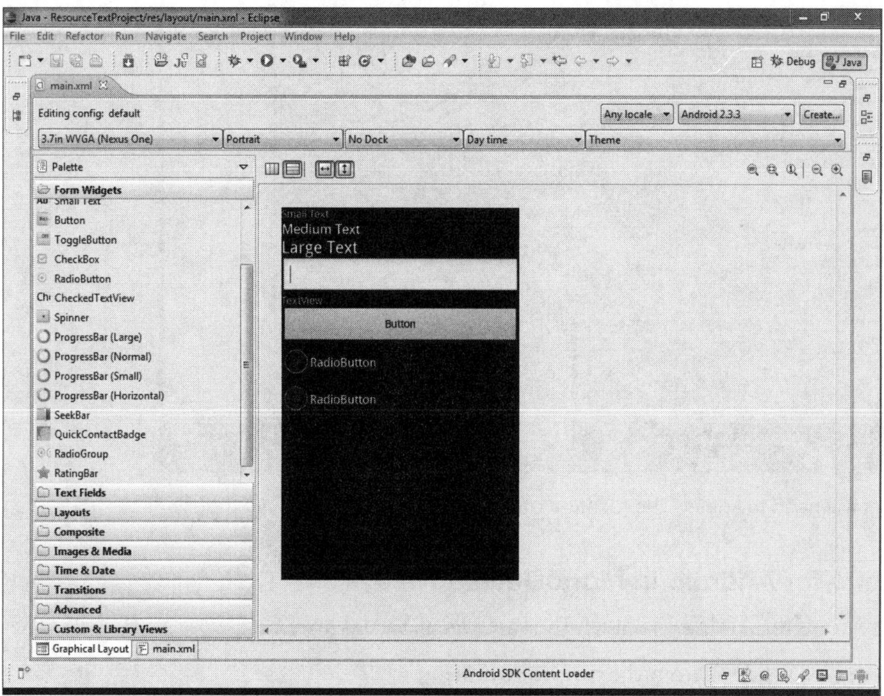

FIGURE 3-25: Use Eclipse with an Android plug-in to test out your Layout files.

Installing Mono for Android

Download and install Mono for Android from `http://xamarin/trial`. Click **Run**.

Configuring Mono for Android in Visual Studio

Configure the Android SDK location by first starting Visual Studio 2010.

1. Select **Tools ➪ Options** from the drop-down menu.
2. In the left pane, scroll down until you find **Mono for Android**, and select it.
3. Either type in or use the browse file dialog to locate your specific Android SDK Location, as shown in Figure 3-26.

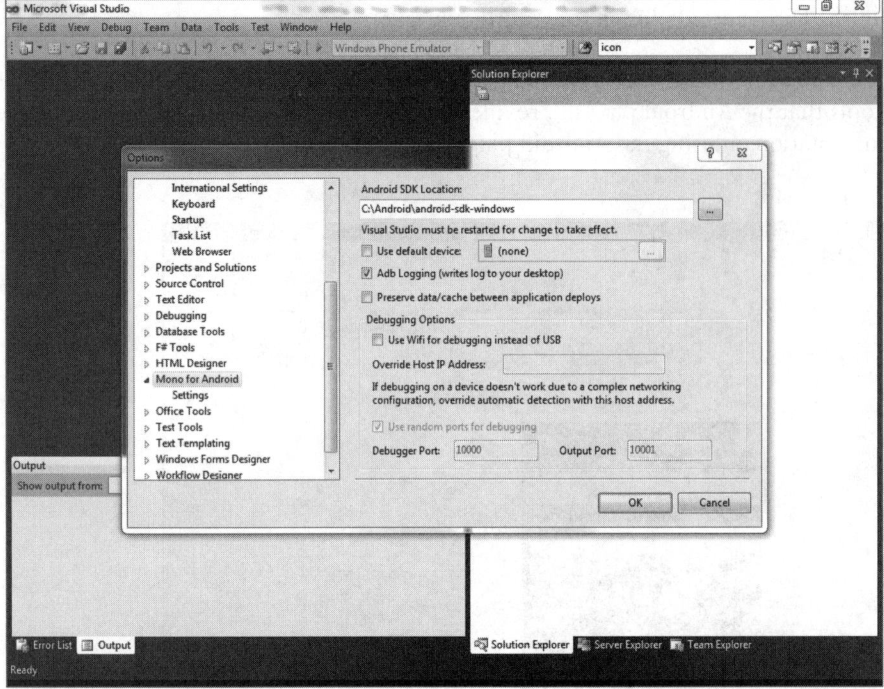

FIGURE 3-26: You will need to specify the location of the Android SDK for Visual Studio.

Configuring Mono for Android in MonoDevelop

Configuring the Mono for Android is much the same as in Visual Studio.

1. Select **Tools ⇨ Options** from the drop-down menu.
2. In the left pane, scroll down until you find **Mono for Android** located under the **Other** section, and select it.
3. Either type in or use the browse file dialog to locate your specific Android SDK location. Figure 3-27 shows the Options configuration dialog.

At this point you can create Mono for Android projects and build and run your code.

Installing MonoCross Project Templates

The majority of samples in this book revolve around a Model View Controller (MVC) cross-platform framework called *MonoCross*. As a convenience, project templates have been built that can add the appropriate references and add stub code for you to do your own implementations. You can either extend the provided samples as a starting point or use the templates; how you want to utilize the code and the templates is up to you.

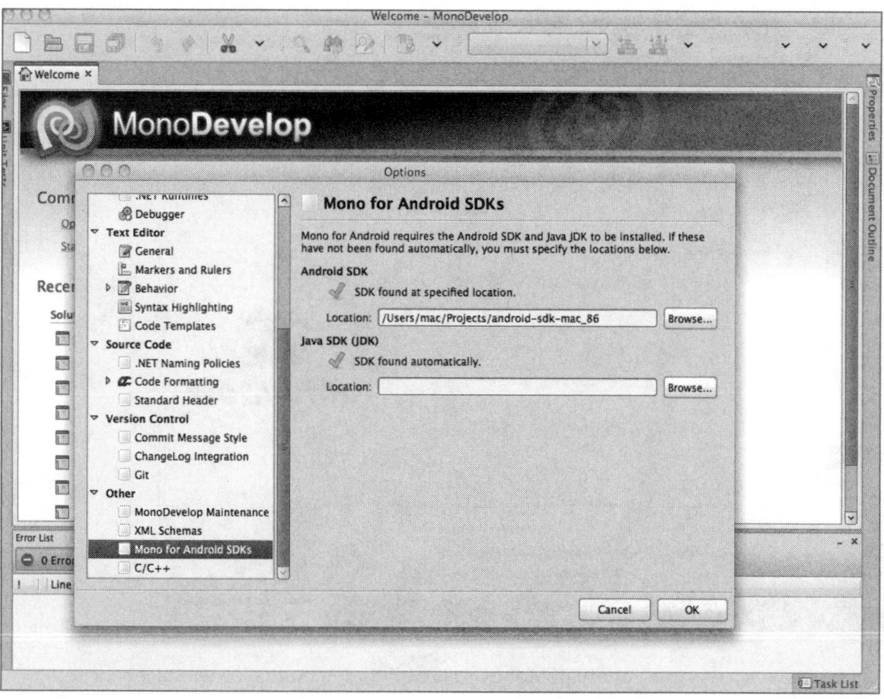

FIGURE 3-27: MonoDevelop requires you to specify the location of the Android SDK.

The latest versions of the MonoCross templates for Visual Studio are available from the MonoCross code repository at `www.monocross.net`, in the Downloads section, and should be labeled appropriately. The MonoCross templates for MonoDevelop are available through the MonoDevelop Add-in Manager.

Installing MonoCross Templates for Visual Studio 2010

The MonoCross templates for Visual Studio contain project templates for Android, Windows Phone, WebKit, and Console MonoCross bindings. In addition, there are class templates for the base classes exposed for these platforms.

1. Download the latest version of `MonoCross Templates.zip`.
2. Extract the `MonoCross Templates.vsix` package from the zip file.
3. Double-click on the `MonoCross Templates.vsix` file from the Download folder.
4. Follow the installation instructions displayed by the Visual Studio Extension Manager.
5. Start **Visual Studio**, or restart if you already had it running.
6. In Visual Studio, select **Tools ➪ Extension Manager**. You should now see the MonoCross Templates for Visual Studio in the list of installed extensions, as shown in Figure 3-28.

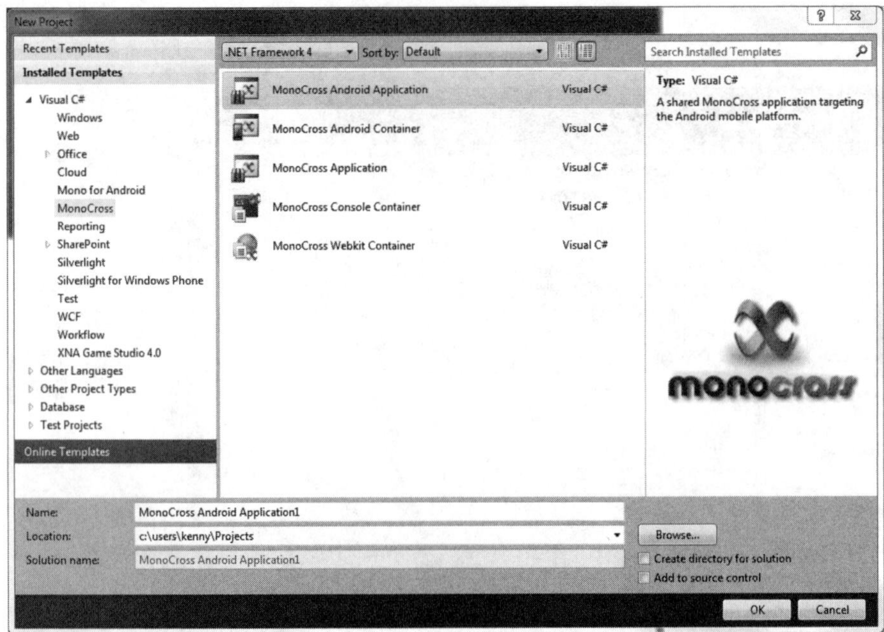

FIGURE 3-28: You now have access to a variety of MonoCross project templates for Visual Studio.

Installing the MonoCross Templates for MonoDevelop

The MonoCross templates for MonoDevelop contain the project and class templates for Mono for Android and MonoTouch MonoCross bindings.

1. Start **MonoDevelop.**
2. In MonoDevelop, select **Tools ⇨ Add-in Manager** and select the **Gallery** tab.
3. Select the **MonoCross MonoDevelop Templates** installation package for Mac OS.

A number of templates are available to you for building your cross-platform solutions from the new Project dialog.

Installing the MonoCross Utilities

Over time the authors have made an attempt to insulate the developer from platform differences that manage to make their way through the use of a single unified framework running on different platforms. The results of this effort are the MonoCross Utilities. This library is available for download from `www.monocross.net`. Usage of the library is covered extensively in Chapter 10, "Using MonoCross Utilities."

ORGANIZING YOUR SOLUTIONS

When you are developing multiplatform solutions, the organization of the code base is important. If you don't have a standard in place from the start, your code base will become hard to navigate, and adding multiple platforms and project types into the mix can make it even worse. Following standard practices such as having your project names match your assembly names and your assembly names match their directory names goes a long way toward keeping track of what you're working on and where it resides in a source control tree hierarchy and on disk.

The biggest issues that break the standard project in terms of maintaining a common code base with shared code across multiple platforms are as follows:

- Different platforms sharing the same code in the same directory/project
- The same application with separate implementations
- Similar assemblies with platform-specific code
- Code files with the same class name targeted for different platforms

To solve the first issue, different platforms sharing code in the same directory, it is possible to keep multiple projects files in the same directory as the shared code, but to clarify what code goes with what platform, add a two-letter platform name to the end of the project. For example, MonoCross has an assembly of shared code with the directory name and name space of `MonoCross.Navigation`. The project name for common Windows targets keeps that same name, with the Android version taking the name `MonoCross.Navigation.MD` and the iOS version taking the name `MonoCross.Navigation.MT`, and so on. In addition, the assemblies take on the name of the project to reduce the chance of mixing up the platform that the assembly is built for when copying around assemblies built for different platforms. This naming convention also enables you to keep the assemblies in the same directory when statically referencing them.

Table 3-2 shows the extensions and platform names used in the examples provided here.

TABLE 3-2: Platform Names and Abbreviations

SHORT PLATFORM NAME	ABBREVIATION
Windows	None (WebKit, Console, Windows Forms)
Droid	MD (Android [MonoDroid])
Touch	MT (MonoTouch)
WindowsPhone	WP
Windows Presentation Foundation	WPF

To solve the second issue, in which the same application may have several implementations, add a prefix to the directory. The application had its own directory, and each platform that the application is built for has its own directory beneath it, so prefix the full common platform name. Take an application named `CustomerManangement` having an implementation for WebKit, Android, and Windows Phone. Under a directory `CustomerManagement` you can have three directories named `WindowsPhone.Container`, `WebKit.Container`, and `Droid.Container` that have the project and code files for each platform.

When you have similar assemblies with platform-specific code, the third issue, use the platform name to designate unshared code in a similar assembly with a common name followed by the platform name. For example, in MonoCross you can have platform-specific implementations that derive from a common base. So use the common base `MonoCross` and append the platform names, resulting in `MonoCross.Touch`, `MonoCross.Droid`, and `MonoCross.WindowsPhone`.

To solve the fourth issue, having code files with the same class name targeted for different platforms, use the same convention as the first. If you have an implementation of the `BarcodeReader` class that will have different implementations on different platforms, you can use the same name and interface across those platforms and keep the files in the same directory, for example, `BarcodeReader.MD.cs` and `BarcodeReader.WP.cs` would house the same classes but with platform-specific implementations.

Figure 3-29 shows how items referenced with this naming convention appear in the Visual Studio Solution Explorer.

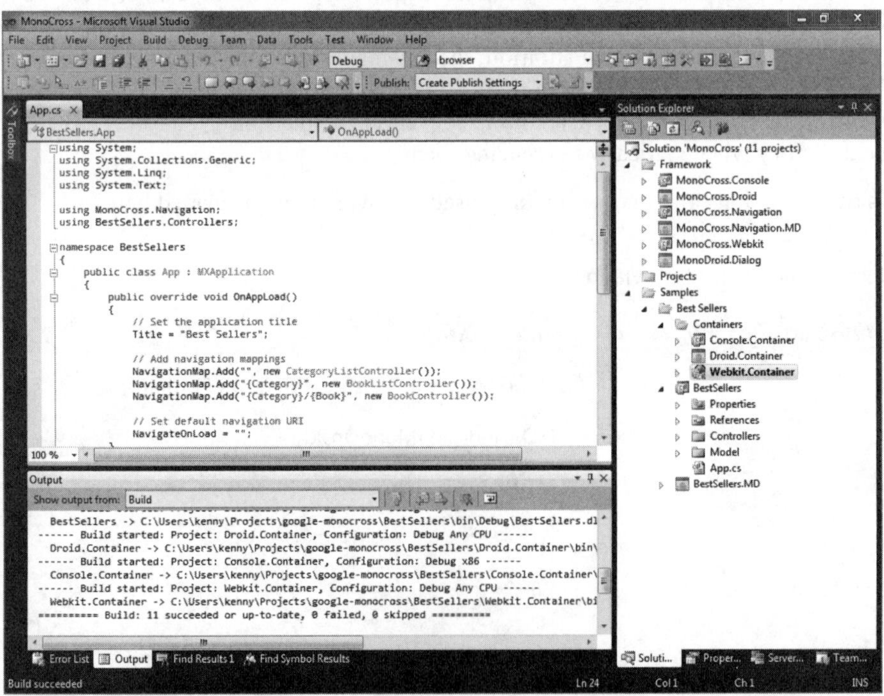

FIGURE 3-29: Naming conventions help organize your cross platform projects and solutions.

NAVIGATING THE SAMPLE CODE

As you work through the examples in this book, you may choose either to type in all the code manually, or to use the source code files that accompany the book. All the source code used in this book is available for download at `www.wrox.com`. When at the site, simply locate the book's title (use the Search box or one of the title lists) and click the **Download Code** link on the book's detail page to obtain all the source code for the book. Code that is included on the website is highlighted by the following icon:

Available for download on Wrox.com

The code in the book is largely organized as we suggest you organize your completed projects and follows the conventions set forth in the section "Organizing Your Solutions." Figure 3-30 shows the project structure and the solution files for all the sample applications. Unfortunately this isn't the easiest to follow as you go through the chapters because the files are a final product instead of snippets that follow from chapter to chapter as they would for a book dedicated to teaching individual coding concepts. So if you want to look over and run the code before a particular section is wrapped up in an application, you can build and run any of the code at any time.

The Chapter 4, "The MonoCross Pattern," introduces the Model-View-Controller concepts with a cross-platform concept, and Chapter 5, "Building Shared Applications," covers building the platform independent code, which iswrapped up in Chapter 6, "Building MonoCross Containers." If you want to sample the code and concepts from those chapters, you can build and run the code from the `CustomerManagement.Console`, `CustomerManagement.Touch`, `CustomerManagement.Droid` or `CustomerManagement.WebKit` directory. The solution files in these folders are independent and complete and can be run individually.

Chapter 7, "Designing and Building Data Services," covers the server-side services built and consumed by the mobile applications and can be found in the solution files in the `CustomerManagement.Data` directory.

Chapter 8, "Consuming Data Services," and Chapter 10 "Using the MonoCross Utilities" code the client side consumption, storage, and manipulation data. The sample code from those chapters can be found in the `CustomerManagement.DataServices` and `CustomerManagement.Samples` directories.

Chapter 9, "Accessing the Device," covers different aspects of direct device access and how you can use mobile specific aspects found in most mobile applications within your applications in a consistent manner, making your applications easier to manage.

Chapter 11, "Hybrid Applications," covers web hybrid applications. The sample code for those is available in the `WebHybrid` solutions directories `WebHybrid.Touch`, `WebHybrid.Droid` and `WebHybrid.WindowsPhone`.

Chapter 12, "Delivering Applications to the Enterprise," covers extending the concepts beyond mobile devices and shows how you can move your server side services into the cloud and your applications to Windows Presentation Foundation.

Explore the sample code and the chapters in any order you find of interest to you, either before or after reading the chapters that cover the code within.

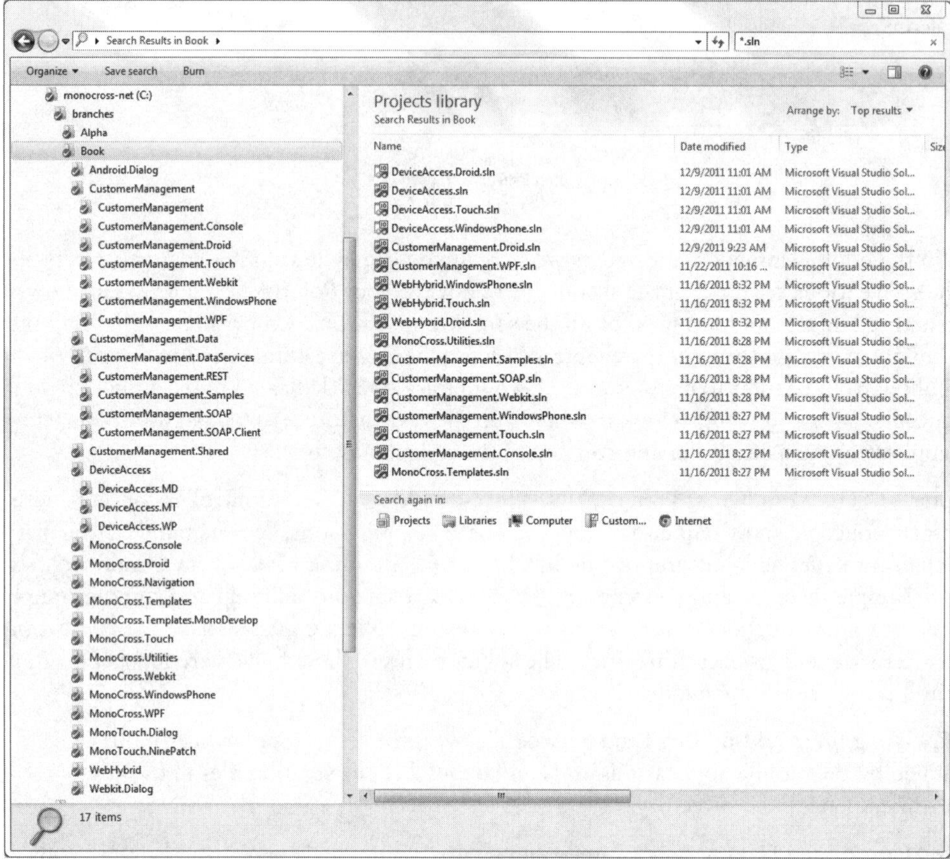

FIGURE 3-30: If you are looking for a Visual Studio Solution from the book, you can find it here.

CONTINUOUS INTEGRATION

Continuous Integration (CI) generally consists of a combination of building, running unit tests, and deploying finished applications. Both Visual Studio and MonoDevelop come with command-line tools that enable solutions and projects to be built and deployed automatically. These tools also work for solutions that contain the additional platforms discussed in this book. In addition, although not covered here, these tools support the creation and signing of a redistributable application via project settings. As a result, with effort, you can work multiple platform builds into your normal CI work flow.

SUMMARY

In this chapter, you learned how to install all the platforms and frameworks needed for mobile development. You've gone through installing the Visual Studio and MonoDevelop development environments needed to build your mobile solutions. You've installed the mobile frameworks and mobile SDKs for the Android, iOS, and Windows Phone. You've also seen each of the device emulators for these platforms and how they can be of use in testing mobile websites.

Just keep reading, and in the next chapter, you'll be introduced to the MonoCross pattern. The chapter discusses the problems you are likely to face in developing for multiple platforms and supply you with answers. You'll find observations that can help you be successful in developing and deploying your solutions.

The MonoCross Pattern

WHAT'S IN THIS CHAPTER?

- Recognizing cross-platform development challenges
- Making your code portable with Mono
- Developing for multiple platforms
- Implementing the Model-View-Controller pattern in MonoCross
- Building shared applications in MonoCross
- Developing platform containers in MonoCross

Now that you've evaluated your architectural options, designed your user experience, and set up your environment, you're ready to begin coding. But before you dive in, it is crucial to understand the problems inherent to cross-platform mobile development and the approach necessary to solve them. By reading this chapter you can achieve a greater understanding of some of the challenges developers face when attempting to write cross-platform mobile applications and explore the MonoCross open-source pattern as a solution to those challenges. You see how MonoCross enables sharing of business logic and data access code across platforms using proven enterprise software patterns, such as the Model-View-Controller (MVC) and Separated Interface patterns. Finally, you learn how MonoCross uses a shared application to define application workflow using URI-based navigation and platform containers to create sophisticated user experiences that can be deployed to multiple platforms and rendered from the shared application.

UNDERSTANDING THE CROSS-PLATFORM PROBLEM

With the introduction of so many new smartphone platforms in recent years, more enterprise developers are being asked to develop mobile applications. When the application requirements dictate cross-platform support, many enterprise developers find themselves in unfamiliar territory. Before you begin developing cross-platform mobile applications, you should consider how you might handle several problems to ensure an effective solution.

Understanding Native Platform Differences

Often, the first question an enterprise developer asks is, "What mobile platform should I choose?" Most of the time, the decision is based on the developer's skills. Java developers are drawn to Android, Mac developers to iOS, and .NET developers to Windows Phone because they already possess the basic knowledge of the language and platform needed to succeed. There are new APIs and some mobile-specific concepts, but knowing the language and conventions of a particular technology can significantly shorten and flatten the mobile development learning curve.

For cross-platform development, these technology differences present a problem. Most large enterprise software organizations tend to create homogeneous development environments, which is why most enterprise developers become specialists in a single technology. "One Language, One Platform" has been the mantra of most enterprise development shops because it's easier to manage things that way. They settle on a single technology, hire developers with those technology skills, and build their applications. The organization also dictates the infrastructure needed and the devices that will be supported — but most of these decisions are made *after* the technology is chosen.

When Apple came along with the iPhone — and Google introduced the Android operating system — enterprises started having their technology decisions made for them. Employees started demanding that IT support their personal devices and give them apps with which to do their work. This consumerization trend has turned corporate IT on its head. The status quo is no longer sufficient. "One Language, One Platform" doesn't work anymore in the rapidly changing world of mobility. Enterprises now face problems they never had before. Supporting multiple, heterogeneous platforms has become a necessity that few organizations have the expertise to address because of the homogeneous platform strategies they followed in the past.

Acknowledging HTML 5 Limitations

Many clients today look to HTML 5 as the answer to their cross-platform mobile problems. Most of the leading mobile browsers support HTML 5, which brings incredible flexibility and power to mobile web applications. Many commercial HTML 5 frameworks, such as Sencha Touch and JQuery Mobile, are designed for mobile form factors, and the apps you can write with these frameworks are truly impressive. But there are just some things a web-based application cannot do. The HTML 5 Cache Manifest standard provides for disconnected capabilities, but it is still difficult to support offline transactions without some intelligence to manage them outside the browser. Access to the device's native features, (GPS, camera, accelerometer, file, and storage), all require interaction via native frameworks such as PhoneGap. Despite the advances in the HTML 5 user experience, it still cannot provide the same richness that the native platforms can.

HTML 5 can provide an elegant, cost-effective solution to many cross-platform problems, and to taking a long, hard look at it should be the first step in any assessment of an enterprise mobile application strategy. Most enterprises already have an army of web developers who can be retrained to develop mobile-optimized web applications. For many of them, developing mobile web applications can often provide a critical first step into the cross-platform mobile world. But as soon as the problem at hand requires disconnected transactions, access to native device functions, or a rich user experience that HTML cannot provide, developers find they must consider native options.

Taking a Hybrid Approach

As mentioned previously, HTML 5 has no specification for access to native mobile device features. These features are only available via native APIs. To access these services, an abstraction layer must be written — usually in JavaScript — that exposes the native functions to the browser. This can be done with commercial frameworks, but enterprise applications often require integration with non-standard device functions or device peripherals, such as barcode scanners. To support this kind of device integration, developers can use a hybrid approach that integrates both web and native components. But this approach still requires knowledge of and skill with the native language and SDK of multiple platforms and peripherals, raising the same issues of language and platform support mentioned previously using a purely native approach.

In many situations, taking a hybrid approach makes sense, but changing requirements around user interaction or disconnected ability may force developers to refactor HTML and JavaScript features to run natively on the device. This kind of refactoring can be expensive and time-consuming when supporting multiple devices with disparate platform languages and APIs.

ENABLING CODE PORTABILITY WITH MONO

Fortunately for most organizations who have already made significant investments in C# and .NET, Mono provides a compelling path forward. Developers have been talking about code reuse and portability for decades, but the discussions have been largely theoretical — until now. With the release of MonoTouch and Mono for Android, a new world of possibilities has been opened.

We have been working with C# and .NET for years, and the foundation of our mobile practice has always been Windows Mobile development in CE and .NET Compact Framework. Within a few days of downloading the MonoTouch evaluation, we had ported several client projects from .NET Compact Framework into MonoTouch and actually proved the concept of code portability in a real-world application. For the first time in our careers, we saw true code reuse occurring in heterogeneous platforms — it was exciting! The theoretical discussions around layered architectures and reuse of code became real, and the benefits are apparent in this new world order.

So we began to put together a vision for cross-platform mobile development. With MonoTouch and Mono for Android, we could clearly demonstrate that the millions of dollars our clients had invested in existing applications could be brought to these new platforms, and with the application of a few proven enterprise design patterns, significant modules could be shared across them all.

.NET Developers now had a choice: They could deliver native applications in MonoTouch and Mono for Android, or they could deliver web applications using HTML 5 and ASP.NET — but a new choice was also available. From experience delivering hybrid applications with ASP.NET, a new pattern emerged. Native device integration could be achieved in HTML 5 via JavaScript interface and custom URI schemes. Developers could now build applications across the hybrid spectrum, delivering as much or as little native versus web functionality as their use-case required. Web techniques could be used where they were strongest and native techniques where they excelled. Not only had Mono enabled cross-platform development, but it also enabled *cross-architecture* development.

Figure 4-1 illustrates this idea by showing various technologies plotted across two dimensions: device platform and application architecture. On the native application end of the architecture spectrum, you see the native device technologies, Objective-C for iOS, Java for Android, and Silverlight for Windows Phone. These technologies are great for delivering native experiences on each platform individually, but offer no cross-platform benefits. On the web application end of the spectrum, you see HTML 5, with PhoneGap providing some access to the device. These technologies provide cross-platform benefits, but can't deliver the full benefits of a native experience. By combining HTML 5 with C#, .NET, and Mono, you can achieve cross-platform benefits across the entire application architecture spectrum. Only the code-portability of Mono makes this approach possible.

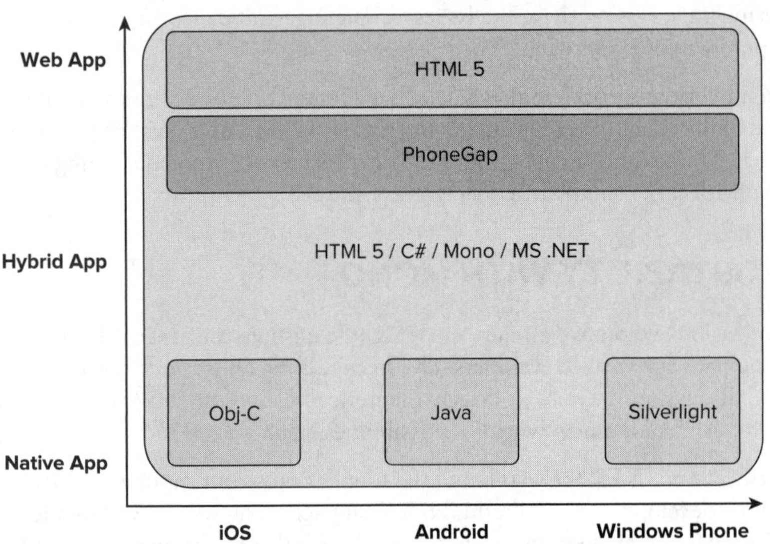

FIGURE 4-1: Cross-platform and cross-architecture development has been enabled with the convergence of HTML 5 with C#/.NET and Mono.

This code portability model has become the foundation upon which we built the MonoCross pattern. The core principles of code reuse not only across platforms, but also across architectures became our rallying cry. It remains our vision moving forward.

DEVELOPING FOR MULTIPLE PLATFORMS

There are many considerations when developing cross-platform mobile applications. Although Mono provides a unified language and portability of code across platforms, there are still significant architectural problems that remain to be solved.

Defining a Cross-Platform Architecture

The realization of code portability across both the platform and architecture dimensions was exciting, but there were some practical architectural problems that still needed to be solved. Most business and data access code could be ported and shared easily. This was proven in our initial experiments with MonoTouch. But the UI paradigms exposed by the various native SDKs were decidedly different. Beyond that the problem of workflow and navigation needed to be solved. How do you enable cross-architecture development when the fundamental construction of application screens varies so much between web and native implementations? Finally, a mechanism was needed to handle differences in presentation of objects in-play and successfully communicate those differences across the UI and to the shared application.

Separating the User Interface

The solution to the mismatch in UI paradigms was obvious. Developers needed fully customized views in the presentation layer, while sharing as much of the other application code as possible. Figure 4-2 illustrates this concept using a layered application architecture in which your application and data layers are shared, but your presentation layer is fully customized.

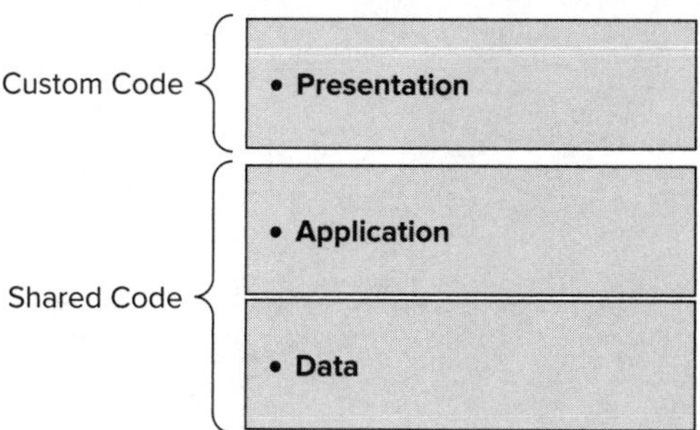

FIGURE 4-2: By separating the user interface, you can share business logic and data access code across platforms.

This concept of separated application layers has been used successfully by enterprise developers for years. Following this approach, developers can build a platform-specific user interface and take full advantage of native device controls and capabilities. All business logic and data access code can be written once and referenced by each platform-specific user interface. New devices can be added by simply writing a new presentation layer for that platform, which is just what the separated layer pattern was designed for.

UNDERSTANDING THE MONOCROSS SOLUTION

To accomplish this separation of business and data logic from the presentation layer we combined two tried-and-true patterns of enterprise development: Model-View-Controller (MVC) and Separated Interface.

Using the Model-View-Controller Pattern

The MonoCross MVC pattern builds upon the traditional MVC pattern, shown in Figure 4-3.

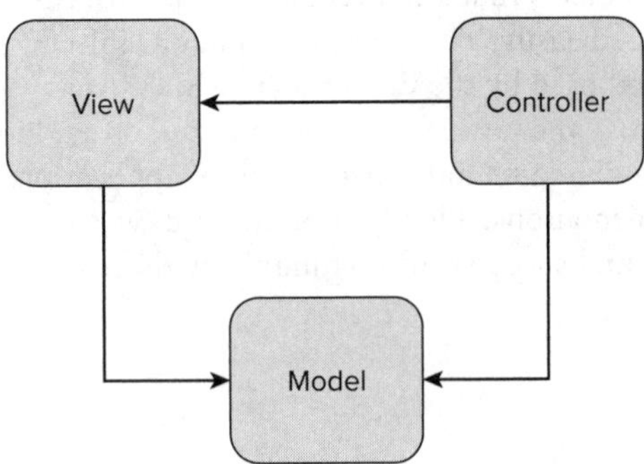

FIGURE 4-3: The traditional Model-View-Controller pattern is straightforward.

But in the MonoCross implementation, we added a Separated Interface between the view and controller to facilitate the separation of platform-specific presentations from the cross-platform application code. This pattern is illustrated in Figure 4-4.

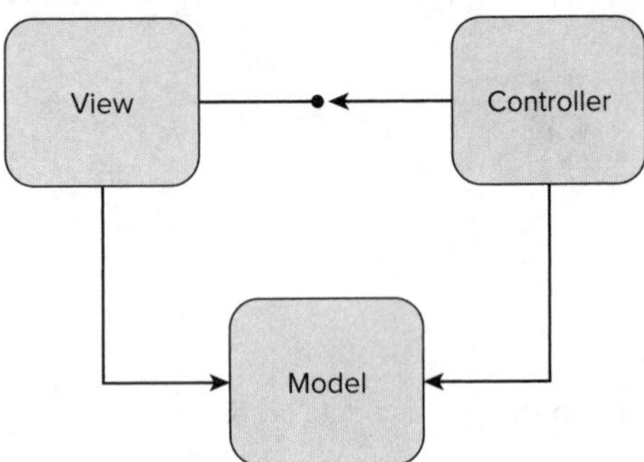

FIGURE 4-4: This version of the MonoCross Model-View-Controller pattern includes a separated interface.

This modification of the pattern decouples the platform-specific presentation views from the common code in the shared application. This enables developers to build whatever customized views are required for the platforms they intend to support without regard to how those views will be bound to the model and rendered in the application. As long as the views implement the Separated Interface definition, they will be processed by the controller and appropriately rendered. This concept is illustrated in more detail in the "Building a Platform-Specific View" section of this chapter.

Defining a Simple Model

Now that you understand the fundamental MonoCross MVC pattern, look at an example implementation, starting with the model. The model represents any business objects being acted upon in your application. For example, you may want to represent a customer in a customer management system using the code in Listing 4-1.

LISTING 4-1: A simple Customer class

Available for download on Wrox.com

```
public class Customer
{
  public Customer()
  {
    ID = "0";
    Name = string.Empty;
    Website = string.Empty;
    PrimaryAddress = new Address();
    Addresses = new List<Address>();
    Contacts = new List<Contact>();
    Orders = new List<Order>();
  }

  public string ID { get; set; }
  public string Name { get; set; }
  public string Website { get; set; }
  public string PrimaryPhone { get; set; }
  public Address PrimaryAddress { get; set; }
  public List<Address> Addresses { get; set; }
  public List<Contact> Contacts { get; set; }
  public List<Order> Orders { get; set; }
}
```

Found in the CustomerManagement.Shared/Model/Customer.cs file of the download

The `Customer` class contains all the properties necessary to describe a customer in your application. Any methods needed to provide business or processing logic for a customer can be added as needed, but you need only a simple data representation for this example.

Creating a MonoCross Controller

Now that you've defined your model object, you need to create a controller that can load the model from your system-of-record and make any business decisions about processing of the model for presentation in your views. Controllers in a MonoCross application are inherited from the abstract `MXController<T>` class.

Listing 4-2 shows the `IMXController` interface definition, and the `MXController<T>` generic implementation. The controller definition contains methods and properties used by the MonoCross framework to load controllers, process model logic, and render views.

LISTING 4-2: The MXController class

Available for download on Wrox.com

```
using System;
using System.Collections.Generic;

namespace MonoCross.Navigation
{
  public interface IMXController
```

continues

LISTING 4-2 *(continued)*

```
  {
    Dictionary<string, string> Parameters { get; set; }
    String Uri { get; set; }
    IMXView View { get; set; }
    Type ModelType { get; }
    object GetModel();

    string Load(Dictionary<string, string> parameters);
    void RenderView();
  }

  public abstract class MXController<T> : IMXController
  {
    public string Uri { get; set; }
    public Dictionary<string, string> Parameters { get; set; }
    public T Model { get; set; }
    public Type ModelType { get { return typeof(T); } }

    public virtual IMXView View { get; set; }

    public object GetModel() { return Model; }
    public abstract string Load(Dictionary<string, string> parameters);
    public virtual void RenderView() { if (View != null) View.Render(); }
    }
}
```

MonoCross.Navigation/MXController.cs

The `MXController<T>` *class implements the* `IMXController` *interface, which defines the contract for a MonoCross controller. The interface consists of the properties, methods, and events necessary for the MonoCross framework to manipulate the model and trigger the rendering of platform-specific views.*

Each controller class can handle all the business and data logic for a particular model type. You can create controllers at any level of your model hierarchy, but it is a best practice to create your controllers at the level that makes the most sense for the specific needs of your application and for the use cases described by your application's workflow requirements.

Techniques for implementing your model and controllers are covered in more detail in Chapter 5, "Building Shared Applications."

The generic type you specify in your implementation will be the model type that will be acted upon by the controller. So define a controller for your `Company` class using the code in Listing 4-3.

Available for download on Wrox.com

LISTING 4-3: The Customer controller

```
using System;
using System.Collections.Generic;
using System.IO;
```

```
using System.Linq;
using System.Text;
using System.Net;
using System.Xml.Serialization;

using MonoCross.Navigation;

using CustomerManagement.Shared;
using CustomerManagement.Shared.Model;

namespace CustomerManagement.Controllers
{
  public class CustomerController : MXController<Customer>
  {
    public override string Load(Dictionary<string, string> parameters)
    {
      string perspective = ViewPerspective.Default;

      string customerId = null;
      parameters.TryGetValue("CustomerId", out customerId);

      // get the action, assumes
      string action;
      if (!parameters.TryGetValue("Action", out action))  {
        // set default action if none specified
        action = "GET";
        }

      switch (action)
      {
        case "EDIT":
        case "GET":
        // populate the customer model
        if (customerId == null)
          throw new Exception("No Customer Id found");
          if (string.Equals(customerId.ToUpper(), "NEW")) {
            // assign Model a new customer for editing
            Model = new Customer();
            perspective = ViewPerspective.Update;
          } else {
            Model = GetCustomer(customerId);
            if (String.Equals(action, "EDIT"))
              perspective = ViewPerspective.Update;
            else
              perspective = ViewPerspective.Default;
            }
          break;

        case "DELETE":
          if (customerId == null)
            customerId = Model.ID;
            // post delete request to the server
            DeleteCustomer(customerId);

            // return and let redirected controller execute,
```

continues

LISTING 4-3 *(continued)*

```
            // remaining navigation is ignored
            MXContainer.Instance.Redirect("Customers");
            return ViewPerspective.Delete;

          case "CREATE":
            // process addition of new model
            if(AddNewCustomer(Model))
              MXContainer.Instance.Redirect("Customers");
            break;

          case "UPDATE":
            if(UpdateCustomer(Model))
              MXContainer.Instance.Redirect("Customers");
            break;
        }

        return perspective;
      }

      public static Customer GetCustomer(string customerId)
      {
#if LOCAL_DATA
        return CustomerManagement.Data.XmlDataStore.GetCustomer(customerId);
#else
        string urlCustomers =
          string.Format("http://localhost/MXDemo/customers/{0}.xml", customerId);

        HttpWebRequest request = (HttpWebRequest)HttpWebRequest.Create(urlCustomers);
        XmlSerializer serializer = new XmlSerializer(typeof(Customer));
        using (StreamReader reader = new StreamReader(request.GetResponse()
                                                   .GetResponseStream(), true))
        {
          return (Customer)serializer.Deserialize(reader);
        }
#endif
      }

      public static bool UpdateCustomer(Customer customer)
      {
#if LOCAL_DATA
        CustomerManagement.Data.XmlDataStore.UpdateCustomer(customer);
#else
        string urlCustomers = "http://localhost/MXDemo/customers/customer.xml";

        HttpWebRequest request = (HttpWebRequest)HttpWebRequest.Create(urlCustomers);
        request.Method = "PUT";
        request.ContentType = "application/xml";

        using (Stream dataStream = request.GetRequestStream())
        {
          XmlSerializer serializer = new XmlSerializer(typeof(Customer));
          serializer.Serialize(dataStream, customer);
        }

        request.GetResponse();
```

```
#endif
        return true;
      }

      public static bool AddNewCustomer(Customer customer)
      {
#if LOCAL_DATA
        CustomerManagement.Data.XmlDataStore.CreateCustomer(customer);
#else
        string urlCustomers = "http://localhost/MXDemo/customers/customer.xml";

        HttpWebRequest request = (HttpWebRequest)HttpWebRequest.Create(urlCustomers);
        request.Method = "POST";
        request.ContentType = "application/xml";

        using (Stream dataStream = request.GetRequestStream())
        {
          XmlSerializer serializer = new XmlSerializer(typeof(Customer));
          serializer.Serialize(dataStream, customer);
        }

        request.GetResponse();
#endif
        return true;
      }

      public static bool DeleteCustomer(string customerId)
      {
#if LOCAL_DATA
        CustomerManagement.Data.XmlDataStore.DeleteCustomer(customerId);
#else
        string urlCustomers = "http://localhost/MXDemo/customers/" + customerId;

        HttpWebRequest request = (HttpWebRequest)HttpWebRequest.Create(urlCustomers);
        request.Method = "DELETE";
        request.GetResponse();
#endif
        return true;
      }
    }
}
```

CustomerManagement/CustomerManagement/Controllers/CustomerController.cs

The `Load()` method of the `CustomerController` is where you write any logic necessary to initialize and prepare your `Company` object for presentation. The `Load()` method receives a dictionary of parameters on the argument that contains any model-specific information passed in the navigation call that loads the controller. In this case, you pass the unique `"Customer"` identifier for the company you want to load, make a call to the data service to retrieve the company data, and then set the `model` property of the `CustomerController` to a new `Company` object instance.

Building a Platform-Specific View

So now that you defined your company model and created a controller to handle company initialization, you're ready to build a platform-specific view to display that customer's information to the user. As mentioned previously in this chapter, the MonoCross pattern implements a Separated Interface pattern to provide a loose-coupling of the presentation layer to the shared application code. This separation is accomplished through the `IMXView` interface, as shown in Listing 4-4:

LISTING 4-4: The IMXView interface

Available for download on Wrox.com

```
public interface IMXView
{
  Type ModelType { get; }
  void SetModel(object model);

  void Render();
}
```

Found in the MonoCross.Navigation/MXView.cs file of the download

The `IMXView` interface defines the implementation contract for all MonoCross views. The interface consists of the properties, methods, and events necessary for the MonoCross navigation framework to initialize the rendering of a view from a controller in the shared application.

This approach offers great flexibility in defining views across multiple mobile platforms. You can implement your views using whatever approach is required by the target platform, provided you implement the `IMXView` interface.

Techniques for implementing platform-specific views are covered in Chapter 6, "Building MonoCross Containers."

The MonoCross `MXView<T>` abstract generic class provides a base implementation of the `IMXView` interface, as shown in Listing 4-5.

LISTING 4-5: The MXView class

Available for download on Wrox.com

```
using System;

namespace MonoCross.Navigation
{
  public delegate void ModelEventHandler(object model);
  public interface IMXView
  {
    Type ModelType { get; }
    void SetModel(object model);

    void Render();
  }

  public abstract class MXView<T> : IMXView
  {
```

```
    public Type ModelType { get { return typeof(T); } }
    public virtual void SetModel(object model)
    {
      Model = (T)model;
    }

    public virtual void Render() { }
    public virtual T Model { get; set; }
  }
}
```

MonoCross.Navigation/MXView.cs

Use the `MXView<T>` class to create a view for your Customer model class. For simplicity in illustrating the concept, the view in Listing 4-6 has been created for the Windows Console target.

LISTING 4-6: A simple Customer view

Available for download on Wrox.com

```
using System;
using System.Collections.Generic;
using System.Linq;
using System.Text;

using MonoCross.Navigation;
using MonoCross.Console;
using CustomerManagement.Shared.Model;

namespace CustomerManagement.Console.Views
{
  class CustomerView : MXConsoleView<Customer>
  {
    public override void Render()
    {
      System.Console.Clear();
      System.Console.WriteLine("Customer Details");
      System.Console.WriteLine();

      System.Console.WriteLine(Model.Name);
      System.Console
        .WriteLine(string
          .Format("{0} {1}",
            Model.PrimaryAddress.Street1,
            Model.PrimaryAddress.Street2));
      System.Console
        .WriteLine(string
          .Format("{0}, {1}  {2}",
            Model.PrimaryAddress.City,
            Model.PrimaryAddress.State,
            Model.PrimaryAddress.Zip));
      System.Console
        .WriteLine("Previous Orders: " + Model.Orders.Count.ToString());
```

continues

LISTING 4-6 *(continued)*

```
            System.Console
              .WriteLine("Addresses:" + Model.Addresses.Count.ToString());
            System.Console
              .WriteLine("Contacts: " + Model.Contacts.Count.ToString());
            System.Console.WriteLine();
            System.Console.WriteLine("Web: " + Model.Website);
            System.Console.WriteLine("Phone: " + Model.PrimaryPhone);
            System.Console.WriteLine();
            System.Console.WriteLine("Enter to Continue, (D)elete or (E)dit");

            while (true)
            {
              string input = System.Console.ReadLine().Trim();
              if (input.Length == 0)
              {
                this.Back();
                return;
              }
              else if (input.StartsWith("E"))
              {
                this.Navigate("Customers/" + Model.ID + "/EDIT");
              }
              else if (input.StartsWith("D"))
              {
                this.Navigate("Customers/" + Model.ID + "/DELETE");
              }
            }
        }
    }
}
```

CustomerManagement/CustomerManagement.Console/Views/CustomerView.cs

The `Render()` method of the `CustomerView` class is where you define the logic to display your model customer instance to the user. In this case the model property values are simply displayed in the appropriate format using the `Console.WriteLine()` method.

Although this particular view may not be terribly glamorous, it quite nicely illustrates the MonoCross view concept. The model instance you created in your `CustomerController.Load()` method is made available in the `CustomerView.Render()` method where it can be displayed and manipulated according to your application requirements. Figure 4-5 shows the rendered console view.

At this point you've defined your company model class, a controller to load a company from your back-end data store, and a view to display the company information in your presentation layer. You can use this approach to define model/controller combinations for every entity in your business domain according to your application requirements and define views for each action required by the presentation layer for the model. These MVC combinations represent discreet modules of application functionality, and can be used and reused in any workflow combinations your application requirements dictate. These workflows will be defined using the MonoCross navigation framework.

```
file:///C:/Projects/MonoCross/Alpha/CustomerManagement/CustomerManagement.Console/bin/...

Enter Customer Index, <N>ew Customer or Enter to go Back
1
Customer Details

Abf Freight System, Inc.
3801 Old Greenwood Rd.
Fort Smith, AR  72903
Previous Orders: 0
Addresses:1
Contacts: 1

Web: http://www.abfs.com
Phone: 479-785-6000

Enter to Continue - <E>dit, <D>elete
```

FIGURE 4-5: The rendered console customer view shows customer detail information.

Using URI-Based Navigation

Until now you've learned about the MonoCross MVC pattern you can use to build cross-platform mobile applications, but the core MVC pattern is only part of what's needed to construct and deploy to multiple device platforms. To turn your MVC combinations into a cohesive application, you need a mechanism to bind them together. The MonoCross navigation framework provides that mechanism using a URI-based navigation structure. Each controller in your application is associated with one or more URI endpoints that uniquely identify its place or places in the application workflow. Each action in your application, whether selecting an item from a list or saving a form, is represented as a navigation to one of these controller endpoints. By using this technique, MonoCross enables the definition of any number of complex workflows, while at the same time encapsulating and reusing as much controller business logic as possible. MonoCross navigation also builds upon the loosely coupled MVC pattern described previously with the addition of two important concepts: a shared application and a platform container.

Building the Shared Application

The shared application in MonoCross encapsulates your MVC modules into a logical, cohesive structure. All the business and data access logic for your application will be shared across mobile platform targets, so the basic workflow navigation is defined in this same structure. The abstract `MXApplication` class in Listing 4-7 defines the base implementation used for your MonoCross shared application.

LISTING 4-7: The MXApplication class

Available for download on Wrox.com

```
using System;
using System.Collections.Generic;
using System.Linq;

namespace MonoCross.Navigation
```

continues

LISTING 4-7 *(continued)*

```
{
  public abstract class MXApplication
  {
    public string NavigateOnLoad { get; set; }
    public string Title { get; set; }
    public NavigationList NavigationMap = new NavigationList();

    protected MXApplication()
    {
      NavigateOnLoad = string.Empty;
      OnAppLoad();
    }

    public virtual void OnAppLoad() { }
    public virtual void OnAppLoadComplete() { }

    public class NavigationList : List<MXNavigation>
    {
      public void Add(string pattern, IMXController controller)
      {
        this.Add(pattern, controller, new Dictionary<string, string>());
      }

      public IMXController GetControllerForPattern(string pattern)
      {
        return this.Contains(pattern)
          ? this.Where(m => m.Pattern == pattern)
            .First().Controller
          : null;
      }
      public String GetPatternForModelType(Type modelType)
      {
        return this.Where(m => m.Controller.ModelType == modelType)
          .First().Pattern;
      }
      public bool Contains(string pattern)
      {
        return this.Where(m => m.Pattern == pattern).Count() > 0;
      }

      public void Add(string pattern,
                      IMXController controller,
                      Dictionary<string, string> parameters)
      {
#if DROID
        Android.Util.Log.Debug("NavigationList", "Adding: '" + pattern + "'");
#endif
        // Enforce uniqueness
        MXNavigation currentMatch = this
          .Where(m => m.Pattern == pattern)
          .FirstOrDefault();
        if (currentMatch != null)
        {
```

```
#if DEBUG
          string text = string
           .Format("MapUri \"{0}\" is already matched to Controller type {1}",
                   pattern, currentMatch.Controller);
          throw new Exception(text);
#else
          return;
#endif
        }

        this.Add(new MXNavigation(pattern, controller, parameters));
      }
    }
  }
}
```

MonoCross.Navigation/MXApplication.cs

You inherit from the `MXApplication` class to create your MonoCross application and register your workflow endpoints for navigation. Listing 4-8 shows the shared application for the customer management example.

LISTING 4-8: A simple shared application

Available for download on Wrox.com

```
using System;
using System.Collections.Generic;
using System.Linq;
using System.Text;

using MonoCross.Navigation;

using CustomerManagement.Controllers;

namespace CustomerManagement
{
  public class App : MXApplication
  {
    public override void OnAppLoad()
    {
      // Set the application title
      Title = "Customer Management";

      // Add navigation mappings
      NavigationMap.Add("Customers", new CustomerListController());

      CustomerController customerController = new CustomerController();
      NavigationMap.Add("Customers/{CustomerId}", customerController);
      NavigationMap.Add("Customers/{CustomerId}/{Action}", customerController);

      // Set default navigation URI
```

continues

LISTING 4-8 *(continued)*

```
            NavigateOnLoad = "Customers";
        }
    }
}
```

CustomerManagement/CustomerManagement/App.cs

Adding Controllers to the Navigation Map

The MonoCross navigation framework is based on RESTful routing principles. Each unique point in your application workflow is defined by a parameterized URI endpoint that corresponds to a controller associated with one or more views used for presentation of the model. Navigation endpoints are registered in the `NavigationMap` found in the `MXApplication` class.

By carefully constructing your `NavigationMap` to model your application's many workflows, you can support even the most complex use cases using the functionality of your application controllers. Each controller in your application can have multiple endpoints defined in your `NavigationMap`. These endpoints reflect the workflow for each specific case defined in your application requirements and enable reuse of existing controller functionality wherever possible.

Now consider a scenario in your customer management application. You want to display and manage customers, and you've already created a controller. Now we need to add the controller to your `NavigationMap`:

```
CustomerController customerController = new CustomerController();
NavigationMap.Add("Customers/{CustomerId}", customerController);
```

This establishes the default entry point for an individual order. The URI template shown uses the squiggly bracket syntax (`{ }`) to indicate a substituted value, (in this case `"CustomerId"`) in the navigation URI. So a URI of `Customers/1234` loads the `CustomerController` from your `NavigationMap`. At runtime, the navigation framework extracts the individual customer identifier, and places it in the controller parameters argument passed to the `CustomerController.Load()` method as a name/value pair, (`CustomerId=1234`).

Now say you want to add a new customer from your customer list view as a part of a different workflow. You want to reuse the existing `CustomerController` because it contains all the business and data logic needed for a customer, so you add the following entry to the `NavigationMap`:

```
CustomerController customerController = new CustomerController();
...
NavigationMap.Add("Customers/{CustomerId}/{Action}", customerController);
```

Now when you request the `CustomerController`, you pass the `Action` identifier for the action you wish to perform. So a URI of `"Customers/0/CREATE"` passed to the application loads the same `CustomerController` as before, but this time you have an additional name-value pair in the `CustomerController.Load()` parameters argument, (`Action=CREATE`), which you can then use to create a new customer . Listing 4-9 shows the `CustomerController.Load()` method.

LISTING 4-9: The CustomerController.Load() method

Available for download on Wrox.com

```
public override string Load(Dictionary<string, string> parameters)
{
  string perspective = ViewPerspective.Default;

  string customerId = null;
  parameters.TryGetValue("CustomerId", out customerId);

  // get the action, assumes
  string action;
  if (!parameters.TryGetValue("Action", out action))  {
    // set default action if none specified
    action = "GET";
    }

  switch (action)
  {
    case "EDIT":
    case "GET":
    // populate the customer model
    if (customerId == null)
      throw new Exception("No Customer Id found");
      if (string.Equals(customerId.ToUpper(), "NEW")) {
        // assign Model a new customer for editing
        Model = new Customer();
        perspective = ViewPerspective.Update;
      } else {
        Model = GetCustomer(customerId);
        if (String.Equals(action, "EDIT"))
          perspective = ViewPerspective.Update;
        else
          perspective = ViewPerspective.Default;
        }
      break;

    case "DELETE":
      if (customerId == null)
        customerId = Model.ID;
        // post delete request to the server
        DeleteCustomer(customerId);

        // return and let redirected controller execute,
        // remaining navigation is ignored
        MXContainer.Instance.Redirect("Customers");
        return ViewPerspective.Delete;

    case "CREATE":
      // process addition of new model
      if(AddNewCustomer(Model))
        MXContainer.Instance.Redirect("Customers");
```

continues

LISTING 4-9 *(continued)*

```
            break;

          case "UPDATE":
            if(UpdateCustomer(Model))
              MXContainer.Instance.Redirect("Customers");
            break;
        }

        return perspective;
      }
```

CustomerManagement/CustomerManagement/Controllers/CustomerController.cs

Adding a Platform Container

To run your shared application, you must deploy it to a specific platform and write the necessary views to present the application to your users. In MonoCross, you do this by creating a platform container. You can have as many platform containers as you have platforms that you want to support. Inside the container you define your views, and your shared controllers render them as defined in your application workflow.

The abstract `MXContainer` class provides a default implementation of a platform container. Each supported platform in MonoCross has a concrete implementation that inherits from the `MXContainer` class and provides platform-specific helper methods and utilities. For the Windows Console example in this chapter, use the `ConsoleContainer` class to initialize your application and register your views, as shown in Listing 4-10.

Available for download on Wrox.com

LISTING 4-10: The ConsoleContainer class

```
using System;
using System.Collections.Generic;
using System.Linq;
using System.Text;
using System.Text.RegularExpressions;

using MonoCross.Navigation;

namespace MonoCross.Console
{
  public static class MXConsoleNavigationExtensions
  {
    public static void Back(this IMXView view)
    {
      MXConsoleContainer.Back(view);
    }
  }

  public class MXConsoleContainer : MXContainer
  {
    public MXConsoleContainer(MXApplication theApp)
```

```
      : base(theApp)
    { }

    private class NavDetail
    {
      public string Path { get; set; }
      public Dictionary<string, string> Parameters { get; set; }

      public NavDetail(string path, Dictionary<string, string> parameters)
      {
        Path = path;
        Parameters = parameters;
      }
    }

    static Stack<NavDetail> NavHistory = new Stack<NavDetail>();

    public static void Initialize(MXApplication theApp)
    {
      MXContainer.InitializeContainer(new MXConsoleContainer(theApp));

      // non-threaded container, not needed as all input is blocking (old-school)
      MXContainer.Instance.ThreadedLoad = false;
    }

    public static void Back(IMXView view)
    {
      // exit if we try to go back too far
      if (!CanGoBack())
      {
        Environment.Exit(0);
      }
      else
      {
        // pop off the current view
        NavHistory.Pop();

        // prepare to re-push the current view
        NavDetail backTo = NavHistory.Pop();

        // re-display the view
        Navigate(view, backTo.Path, backTo.Parameters);
      }
    }

    public static bool CanGoBack()
    {
      if (NavHistory.Count > 1)
        return true;
      else
        return false;
    }

    protected override void OnControllerLoadComplete(
        IMXView fromView,
        IMXController controller,
```

continues

LISTING 4-10 *(continued)*

```
            MXViewPerspective perspective)
        {
          // store of the stack for later
          NavHistory.Push(new NavDetail(controller.Uri, controller.Parameters));

          // render the view
          MXConsoleContainer.RenderViewFromPerspective(controller, perspective);
        }

        protected override void OnControllerLoadFailed(IMXController controller,
            Exception ex)
        {
          System.Console.WriteLine("Failed to load controller: " + ex.Message);
          System.Console.WriteLine("Stack Dump");
          System.Console.WriteLine(ex.StackTrace.ToString());

          System.Diagnostics.Debug.WriteLine("Failed to load controller: "
                                          + ex.Message);
          System.Diagnostics.Debug.WriteLine("Stack Dump");
          System.Diagnostics.Debug.WriteLine(ex.StackTrace.ToString());
        }

        public override void Redirect(string url)
        {
          Navigate(null, url);
          CancelLoad = true;
        }
      }
    }
```

MonoCross.Console/MXConsoleContainer.cs

Listing 4-11 shows the code for initializing your container. You need to start by providing it an instance of your shared app. You also register the views for your application by calling the `AddView()` method on the container and passing a new instance of each view to be placed in the view map. In this case, you register two views: The first displays a list of customers in the system and the second displays the details of a single customer, which is an instance of the `CustomerView` class discussed earlier in this chapter.

LISTING 4-11: Initializing your Console container

Available for download on Wrox.com

```
using System;
using System.Collections.Generic;
using System.Linq;
using System.Text;

using MonoCross.Navigation;
using MonoCross.Console;

using CustomerManagement;
using CustomerManagement.Controllers;
```

```
using CustomerManagement.Shared;
using CustomerManagement.Shared.Model;

namespace CustomerManagement.Console
{
  class Program
  {
    static void Main(string[] args)
    {
      // initialize container
      MXConsoleContainer.Initialize(new CustomerManagement.App());

      // customer list view
      MXConsoleContainer.AddView<List<Customer>>(new Views.CustomerListView(),
                                          ViewPerspective.Default);

      // customer view and customer edit/new
      MXConsoleContainer.AddView<Customer>(new Views.CustomerView(),
                                      ViewPerspective.Default);
      MXConsoleContainer.AddView<Customer>(new Views.CustomerEdit(),
                                      ViewPerspective.Update);

      // navigate to first view
      MXConsoleContainer.Navigate(MXContainer.Instance.App.NavigateOnLoad);
    }
  }
}
```

CustomerManagement/CustomerManagement/Containers/Console.Container/Program.cs

As you build out your application and create more views, you can add them to this block of initialization code for each presentation case in your requirements.

Working with View Perspectives

An important part of defining your container view structure is indicating the intended purpose of each view. As you build out your workflow, you may have multiple views that correspond to a particular model type, such as a form view for creating an order and another for displaying the order details. To register these views, you need a way to specify the purpose for each view; you can accomplish this in MonoCross using view perspectives.

A view perspective is simply a string that describes the intended purpose of your view. The `ViewPerspective` class in Listing 4-12 defines five string constants for the most common view perspective values.

Available for download on Wrox.com

LISTING 4-12: The ViewPerspective class

```
public static class ViewPerspective
{
  public const string Default = "";
  public const string Read = "GET";
```

continues

LISTING 4-12 *(continued)*

```
    public const string Create = "POST";
    public const string Update = "PUT";
    public const string Delete = "DELETE";
  }
```

MonoCross.Navigation/MXViewPerspective.cs

View perspectives are used to uniquely register views in your container and are also used by your controllers to indicate to the container which view to render at a given point in your application.

Although view perspectives provide great flexibility in defining your application presentation layer, you may identify perspectives that are appropriate for some platforms, but not for others. Rendering of your views occurs from the shared controllers, where you must account for view perspectives, across all target platforms.

This is the reason you need to complete a mobile application design, using the steps outlined in Chapter 2, "Designing Your User Experience", to clearly define your application workflow using a platform-agnostic approach and develop the user experience for each platform to support that workflow.

Your simple console container uses only the `ViewPerspective.Default` constant because the two views you initially registered are used to simply display customer information. But as you expand the functionality of your application, you will likely add views for additional operations. For example, Listing 4-13 shows the action of adding a new customer included in the `CustomerController` class:

Available for download on Wrox.com

LISTING 4-13: Adding a new customer

```
public override string Load(Dictionary<string, string> parameters)
{
  string perspective = ViewPerspective.Default;

  string customerId = null;
  parameters.TryGetValue("CustomerId", out customerId);

  // get the action, assumes
  string action;
  if (!parameters.TryGetValue("Action", out action))  {
    // set default action if none specified
    action = "GET";
    }

  switch (action)
  {
    case "EDIT":
    case "GET":
```

```
        // populate the customer model
        if (customerId == null)
          throw new Exception("No Customer Id found");
          if (string.Equals(customerId.ToUpper(), "NEW")) {
            // assign Model a new customer for editing
            Model = new Customer();
            perspective = ViewPerspective.Update;
          } else {
            Model = GetCustomer(customerId);
            if (String.Equals(action, "EDIT"))
              perspective = ViewPerspective.Update;
            else
              perspective = ViewPerspective.Default;
            }
          break;

        case "DELETE":
          if (customerId == null)
            customerId = Model.ID;
            // post delete request to the server
            DeleteCustomer(customerId);

            // return and let redirected controller execute,
            // remaining navigation is ignored
            MXContainer.Instance.Redirect("Customers");
            return ViewPerspective.Delete;

        case "CREATE":
          // process addition of new model
          if(AddNewCustomer(Model))
            MXContainer.Instance.Redirect("Customers");
          break;

        case "UPDATE":
          if(UpdateCustomer(Model))
            MXContainer.Instance.Redirect("Customers");
          break;
      }

      return perspective;
    }
```

Found in the CustomerManagement/CustomerManagement/Controllers/CustomerController.cs file of the download

In this case, the `CustomerController.Load()` method conditionally returns the `ViewPerspective.Update` value when a new order is created. Now, when the `CustomerController` is loaded to create a new customer, the `EditCustomerView` renders to the user, and enables input of customer information.

The view perspective concept is designed for maximum flexibility. You can register your views with whatever string value adequately describes the intended function. When you want to display that view from your controller, simply return the corresponding view perspective value to your container, and the desired view renders.

SUMMARY

In this chapter you briefly explored the problems encountered in cross-platform mobile development. You learned about the impact of differences in mobile platforms, the limitations of HTML 5 as a solution, and some of the challenges when using a hybrid approach. You then explored the MonoCross open-source project as a solution to these challenges by using the MVC and Separated Interface patterns. You also learned how to share business and data logic in your shared application and create platform-specific views in C# and .NET.

In the next chapter, you learn more about building a shared application and explore the details of business logic and data access for the customer management application.

Building Shared Applications

WHAT'S IN THIS CHAPTER?

- Reviewing how to drive model design from user experience
- Walking through explicit model examples
- Understanding the controller's function

The model and controller are at the heart of an MVC application. For cross-platform applications, developers can reap more benefits from code portability by leveraging the model and controller classes to do the heavy lifting. Routines for verifying data input, logic trees, navigations flows, and data loading are all best placed in either the controller or the model. Such a practice results in the most reusable code.

Because you implement views independently on each platform, you can rarely leverage code written for one view when writing that same view for another platform. This is because each platform's UI classes and constructs are not shared. In iOS the `UIView` and its subclasses make up the large portion of the built-in controls. As might be expected, Android and Windows Phone 7 don't have a `UIView` class. For Android OS the `Activity` class serves as the root container for UI controls. In Windows Phone 7 the Silverlight `Canvas` classes sit at the base of UI controls.

At first it can seem obvious and easy to keep business logic out of the view. But every time a control verifies a value entered, every time a UI action updates a model's value, and every time a touch event causes a navigation event, the code must be rewritten in each platform's view. The navigation events are the secret sauce to wiring up a portable MVC application. Navigating to an endpoint is simple; writing code to verify values can be complex. Put the complex code in the models and controllers; put the simple stuff, such as navigation events, in the views.

You can create abstract UI constructs that can be used to represent UI controls and then rendered using native UI objects. The most popular open-source presentation micro framework is MonoDialog. Originally written by Miguel de Icaza, the dialog framework initially spread through the open source community as a rapid development dialog framework for MonoTouch applications. As Mono for Android materialized, the dialog framework was ported to Android. The spread of the dialog framework to multiple platforms has proven the theory that abstract dialog concepts could be used to share application-specific UI code between wildly different native UI SDKs.

Although HTML 5 development enables greater flexibility on code placement in the view, the overall maturity of the language and technology stack to handle device-side storage and interact with device hardware is limited. Like most technologies, you can create solutions to hurdle these obstacles, but using the MVC pattern and C# can provide more robust solutions to meet your enterprise's needs.

HTML became a popular mobile development technology shortly after Apple released the iPhone. Just as popular mobile phones were being released with software development kits, Apple chose to keep the iOS platform closed. The WebKit HTML rendering engine under the hood of the Mobile Safari browser gave solution designers a gateway into application deployment for Apple's instant success. *Connected applications* quickly spread across the web, and websites targeted for consumption on mobile devices were launched.

The ability to host web applications for mobile devices is relatively new. Historically, mobile platforms have not been connected devices. As cellular technology has spread, many people are being introduced to mobile computing for the first time. Moving from web applications to native applications has not nullified the advantage of a data connection. Running a native (disconnected) application can bring real advantages, but much of the power in today's mobile apps comes from their ability to retrieve current information from online data sources. Users reach for today's applications because of an app's ability to display relevant information. The data can be trivial, for example sports scores, or vital business data, such as real-time stock quotes or inventory levels. Getting your user his or her information will often be at the heart of the application's functionality. Strategically designing your over-the-wire data pulls can be the difference between a responsive application and a slow one.

A data connection empowers applications to pull data of all sizes, and the speed of today's networks means there is no need to be concerned about pulling kilobytes of data. In addition, WiFi and high-speed cellular data speeds enable sub-second round trips for data. The same is true for retrieving megabytes of data. In a background thread, it is easy to achieve download times well under a minute for a megabyte of data. Compressing the data can decrease download times even more. The size of the data is less important than how it interrupts the user experience. If the application pulls 100MB of serialized `.xml` data seamlessly in the background, users will likely not complain. If, however, the user must wait for data too often, their experience will suffer. Keeping data pulls smaller when occurring between screen transitions helps the application feel responsive. Utilize background processes for pulling large data sets before the user needs them.

Make sure to test on slower data connections when prototyping, developing, and regression testing your applications. Mobile users often find themselves connected to different data connections, some maxing out around 15 Kbps. Testing the application in a sheltered environment with a high-speed Internet connection may not reflect reality when the app is in production. Take time during the development phase to verify the user experience is not too heavily degraded when the device has a slower network connection.

DEFINING YOUR MODEL

As stressed in Chapter 2, "Designing Your User Experience," the model's properties and methods should have a direct correlation to the data that is necessary for the view to render. If you render a list of customers, you do not need to pull every detail about each customer. It is enough to simply pull the details you want to display. The properties of the model and its methods should support this "just enough" approach. Perhaps your list includes each customer's name, region, and account number. Your model should provide a corresponding list property for each. In the customer look up example workflow discussed in Chapter 2, the rendering of the customer list did not require many details about the customer. Those details are not necessary until after a user chooses to view an individual customer from the customer list. At that point the application will need access to more details about that individual customer by using a customer detail property in your model. This is an example of how the desired behavior of the view drives the design of the model.

Starting from Your User Experience Design

Chapter 2 looks at an initial customer management and order entry application workflow. The workflow, illustrated in Figure 5-1, includes searching for a customer, viewing a customer, and starting an order.

For your first dive into what the supporting model might look like, consider a possible customer model. The customer is the central object of the workflow because the process starts off with a list of customers. Figure 5-2 shows that the customer object has several attributes.

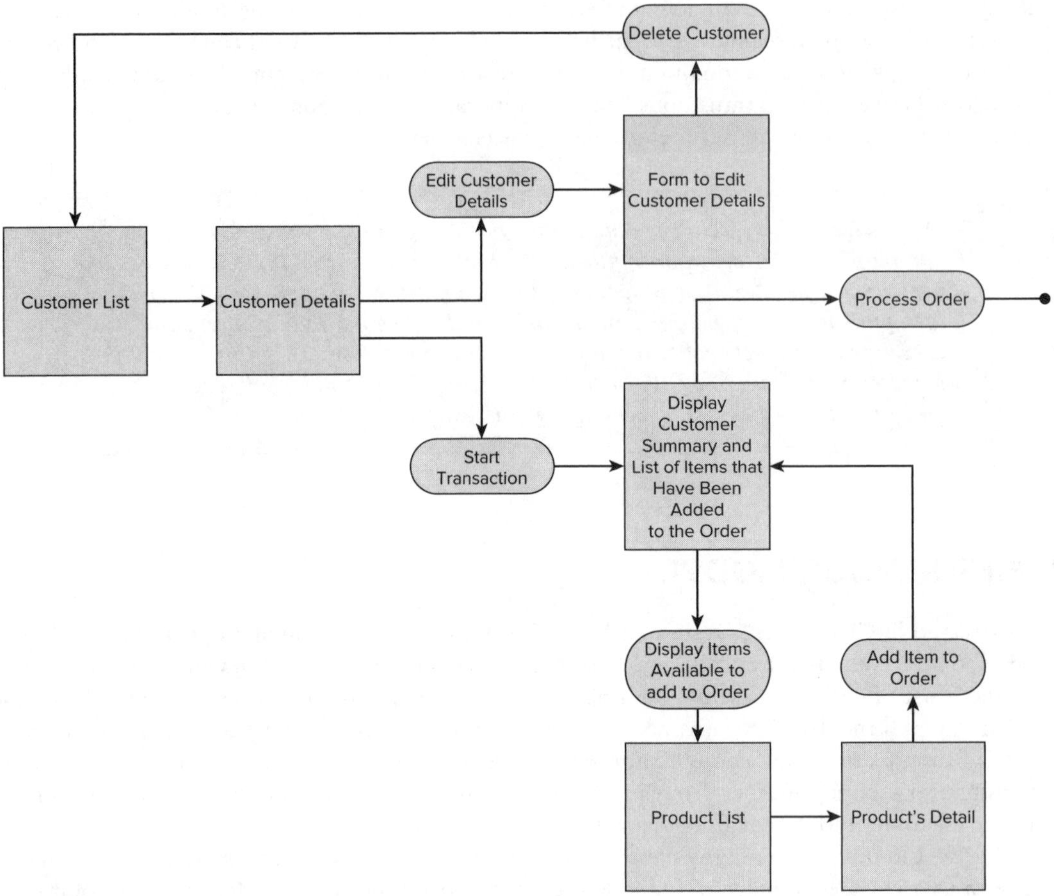

FIGURE 5-1: Activity diagram.

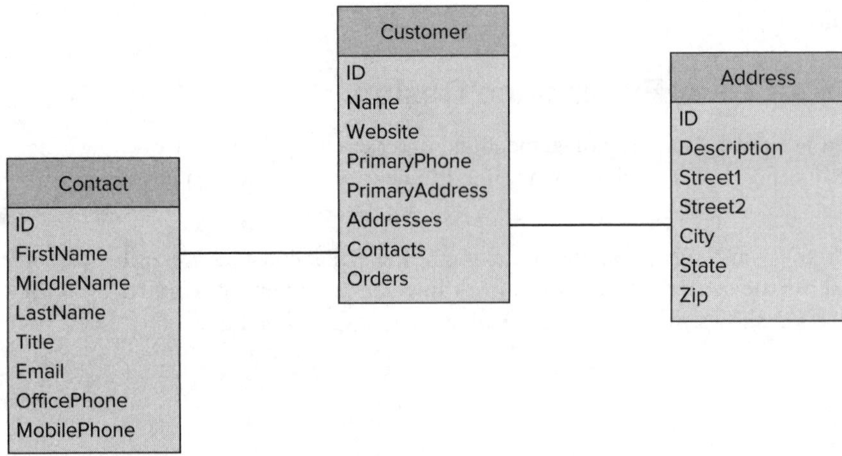

FIGURE 5-2: Simple customer data model diagram.

Listing 5-1 shows how the Customer model translates to a C# object that the view can leverage for displaying the list.

Available for download on Wrox.com

LISTING 5-1: Customer model

```
public class Customer
{
  public string ID { get; set; }
  public string Name { get; set; }
  public string Website { get; set; }
  public string PrimaryPhone { get; set; }
  public Address PrimaryAddress { get; set; }
  public List<Address> Addresses { get; set; }
  public List<Contact> Contacts { get; set; }
  public List<Order> Orders { get; set; }
}
```

Found in the CustomerManagement.Shared/Model/Customer.cs file of the download

In the code you see several properties necessary for displaying a list, including `ID` and `Name`. Those properties are either critical to identifying the account or represent pieces of identifying information that the users might commonly use to query the customer. In the `Customer` model object, you also see several properties that would not be necessary for displaying the customer list, for example the list of orders. If the entire model and associated collections had to be populated for every customer before the list could be displayed, it's likely the user experience would be diminished by slow load times.

Over the history of mobile devices, connectivity has been lacking, in general, and high-bandwidth connectivity has been missing until very recently. Today's smartphones and cellphone-enabled tablets introduce a new connectivity paradigm. Developers can assume most devices are generally connected and have reasonable data bandwidths. The end result is that small data grabs can seamlessly occur between screen transitions, and larger data grabs can often occur within tolerable durations.

Ultimately it's the user base that defines what reasonable wait times are. With second and third generation cellular data networks, pulling 10KB of data can be accomplished in well under a one second. That small download can occur easily between screen transitions. One second is acceptable for most users, as long as a touch or click indication can provide feedback that their user interaction has been recognized by the application. Often screens that require larger data pulls that take approximately 10 seconds are tolerable, but the user needs to see a wait spinner displayed. Be careful of screens requiring extremely large data downloads, such as a 5MB download. Users tire of using the app if they must routinely wait 20 seconds for the UI to render.

Building for Lightly Loaded Lists

To match the new data connectivity paradigm, lightly loaded lists that are seamlessly integrated through the RESTful services can help shorten the duration of data pulls for larger lists. Lightly loaded lists contain a subset of information contained within the model. The subset should include key identifiable information the user might expect to see displayed on the screen, choose to query for in a search box, or need to complete calculations performed on the list. RESTful services provide an easy way to expose this type of information. JSON or XML endpoints are easily and securely exposed using WCF and SSL. Applications can use simple HTML `GET` and `PUT` actions to retrieve and post information to a data server. A simple `GET` request to an endpoint can provide a list of customers with just a few details of each customer. Listing 5-2 shows a slimmed down customer object with just a few properties for a lightly loaded list.

LISTING 5-2: Lightly loaded Customer model

Available for download on Wrox.com

```
public class Customer
{
  public string ID { get; set; }
  public string Name { get; set; }
  public string Website { get; set; }
  public Date_LastOrder { get; set; }
}
```

Found in the CustomerManagement.Shared/Model/Customer.cs file of the download

In the lightly loaded customer model, the `Name` field would most likely be the identifiable information a user might want to see about the customer. In addition, the model contains a customer `ID` field that provides easy reference to the customer from a single identifier.

In the hypothetical customer model shown in Listing 5-2, there is an additional property for the date of the last order (`Date_LastOrder`). The last order date might not be a necessary property for display in a list of search results, but it serves as an example of key information that you might also include in your lightly loaded list. If the customer management application performs a lot of business logic around who the last customer was to order, having that information on the lightly loaded object can spare the application from downloading every customer record before completing that calculation.

Using lightly loaded list endpoints can be a great way to get the application up and running with a basic set of essential data for the application workflow. In the customer workflow in Figure 5-1 the user workflow does not require any real detailed information on the first screen. In the customer management workflow, the second screen transitions to the details of a specific customer. This can require an additional call to the data server to retrieve a more extensive set of information on that particular customer. The advantage of the lightly loaded list approach is that the customer list screen can load significantly faster because the details of each customer do not need to be downloaded first. Additionally, in this approach, the customer's detailed information is not retrieved until it is necessary to complete the screen render. This prevents unnecessary data from being transferred and speeds up the application's execution for the user.

Plan for Lazy-Loaded Details

Lazy-loading data is the simplest option to implement when utilizing RESTful services. This technique is accomplished by waiting to load a particular dataset until it is necessary for screen rendering. The technique works well for individual objects, because their data sizes are relatively small. When downloading lightly loaded lists, the data size can be large, simply due to the number of entities represented in the list. To prevent over engineering, start by completing RESTful service calls at the time of screen rendering. If the screen transitions or interactions are slow because of data loads, look at pulling the data earlier in the application's execution flow.

To accelerate the screen transitions more, pre-fetching models can help leverage times of idle network activity by initiating background data pulls when users are not accessing portions of the application requiring data — or are accessing screens that already have their supporting data cached to the device.

Techniques to lazy loading depend completely on the model. In the customer example, you can build in functionality to help users facilitate pre-fetching the model. You wouldn't have to build a UI queueing mechanism for your users. You can subtly build in benchmarks for your pre-fetching engine to determine which models to fetch first.

One subtle way to introduce a priority ordering mechanism is by identifying user preference "favorites." Building on your Customer model in Listing 5-1, you can add a new `Favorite` property, as shown in Listing 5-3.

LISTING 5-3: Favorite property added to the Customer model

Available for download on Wrox.com

```
public class Customer
{
  public string ID { get; set; }
  public string Name { get; set; }
  public string Website { get; set; }
  public Date LastOrder { get; set; }
  public string Favorite { get; set; }
}
```

Found in the CustomerManagement.Shared/Model/Customer.cs file of the download

The `Favorite` property on a Customer model provides the user a way to provide feedback into prefetch queueing logic. When a customer is identified as a user's favorite, the underlying logic can prioritize that customer in the queue above customers who are not the user's favorite.

The favorite customer approach works well in applications with large backend servers, where individual users are uniquely identified within the ecosystem. For smaller applications without individual user's, lazy-load prioritizing can be determined by other available information. One of the nice hardware items packaged in today's breed of smartphones is a GPS chip. By leveraging location services, the current location of the user can be determined and data pre-fetched based on proximity. In the Customer model in Listing 5-1, you see a primary address. If the primary address is included in the lightly loaded model, queueing your models for pre-fetching by proximity may serve as a reasonable way to prioritize the order in which data is queued.

Implementing a pre-fetcher should not be necessary out-of-the-box. The first order of business is to let the application lazy load everything. If performance is not sufficient, then create a background thread to do the pre-fetching. Prioritizing can be as simple as sequentially walking through the individual list items from top to bottom. Only when performance is being compromised should additionally prioritized queuing become necessary.

Advanced Techniques

The exchange of data between the data source and device generally occurs using either text representations or bytes, and at the most rudimentary level even text streams are byte streams. Traditional database synchronization engines are an example of data source interactions using byte streams. These engines analyze the underlying data structures and transfer "unsynced" information between the two data storage repositories. RESTful services provide another paradigm for data access. With REST data entities are transferred in their entirety to requesting clients. The clients do not house their own data repositories, but they cache snapshots of the database and, in turn, post all change requests to the server. When data discrepancies exist, the client relies on the server as the source of truth. These kinds of RESTful transactions typically occur using XML or JSON transferred in an HTTP `GET` request. The advantages of REST in mobile applications are discussed at length in later chapters, but you can see serialization techniques for interacting with models here.

JSON Versus XML

XML can be a great tool for data exchange in your mobile applications. It's human readable, easily serialized, and has solid parsing libraries for most platforms and frameworks. XML provides many nice advantages, especially legibility. Following is a trimmed-down version of the server's Customer list response in your Customer management example. The sample code provided returns 100 customers, but the output has been shortened to only four for the examples shown here:

```
<?xml version="1.0" encoding="utf-8"?>
<ArrayOfCompany xmlns:xsd="http://www.w3.org/2001/XMLSchema"
    xmlns:xsi="http://www.w3.org/2001/XMLSchema-instance">
  <Company>
    <ID>1</ID>
    <Name>Stein Mart, Inc.</Name>
    <PrimaryPhone>904-346-1500</PrimaryPhone>
    <PrimaryAddress>
      <ID>1-a1</ID>
      <Description>World Headquarters</Description>
      <Street1>1200 Riverplace Blvd.</Street1>
      <City>Jacksonville</City>
      <State>FL</State>
      <Zip>32207</Zip>
    </PrimaryAddress>
  </Company>
  <Company>
```

```
      <ID>2</ID>
      <Name>Bgc Partners, Inc.</Name>
      <PrimaryPhone>212-938-5000</PrimaryPhone>
      <PrimaryAddress>
        <ID>2-a1</ID>
        <Description>World Headquarters</Description>
        <Street1>499 Park Ave.</Street1>
        <City>New York</City>
        <State>NY</State>
        <Zip>10022</Zip>
      </PrimaryAddress>
    </Company>
    <Company>
      <ID>3</ID>
      <Name>Carpenter Technology Corporation</Name>
      <PrimaryPhone>610-208-2000</PrimaryPhone>
      <PrimaryAddress>
        <ID>3-a1</ID>
        <Description>World Headquarters</Description>
        <Street1>2 Meridian Blvd.</Street1>
        <City>Wyomissing</City>
        <State>PA</State>
        <Zip>19610</Zip>
      </PrimaryAddress>
    </Company>
    <Company>
      <ID>4</ID>
      <Name>Tri Marine International, Inc.</Name>
      <PrimaryPhone>425-688-1288</PrimaryPhone>
      <PrimaryAddress>
        <ID>4-a1</ID>
        <Description>World Headquarters</Description>
        <Street1>10500 N.E. 8th St.</Street1>
        <Street2>Ste. 1888</Street2>
        <City>Bellevue</City>
        <State>WA</State>
        <Zip>98004</Zip>
      </PrimaryAddress>
    </Company>
  </ArrayOfCompany>
```

JSON is an excellent and efficient data serialization standard. It is widely used in enterprise applications. In most situations, JSON can provide a great solution in your run-time environment. Debugging with JSON can be a headache. There are several JSON parsing tools, but neither Visual Studio nor MonoDevelop have any parsing built into the debugger's user interface. The following is the same server response serialized to JSON (and condensed to four entries):

```
[
 {
   "<Addresses>k__BackingField":null,
   "<Contacts>k__BackingField":null,
   "<ID>k__BackingField":"1",
   "<Name>k__BackingField":"Stein Mart, Inc.",
   "<Orders>k__BackingField":null,
```

```
  "<PrimaryAddress>k__BackingField":{
     "<City>k__BackingField":"Jacksonville",
     "<Description>k__BackingField":"World Headquarters",
     "<ID>k__BackingField":"1-a1",
     "<State>k__BackingField":"FL",
     "<Street1>k__BackingField":"1200 Riverplace Blvd.",
     "<Street2>k__BackingField":null,
     "<Zip>k__BackingField":"32207"
  },
  "<PrimaryPhone>k__BackingField":"904-346-1500",
  "<Website>k__BackingField":null
},
{
  "<Addresses>k__BackingField":null,
  "<Contacts>k__BackingField":null,
  "<ID>k__BackingField":"2",
  "<Name>k__BackingField":"Bgc Partners, Inc.",
  "<Orders>k__BackingField":null,
  "<PrimaryAddress>k__BackingField":{
     "<City>k__BackingField":"New York",
     "<Description>k__BackingField":"World Headquarters",
     "<ID>k__BackingField":"2-a1",
     "<State>k__BackingField":"NY",
     "<Street1>k__BackingField":"499 Park Ave.",
     "<Street2>k__BackingField":null,
     "<Zip>k__BackingField":"10022"
  },
  "<PrimaryPhone>k__BackingField":"212-938-5000",
  "<Website>k__BackingField":null
},
{
  "<Addresses>k__BackingField":null,
  "<Contacts>k__BackingField":null,
  "<ID>k__BackingField":"3",
  "<Name>k__BackingField":"Carpenter Technology Corporation",
  "<Orders>k__BackingField":null,
  "<PrimaryAddress>k__BackingField":{
     "<City>k__BackingField":"Wyomissing",
     "<Description>k__BackingField":"World Headquarters",
     "<ID>k__BackingField":"3-a1",
     "<State>k__BackingField":"PA",
     "<Street1>k__BackingField":"2 Meridian Blvd.",
     "<Street2>k__BackingField":null,
     "<Zip>k__BackingField":"19610"
  },
  "<PrimaryPhone>k__BackingField":"610-208-2000",
  "<Website>k__BackingField":null
},
{
  "<Addresses>k__BackingField":null,
  "<Contacts>k__BackingField":null,
  "<ID>k__BackingField":"4",
  "<Name>k__BackingField":"Tri Marine International, Inc.",
  "<Orders>k__BackingField":null,
```

```
        "<PrimaryAddress>k__BackingField":{
          "<City>k__BackingField":"Bellevue",
          "<Description>k__BackingField":"World Headquarters",
          "<ID>k__BackingField":"4-a1",
          "<State>k__BackingField":"WA",
          "<Street1>k__BackingField":"10500 N.E. 8th St.",
          "<Street2>k__BackingField":"Ste. 1888",
          "<Zip>k__BackingField":"98004"
        },
        "<PrimaryPhone>k__BackingField":"425-688-1288",
        "<Website>k__BackingField":null
      },
      {
        "<Addresses>k__BackingField":null
      }
    ]
```


Whether to use JSON or XML can be a decision made by the developer. With smaller data items, the extra bloat of the XML element scheme is easily masked by the speed of today's data connections. Additionally, XML can be much easier to read during a debug session. In general, JSON is a lighter-weight data serialization scheme. Ultimately, JSON can probably produce smaller serialized data sizes. In addition, JSON can compress larger payload sizes before they are sent.

A few considerations to keep in mind when choosing a serialization method are bandwidth, serialization time, and frequency of use. Upload and download bandwidths differ on most mobile devices. Nearly 100 percent of the time, you can count on a considerably faster download speed than upload speed. Keeping requests small can help in the upload request times.

Serialization time is worth evaluating within an enterprise application. There can be tremendous differences in serialization times based on complexity and size of the data being serialized. Picking a serialization scheme can have dramatic ramifications for both server and client execution. Expensive serialization routines on the server can cause a lag in the server's response time. In some situations serialization can take longer than the over-the-wire time saved from the smaller payload size. The reverse can be true on the device. It's possible that a particular serialization routine can execute within tolerance levels on a high-powered server but bog down on the less-powerful processors, which power most of today's mobile devices.

A model's frequency of use can be another factor you consider when selecting its serialization method. If the object is not used a lot, don't waste time analyzing its serialization method. Simply use the project's default serialization method and optimize only if bottlenecks show up.

You do not need to use the same serialization techniques across all models in an application. The .NET framework provides many libraries for data serialization and compression. That depth of qualified libraries means a development team does not need to spend a lot of time building libraries to assist with data transfer. With just a flip of an enumeration, teams can experiment with vastly different serialization schemes.

Don't Serialize What You Don't Need

Regardless of whether the data is serialized using JSON or XML, serializing unnecessary information is a waste of bandwidth and time. The number one piece of wasted data often transferred is data with values for objects that default to that value. If the item count is zero and the object defaults to an initialized value of zero, it's not necessary to serialize and transfer that value over the wire. You can take the same kind of optimization to the next level by wiring default values into the constructor of those objects.

Additionally, sending objects with greater resolution than necessary can cause wasted bandwidth. The most popular example is with `DateTime` values. The values are best serialized by their tick value. You can easily construct and manipulate `DateTime` objects using ticks. Ticks are a representation of 100 nanosecond time intervals stored in a `Long`. Chances are the business logic does not require fidelity down to the 100th nanosecond. Serializing a `DateTime` object to ticks and dividing that by 10000000 can shrink your `DateTime` object by 7 bytes and still provide 1-second fidelity. Considering an object's resolution and data fidelity when serializing can help shave precious bytes from large data payloads.

Additional Tips and Tricks

One of the advantages of using C# and .NET to build your application is the ability to carry your data-model objects with you when building the backend services. If using WCF to build RESTful services, the `Model` classes can be leveraged within the data server code too. This makes it easier to communicate data requirements and leverage more shared code.

Delayed instantiation is another trick to keep in mind if you are pre-fetching data objects. The concept of delayed instantiation is to prevent over consumption of large data items until the application run-time requires it. Because larger data objects require lengthier downloads, it can be advantageous to retrieve them in a background thread with the intent to them accessible on the device before the user needs them. When downloading data with a large number of objects, deserialization of the data can bog down the CPU. If the device is idle, it won't be a problem; but, if a screen rendering is occurring, the user could notice a significant delay in screen animations. For that reason, cache the resource to disk, but avoid deserializing the resource into objects until necessary.

BUILDING YOUR CONTROLLERS

Just as the heart of your application's responsiveness is in the model, the capability to leverage shared business logic exists within the controller. Business logic is the root of your application. It's the logic specific to your application's objects. Leveraging a shared code base for this logic allows you to reuse tested code as you take your application to new platforms.

The controller code provides an opportunity for the business logic to evaluate the current state of the model and execute a decision tree. You can find an example of this in your customer management workflow. Your customer management example provides a workflow where an order is processed. Order processing often includes business logic such as payment validation, in-stock status, and saving the order to the backend system. And, because the order processing code must execute on every platform, the controller is an ideal spot to place the code. Alternatively, you can place the order-processing code in the button or keystrokes' event handlers, but UI code cannot be compiled by each platform. The controller code is compiled into the application assembly and executed from a shared code base on each platform. If the logic were placed inside an event handler of a UI control, the majority of that platform-agnostic validation code would need to be copied and pasted between platform assemblies. To ensure the easiest code maintenance, compiling assemblies with shared code files is a far superior structure than copying and pasting C# code between source code files.

The word platform *can be an indicator of exponential work. Every piece of code written in a platform-specific implementation must be re-implemented each time the application is moved to a new platform. This includes the use of .NET libraries available for one target's compiler and not another's.*

Implementing Your Workflow

Within the MonoCross pattern, the Controller code must accomplish a couple of tasks. It must identify and process any parameters passed within the navigation URI, perform business logic related to the state of the application, and return a view perspective that can be leveraged by each platform's container. The platform container uses that perspective to determine what view to display.

Perhaps the easiest way to explore a controller's jobs is in code. You can break down the controller's three responsibilities into individual code segments. Within the customer management example you've been working through, you can pull out workflows to help highlight the concepts.

Looking back at Figure 5-1, you can see the customer management example has several screen transitions. Those screen transitions manifest as URIs in its navigation map. The relationship may be a one-to-one, view-to-URI relationship or a one-to-many relationship. The navigation map is discussed and displayed later in the chapter. A basic controller flow might look like the following if a view executes the navigation:

```
MXContainer.Navigate("Customer");
```

Listing 5-4 demonstrates the basic functionality of the controller logic. The `Load()` method populates the model and returns a view perspective related to the availability of the model. There is no business logic to execute on the list, in this functionality you just determine if it's immediately available.

LISTING 5-4: Customer List controller

Available for download on Wrox.com

```
public class CustomerListController : MXController<List<Company>>
{
  public override string Load(Dictionary<string, string> parameters)
  {
    // populate model
    Model = new List<Company>();

    // determine current view perspective
```

continues

LISTING 5-4 *(continued)*

```
        string perspective = ViewPerspective.Default;
        if (Model == null) { perspective = "No Data"; }
        return perspective;
    }
}
```

Found in the CustomerManagement/Controllers/CustomerListController.cs file of the download

Controllers have the option to return view perspectives and perform redirects. If the current state of the model does not support the default view, an alternative view perspective can be returned. If the data is not cached yet, you have the option to return a view perspective for data loading. If the current model has invalidated its state execution, flow can be directed to a new controller/model pair to initiate or restart a workflow.

Another task the controller performs is handling any parameters passed in the navigation URI. In the supporting MonoCross framework (`MonoCross.Navigation`) a simple regular expression (regex) extracts them from the navigated URI. When the controller's `Load()` method is called, the parameters are nicely packaged in the parameter dictionary collection.

When selecting a customer from the list, the Customer controller can perform a little bit more business logic based on the parameters provided by the navigation event, as shown in Listing 5-5.

LISTING 5-5: Customer controller

Available for download on Wrox.com

```
public override string Load(Dictionary<string, string> parameters)
{
  if (parameters.ContainsKey("Customer"))
  {
    Model = Company.GetCompany(parameters["Customer"]);
    perspective = CustomerDetail;
  }
  return ViewPerspective.Default
}
```

Found in the CustomerManagement/Controllers/CustomerController.cs file of the download

The preceding Customer controller code contains a basic example of retrieving parameters from the URI. When you navigate from the Customer list screen, the ID of the customer to be represented on the next screen is placed in the URI. Parameters provide a simple mechanism to pass information necessary to facilitate screen transition. In this example, the parameter contains information related to which customer to view.

Generally, controllers are more complex than just data loaders. Often, a controller can encapsulate all the functionality around an object. The preceding Customer controller can easily be extended to handle basic operations to a customer. In Listing 5-6, the customer controller handles the business logic for both viewing a customer and creating a new one.

LISTING 5-6: Customer controller with Partial CRUD implemented

```
public override string Load(Dictionary<string, string> parameters)
{
  string perspective = ViewPerspective.Default;

  string customer = null;
  parameters.TryGetValue("Customer", out customer);

  string action;
  if (!parameters.TryGetValue("Action", out action))
  {
    // set default action if none specified
    action = "VIEW";

    if (customer == null)
      throw new Exception("No Customer Id found");
  }

  switch (action)
  {
    case "VIEW":
      // populate the customer model
      Model = GetCustomer(customer);
      perspective = CustomerDetail;
      break;
    case "ADD":
      // process addition of new model
      Model = new Company();
      perspective = ViewPerspective.Create;
      break;

      // return and let redirected controller execute
      return ViewPerspective.Delete;
  }
  return perspective;
}
```

Found in the CustomerManagement/Controllers/CustomerController.cs file of the download

The code snippet includes two business flows. If you want to create a new customer, simply instantiate a new instance of the model. If you want to view information about a customer, the information is loaded into the model. After the model is successfully prepared for the view, the perspective is returned. Each platform's container can then leverage that perspective to render the correct view.

These workflows introduce simple screens into the workflow. Although basic database functions of Create, Retrieve, Update, and Delete (CRUD) on a customer might not be too exciting, the simple customer activity diagram introduced in Chapter 2 illustrates areas of more complex business logic.

Generally, starting a transaction takes a little set up for the business logic and typically results in a more dynamic model setup. There may or may not be items added to the order. There could be additional order details present, such as shipping or payment information. Listing 5-7 shows the basic controller's `Load()` method for starting an order.

LISTING 5-7: Order controller

Available for download on Wrox.com

```
public class OrderController : MXController<Order>
{
  public override string Load(Dictionary<string, string> parameters)
  {
    string actionParameter;
    if (parameters.TryGetValue("Order", out actionParameter))
    {
      Model = GetOrder(actionParameter);
    }
    else if (parameters.TryGetValue("Item", out actionParameter))
    {
      Order.Item item = new Order.Item();
      item.Product = Product.GetProduct(actionParameter);
      if (parameters.TryGetValue("Quantity", out actionParameter))
      {
        try { item.Quantity = Convert.ToInt32(actionParameter); }
        catch { }
      }
      Model.Items.Add(item);
    }
    else
    {
      Model = new Order();

      string customerId;
      if (parameters.TryGetValue("Customer", out customerId))
      {
        Model.Customer = CustomerController.GetCustomer(customerId);
      }
      return ViewPerspective.Create;
    }
    return ViewPerspective.Default;
  }

  private Order GetOrder(string orderId)
  {
    return null;
  }
}
```

Found in the CustomerManagement/Controllers/OrderController.cs file of the download

The Order controller does a little more heavy lifting than the Customer controller. The Order controller fetches the existing order, or creates a new one. If a new order is created, it populates the `Customer` property. If a product is passed in the URI, it's added to the current order. The controller performs all the necessary logic. It handles the parameters passed within the navigation URI, it conditionally populates the model, and it returns an appropriate view perspective.

Basic Workflow Summary

At this point there is a controller/model combination for every entity identified in your workflow from Figure 5-1. The Customer controller loads the list of customers or returns a view perspective indicating no data is available. The Customer controller handles creating a new customer and loading existing customer information for the view. The Order controller can create a new order, load an existing order, or add an item to an order.

The `Load()` method of the controllers within the MonoCross pattern helps encapsulate business logic and data access into logical code modules. The MonoCross navigation framework is built on RESTful routing principles that feed the controller with all the information necessary to process business logic. Navigation endpoints will be generated from screens identified in your paper prototyping. Each screen will have one or more endpoint.

To recap each controller's execution flow for the previous workflow, you can identify a workflow strung together by the following navigation URIs in Listing 5-8.

Available for download on Wrox.com

LISTING 5-8: Navigation map setup

```
public class App : MXApplication
{
  public override void OnAppLoad()
  {
    // Set the application title
    Title = "Customer Management";

    // Add navigation mappings for customer controller
    NavigationMap.Add("Customers", new CustomerListController());
    CustomerController customerController = new CustomerController();
    NavigationMap.Add("Customers/{CustomerId}", customerController);
    NavigationMap.Add("Customers/{CustomerId}/{Action}", customerController);

    // for the order controller
    OrderController orderController = new OrderController();
    NavigationMap.Add("Orders/{Order}", orderController);
    NavigationMap.Add("Orders/New/{Customer}", orderController);
    NavigationMap.Add("Orders/Add/{Order}/", orderController);

    // Set default navigation URI
    NavigateOnLoad = "Customers";
  }
}
```

Found in the CustomerManagement /App.cs file of the download

You can view the customer list by navigating to a parameter-less URI. But when navigating to a customer's details, the URI must contain a parameter that identifies the customer to view. When navigating to the Order controller, it requires several different pieces of information. And, as you found when you explored the Order controller's code, depending on the parameters the URI contains, one of several code paths are executed.

Stringing Together Controllers

At this point, the customer management example has laid out some straightforward workflows. Users can walk through basic workflows to view customers, create orders, and add items to an order. All these tasks are accomplished by stepping through a systematic workflow. For more advanced workflows, the MonoCross navigation pattern provides a redirect method for the controller to use. The purpose of the redirect is to cancel the loading of a model/view pairing and redirect business logic execution to another controller.

To better explain the navigation concept, explore another workflow in your customer management example. In the workflow laid out in Figure 5-1, the user can select a customer from the list to view details. Expanding on the workflow a little, you can assume the customer's detail screen also includes a delete customer option. Adding these two customer URIs to the navigation map sets up an illustration of the Redirect functionality.

The first two URIs leads to the same endpoint. One omits the `Action` parameter, which defaults to the `GET` option in the controller. The second enables a specific set of verbs to be acted on by the controller. Navigating from a view to the second URI shown in Listing 5-9 and specifying the `DELETE` action string can delete the customer model, and because that customer is deleted, the controller can redirect to another controller.

LISTING 5-9: Sample navigation map entries

Available for download on Wrox.com

```
CustomerController customerController = new CustomerController();
NavigationMap.Add("Customer/{Customer}", customerController);
NavigationMap.Add("Customer/{Customer}/{Action}/", customerController);
NavigationMap.Add("Customer", new CustomerListController());
```

Found in the CustomerManagement/App.cs file of the download

In Listing 5-10, the direct is back to the list of customers.

LISTING 5-10: CustomerController load method

Available for download on Wrox.com

```
using System;
using System.Collections.Generic;
using System.IO;
using System.Linq;
using System.Text;
using System.Net;
using System.Xml.Serialization;

using MonoCross.Navigation;

using CustomerManagement.Shared;
using CustomerManagement.Shared.Model;

namespace CustomerManagement.Controllers
{
  public class CustomerController : MXController<Customer>
```

```
{
  public override string Load(Dictionary<string, string> parameters)
  {
    string perspective = ViewPerspective.Default;

    string customerId = null;
    parameters.TryGetValue("CustomerId", out customerId);

    // get the action, assumes
    string action;
    if (!parameters.TryGetValue("Action", out action))
    {
      // set default action if none specified
      action = "GET";
    }

    switch (action)
    {
      case "EDIT":
      case "GET":
        // populate the customer model
        if (customerId == null)
          throw new Exception("No Customer Id found");
        if (string.Equals(customerId.ToUpper(), "NEW"))
        {
          // assigm Model a new customer for editing
          Model = new Customer();
          perspective = ViewPerspective.Update;
        }
        else
        {
          Model = GetCustomer(customerId);
          if (String.Equals(action, "EDIT"))
            perspective = ViewPerspective.Update;
          else
            perspective = ViewPerspective.Default;
        }
        break;

      case "DELETE":
        if (customerId == null)
          customerId = Model.ID;
        // post delete request to the server
        DeleteCustomer(customerId);

        // return and let redirected controller execute, remaining
        // navigation is ignored
        MXContainer.Instance.Redirect("Customers");
        return ViewPerspective.Delete;

      case "CREATE":
        // process addition of new model
        if (AddNewCustomer(Model))
          MXContainer.Instance.Redirect("Customers");
```

continues

LISTING 5-10 *(continued)*

```
          break;

        case "UPDATE":
          if (UpdateCustomer(Model))
            MXContainer.Instance.Redirect("Customers");
          break;
      }

      return perspective;
    }

    public static Customer GetCustomer(string customerId)
    {
      return CustomerManagement.Data.XmlDataStore.GetCustomer(customerId);
    }

    public static bool UpdateCustomer(Customer customer)
    {
      CustomerManagement.Data.XmlDataStore.UpdateCustomer(customer);
      return true;
    }

    public static bool AddNewCustomer(Customer customer)
    {
      CustomerManagement.Data.XmlDataStore.CreateCustomer(customer);
      return true;
    }

    public static bool DeleteCustomer(string customerId)
    {
      CustomerManagement.Data.XmlDataStore.DeleteCustomer(customerId);
      return true;
    }
  }
}
```

Found in the CustomerManagement/Controllers/CustomerController.cs file of the download

Code Summary

To complete the preceding example code, Listing 5-11 provides the underlying layouts of the sample application's classes. As described in Chapter 4, "The MonoCross Pattern," the thread tying the application together is the `MXApplication` class. When the application loads, the `OnAppLoad()` method is called, and the navigation map is built. For the preceding example controllers, the `MXApplication` class is laid out here.

LISTING 5-11: MXApplication

Available for download on Wrox.com

```
public class App : MXApplication
{
  public override void OnAppLoad()
  {
    // Set the application title
    Title = "Customer Management";

    // Add navigation mappings for customer controller
    NavigationMap.Add("Customers", new CustomerListController());
    CustomerController customerController = new CustomerController();
    NavigationMap.Add("Customers/{CustomerId}", customerController);
    NavigationMap.Add("Customers/{CustomerId}/{Action}", customerController);

    // for the order controller
    OrderController orderController = new OrderController();
    NavigationMap.Add("Orders/{Order}", orderController);
    NavigationMap.Add("Orders/New/{Customer}", orderController);
    NavigationMap.Add("Orders/Add/{Order}/", orderController);

    // Set default navigation URI
    NavigateOnLoad = "Customers";
  }
}
```

Found in the CustomerManagement/App.cs file of the download

The customer management workflow starts with the loading of the customer list. Listing 5-12 shows the Customer List controller code.

LISTING 5-12: CustomerListController

Available for download on Wrox.com

```
public class CustomerListController : MXController<List<Customer>>
{
  public override string Load(Dictionary<string, string> parameters)
  {
    // populate model
    Model = GetCustomerList();

    return ViewPerspective.Default;
  }

  public static List<Customer> GetCustomerList()
  {
    List<Customer> customerList = new List<Customer>();
    // XML Serializer
```

continues

LISTING 5-12 *(continued)*

```
    System.Xml.Serialization.XmlSerializer serializer = new
XmlSerializer(typeof(List<Customer>));

    // web request
    string urlCustomers = "http://localhost/MXDemo/customers.xml";
    HttpWebRequest request = (HttpWebRequest)HttpWebRequest.Create(urlCustomers);
    using (StreamReader reader = new
StreamReader(request.GetResponse().GetResponseStream(), true))
    {
        // XML serializer
        customerList = (List<Customer>)serializer.Deserialize(reader);
    }
    return customerList;
  }
}
```

Found in the CustomerManagement/Controllers/CustomerListController.cs file of the download

Applying Changes to the Model

As briefly seen in the Order controller, the controller provides an opportunity for the business logic to update the Model. The MonoCross pattern does not force controllers to save data to the model. As items are selected in a view, the view can write directly to the model. However, the purpose of the MonoCross pattern is to facilitate the development of a shared code base. The purpose of the MVC pattern is to keep business logic out of the view code.

In the previous example, the view could easily add a selected item to an order. The code used to demonstrate how to update the model was not complex. But often each piece of data gets validated. Validation code usually involves business logic specific to that application. Performing that validation in the controller allows the code base to be utilized on all platforms without copying and pasting code between code files that can be compiled only on a single platform. Each source code file for a controller can be compiled, in its entirety, by each compiler utilized for the MonoCross targets.

SUMMARY

In this chapter, you learned about the model and controller pieces of the MVC pattern that MonoCross uses to create a shared code base. You learned how to create the models based on data either necessary to create views they support or to complete calculations based on business rulesets. The chapter also addressed the importance of coding business rules into the controller whenever possible. Code placed in the model and controller classes are the heart of your shared code base.

In the next chapter you take a look at building views for the customer management application. You explore the different UI objects within the various SDKs, as well as looking at how to leverage the

MonoCross framework to pass execution from the controller's `Load()` method to the container's `Render()` method.

The link between the controller and the view is the model and view perspective. One option for data loading is to kick off the data load in the controller and let the view pick it up when the `Render()` method is called. In the case of the Customer List controller, there would be no logic executed in the controller. The default view perspective could be returned and execution passed on. The advantage of that approach comes when the view takes a while to render, or the wait spinner can display in the view until the model is populated. That flow of execution works well in cases where no business logic execution needs to occur after the model is populated.

Building MonoCross Containers

WHAT'S IN THIS CHAPTER?

- Tying together your models, controllers, and views
- Understanding MonoCross platform containers
- Defining your platform-specific views
- Implementing navigation between views

This chapter integrates the user interface designed in Chapter 2, "Designing Your User Experience," with the models and controllers built in Chapter 5, "Building Shared Applications," and ties it all together for five different platform implementations. The chapter starts with an explanation of how the views, models, and controllers are set up and managed by MonoCross and moves into how each platform implements the management of the views and controllers.

Following an introduction to how this portion of the framework functions, you learn how to implement views for the customer list and for displaying, adding, changing, and deleting a customer (standard CRUD operations). The sample code includes implementations for Windows console, iOS, Android, Windows Phone, and a WebKit server implementation.

UNDERSTANDING HOW IT ALL FITS TOGETHER

The Model-View-Controller (MVC) pattern describes a single screen and its data in an application, and applications consist of many views, even more data, and some form of navigation between the views. Up to this point you defined a high-level user interface, modeled your data, and constructed a navigational framework as defined in your application and implemented in controllers. The next step is to define your platform-specific views and implement the navigation between them for each platform you plan to support.

Figure 6-1 illustrates how the code built in the previous chapter is shared. The left side of the figure shows the relationship of the application object, the controllers, and the models.

The right side shows the platform-specific bits we will concentrate on to build our views and defines them within platform-specific containers.

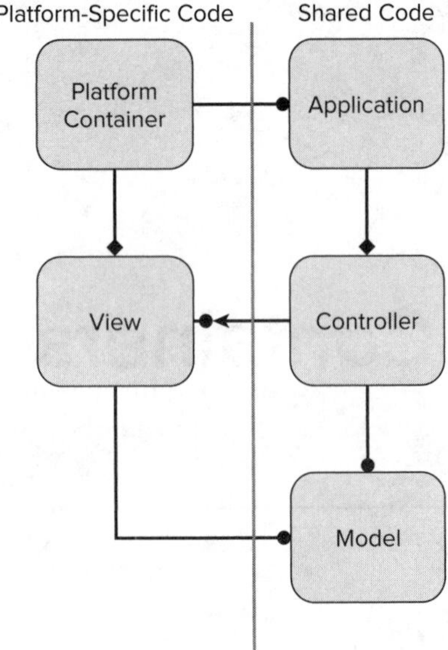

FIGURE 6-1: A UML diagram illustrates the object relationships and platform code boundaries.

To this end we now create platform-specific view object classes using MonoCross framework convenience classes to simplify the implementation and make that implementation as consistent as possible across all your platforms. We still utilize all the platform-specific interfaces to give end users an application that looks and behaves as if it were designed just for the device they use.

At the base of your platform implementations are the platform-specific containers. The container for each platform is responsible for the following:

- Implementing the navigational structure
- Creating and loading your model via its controller
- Creating your view and assigning it the model
- Placing your view in its platform hierarchy

You may have noticed in the controllers that no consideration was given to making the controllers or their `Load()` methods multithreaded or asynchronous. At first thought, this is counter to how you would expect most user interfaces to function. An interface should always be responsive and as fast as possible, and long-running tasks in the foreground is a major affront to this need. In reality, all the navigation calls implemented in MonoCross are implemented as asynchronous on the platforms that need them. You can even hook into events that enable you to interact in various ways with the user to provide feedback on longer-running operations, for example, pulling relatively large amounts of data over a slow Internet connection.

Building your applications using a shared structure gives you an advantage over implementing separate applications for each platform. You can get consistency in design; you built your models and controllers and then defined views for each. These views have the same functionality across all platforms and have the same navigational structure. In addition, using a shared structure keeps you from going too far astray from your design. If changes are made, you need only change the model, application, and controller in one place. This change helps you keep consistency in all platforms.

For the remainder of the chapter, you create three views from two Model and Controller pairs for each platform. Those views are the Customer List View, the Customer View, and the Customer Edit View. You start with the most simplistic platform possible, a text-based console view, to highlight the aspects and responsibilities of the Models, Controllers, Application, Container, and Views. It helps to run and step through the code of each sample as they are presented here to further your understanding of the patterns and their implementations.

When designing and building your platform views, consider keeping the implementations of your views as consistent as possible while still utilizing the native user experience your chosen platforms provide. For example, when building the views, we can offer all the same data and functionality on each view; you can also name the views the same. The views need to be consistent with the platform and across platforms. This aids users in moving from one platform to another as well as in maintaining the code and allowing developers to easily identify where in the code to look when they need to perform maintenance tasks.

IMPLEMENTING A SIMPLE APPLICATION

To explore how to implement a simple application, let's start with the oldest and simplest user interface target, the command prompt. Even if you never need a text-based interface as a target you would give an end user, such a simple interface goes a long way in explaining the general concepts. Consisting of only text input and text output, it requires you to keep your views simple. Although it isn't an application you would ever deploy to an end user, this simple application can help you prove your model and controller implementation as well as your URI navigation and can sometimes test changes to your controllers.

Initializing the Container

All Mono and .NET console applications start from a single static function named `Main()`. (Yes, this application can run on Mac OS, Windows, and even Linux.) In `Main()` you initialize your application and then proceed to your first view. Initialization consists of creating an instance of the Application object you defined in Chapter 5. Listing 6-1 shows the implementation of `Main()` for the Customer Management application.

LISTING 6-1: Console Main application

Available for download on Wrox.com

```
namespace CustomerManagement.Console
{
  class Program
  {
    static void Main(string[] args)
    {
      // initialize container
      MXConsoleContainer.Initialize(new CustomerManagement.App());
```

continues

LISTING 6-1 *(continued)*

```
            // customer list view
            MXConsoleContainer.AddView<List<Customer>>(new Views.CustomerListView(),
              ViewPerspective.Default);

            // customer view and customer edit/new
            MXConsoleContainer.AddView<Customer>(new Views.CustomerView(),
              ViewPerspective.Default);
            MXConsoleContainer.AddView<Customer>(new Views.CustomerEdit(),
              ViewPerspective.Update);

            // navigate to first view
            MXConsoleContainer.Navigate(MXContainer.Instance.App.NavigateOnLoad);
        }
    }
}
```

Found in the CustomerManagement/CustomerManangement.Console/Program.cs file of the download

The Application object we defined in Chapter 5 holds the URI navigational mapping to your controllers and models, the platform-independent title of your application, and your entry point into the application that passes it into the console containers static `Initialization()` method. The code then adds each view to the container and specifies the model type for an associated view using a template parameter. The view type gives the container enough information to associate the model, the controller, and the view together. Note the second parameter of the `AddView()` method — the view perspective. It is sometimes important to have two or more views associated with the same model and controller. For example, you can use separate views for viewing and editing the Customer object, which allows you latitude in how you would edit a view as opposed to just showing it to the end user without having to force that functionality into the same form. The last step is to initiate the navigation to the first view from the URI specified in the `NavigateOnLoad` property from the application.

The Console container is not asynchronous in any way, which enables you to step through all the code if you want to.

Building the Customer List View

Now that you have initialized the container, you can implement the first view. Listing 6-2 shows the implementation of `CustomerListView`. Some lines are bolded to highlight key lines of code. In MonoCross, all views must implement the interface `IMXView`, which is required to allow the container to track the views, initialize the view with its model, and tell the view to render itself. All the platform containers provide basic template classes that attempt to simplify implementation of the views for each platform. The console container provides just one view type, `MXConsoleView<ModelT>`, which implements the basics that the console container needs to keep track of it and exposes a single abstract method, `Render`, to do its input and output.

LISTING 6-2: Console Customer List View

Available for download on Wrox.com

```
namespace CustomerManagement.Console.Views
{
  public class CustomerListView : MXConsoleView<List<Customer>>
  {
    public override void Render()
    {
      // Output Customer List to Console
      System.Console.Clear();
      System.Console.WriteLine("Customers");
      System.Console.WriteLine();

      int index = 1;
      foreach (Customer customer in Model)
      {
        System.Console.WriteLine(index.ToString() + ". " + customer.Name);
        index++;
      }

      System.Console.WriteLine();
      System.Console.WriteLine(
          "Enter Customer Index, (N)ew Customer or Enter to go Back");

      // Input Actions from Console
      do
      {
        string input = System.Console.ReadLine().Trim();

        if (input.Length == 0)
        {
          this.Back();
          return;
        }

        if (int.TryParse(input, out index) && index > 0 && index <= Model.Count)
        {
          this.Navigate(string.Format("Customers/{0}", Model[index - 1].ID));
          return;
        }
        else if (string.Equals(input, "N"))
        {
          this.Navigate("Customers/NEW");
          return;
        }
        else
        {
          System.Console.WriteLine("Invalid input, retry input or Enter to go back");
        }

      } while (true);
    }
  }
}
```

Found in the CustomerManagement/CustomerManangement.Console/Views/CustomerListView.cs file of the download

The first view from the initial design you completed in Chapter 2 is your Customer list; it has three functions: to display all your customers, to enable your user to get more information on a customer, and to create a new customer. To implement these functions, you utilize the only two methods for input and output that you have: `Console.Write()` and `Console.Read()`. You can define the view as `CustomerListView`, deriving from `MXConsoleView<List<Customer>>`, specifying your Model type, and overriding the `Render` method to do all the required work. Your implementation can output the customer name with an index. Upon completion, you can wait for one of two inputs: the index of the customer the user wants to see more information about or an "N" to add a new customer, to make the view a little friendlier. Users can exit the application by pressing Enter, giving no input. The application prompts them to re-enter a number or "N" for new. After that input, the user can navigate to another view, either the Customer View if an existing customer is specified or the Customer Edit View if the user is creating a new customer.

Navigation is implemented in the base container (`MXContainer`) upon which you base all platform-specific containers. The base container initiates navigation by matching the navigation URI against the patterns given in the base application. If a match is found, the associated controller's `Load()` method is called with the parameters from the URI to load the model. The platform-specific container is then used to find the associated view, and then render and complete the platform-specific steps needed to show the view.

In Listing 6-2, the navigate functions are static methods on the base container class. These particular calls are extension methods specific to the platform. Each platform can add extension methods that define additional parameters and functionality. For example, in platforms that support it, animations and transitions could be specified as additional information. Figure 6-2 shows the resulting view.

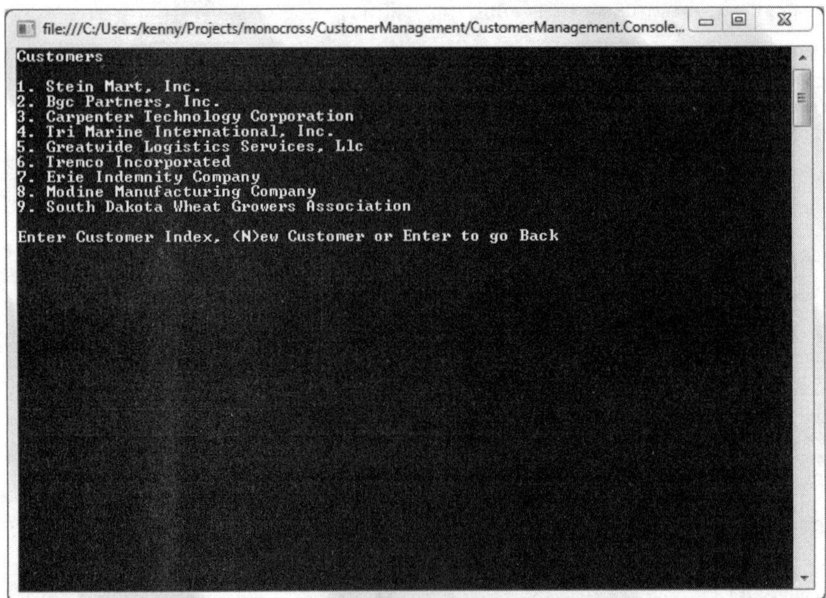

FIGURE 6-2: Implementing the code generates this console application Customer List View.

Building the Customer View

Building the Customer View is even simpler than building the Customer List View. Again you derive a view class from `MXConsoleView`. This time, however, Customer is the template model parameter.

The functionality enables the user to see the customer details, such as the primary phone number, address, and other information, and enables the user to change the customer details by navigating to the Customer Edit View. A user can enter a blank response to return to the list or "E" to edit the customer details in the Customer Edit View. Listing 6-3 highlights the `Navigate()` method and shows the code for the Customer View. Figure 6-3 shows the view output.

Available for download on Wrox.com

LISTING 6-3: Console Customer View

```
namespace CustomerManagement.Console.Views
{
  class CustomerView : MXConsoleView<Customer>
  {
    public override void Render()
    {
      System.Console.Clear();
      System.Console.WriteLine("Customer Details");
      System.Console.WriteLine();

      System.Console.WriteLine(Model.Name);
      System.Console.WriteLine(string.Format("{0} {1}", Model.PrimaryAddress.Street1,
        Model.PrimaryAddress.Street2));
      System.Console.WriteLine(string.Format("{0}, {1}  {2}", Model.PrimaryAddress.City,
        Model.PrimaryAddress.State, Model.PrimaryAddress.Zip));
      System.Console.WriteLine("Previous Orders: " + Model.Orders.Count.ToString());
      System.Console.WriteLine("Addresses:" + Model.Addresses.Count.ToString());
      System.Console.WriteLine("Contacts: " + Model.Contacts.Count.ToString());
      System.Console.WriteLine();
      System.Console.WriteLine("Web: " + Model.Website);
      System.Console.WriteLine("Phone: " + Model.PrimaryPhone);
      System.Console.WriteLine();
      System.Console.WriteLine("Enter to Continue, (D)elete or (E)dit");

      while (true)
      {
        string input = System.Console.ReadLine().Trim();
        if (input.Length == 0)
        {
          this.Back();
          return;
        }
        else if (input.StartsWith("E"))
        {
          this.Navigate("Customers/" + Model.ID + "/EDIT");
        }
        else if (input.StartsWith("D"))
        {
          this.Navigate("Customers/" + Model.ID + "/DELETE");
        }
      }
    }
  }
}
```

Found in the CustomerManagement/CustomerManangement.Console/Views/CustomerView.cs file of the download

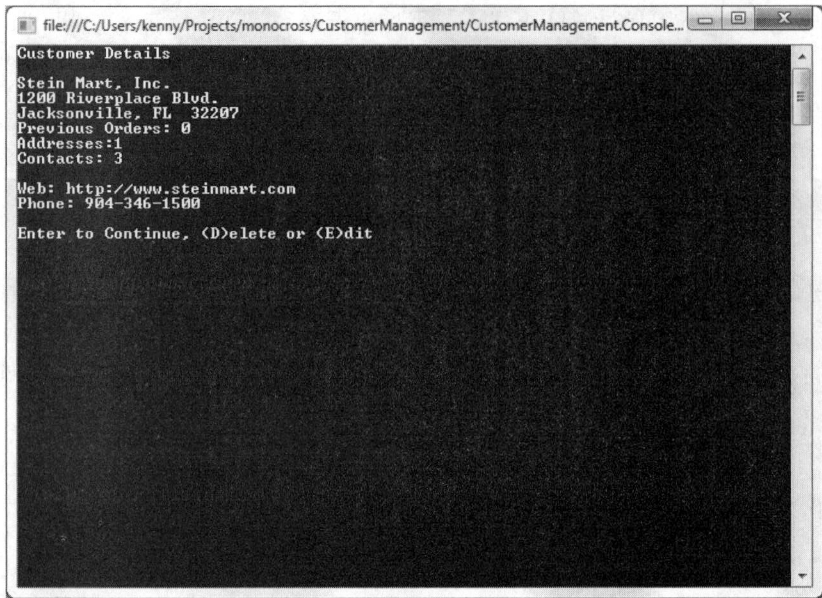

FIGURE 6-3: The code generates a console application Customer View.

Building the Customer Edit View

The Customer Edit View is also a simple implementation; you simply prompt the user to type an overriding value, or nothing, and set the model value to the data entered by the user. If you look carefully at Listing 6-4, you can see the code updating the model and making a navigation call to the same URI that brought you here, with the exception that you appended either `UPDATE` or `CREATE` as an additional parameter. This tells the controller what the intent is. When the controller sees these parameters, it knows to take the values from the model it shares with the view and either updates an existing customer or creates a new one. After the controller updates the customer record, the controller issues its own navigation call to return to the Customer List View. You can see the final resulting view in Figure 6-4.

Available for download on Wrox.com

LISTING 6-4: Console Customer Edit View

```
{
  class CustomerEdit: MXConsoleView<Customer>
  {
    public override void Render()
    {
      System.Console.Clear();
      System.Console.WriteLine("Customer Details");
      System.Console.WriteLine();

      System.Console.Write("Name: (" + Model.Name + ") New Name: ");
      string input = System.Console.ReadLine();
      if (!string.IsNullOrWhiteSpace(input))
          Model.Name = input;
```

```
        System.Console.Write("Website: (" + Model.Website + ") New Website: ");
        input = System.Console.ReadLine();
        if (!string.IsNullOrWhiteSpace(input))
            Model.Website = input;

        System.Console.Write(
                "Primary Phone: (" + Model.PrimaryPhone + ") New Primary Phone: ");
        input = System.Console.ReadLine();
        if (!string.IsNullOrWhiteSpace(input))
            Model.PrimaryPhone = input;

        System.Console.WriteLine();
        System.Console.WriteLine("New Customer Info");
        System.Console.WriteLine("Name: " + Model.Name);
        System.Console.WriteLine("Web: " + Model.Website);
        System.Console.WriteLine("Phone: " + Model.PrimaryPhone);
        System.Console.WriteLine();
        System.Console.WriteLine("Enter to Cancel - (S)ave");
        input = System.Console.ReadLine();
        if (!string.IsNullOrWhiteSpace(input) && string.Equals(input, "S")) {
           string action = string.Equals(Model.ID, "0") ? "CREATE": "UPDATE";
           this.Navigate("Customers/" + Model.ID + "/" + action);
        } else {
           this.Back();
        }
      }
    }
  }
}
```

Found in the CustomerManagement/CustomerManangement.Console/Views/CustomerEdit.cs file of the download

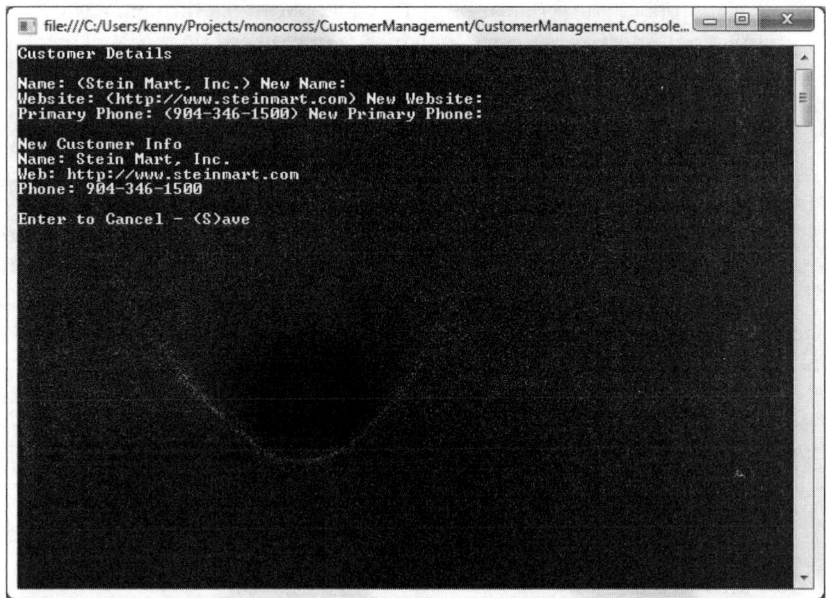

FIGURE 6-4: Implementing the code results in the console application Customer Edit View.

IMPLEMENTING AN IOS PLATFORM CONTAINER

In the previous section, you built a simple application that provides the bare minimum of user interaction. Now you build a fully functional iOS application that provides all the expected interface features a user of your application would expect. For brevity in the code discussed, we leave out data validation and multilingual features, but you can easily extend the sample to implement that functionality.

For those of you reading this that haven't written MonoTouch applications yet, and even for those that haven't programmed for iOS, the best way to describe MonoTouch is to say it's a slimmed-down version of Microsoft's .NET desktop libraries with the addition of bindings to the native iOS programming APIs that Apple provides to C/Objective-C developers (Cocoa Touch). It does not provide an abstracted UI that you can run cross platform; instead it provides bindings to the native API of the device. There is no System.Graphics support beyond a few needed definitions, and there is no Microsoft.Windows.Forms support for windowing. If you need either of these types of functionality, you need to use the MonoTouch bindings for the user interface. The MonoTouch bindings to Cocoa Touch match Cocoa Touch's classes one for one and map directly to the MonoTouch class. MonoTouch provides only the wrapper around the MonoTouch classes and does not implement any of the Cocoa Touch functionality itself. Essentially, anything you can do with a native Objective-C interface you can do in MonoTouch; plus you get all the built-in .NET class libraries.

Initializing a Container in MonoTouch

Almost identically to the console application, you can initiate iOS applications through a static Main function. The Main function generally has one job, which is to call a static function on the `UIApplication` class and specify the class name that iOS is to create to control the application. Listing 6-5 shows you the definition of the application delegate class aptly named `AppDelegate`. In Cocoa Touch terms, applications generally consist of a single Window (UIWindow) upon which all views and user interactions reside. The application delegate class has an override for a virtual method, `FinishedLaunching()`, which handles the initialization of the MonoCross application, sets up the Model-View mapping, and initiates navigation. In initializing the platform container this time, there are additional parameters passed to the container. Because the platform container handles creating and manipulating the views, it requires additional information to function in iOS. The additional items it needs are a reference to your application delegate and a reference to the window the application runs in.

Available for download on Wrox.com

LISTING 6-5: iOS AppDelegate.cs

```
namespace CustomerManagement.Touch
{
  [MXTouchTabletOptions(TabletLayout.MasterPane,
    MasterShowsinLandscape = true,
```

```
        MasterShowsinPotrait = true,
        AllowDividerResize = false)]
    [MXTouchContainerOptions(SplashBitmap = "Images/splash.jpg")]
    [Register ("AppDelegate")]
    public partial class AppDelegate : UIApplicationDelegate
    {
        UIWindow window;

        public override bool FinishedLaunching (UIApplication app, NSDictionary options)
        {
            // create a new window instance based on the screen size
            window = new UIWindow (UIScreen.MainScreen.Bounds);

            MXTouchContainer.Initialize(new CustomerManagement.App(), this, window);

            // add Views
            MXTouchContainer.AddView<List<Customer>>(typeof(CustomerListView),
                ViewPerspective.Default);
            MXTouchContainer.AddView<Customer>(typeof(CustomerView),
                ViewPerspective.Default);
            MXTouchContainer.AddView<Customer>(typeof(CustomerEditView),
                ViewPerspective.Update);

            MXTouchContainer.Navigate(null, MXContainer.Instance.App.NavigateOnLoad);

            UIDevice.CurrentDevice.BeginGeneratingDeviceOrientationNotifications();

            return true;
        }
    }
}
```

Found in the CustomerManagement/CustomerManangement.Touch/AppDelegate.cs file of the sample code

The initialization of the container is nearly identical to the initialization of the container in the console application: the base initialization is called, the Model-View mappings are added, and then the first navigation is presented. This pattern persists across all the containers, but it is called at different points in the platforms' execution because of differences in the platforms themselves.

In addition to completing the initialization of the container, you have also added attributes on the `AppDelegate` class to describe how the views behave when displayed on a tablet. By default, the iOS container (`MXTouchContainer`) behaves and displays the same on an iPad as it would on an iPhone and iPod, making it function like a large phone. However, by specifying attributes on the `AppDelegate` class, the Touch Container can use a master-detail pane layout similar to the ones you see in the iPad Settings or e-mail apps. Because we target both the iPad and iPhone in this sample, you also need to provide a little more information on the views to allow the container to figure out where to put the views when a user navigates to a view. You address that aspect of each view when implementing each view. For this implementation, you specify the `MXTabletOptions` attribute with values for the layout style (`MasterPane`) and flags for when you want the master pane to show — in this case, both landscape and portrait. In addition to the properties used in the sample, additional properties enable you to specify the navigation bar color and a few other behaviors of the container.

The console section, "Implementing a Simple Application," mentioned that navigation is either synchronous or asynchronous, depending on the platform. The Touch Container navigation is asynchronous, meaning that the navigation call at the end of `AppDelegate` initialization and the navigation in the views start a thread that loads the model data on a background thread and then shows the view when the controller finishes loading the data for the view.

Building the Customer List View in MonoTouch

In iOS applications, the top-level views are `UIViewController`-derived classes that contain the user interface elements (`UIView`-derived elements). Following that pattern for the MonoTouch platform container, all the view classes derive indirectly from `UIViewController`. MonoCross provides three base classes from which to derive your views:

- `MXTouchViewController`: A basic view with no functionality that is derived directly from `UIViewController`. It is intended to contain basic views and show the minimal functionality needed for a view in the Touch container. Possible uses include placing a `UIImageView` to show an image, or your own `UIView`-derived class.
- `MXTouchTableViewController`: A `UITableViewController`-derived class for implementing lists and tables. You can use this class to build your Customer List View.
- `MXTouchDialogViewController`: A view derived from `DialogViewController`, an open source project built and maintained by Miguel de Icaza. This class indirectly derives from `UITableViewController` and builds dialog-like views generally found in the iPhone and iPad Settings app. Your Customer View and Customer Edit View use this view class as its base.

  You can find more detailed information at the following location on GitHub: `https://github.com/migueldeicaza/MonoTouch.Dialog`.

Listing 6-6 shows the view for the Customer List derived from `MXTouchTableViewController`, a convenience class that derives from `UITableViewController`, the class upon which all the lists in iOS are based. In the Customer List View, the overridden `Render()` method assigns a delegate class and a data source class based on the Customer List and adds a new Customer button. The delegate handles the user selecting a customer, and the data source assigns data to the cells that the table view uses to display the customers as the user scrolls through the list. Figure 6-5 shows the resulting view.

LISTING 6-6: iOS Customer List View

Available for download on Wrox.com

```
namespace CustomerManagement.Touch
{
  [MXTouchViewAttributes(ViewNavigationContext.Master)]
```

```
public class CustomerListView : MXTouchTableViewController<List<Customer>>
{
  public CustomerListView()
  {
  }

  public override void Render()
  {
    Title = "Customers";

    TableView.Delegate = new TableViewDelegate(this, Model);
    TableView.DataSource = new TableViewDataSource(Model);
    TableView.ReloadData();

    if (MXTouchNavigation.MasterDetailLayout && Model.Count > 0)
    {
      // we have two available panes, fill both (like the email application)
      this.Navigate(string.Format("Customers/{0}", Model[0].ID));
    }
  }

  public override void ViewDidLoad()
  {
    base.ViewDidLoad();
    NavigationItem.SetRightBarButtonItem(
      new UIBarButtonItem(UIBarButtonSystemItem.Add,
        (sender, e) => { NewCustomer(); }), false);
  }

  public void NewCustomer()
  {
    MXTouchContainer.Navigate(this, "Customers/NEW");
  }

  public override void ViewWillAppear(bool animated)
  {
  }

  public override bool ShouldAutorotateToInterfaceOrientation(
    UIInterfaceOrientation toInterfaceOrientation)
  {
    return true;
  }

  private class TableViewDelegate : UITableViewDelegate
  {
    private CustomerListView _parent;
    private List<Customer> _clientList;

    public TableViewDelegate(CustomerListView parent, List<Customer> list)
    {
```

continues

LISTING 6-6 *(continued)*

```
          _parent = parent;
          _clientList = list;
        }
        public override void RowSelected(UITableView tableView, NSIndexPath indexPath)
        {
          Customer client = _clientList[indexPath.Row];
          _parent.Navigate(String.Format("Customers/{0}", client.ID));
        }
      }

      private class TableViewDataSource : UITableViewDataSource
      {
        static NSString kCellIdentifier = new NSString("ClientCell");
        private List<Customer> _list;

        public TableViewDataSource(List<Customer> list)
        {
          this._list = list;
        }
        public override int RowsInSection(UITableView tableview, int section)
        {
          return _list.Count;
        }
        public override UITableViewCell GetCell(UITableView tableView,
          NSIndexPath indexPath)
        {
          UITableViewCell cell = tableView.DequeueReusableCell(kCellIdentifier);
          if (cell == null)
          {
            cell = new UITableViewCell(UITableViewCellStyle.Subtitle, kCellIdentifier);
            if (!MXTouchNavigation.MasterDetailLayout)
              cell.Accessory = UITableViewCellAccessory.DisclosureIndicator;
            else
              cell.Accessory = UITableViewCellAccessory.None;
          }
          cell.TextLabel.Text = _list[indexPath.Row].Name;
          cell.DetailTextLabel.Text = _list[indexPath.Row].Website;
          return cell;
        }
        public override string TitleForHeader(UITableView tableView, int section)
        {
          return string.Empty;
        }
        public override int NumberOfSections(UITableView tableView)
        {
          return 1;
        }
      }
    }
  }
```

Found in the CustomerManagement/CustomerManangement.Touch/Views/CustomerListView.cs file of the download

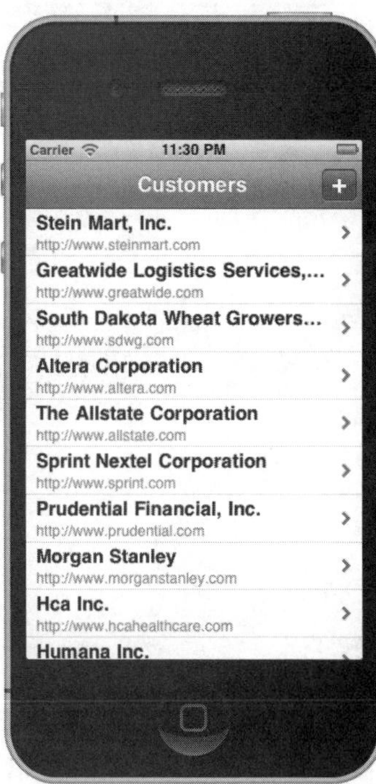

FIGURE 6-5: The result of code implementation for the iOS iPhone application Customer List View should look similar.

Building the Customer View in MonoTouch

Your Customer View is just a simple view to display all the basic information about your customer in a form that looks much like one of the settings pages in the Settings app. Building upon the `DialogViewController` mentioned at the start of this section, you can add simple sections for Contact Info and General Info (contrived, yes). These sections place the contact information for your customer, including the customer's website address, main phone number, and main address. For these items you can also add simple embellishments that make sense for each by adding an anonymous delegate to handle a click event for each. Review Listing 6-7 for all the details involved in dialing a phone number, launching maps with an address, and launching a web link. Figure 6-6 shows the final implementation of the Customer View.

LISTING 6-7: iOS Customer View

Available for download on Wrox.com

```
namespace CustomerManagement.Touch
{
  [MXTouchViewAttributes(ViewNavigationContext.Detail)]
  public class CustomerView : MXTouchDialogView<Customer>
  {
    public CustomerView()
      : base(UITableViewStyle.Grouped, null, true)
    {
    }
```

continues

LISTING 6-7 *(continued)*

```
public override void ViewDidLoad()
{
  base.ViewDidLoad();

  NavigationItem.SetRightBarButtonItem(
    new UIBarButtonItem(UIBarButtonSystemItem.Action,
      (sender, e) => { ActionMenu(); }), false);
}

public override void Render()
{
  string addressString = Model.PrimaryAddress != null ?
    Model.PrimaryAddress.ToString() : string.Empty;
  this.Root = new RootElement("Customer Info")
  {
    new Section("Contact Info")
    {
      new StringElement("ID", Model.ID),
      new StringElement("Name", Model.Name ?? string.Empty),
      new StringElement("Website", Model.Website ?? string.Empty,
        delegate { LaunchWeb();}),
      new StringElement("Primary Phone", Model.PrimaryPhone ?? string.Empty,
        delegate { LaunchDial();})
    },
    new Section("General Info")
    {
      new StyledMultilineElement("Address", addressString,
        UITableViewCellStyle.Subtitle,
          delegate { LaunchMaps(); } ),
      new StringElement("Previous Orders ", Model.Orders != null ?
         Model.Orders.Count.ToString() : string.Empty),
      new StringElement("Other Addresses ", Model.Addresses != null ?
         Model.Addresses.Count.ToString() : string.Empty),
      new StringElement("Contacts ", Model.Contacts != null ?
         Model.Contacts.Count.ToString() : string.Empty),
    },
  };
}

void ActionMenu()
{
  //_actionSheet = new UIActionSheet("");
  UIActionSheet actionSheet = new UIActionSheet(
    "Customer Actions", null, "Cancel", "Delete Customer",
       new string[] { "Change Customer" });
  actionSheet.Style = UIActionSheetStyle.Default;
  actionSheet.Clicked += delegate(object sender, UIButtonEventArgs args)
  {
    switch (args.ButtonIndex)
    {
      case 0: DeleteCustomer(); break;
      case 1: ChangeCustomer(); break;
    }
```

```
  };

  if (UIDevice.CurrentDevice.UserInterfaceIdiom == UIUserInterfaceIdiom.Phone)
    actionSheet.ShowFromToolbar(NavigationController.Toolbar);
  else
    actionSheet.ShowFrom(NavigationItem.RightBarButtonItem, true);
}

void ChangeCustomer()
{
  this.Navigate(string.Format("Customers/{0}/EDIT", Model.ID));
}

void DeleteCustomer()
{
  var alert = new UIAlertView("Delete Client","Are you sure?",null,"OK","Cancel");
  alert.Show();
  alert.Clicked += (sender, buttonArgs) =>
  {
    if (buttonArgs.ButtonIndex == 0)
    {
      this.Navigate(string.Format("Customers/{0}/DELETE", Model.ID));
    }
  };
}

void LaunchWeb()
{
  UIApplication.SharedApplication.OpenUrl(new NSUrl(Model.Website));
}

void LaunchMaps()
{
  string googleAddress = string.Format("{0} {1}\n{2}, {3}  {4}",
        Model.PrimaryAddress.Street1, Model.PrimaryAddress.Street2,
        Model.PrimaryAddress.City, Model.PrimaryAddress.State,
        Model.PrimaryAddress.Zip);

  googleAddress = System.Web.HttpUtility.UrlEncode(googleAddress);

  string url = string.Format("http://maps.google.com/maps?q={0}", googleAddress);

  UIApplication.SharedApplication.OpenUrl(new NSUrl(url));
}

void LaunchDial()
{
  string url = string.Format("tel:{0}", Model.PrimaryPhone);
  UIApplication.SharedApplication.OpenUrl(new NSUrl(url));
}

void ViewOrders()
{
}
```

continues

LISTING 6-7 *(continued)*

```
        void NewOrder()
        {
        }
    }
}
```

Found in the CustomerManagement/CustomerManangement.Touch/Views/CustomerView.cs file of the download

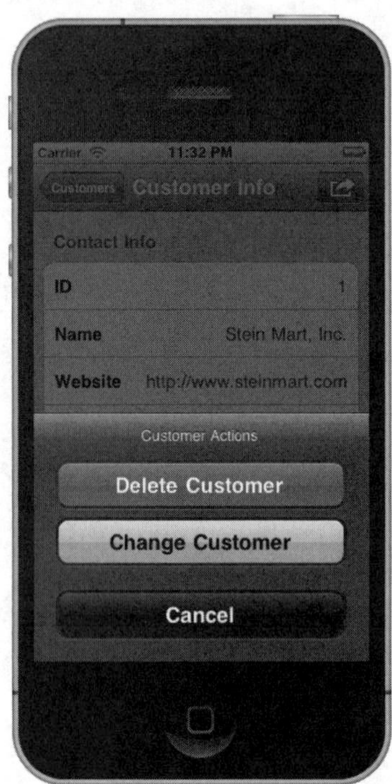

FIGURE 6-6: This iOS iPhone application Customer View is created using the code provided.

Following are some other details shown in Listing 6-7 you should consider in your own implementations:

- The `CustomerView` class is decorated with `MXTouchViewAttributes`. Here you can specify that the Customer View should display in the detail pane when displaying on an iPad.
- You added a button on the right of the navigation bar to show an action bar that enables you to go to the Customer Edit View or to delete this customer; both actions are navigations back to the customer controller.

Building the Customer Edit View in MonoTouch

The final view is nearly identical to the last with two exceptions. First, replacing the label elements with data entry elements allows the user to change the values of the fields you give them access to. Secondly, you need to keep references to the elements so that you can update the model and save it. Listing 6-8 shows the complete implementation for the Customer Edit View.

Available for download on Wrox.com

LISTING 6-8: iOS Customer Edit View

```
namespace CustomerManagement.Touch
{
  [MXTouchViewAttributes(ViewNavigationContext.Detail)]
  public class CustomerEditView : MXTouchDialogView<Customer>
  {
    EntryElement _nameEntry;
    EntryElement _webEntry;
    EntryElement _phoneEntry;
    EntryElement _address1Entry;
    EntryElement _address2Entry;
    EntryElement _cityEntry;
    EntryElement _stateEntry;
    EntryElement _zipEntry;

    public CustomerEditView()
      : base(UITableViewStyle.Grouped, null, true)
    {
    }

    public override void ViewDidAppear(bool animated)
    {
      base.ViewDidAppear(animated);

      this.NavigationItem.SetRightBarButtonItem(
        new UIBarButtonItem("Save", UIBarButtonItemStyle.Done, null), false);
      this.NavigationItem.RightBarButtonItem.Clicked += delegate
      {
        SaveCustomer();
      };
      this.NavigationItem.SetLeftBarButtonItem(
        new UIBarButtonItem("Cancel", UIBarButtonItemStyle.Bordered, null), false);
      this.NavigationItem.LeftBarButtonItem.Clicked += delegate
      {
        if (string.Equals("0", Model.ID))
          this.Navigate(string.Format("Customers", Model.ID));
        else
          this.Navigate(string.Format("Customers/{0}", Model.ID));
      };
```

continues

LISTING 6-8 *(continued)*

```
    }

    public override void Render()
    {
      if (Model.PrimaryAddress == null)
        Model.PrimaryAddress = new Address();

      _nameEntry = new EntryElement("Name", "Name", Model.Name ?? string.Empty);
      _webEntry = new EntryElement("Website", "Website", Model.Website ?? string.Empty);
      _phoneEntry = new EntryElement("Primary Phone", "Phone",
         Model.PrimaryPhone ?? string.Empty);
      _address1Entry = new EntryElement("Address", "",
         Model.PrimaryAddress.Street1 ?? string.Empty);
      _address2Entry = new EntryElement("Address2", "",
         Model.PrimaryAddress.Street2 ?? string.Empty);
      _cityEntry = new EntryElement("City ", "",
         Model.PrimaryAddress.City ?? string.Empty);
      _stateEntry = new EntryElement("State ", "",
         Model.PrimaryAddress.State ?? string.Empty);
      _zipEntry = new EntryElement("ZIP", "", Model.PrimaryAddress.Zip ?? string.Empty);

      this.Root = new RootElement("Customer Info")
      {
        new Section("Contact Info")
        {
          new StringElement("ID", Model.ID ?? string.Empty),
            _nameEntry,
            _webEntry,
            _phoneEntry,
        },
        new Section("Primary Address")
        {
          _address1Entry,
          _address2Entry,
          _cityEntry,
          _stateEntry,
          _zipEntry,
        },
      };
    }

    void SaveCustomer()
    {
      Model.Name = _nameEntry.Value;
      Model.Website = _webEntry.Value;
      Model.PrimaryPhone = _phoneEntry.Value;

      Model.PrimaryAddress.Street1 = _address1Entry.Value;
      Model.PrimaryAddress.Street2 = _address2Entry.Value;
      Model.PrimaryAddress.City = _cityEntry.Value;
```

```
            Model.PrimaryAddress.State = _stateEntry.Value;
            Model.PrimaryAddress.Zip = _zipEntry.Value;

            // Save
            if (string.Equals(Model.ID, "0"))
              this.Navigate(string.Format("Customers/{0}/CREATE", Model.ID));
            else
              this.Navigate(string.Format("Customers/{0}/UPDATE", Model.ID));
        }
    }
}
```

Found in the CustomerManagement/CustomerManangement.Touch/Views/CustomerView.cs file of the download

The `SaveCustomer()` method places the field values into the model and navigates to the controller; this is where sharing the model between the view and the controller simplifies your implementation. You can place validation in the view, the controller, or both, whichever suits the needs of your implementation.

Figure 6-7 shows the Customer Edit View in action.

FIGURE 6-7: The sample code generates an iOS iPhone application Customer Edit View.

Figure 6-8 shows the sample iOS application running on an iPad with the Customer List in the master pane and the Customer View in the detail pane.

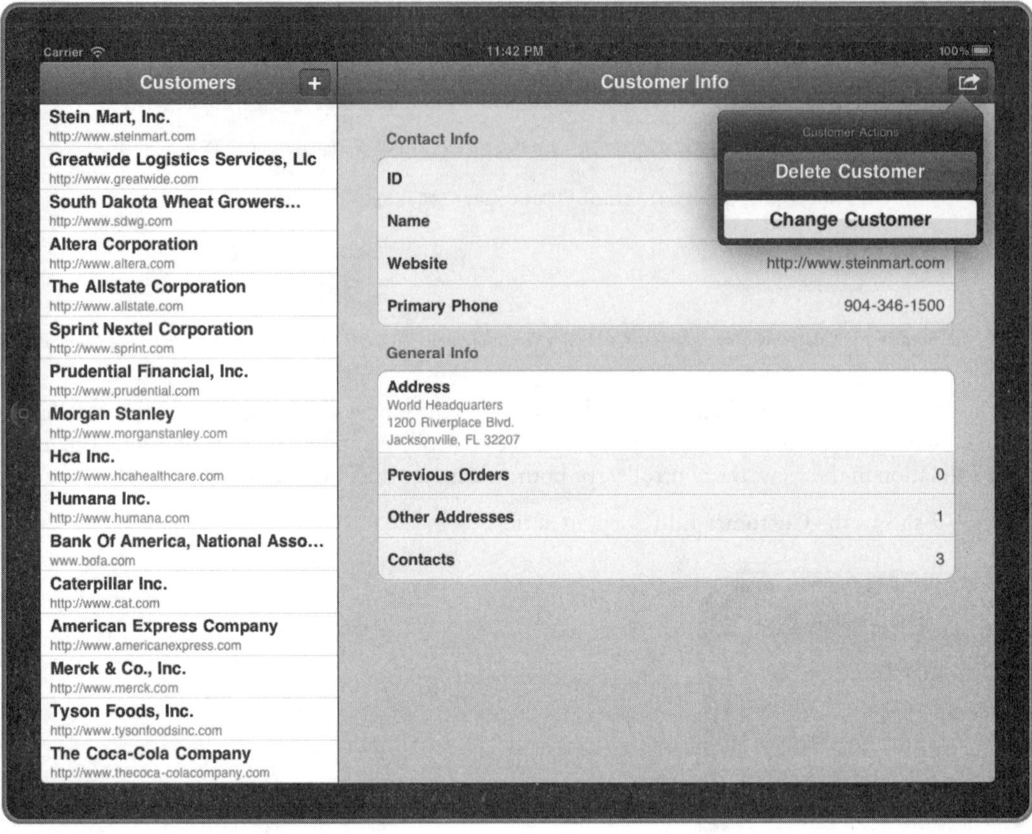

FIGURE 6-8: The iOS application runs on an iPad.

That completes the Customer Management sample for the iOS platform. It implements the bare minimum required to fully show how a MonoCross application can implement your requirements.

IMPLEMENTING AN ANDROID PLATFORM CONTAINER

The next code sample is an Android phone-based application. Although Android now supports both tablet and phone devices, the Mono for Android toolset began supporting tablet APIs only recently, so currently the sample runs on an Android tablet, but as a single-view application just like the phone implementation. By the time this book is published, this sample should have the similar features to its MonoTouch cousin.

The Android sample is nearly identical to the iOS version of your sample code with the exception of where and how you initialize the platform container.

Initializing the Container for Android

At a simple level, Android applications consist of one or more activities, and any activity can potentially be the entry point of the application. The developer specifies which activity is the entry point for the application; there is no handy main application to do your initialization. In addition, an

Android application creates your views for you in response to a navigation-like call. To do your initialization, you must work within the context of an initial view. We typically do our initialization in a Splash Screen activity. You can leave the splash screen blank or give it an image; in either case, it displays a short time while you do your initial navigation.

Remember in the initialization of the iOS container you passed references to some platform-specific properties to allow the container to do proper navigation and deal with platform specifics. On the Android platform, the context is the common thread throughout an application. You need the context to do any navigation or create activities, so pass the application context on to the initialization of the Android container.

Moving on to the views and view navigation, you need to know that navigation is asynchronous, as it is in iOS. This is important because you don't need to worry about maintaining background threads in your view. They are handled by default by the MonoCross framework. Should it be important on a long-running controller load, you can add a handler to the platform container to show a message while the controller loads. Listing 6-9 shows the code for a splash screen that is used to show an initial view and initialize the MonoCross components.

LISTING 6-9: Android SplashScreen Activity

Available for download on Wrox.com

```
namespace CustomerManagement.Droid
{
  [Activity(Label = "SplashScreenActivity",
    Theme = "@android:style/Theme.Black.NoTitleBar",
    MainLauncher = true,
    Icon = "@drawable/icon", NoHistory = true)]
  public class SplashScreenActivity : Activity
  {
    protected override void OnCreate(Bundle savedInstanceState)
    {
      base.OnCreate(savedInstanceState);

      // assign a layout with an image
      SetContentView(Resource.Layout.Splash);

      CheckFiles(ApplicationContext);

      // initialize app
      MXDroidContainer.Initialize(new CustomerManagement.App(),
        this.ApplicationContext);

      // initialize views
      MXDroidContainer.AddView<List<Customer>>(typeof(Views.CustomerListView),
        ViewPerspective.Default);
      MXDroidContainer.AddView<Customer>(typeof(Views.CustomerView),
        ViewPerspective.Default);
      MXDroidContainer.AddView<Customer>(typeof(Views.CustomerEditView),
        ViewPerspective.Update);

      // navigate to first view
      MXDroidContainer.Navigate(null, MXContainer.Instance.App.NavigateOnLoad);
    }
```

continues

LISTING 6-9 *(continued)*

```
    protected override void OnResume()
    {
      base.OnResume();

    }

    /// <summary>
    /// Copies the contents of input to output. Doesn't close either stream.
    /// </summary>
    public void CopyStream(Stream input, Stream output)
    {
      byte[] buffer = new byte[8 * 1024];
      int len;
      while ((len = input.Read(buffer, 0, buffer.Length)) > 0)
      {
        output.Write(buffer, 0, len);
      }
    }

    public void CheckFiles(Context context)
    {
      string documents =
System.Environment.GetFolderPath(System.Environment.SpecialFolder.MyDocuments);

      string dataDirectory = Path.Combine(documents, "Xml");
      if (!Directory.Exists(dataDirectory))
        Directory.CreateDirectory(dataDirectory);

      string dataFile = Path.Combine(documents, @"Xml/Customers.xml");
      if (File.Exists(dataFile))
        return;

      Stream input = context.Assets.Open(@"Xml/Customers.xml");
      FileStream output = File.Create(dataFile);
      CopyStream(input, output);
      input.Close();
      output.Close();
    }
  }
}
```

Found in the CustomerManagement/CustomerManangement.Droid/SplashScreenActivity.cs file of the download

Building the Customer List View for Android

As mentioned in the previous section, in Android applications the top-level views derive from the Activity class, either directly or indirectly. Following that pattern for the Android platform container, all the View classes derive from Activity classes. The MonoCross Android container provides three base classes from which to derive your views:

- `MXActivityView`: A basic view with no added functionality, derived directly from Activity, intended to contain basic views and show the minimal functionality needed for a view in the Android container. Possible uses include placing an `ImageView` to show an image or your own view-derived class.
- `MXListActivityView`: A `ListActivity`-derived class for implementing lists and tables. Use this class to build your Customer List View. This class is analogous to the `UITableView` in the iOS platform.
- `MXDialogActivityView`: Built to be close to the `MonoTouch.Dialog` classes, they provide a set of classes for easily building Form classes to display and edit data in a similar pattern as the Android settings application. The Android-based Customer View and the Customer Edit View sections go into more detail.

Listing 6-10 shows the view for the Customer List derived from `MXListActivityView`, a convenience class that derives from `ListActivity`, the class upon which nearly all the lists in Android are based. In the Customer List View, the overridden `Render()` method assigns an Adapter class that is responsible for returning views to the list as the user scrolls through the list. Items are recycled as they are scrolled through. For simplicity you can implement a simple adapter that populates the list using a predefined view. In addition to viewing the customers in the list, a menu that includes an `Add` Customer item similar to the functionality added to the iOS application displays.

LISTING 6-10: Android Customer List View

Available for download on Wrox.com

```
namespace CustomerManagement.Droid.Views
{
  [Activity(Label = "Customer List", Icon = "@drawable/icon")]
  public class CustomerListView : MXListActivityView<List<Customer>>
  {
    class CustomerAdapter : ArrayAdapter<Customer>
    {
      List<Customer> items;

      public CustomerAdapter(Context context,
                             int textViewResourceId,
                             List<Customer> items)
            : base(context, textViewResourceId, items)
      {
        this.items = items;
      }

      public override View GetView(int position, View convertView, ViewGroup parent)
      {
        View v = convertView;
        if (v == null)
        {
          LayoutInflater li = (LayoutInflater)this.Context.GetSystemService(
            Context.LayoutInflaterService);
          v = li.Inflate(Android.Resource.Layout.SimpleListItem2, null);
        }
```

continues

LISTING 6-10 *(continued)*

```
            Customer o = items[position];
            if (o != null)
            {
              TextView tt = (TextView)v.FindViewById(Android.Resource.Id.Text1);
              if (tt != null)
                tt.Text = o.Name;
              TextView bt = (TextView)v.FindViewById(Android.Resource.Id.Text2);
              if (bt != null && o.Website != null)
                bt.Text = o.Website;
            }
            return v;
          }
        }

        protected override void OnListItemClick(ListView l, View v, int position, long id)
        {
          base.OnListItemClick(l, v, position, id);
          this.Navigate(string.Format("Customers/{0}", Model[position].ID));
        }

        public override bool OnCreateOptionsMenu(IMenu menu)
        {
          MenuInflater.Inflate(Resource.Menu.customer_list_menu, menu);
          return true;
        }

        public override bool OnOptionsItemSelected(IMenuItem item)
        {
          switch (item.ItemId)
          {
            case Resource.Id.add_customer:
              AddCustomer();
              return true;
          }
          return base.OnOptionsItemSelected(item);
        }

        public override void Render()
        {
          ListView.Adapter = new CustomerAdapter(this, 0, Model);
        }

        void AddCustomer()
        {
          this.Navigate("Customers/NEW");
        }
      }
    }
```

Found in the CustomerManagement/CustomerManangement.Droid/Views/CustomerListView.cs file of the download

Figure 6-9 shows the running Customer List View and the Menu item for adding a new customer.

FIGURE 6-9: The Android application Customer List View as developed provides a menu item to add a new customer.

Building the Customer View for Android

Next, you create the simple Customer View based on the `MXDialogActivityView` mentioned in the previous section. To build this view, you literally cut and paste the code from the iOS view's `Render` method and use it as your starting point. Then, change the event handlers and a menu for the `Add` and `Delete` commands, and you are done in short order. Listing 6-11 shows the code for the Customer View; compare the `Render` method to the implementation in Listing 6-7, and you can see the similarities. Figure 6-10 shows the result of implementing the code.

Available for download on Wrox.com

LISTING 6-11: Android Customer View

```
namespace CustomerManagement.Droid.Views
{
  [Activity(Label = "Customer Info", WindowSoftInputMode = SoftInput.AdjustPan)]
  public class CustomerView : MXDialogActivityView<Customer>
  {
    public override void Render()
    {
      this.Root = new RootElement("Customer Info")
      {
        new Section("Contact Info")
        {
```

continues

LISTING 6-11 *(continued)*

```
            new StringElement("Name", Model.Name,
              (int)DroidResources.ElementLayout.dialog_labelfieldbelow),
            new StringElement("Website", Model.Website,
                (int)DroidResources.ElementLayout.dialog_labelfieldbelow)
                {
                  Click = (o, e) => { LaunchWeb(); },
                },
            new StringElement("Primary Phone", Model.PrimaryPhone,
                (int)DroidResources.ElementLayout.dialog_labelfieldbelow)
              {
                 Click = (o, e) => { LaunchDial(); },
              },
          },
          new Section("General Info")
          {
            new StringMultilineElement("Address", Model.PrimaryAddress.ToString())
            {
              Click = (o, e) => { LaunchMaps(); },
            },
            new StringElement("Previous Orders ", Model.Orders.Count.ToString()),
            new StringElement("Other Addresses ", Model.Addresses.Count.ToString()),
            new StringElement("Contacts ", Model.Contacts.Count.ToString()),
          },
      };
    }

    void LaunchWeb()
    {
      Intent newIntent = new Intent(Intent.ActionView,
        Android.Net.Uri.Parse(Model.Website));
      StartActivity(newIntent);
    }

    void LaunchMaps()
    {
      string googleAddress = Model.PrimaryAddress.ToString();
      googleAddress = System.Web.HttpUtility.UrlEncode(googleAddress);

      string url = string.Format("http://maps.google.com/maps?q={0}", googleAddress);
      Intent newIntent = new Intent(Intent.ActionView, Android.Net.Uri.Parse(url));
      StartActivity(newIntent);
    }

    void LaunchDial()
    {
      string phoneNumber = PhoneNumberUtils.FormatNumber(Model.PrimaryPhone);
      Intent newIntent = new Intent(Intent.ActionDial,
        Android.Net.Uri.Parse("tel:" + phoneNumber));
      StartActivity(newIntent);
    }

    public override bool OnCreateOptionsMenu(IMenu menu)
    {
```

```
            MenuInflater.Inflate(Resource.Menu.customer_menu, menu);
            return true;
        }

        public override bool OnOptionsItemSelected(IMenuItem item)
        {
            switch (item.ItemId)
            {
                case Resource.Id.change_customer:
                    this.Navigate(string.Format(@"Customers/{0}/EDIT", Model.ID));
                    return true;
                case Resource.Id.delete_customer:
                    this.Navigate(string.Format(@"Customers/{0}/DELETE", Model.ID));
                    return true;
            }
            return base.OnOptionsItemSelected(item);
        }
    }
}
```

Found in the CustomerManagement/CustomerManangement.Droid/Views/CustomerView.cs file of the download

FIGURE 6-10: The code generates the Android application Customer View.

Building the Customer Edit View for Android

The Customer Edit View is nearly identical to the Customer View with two exceptions. First you need to replace the label elements you used in the Customer View with data entry elements so the user can change the values of the Name, Website, and other editable fields. Secondly, you need to keep references to the elements so that you can get the changed values from the edit elements, update the model, and save it.

The SaveCustomer() method places the field values into the Model and navigates to the controller, which is where sharing the model between the view and the controller simplifies your implementation. You can place validation in the view, the controller, or both, whichever suits the needs of your implementation. Listing 6-12 has the complete implementation for the Customer Edit View.

LISTING 6-12: Android Customer Edit View

Available for download on Wrox.com

```
namespace CustomerManagement.Droid.Views
{
  [Activity(Label = "Customer Changes", WindowSoftInputMode = SoftInput.AdjustPan)]
  public class CustomerEditView : MXDialogActivityView<Customer>
  {
    EntryElement _nameEntry, _webEntry, _phoneEntry, _address1Entry, _address2Entry;
    EntryElement _cityEntry, _stateEntry, _zipEntry;

    public override void Render()
    {
      if (Model.PrimaryAddress == null)
        Model.PrimaryAddress = new Address();

      _nameEntry = new EntryElement("Name", Model.Name ?? string.Empty,
        (int)DroidResources.ElementLayout.dialog_textfieldbelow);
      _webEntry = new EntryElement("Website", Model.Website ?? string.Empty,
        (int)DroidResources.ElementLayout.dialog_textfieldbelow);
      _phoneEntry = new EntryElement("Primary Phone", Model.PrimaryPhone ??
        string.Empty, (int)DroidResources.ElementLayout.dialog_textfieldbelow);

      _address1Entry = new EntryElement("Address", Model.PrimaryAddress.Street1 ??
        string.Empty, (int)DroidResources.ElementLayout.dialog_textfieldbelow);
      _address2Entry = new EntryElement("Address2", Model.PrimaryAddress.Street2 ??
        string.Empty, (int)DroidResources.ElementLayout.dialog_textfieldbelow);
      _cityEntry = new EntryElement("City ", Model.PrimaryAddress.City ??
        string.Empty, (int)DroidResources.ElementLayout.dialog_textfieldbelow);
      _stateEntry = new EntryElement("State ", Model.PrimaryAddress.State ??
        string.Empty, (int)DroidResources.ElementLayout.dialog_textfieldbelow);
      _zipEntry = new EntryElement("ZIP", Model.PrimaryAddress.Zip ?? string.Empty,
        (int)DroidResources.ElementLayout.dialog_textfieldbelow);

      this.Root = new RootElement("Customer Info")
      {
        new Section("Contact Info")
        {
          new StringElement("ID", Model.ID ?? string.Empty),
          _nameEntry,
          _webEntry,
          _phoneEntry,
        },
```

```
          new Section("Primary Address")
          {
            _address1Entry,
            _address2Entry,
            _cityEntry,
            _stateEntry,
            _zipEntry,
          },
        };
      }

      public override bool OnCreateOptionsMenu(IMenu menu)
      {
        MenuInflater.Inflate(Resource.Menu.customer_edit_menu, menu);
        return true;
      }

      public override bool OnOptionsItemSelected(IMenuItem item)
      {
        switch (item.ItemId)
        {
          case Resource.Id.save_customer:
            SaveCustomer();
            return true;
        }
        return base.OnOptionsItemSelected(item);
      }

      void SaveCustomer()
      {
        Model.Name = _nameEntry.Value;
        Model.Website = _webEntry.Value;
        Model.PrimaryPhone = _phoneEntry.Value;

        Model.PrimaryAddress.Street1 = _address1Entry.Value;
        Model.PrimaryAddress.Street2 = _address2Entry.Value;
        Model.PrimaryAddress.City = _cityEntry.Value;
        Model.PrimaryAddress.State = _stateEntry.Value;
        Model.PrimaryAddress.Zip = _zipEntry.Value;

        // Save
        if (string.Equals(Model.ID, "0"))
          this.Navigate(string.Format("Customers/{0}/UPDATE", Model.ID));
        else
          this.Navigate(string.Format("Customers/{0}/CREATE", Model.ID));
      }
    }
  }
```

Found in the CustomerManagement/CustomerManangement.Droid/Views/CustomerEditView.cs file of the download

Figure 6-11 shows a screen capture of the Customer Edit View.

FIGURE 6-11: The code generates the Android application Customer Edit View.

IMPLEMENTING A WINDOWS PHONE PLATFORM CONTAINER

Still a relative newcomer, Windows Phone will likely begin to gain popularity as Microsoft brings on additional manufacturers to support it. Windows Phone native application development is done in a Windows Phone-specific version of Silverlight. View layout, formatting, and data binding are done in XAML. Every page needs a XAML file; dynamic views are not supported on Windows Phone. Following is a quick tour of the Windows Phone implementation of the Customer Management sample.

Initializing a Container for Windows Phone

Windows Phone handles application initialization and application events via an Application-derived class generally named App. The MonoCross application initialized in the application constructor is the exception of the initial application navigation. Initial navigation is, instead, handled in the `Application_Launching` event to allow the application to initialize because many of the services used in a Silverlight application are not available until then. This is so because most useful APIs are asynchronous and require views to be available for internal messaging. Listing 6-13 shows the initialization of the application.

Available for download on Wrox.com

LISTING 6-13: Windows Phone initialization

```
namespace CustomerManagement.WindowsPhone
{
  public partial class App : Application
  {
    /// <summary>
    /// Provides easy access to the root frame of the Phone Application.
    /// </summary>
    /// <returns>The root frame of the Phone Application.</returns>
    public PhoneApplicationFrame RootFrame { get; private set; }

    /// <summary>
    /// Constructor for the Application object.
    /// </summary>
    public App()
    {
      // Global handler for uncaught exceptions.
      UnhandledException += Application_UnhandledException;

      // Standard Silverlight initialization
      InitializeComponent();

      // Phone-specific initialization
      InitializePhoneApplication();

      // Show graphics profiling information while debugging.
      if (System.Diagnostics.Debugger.IsAttached)
      {
        // Display the current frame rate counters.
        Application.Current.Host.Settings.EnableFrameRateCounter = true;

        // Show the areas of the app that are being redrawn in each frame.
        //Application.Current.Host.Settings.EnableRedrawRegions = true;

        // Enable non-production analysis visualization mode,
        // which shows areas of a page that are handed off to GPU with a colored overlay
        // Application.Current.Host.Settings.EnableCacheVisualization = true;

        // Disable the application idle detection by setting the
        // UserIdleDetectionMode property of the
        // application's PhoneApplicationService object to Disabled.
        // Caution:- Use this under debug mode only. Application that disables user idle
        // detection will continue to run
        // and consume battery power when the user is not using the phone.
        PhoneApplicationService.Current.UserIdleDetectionMode =
          IdleDetectionMode.Disabled;
      }

      // initialize app
```

continues

LISTING 6-13 *(continued)*

```
    MXPhoneContainer.Initialize(new CustomerManagement.App(), RootFrame);

    // initialize views
    MXPhoneContainer.AddView<List<Customer>>(
      typeof(CustomerListView), ViewPerspective.Default);
    MXPhoneContainer.AddView<Customer>(
      typeof(CustomerView), ViewPerspective.Default);
    MXPhoneContainer.AddView<Customer>(
      typeof(CustomerEditView), ViewPerspective.Update);
  }

  // Code to execute when the application is launching (eg, from Start)
  // This code will not execute when the application is reactivated
  private void Application_Launching(object sender, LaunchingEventArgs e)
  {
    MXPhoneContainer.Navigate(null, MXContainer.Instance.App.NavigateOnLoad);
  }

  // Code to execute if a navigation fails
  private void RootFrame_NavigationFailed(object sender, NavigationFailedEventArgs e)
  {
    if (System.Diagnostics.Debugger.IsAttached)
    {
      // A navigation has failed; break into the debugger
      System.Diagnostics.Debugger.Break();
    }
  }

  // Code to execute on Unhandled Exceptions
  // private void Application_UnhandledException(object sender,
  // ApplicationUnhandledExceptionEventArgs e)
  {
    if (System.Diagnostics.Debugger.IsAttached)
    {
      // An unhandled exception has occurred; break into the debugger
      System.Diagnostics.Debugger.Break();
    }
  }

  #region Phone application initialization

  // Avoid double-initialization
  private bool phoneApplicationInitialized = false;

  // Do not add any additional code to this method
  private void InitializePhoneApplication()
  {
    if (phoneApplicationInitialized)
      return;

    // Create the frame but don't set it as RootVisual yet; this allows the splash
    // screen to remain active until the application is ready to render.
    RootFrame = new PhoneApplicationFrame();
```

```
            RootFrame.Navigated += CompleteInitializePhoneApplication;

            // Handle navigation failures
            RootFrame.NavigationFailed += RootFrame_NavigationFailed;

            // Ensure we don't initialize again
            phoneApplicationInitialized = true;
        }

        // Do not add any additional code to this method
        private void CompleteInitializePhoneApplication(object sender,
                                                        NavigationEventArgs e)
        {
            // Set the root visual to allow the application to render
            if (RootVisual != RootFrame)
                RootVisual = RootFrame;

            // Remove this handler since it is no longer needed
            RootFrame.Navigated -= CompleteInitializePhoneApplication;
        }

        #endregion
    }
}
```

Found in the CustomerManagement/CustomerManangement.WindowsPhone/App.xaml.cs file of the download

Building the Customer List View for Windows Phone

Consider the XAML view. Listing 6-14 shows that the `CustomerListView` class is specified in XAML XML, as is its namespace. In addition, you can see the base class from which the `CustomerListView` derives. This causes a problem for the model you've used up to this point, which uses a `template` class with the model type as the `template` parameter. You can't use that pattern within an XML file because the < and > symbols that specify that the class name shouldn't be broken up cannot be used in the same manner in XML.

Listing 6-14 also shows highlighted properties from the `Customer model` class, which defines your data binding so that when you assign the `DataContext` for the view, Silverlight automatically populates the model property values from your model to specific display views on the page.

LISTING 6-14: Windows Phone Customer List View XAML

Available for download on Wrox.com

```
<local:BaseCustomerListView
    x:Class="CustomerManagement.WindowsPhone.CustomerListView"
    xmlns:local="clr-namespace:CustomerManagement.WindowsPhone;
        assembly=CustomerManagement.WindowsPhone"
    xmlns="http://schemas.microsoft.com/winfx/2006/xaml/presentation"
    xmlns:x="http://schemas.microsoft.com/winfx/2006/xaml"
    xmlns:phone="clr-namespace:Microsoft.Phone.Controls;assembly=Microsoft.Phone"
    xmlns:shell="clr-namespace:Microsoft.Phone.Shell;assembly=Microsoft.Phone"
    xmlns:d="http://schemas.microsoft.com/expression/blend/2008"
```

continues

LISTING 6-14 *(continued)*

```
    xmlns:mc="http://schemas.openxmlformats.org/markup-compatibility/2006"
    mc:Ignorable="d" d:DesignWidth="480" d:DesignHeight="768"
    FontFamily="{StaticResource PhoneFontFamilyNormal}"
    FontSize="{StaticResource PhoneFontSizeNormal}"
    Foreground="{StaticResource PhoneForegroundBrush}"
    SupportedOrientations="Portrait" Orientation="Portrait"
    shell:SystemTray.IsVisible="True">

  <!--LayoutRoot is the root grid where all page content is placed-->
  <Grid x:Name="LayoutRoot" Background="Transparent">
    <Grid.RowDefinitions>
      <RowDefinition Height="Auto"/>
      <RowDefinition Height="*"/>
    </Grid.RowDefinitions>

    <!--TitlePanel contains the name of the application and page title-->
    <StackPanel x:Name="TitlePanel" Grid.Row="0" Margin="12,17,0,28">
      <TextBlock x:Name="ApplicationTitle" Text="Client Management"
                 Style="{StaticResource PhoneTextNormalStyle}"/>
      <TextBlock x:Name="PageTitle" Text="Client List" Margin="9,-7,0,0"
                 Style="{StaticResource PhoneTextTitle1Style}"/>
    </StackPanel>

    <!--ContentPanel - place additional content here-->
    <Grid x:Name="ContentPanel" Grid.Row="1" Margin="12,6,12,6">
      <!--Double line list with text wrapping-->
      <ListBox Margin="0,0,-12,0" Name="listBox">
        <ListBox.ItemTemplate>
          <DataTemplate>
            <StackPanel Margin="0,0,0,17" Width="432">
              <TextBlock Text="{Binding Name}"
                         Style="{StaticResource PhoneTextExtraLargeStyle}"/>
              <TextBlock Text="{Binding Website}" TextWrapping="Wrap"
                         Margin="12,-6,12,0"
                         Style="{StaticResource PhoneTextSubtleStyle}"/>
            </StackPanel>
          </DataTemplate>
        </ListBox.ItemTemplate>
      </ListBox>
    </Grid>
  </Grid>

  <!--Sample code showing usage of ApplicationBar-->
</local:BaseCustomerListView>
```

Found in the CustomerManagement/CustomerManangement.WindowsPhone/Views/ CustomerListView.xaml file of the download

Listing 6-15 shows a base class derived from the `template` class instead to enable you to use the pattern. Now, instead of `CustomerListView` deriving from `MXPhonePage<List<Customer>>` you use an intermediary class named `BaseCustomerListView`.

LISTING 6-15: Windows Phone Customer List View code

Available for download on Wrox.com

```
namespace CustomerManagement.WindowsPhone
{
  public class BaseCustomerListView : MXPhonePage<List<Customer>> { }

  [MXPhoneView("/Views/CustomerListView.xaml")]
  public partial class CustomerListView : BaseCustomerListView
  {
    // Constructor
    public CustomerListView()
    {
      InitializeComponent();

      ApplicationTitle.Text = MXContainer.Instance.App.Title;
      PageTitle.Text = "Customers";

      InitAppBar();
    }

    private void InitAppBar()
    {
      ApplicationBar appBar = new ApplicationBar();

      var addButton = new ApplicationBarIconButton(
                        new Uri("images/appbar.add.rest.png", UriKind.Relative));
      addButton.Click += new EventHandler(addButton_Click);
      addButton.Text = "Add";
      appBar.Buttons.Add(addButton);

      ApplicationBar = appBar;
    }

    void addButton_Click(object sender, EventArgs e)
    {
      this.Navigate("Customers/NEW");
    }

    public override void Render()
    {
      foreach (var customer in Model)
        listBox.Items.Add(customer);

      listBox.SelectionChanged +=
                    new SelectionChangedEventHandler(listBox_SelectionChanged);

      // remove the splash screen that was shown just before this
      NavigationService.RemoveBackEntry();
    }

    void listBox_SelectionChanged(object sender, SelectionChangedEventArgs e)
    {
      if (e.AddedItems.Count != 1)
        return;
```

continues

LISTING 6-15 *(continued)*

```
            Customer c = e.AddedItems[0] as Customer;

            listBox.SelectedIndex = -1;

            MXPhoneContainer.Navigate(this, "Customers/" + c.ID);
        }
    }
}
```

Found in the CustomerManagement/CustomerManangement.WindowsPhone/Views/CustomerListView.xaml.cs file of the download

Figure 6-12 illustrates the result of the code in Listings 6-14 and 6-15.

FIGURE 6-12: The sample code results in the Windows Phone Customer List View.

Building the Customer View for Windows Phone

Moving on to the Customer View, because of the differences between Windows Phone with XAML and the other platforms, you cannot reuse much code, but you can still keep the functionality similar.

Listing 6-16 shows the layout of the view where you can keep the data fields in the same order as the Customer Views on the other platforms.

LISTING 6-16: Windows Phone Customer View XAML

Available for download on Wrox.com

```
<local:BaseCustomerView
    x:Class="CustomerManagement.WindowsPhone.CustomerView"
    xmlns:local="clr-namespace:CustomerManagement.WindowsPhone;
         assembly=CustomerManagement.WindowsPhone"
    xmlns="http://schemas.microsoft.com/winfx/2006/xaml/presentation"
    xmlns:x="http://schemas.microsoft.com/winfx/2006/xaml"
    xmlns:phone="clr-namespace:Microsoft.Phone.Controls;assembly=Microsoft.Phone"
    xmlns:shell="clr-namespace:Microsoft.Phone.Shell;assembly=Microsoft.Phone"
    xmlns:d="http://schemas.microsoft.com/expression/blend/2008"
    xmlns:mc="http://schemas.openxmlformats.org/markup-compatibility/2006"
    FontFamily="{StaticResource PhoneFontFamilyNormal}"
    FontSize="{StaticResource PhoneFontSizeNormal}"
    Foreground="{StaticResource PhoneForegroundBrush}"
    SupportedOrientations="Portrait" Orientation="Portrait"
    mc:Ignorable="d" d:DesignHeight="768" d:DesignWidth="480"
    shell:SystemTray.IsVisible="True">

    <!--LayoutRoot is the root grid where all page content is placed-->
    <Grid x:Name="LayoutRoot" Background="Transparent">
      <Grid.RowDefinitions>
        <RowDefinition Height="0.231*"/>
        <RowDefinition Height="0.769*"/>
      </Grid.RowDefinitions>

      <!--TitlePanel contains the name of the application and page title-->
      <StackPanel x:Name="TitlePanel" Grid.Row="0" Margin="12,17,0,28">
        <TextBlock x:Name="ApplicationTitle" Text="Customer Management"
          Style="{StaticResource PhoneTextNormalStyle}"/>
        <TextBlock x:Name="PageTitle" Text="Client" Margin="9,-7,0,0"
                      Style="{StaticResource PhoneTextTitle1Style}"/>
      </StackPanel>

      <!--ContentPanel - place additional content here-->
      <Grid x:Name="ContentPanel" Grid.Row="1" Margin="12,0,12,0">
        <ScrollViewer Margin="12,17,0,28" Grid.Row="0">
          <StackPanel x:Name="CustomerPanel" Width="444">
            <TextBlock Text="Name" Style="{StaticResource PhoneTextSubtleStyle}"/>
            <TextBlock Text="{Binding Name}"
                       Style="{StaticResource PhoneTextExtraLargeStyle}"/>
            <TextBlock Text="Website"
                       Style="{StaticResource PhoneTextSubtleStyle}"/>
            <TextBlock x:Name="textWebsite" Text="{Binding Website}"
                       Style="{StaticResource PhoneTextExtraLargeStyle}"/>
            <TextBlock Text="Primary Phone"
                       Style="{StaticResource PhoneTextSubtleStyle}"/>
            <TextBlock x:Name="textPhone"  Text="{Binding PrimaryPhone}"
                       Style="{StaticResource PhoneTextExtraLargeStyle}"/>
            <TextBlock Text="Address"
```

continues

LISTING 6-16 *(continued)*

```
                    Style="{StaticResource PhoneTextSubtleStyle}"/>
          <TextBlock x:Name="textAddress"
                    Text="{Binding PrimaryAddress}" TextWrapping="Wrap"
                    Style="{StaticResource PhoneTextExtraLargeStyle}"/>
        </StackPanel>
      </ScrollViewer>
    </Grid>
  </Grid>
</local:BaseCustomerView>
```

Found in the CustomerManagement/CustomerManangement.WindowsPhone/Views/CustomerView.xaml file of the download

In the code behind the XAML view in Listing 6-17, you can add event handlers for clicking on the items, dialing out for the phone number, launching the maps application for the customer address, and starting up the web browser for the customer's website. The application bar adds the functionality to match the other platforms in your sample code.

LISTING 6-17: Windows Phone Customer View code

Available for download on Wrox.com

```
namespace CustomerManagement.WindowsPhone
{
  public class BaseCustomerView : MXPhonePage<Customer> { }

  [MXPhoneView("/Views/CustomerView.xaml")]
  public partial class CustomerView : BaseCustomerView
  {
    public CustomerView()
    {
      InitializeComponent();

      ApplicationTitle.Text = MXContainer.Instance.App.Title;

      // events for
      this.textAddress.Tap += new EventHandler<GestureEventArgs>(textAddress_Tap);
      this.textPhone.Tap += new EventHandler<GestureEventArgs>(textPhone_Tap);
      this.textWebsite.Tap += new EventHandler<GestureEventArgs>(textWebsite_Tap);

      InitAppBar();
    }

    private void InitAppBar()
    {
      ApplicationBar appBar = new ApplicationBar();

      var backButton = new ApplicationBarIconButton(
                new Uri("images/appbar.back.rest.png", UriKind.Relative));
      backButton.Click += new EventHandler(backButton_Click);
      backButton.Text = "Back";
```

```
    appBar.Buttons.Add(backButton);

    var editButton = new ApplicationBarIconButton(
                  new Uri("images/appbar.edit.rest.png", UriKind.Relative));
    editButton.Click += new EventHandler(editButton_Click);
    editButton.Text = "Edit";
    appBar.Buttons.Add(editButton);

    var deleteButton = new ApplicationBarIconButton(
                  new Uri("images/appbar.delete.rest.png", UriKind.Relative));
    deleteButton.Click += new EventHandler(deleteButton_Click);
    deleteButton.Text = "Delete";
    appBar.Buttons.Add(deleteButton);

    ApplicationBar = appBar;
  }

  void editButton_Click(object sender, EventArgs e)
  {
    this.Navigate(string.Format("Customers/{0}/EDIT", Model.ID));
  }

  void deleteButton_Click(object sender, EventArgs e)
  {
    this.Navigate(string.Format("Customers/{0}/DELETE", Model.ID));
  }

  void backButton_Click(object sender, EventArgs e)
  {
    NavigationService.GoBack();
  }

  public override void Render()
  {
    this.DataContext = Model;
  }

  void textWebsite_Tap(object sender, GestureEventArgs e)
  {
    WebBrowserTask webBrowserTask = new WebBrowserTask();
    webBrowserTask.Uri = new Uri(Model.Website);
    webBrowserTask.Show();
  }

  void textPhone_Tap(object sender, GestureEventArgs e)
  {
    PhoneCallTask pct = new PhoneCallTask();
    pct.DisplayName = Model.Name;
    pct.PhoneNumber = Model.PrimaryPhone;
    pct.Show();
  }

  void textAddress_Tap(object sender, GestureEventArgs e)
  {
    string googleAddress = string.Format("{0} {1}\n{2}, {3}  {4}",
              Model.PrimaryAddress.Street1, Model.PrimaryAddress.Street2,
```

continues

LISTING 6-17 *(continued)*

```
                    Model.PrimaryAddress.City,
                    Model.PrimaryAddress.State,
                    Model.PrimaryAddress.Zip);
            googleAddress = Uri.EscapeUriString(googleAddress);

            string url = string.Format("http://maps.google.com/maps?q={0}", googleAddress);

            WebBrowserTask webBrowserTask = new WebBrowserTask();
            webBrowserTask.Uri = new Uri(url);
            webBrowserTask.Show();
        }
    }
}
```

Found in the CustomerManagement/CustomerManangement.WindowsPhone/Views/CustomerView.xaml.cs file of the download

Figure 6-13 shows the completed view with the menu bar.

FIGURE 6-13: This Windows Phone Customer View shows the menu available.

Building the Customer Edit View for Windows Phone

For the final view you use the XAML from your view and change over the `TextBlocks` to `TextBoxes` and set up the data binding for all the fields as in the Customer View. Because you use the same model type, the data binding is nearly identical; with the exception that you separate the address fields to allow a user to edit them separately. Listing 6-18 shows the resulting XAML template. One feature of the XAML approach using data binding is it greatly simplifies the code needed to update the model. In the previous examples, you maintained references to your edit fields, extracted the data from those fields, and updated the model. Data binding in Silverlight automatically updates the data elements in your model, making the update of the model simple via navigation to the controller via the `UPDATE` or `CREATE` action parameters because you use the shared model.

LISTING 6-18: Windows Phone Customer Edit View XAML

Available for download on Wrox.com

```
<local:BaseCustomerEditView
    x:Class="CustomerManagement.WindowsPhone.CustomerEditView"
    xmlns:local="clr-namespace:CustomerManagement.WindowsPhone;
          assembly=CustomerManagement.WindowsPhone"
    xmlns="http://schemas.microsoft.com/winfx/2006/xaml/presentation"
    xmlns:x="http://schemas.microsoft.com/winfx/2006/xaml"
    xmlns:phone="clr-namespace:Microsoft.Phone.Controls;assembly=Microsoft.Phone"
    xmlns:shell="clr-namespace:Microsoft.Phone.Shell;assembly=Microsoft.Phone"
    xmlns:d="http://schemas.microsoft.com/expression/blend/2008"
    xmlns:mc="http://schemas.openxmlformats.org/markup-compatibility/2006"
    FontFamily="{StaticResource PhoneFontFamilyNormal}"
    FontSize="{StaticResource PhoneFontSizeNormal}"
    Foreground="{StaticResource PhoneForegroundBrush}"
    SupportedOrientations="Portrait" Orientation="Portrait"
    mc:Ignorable="d" d:DesignHeight="768" d:DesignWidth="480"
    shell:SystemTray.IsVisible="True">

    <!--LayoutRoot is the root grid where all page content is placed-->
    <Grid x:Name="LayoutRoot" Background="Transparent">
      <Grid.RowDefinitions>
        <RowDefinition Height="0.231*"/>
        <RowDefinition Height="0.769*"/>
      </Grid.RowDefinitions>

      <!--TitlePanel contains the name of the application and page title-->
      <StackPanel x:Name="TitlePanel" Grid.Row="0" Margin="12,17,0,28">
        <TextBlock x:Name="ApplicationTitle" Text="Customer Management"
                   Style="{StaticResource PhoneTextNormalStyle}"/>
        <TextBlock x:Name="PageTitle" Text="Client" Margin="9,-7,0,0"
                   Style="{StaticResource PhoneTextTitle1Style}"/>
      </StackPanel>

      <!--ContentPanel - place additional content here-->
      <Grid x:Name="ContentPanel" Grid.Row="1" Margin="12,0,12,0">
        <ScrollViewer Margin="12,17,0,28" Grid.Row="0">
          <StackPanel x:Name="CustomerPanel" Width="444">
            <TextBlock Text="Name" Style="{StaticResource PhoneTextSubtleStyle}"/>
            <TextBox x:Name="textName" Text="{Binding Name, Mode=TwoWay}"
                     DataContext="{Binding}" />
            <TextBlock Text="Website" Style="{StaticResource PhoneTextSubtleStyle}"/>
            <TextBox x:Name="textWebsite" Text="{Binding Website, Mode=TwoWay}"/>
            <TextBlock Text="Primary Phone"
```

continues

LISTING 6-18 *(continued)*

```
                    Style="{StaticResource PhoneTextSubtleStyle}"/>
            <TextBox x:Name="textPhone" Text="{Binding PrimaryPhone, Mode=TwoWay}" />
            <TextBlock Height="30" Text="Address" />
            <TextBlock Text="Street" Style="{StaticResource PhoneTextSubtleStyle}"/>
            <TextBox x:Name="textAddress"
                    Text="{Binding PrimaryAddress.Street1, Mode=TwoWay}"/>
          </StackPanel>
        </ScrollViewer>
      </Grid>
    </Grid>
</local:BaseCustomerEditView>
```

Found in the CustomerManagement/CustomerManangement.WindowsPhone/Views/CustomerEditView.xaml file of the download

The code in Listing 6-19 has the navigational details.

LISTING 6-19: Windows Phone Customer Edit View code

Available for download on Wrox.com

```
namespace CustomerManagement.WindowsPhone
{
  public class BaseCustomerEditView : MXPhonePage<Customer> { }

  [MXPhoneView("/Views/CustomerEditView.xaml")]
  public partial class CustomerEditView : BaseCustomerEditView
  {
    public CustomerEditView()
    {
      InitializeComponent();

      InitAppBar();
    }

    public override void Render()
    {
      this.DataContext = Model;
    }

    private void InitAppBar()
    {
      ApplicationBar appBar = new ApplicationBar();

      var backButton = new ApplicationBarIconButton(
        new Uri("images/appbar.back.rest.png", UriKind.Relative));
      backButton.Click += new EventHandler(backButton_Click);
      backButton.Text = "Back";
      appBar.Buttons.Add(backButton);

      var addButton = new ApplicationBarIconButton(
        new Uri("images/appbar.save.rest.png", UriKind.Relative));
      addButton.Click += new EventHandler(saveButton_Click);
```

```
            addButton.Text = "Save";
            appBar.Buttons.Add(addButton);

            ApplicationBar = appBar;
        }

        void saveButton_Click(object sender, EventArgs e)
        {
            this.Navigate("Customers/" + Model.ID +
                          (Model.ID == "0" ? "/CREATE" : "/UPDATE"));
        }

        void backButton_Click(object sender, EventArgs e)
        {
            NavigationService.GoBack();
        }
    }
}
```

Found in the CustomerManagement/CustomerManangement.WindowsPhone/Views/CustomerEditView.xaml.cs file of the download

Figure 6-14 shows the completed screen in action. The gray fields on the screen indicate the fields are editable.

FIGURE 6-14: Windows Phone Customer Edit View looks just a little different from the other Customer Edit View implementations.

IMPLEMENTING A WEBKIT PLATFORM CONTAINER

Up to this point you've largely ignored solutions that target varied platforms, yet there are many reasons that you may need to do so. Smaller budgets or development teams may need to target a large number of platforms in a short amount of time, or you may need to consider a number of platforms if your target audience mostly uses iPhones, but you want to support other platforms until you know which are best to target directly. And of course, there is that Blackberry community that refuses to die and can't be directly targeted with C#. Also remember that with the web implementation access to GPS, barcode scanners and other hardware interfaces that are either required or wanted aren't available, so you must evaluate consistency with a native platform implementation.

MonoCross includes a basic container implemented for Microsoft's ASP.NET MVC framework. You can use WebApp.Net's Web UI framework implementation to give an iPhone-like presentation. If you want to know more about the details of Microsoft's framework, go to `http://webapp-net.com`. You can use other frameworks, such as jQuery mobile and jQTouch; most frameworks use some combination of JavaScript and CSS to generate their look and feel and navigational interface. One big difference between the WebKit container and the other platform-specific containers is that it runs on the server and not on the client. The view and the controller render the HTML for the web pages sent down to the client, which is simple for views that don't require any data entry, such as the Customer List and Customer View, but require a good amount of thought when applied to the Customer Edit View.

Another smaller difference is that navigation on the server is synchronous and not asynchronous, as is navigation on the mobile platform implementations you've used so far. As you might guess, multithreading isn't required in a web interface because all applicable code runs on the server. This sample can leave out chunks of code because much of it is boilerplate ASP.NET MVC code, but it includes the important portions that are applicable to the implementation.

Initializing a Container with WebKit

The WebKit container uses the ASP.NET MVC framework and integrates the URL rewriting mechanisms to the navigational model used by MonoCross. Listing 6-20 shows the implementation of `Global.asax.cs`. Initialization occurs for the web application during the Session Start and runs for each new client that connects to the web server. The minimal state, primarily the URL mapping, is maintained for each client.

LISTING 6-20: ASP.NET Global.asax.cs

Available for download on Wrox.com

```
namespace CustomerManagement.Webkit
{
  public class MvcApplication : System.Web.HttpApplication
  {
    public static void RegisterRoutes(RouteCollection routes)
    {
      routes.Ignore("favicon.ico");
      routes.Ignore("WebApp/{*mapUri}");
      routes.MapRoute("", "{*mapUri}", new { controller = "App", action = "Render" });
    }
```

```
        protected void Application_Start()
        {
          RegisterRoutes(RouteTable.Routes);
        }

        protected void Session_Start()
        {
          // initialize app
          MXWebkitContainer.Initialize(new CustomerManagement.App());
          // add views to container
          MXWebkitContainer.AddView<List<Customer>>(new Views.CustomerListView(),
               ViewPerspective.Default);
          MXWebkitContainer.AddView<Customer>(new Views.CustomerEditView(),
               ViewPerspective.Update);
          MXWebkitContainer.AddView<Customer>(new Views.CustomerView(),
               ViewPerspective.Default);
        }
      }
    }
```

Found in the CustomerManagement/CustomerManangement.WebKit/Global.asax.cs file of the download

Continuing with Listing 6-21, you implement the only controller for the ASP.NET MVC application. There is only a single controller that maps the incoming URL to the MonoCross navigation URI scheme and forwards it to the WebKit container, which in turn routes the request to the appropriately mapped controller.

LISTING 6-21: ASP.NET WebKit Customer List

Available for download on Wrox.com

```
namespace CustomerManagement.Webkit.Controllers
{
  [HandleError]
  public class AppController : Controller
  {
    public ActionResult Render(string mapUri)
    {
      var url = (mapUri == null) ? MXContainer.Instance.App.NavigateOnLoad : mapUri;
      MXWebkitContainer.Navigate(url, this.Request);
      return null;
    }
  }
}
```

Found in the CustomerManagement/CustomerManangement.WebKit/Controllers/AppController.cs file of the download

Building the Customer List View with WebKit

The WebKit container implementation uses a single markup file called `Root.html` for its interface. All common HTML is contained in the `Root.html` file, including CSS and JavaScript includes, header and footer layout, and HTML specific for the WebApp.Net implementation. WebApp.Net uses layers of "div" tags to define a page and the navigational areas on the page, as well as all items on the page. The div tags have class attributes to define their look and feel and are styled according to the included CSS.

The MonoCross WebKit container provides two base classes from which to derive your views:

- `MXWebkitView`: Provides a basic view with a simple helper method for writing the `HtmlGenericControl` hierarchies to the web page.
- `MXWebkitDialogView`: Following the pattern established in the iOS and Android, MonoCross provides a Dialog building class nearly identical to the `MonoTouch.Dialog` and `MonoDroid.Dialog` classes. In addition, it provides a binding functionality that maps HTML form elements back to the model to simplify updates to the model via a form postback. Although not highlighted in this sample, it provides simple form layout for read-only layers as well.

The Customer List View in Listing 6-22 builds the HTML for the client using `HtmlGenericControls`. HTML link elements direct the client to show the view and edit pages, and the additional HTML is formatting for the list and its items.

LISTING 6-22: ASP.NET WebKit Customer List

Available for download on Wrox.com

```
namespace CustomerManagement.Webkit.Views
{
  public class CustomerListView : MXWebkitView<List<Customer>>
  {
    public override void Render()
    {
      HtmlGenericControl button = new HtmlGenericControl("a");
      button.Attributes.Add("href", "Customers/NEW");
      button.Attributes.Add("rel", "action");
      button.Attributes.Add("rev", "async");
      button.Attributes.Add("class", "iButton iBClassic");

      HtmlGenericControl image = new HtmlGenericControl("img");
      image.Attributes.Add("src", "../../WebApp/Img/more.png");

      HtmlGenericControl list = new HtmlGenericControl("div");
      list.Attributes.Add("class", "iList");

      HtmlGenericControl ul = new HtmlGenericControl("ul");
      ul.Attributes.Add("class", "iArrow");
      ul.Attributes.Add("style", "background-color: #FFFFFF; color: #000000");

      foreach (CustomerManagement.Shared.Model.Customer customer in Model)
      {
        HtmlGenericControl li = new HtmlGenericControl("li");
        HtmlGenericControl a = new HtmlGenericControl("a");
        a.Attributes.Add("href", string.Format("/Customers/{0}", customer.ID));
        a.Attributes.Add("rev", "async");
        HtmlGenericControl em = new HtmlGenericControl("em");
        em.InnerText = customer.Name;
```

```
                HtmlGenericControl small = new HtmlGenericControl("small");
                small.Attributes.Add("style", "color:#666666");
                small.InnerText = customer.Website;
                a.Controls.Add(em);
                a.Controls.Add(small);
                li.Controls.Add(a);
                ul.Controls.Add(li);
            }
            button.Controls.Add(image);
            list.Controls.Add(ul);
            WriteToResponse("CustomerList", "Customers", new Control[] { button, list });
        }
    }
}
```

Found in the CustomerManagement/CustomerManangement.Webkit/Views/CustomerListView.cs file of the download

Figure 6-15 shows the page in its final form.

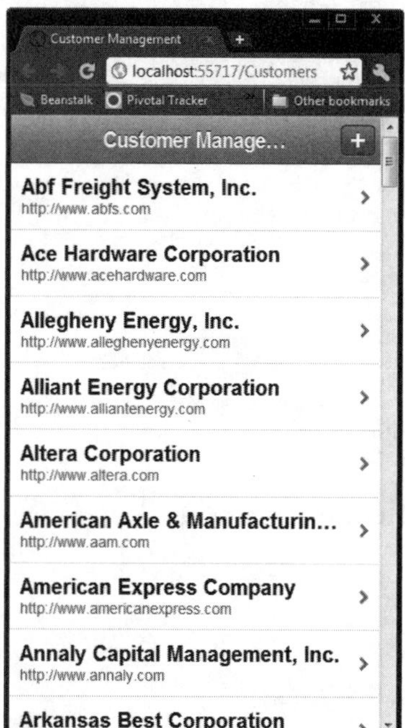

FIGURE 6-15: The sample code generates the WebKit Customer List View.

Building the Customer View with WebKit

The sample code for Customer View for the WebKit in Listing 6-23 shows the appropriate HTML using `HtmlGenericControl` objects and adding appropriate HTML elements for formatting and navigation. Notice the map, call, and customer home page are implemented as links, just as you did in the iOS, Android, and Windows Phone examples.

Available for download on Wrox.com

LISTING 6-23: ASP.NET WebKit Customer View

```
namespace CustomerManagement.Webkit.Views
{
  public class CustomerView : MXWebkitView<Customer>
  {
    public override void Render()
    {
      HtmlGenericControl div = new HtmlGenericControl("div");
      div.Attributes.Add("class", "iMenu");

      HtmlGenericControl contactHeader = new HtmlGenericControl("h3");
      contactHeader.InnerText = "Contact Info";
      HtmlGenericControl contact = new HtmlGenericControl("ul");
      contact.Controls.Add(LabelItem("ID", Model.ID));
      contact.Controls.Add(LabelItem("Name", Model.Name));
      contact.Controls.Add(LinkItem(Model.Website, "Website", Model.Website));
      contact.Controls.Add(LinkItem(string.Format("tel:{0}",
                           Model.PrimaryPhone),
                           "Primary Phone", Model.PrimaryPhone));

      HtmlGenericControl addressHeader = new HtmlGenericControl("h3");
      addressHeader.InnerText = "Primary Address";
      HtmlGenericControl address = new HtmlGenericControl("ul");
      address.Controls.Add(BlockItem("Address",
                           string.Format("{0}<br>{1} {2}<br>{3}, {4}  {5}",
                           Model.PrimaryAddress.Description,
                           Model.PrimaryAddress.Street1,
                           Model.PrimaryAddress.Street2,
                           Model.PrimaryAddress.City,
                           Model.PrimaryAddress.State,
                           Model.PrimaryAddress.Zip
                                                                 )));
      address.Controls.Add(LabelItem("Previous Orders",
                           Model.Orders.Count.ToString()));
      address.Controls.Add(LabelItem("Addresses",
                                     Model.Addresses.Count.ToString()));

      div.Controls.Add(contact);
      div.Controls.Add(address);

      div.Controls.Add(DeleteButton(
        string.Format("/Customers/{0}/{1}", Model.ID, "DELETE"),
                      "Delete Customer", false));
      div.Controls.Add(EditButton(
        string.Format("/Customers/{0}/{1}", Model.ID, "EDIT"),
                      "Change Customer", true));

      WriteAjaxToResponse("ViewCustomer", "Customer Details", div);
    }
    static HtmlGenericControl LabelItem(string caption, string value)
    {
      HtmlGenericControl item = new HtmlGenericControl("li");
      HtmlGenericControl span = new HtmlGenericControl("span");
      span.InnerText = value;
```

```
        item.InnerText = caption;
        item.Controls.Add(span);
        return item;
      }
      static HtmlGenericControl BlockItem(string caption, string html)
      {
        HtmlGenericControl item = new HtmlGenericControl("li");
        HtmlGenericControl div = new HtmlGenericControl("div");
        div.Attributes.Add("class", "iBlock");
        div.Attributes.Add("style", "font-weight:normal");
        div.InnerHtml = html;
        item.InnerText = caption;
        item.Controls.Add(div);
        return item;
      }
      static HtmlGenericControl LinkItem(string link, string caption, string value)
      {
        HtmlGenericControl item = new HtmlGenericControl("li");
        HtmlGenericControl a = new HtmlGenericControl("a");
        HtmlGenericControl span = new HtmlGenericControl("span");
        a.Attributes.Add("href", link);
        a.Attributes.Add("rev", "async");
        span.InnerText = value;
        a.InnerText = caption;
        a.Controls.Add(span);
        item.Controls.Add(a);
        return item;
      }

      static HtmlGenericControl DeleteButton(string link, string caption, bool async)
      {
        HtmlGenericControl a = new HtmlGenericControl("a");
        a.Attributes.Add("href", link);
        if (async) a.Attributes.Add("rev", "async");
        a.Attributes.Add("class", "iPush iBWarn");
        a.Attributes.Add("style", "width:100%");
        a.InnerText = caption;
        return a;
      }

      static HtmlGenericControl EditButton(string link, string caption, bool async)
      {
        HtmlGenericControl a = new HtmlGenericControl("a");
        a.Attributes.Add("href", link);
        if (async) a.Attributes.Add("rev", "async");
        a.Attributes.Add("class", "iPush iBClassic");
        a.Attributes.Add("style", "width:100%");
        a.InnerText = caption;
        return a;
      }
    }
  }
```

Found in the CustomerManagement/CustomerManangement.Webkit/Views/CustomerView.cs file of the download

Figure 6-16 shows the completed view.

FIGURE 6-16: The result is the WebKit Customer View.

Building the Customer Edit View with WebKit

The final view is the most complex; although, it has the least amount of code. Listing 6-24 shows the implementation of the Customer Edit View, using the Dialog builder included in MonoCross to build the page layout almost identically to the Customer Edit Views in the iOS and Android samples. This view, in particular, requires the most thought because you need to handle form updates from the client and must get the form variables from the web page into the model and back to the controller. You can do this in the dialog building class. The Root constructor defines the navigation as in the previous sample, but the elements provide the formatting. Using reflection provides mapping used on postback to populate the model with the values the user may have updated.

LISTING 6-24: ASP.NET WebKit Customer Edit View

Available for download on Wrox.com

```
namespace CustomerManagement.Webkit.Views
{
  public class CustomerEditView : MXWebkitDialogView<Customer>
  {
    public override void Render()
    {
      this.Root = new RootElement("Customer Info", "customerForm", "Customers",
                  string.Format("/Customers/{0}/{1}", Model.ID,
                  Model.ID == "0" ? "CREATE" : "UPDATE"), false)
            {
                new Section("Contact Info")
```

```
                {
                    new StringElement("ID", Model.ID),
                    new TextElement("Name", Model.Name, "Name"),
                    new TextElement("Website", Model.Website, "Website"),
                    new TextElement("Primary Phone", Model.PrimaryPhone, "PrimaryPhone")
                },
                new Section("Primary Address")
                {
                    new TextElement("Address 1", Model.PrimaryAddress.Street1,
                                    "PrimaryAddress.Street1"),
                    new TextElement("Address 2", Model.PrimaryAddress.Street2,
                                    "PrimaryAddress.Street2"),
                    new TextElement("City", Model.PrimaryAddress.City,
                                    "PrimaryAddress.City"),
                    new TextElement("State", Model.PrimaryAddress.State,
                                    "PrimaryAddress.State"),
                    new TextElement("Zip", Model.PrimaryAddress.Zip,
                                    "PrimaryAddress.Zip")
                }
            };
            WriteRootToResponse("EditCustomer", "Edit Customer", Root);
        }
    }
}
```

Found in the CustomerManagement/CustomerManangement.Webkit/Views/CustomerEditView.cs file of the download

Figure 6-17 shows the final view in action.

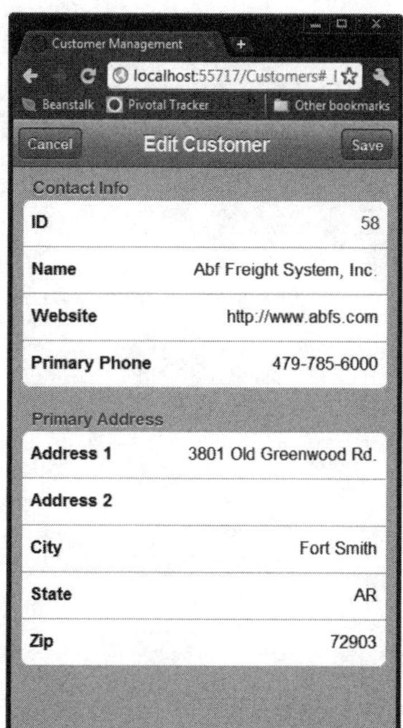

FIGURE 6-17: The WebKit Customer Edit View is now complete.

SUMMARY

In this chapter, you've gone over the basics of showing a list of items, viewing those items, and performing the CRUD operations in a user experience that is unique to each platform but is implemented consistently across those platforms. You've seen in these solutions that you don't need to sacrifice the look and feel of the platform to build solutions that give your users what they expect from an application on their mobile device.

In the next chapter you see how to connect your backend enterprise systems to your cross-platform solutions so your application can consume data without overburdening the slower device.

7

Designing and Building Data Services

WHAT'S IN THIS CHAPTER?

- Understanding web services
- Choosing between SOAP and REST
- Designing services for mobile applications
- Optimizing services for mobile data access
- Creating logical resource endpoints
- Extending your services into the enterprise

Now that you've written your shared application, and built one or more containers for your targeted platforms, you need a way to get information from both your enterprise databases and other back-end systems for consumption on your mobile devices. In this chapter you learn how to build web services that are optimized for mobile applications. You explore examples of both traditional SOAP and RESTful techniques and learn to build services that mirror your application design to best serve data to your application. Finally, you examine techniques for customizing and limiting the volume of data returned to your application according to mobile best practices.

UNDERSTANDING WEB SERVICES PRINCIPLES

Web services and Service Oriented Architectures (SOAs) have become ubiquitous in most large companies. The proliferation of web applications over the past decade or two has resulted in the need for integration between heterogeneous systems in most enterprises. Because SOAs are based upon clear standards with implementations available for the most popular enterprise development frameworks and technologies, they have become the standard for moving information around most organizations.

Generally, two major classes of web services are present in most organizations: SOAP and REST. Each has its strengths and weaknesses, and using either is a viable option for your mobile application. But you should consider some things when deciding what technique is best for your situation.

Using SOAP Services

SOAP-based services are usually easy to find in any organization. This technique of writing web services has been around for a long time and is well established in most companies. As a result, you usually have the benefit of a seasoned team of developers that can help you expose and publish new services easily. Many application frameworks, such as Microsoft .NET, include robust SOAP support in both implementations of the protocol, such as Windows Communication Framework (WCF), or in middleware services, such as Web References in Visual Studio or Language Integrated Query (LINQ), specifically LINQ to XML.

For all these reasons, SOAP can be an attractive option, but you must consider some of the drawbacks of this approach before using it for all your mobile services. First, SOAP is by definition an XML standard. XML has rich support on the server, and in Mono that support is extended to most major mobile platforms. However, XML is also quite verbose, and streaming large blocks of character-based information over limited 2G and 3G connections can result in serious performance issues on a mobile device. SOAP also requires the use of header and body tags in the XML that increase the weight of these services even more. Existing enterprise SOAP services are also often coarse-grained, providing large amounts of information that may or may not be needed in a mobile application. Finally, the Remote Procedure Call (RPC) style used by most SOAP services can be difficult to consume in a mobile context.

Using REST Services

Representational State Transfer (REST) is a technique pioneered by the World Wide Web and adopted to provide a simple way to exchange information between systems, which has become increasingly popular in recent years. RESTful services use the standard HTTP verbs (`GET`, `POST`, `PUT`, and `DELETE`) to specify actions performed on a representation of a specific resource — for example, a customer. The services themselves are defined as resource endpoints that use parameter substitution to convey pertinent information for server-side processing. Most development frameworks, including WCF, now offer REST support, so implementation is becoming more and more widespread.

REST is often the best fit for mobile data services for several reasons. First, it uses HTTP for all interactions. Each request is a standard HTTP Request, and the data is delivered in a standard HTTP Response. As a result, the service response can contain data in any of a number of data formats supported by HTTP, including XML and JSON, as well as other resource formats such as documents, images, and applications. Although resource endpoint definitions can become somewhat complex, they are more easily tailored to mobile application needs. The resource-centric design is often more easily translated into the object-oriented designs used in the sample applications. If you are faced with writing or rewriting existing enterprise services to support your application, put

RESTful services in place, rather than extending existing SOAP architectures. The flexibility and ease of use of RESTful services have most often made it worth the cost of training and development for the organizations we have worked with.

DEFINING A MOBILE SERVICES API

Consider several things when building data services for your mobile application. First and foremost, you should always define an interface that reflects your mobile application use case. As mentioned previously, although SOAs and web services are a part of most organizations' overall data management strategy, existing enterprise services are usually not suitable for mobile applications.

Most organizations tend to take an "inside-out" perspective of data management and services design. That is to say, there is a tendency to start from the data structures defined in the back-end and expose them outward. Most Object-to-Relational Mapping frameworks (ORMs) make it easy to bring relational data constructs, such as tables and joins, into the services architecture. As a result, a single service request often returns a large amount of data pertaining to multiple entities in the problem domain. For example, a customer request may return the basic customer information, along with all addresses, contacts, orders, and order items for that customer — all presented neatly in a relational structure.

Although this technique may work well for many enterprise applications, the storage, bandwidth, and processing limitations can make this approach unusable in a mobile context. Instead, take an outside-in perspective when designing your mobile services. By designing services based on the consumption of the data within the context of the application you are building, you can more finely tune your services to provide only the information needed, at the time it is needed.

Starting with Your User Experience Design

In Chapter 2, "Designing Your User Experience," you learned about some of the techniques for designing your user experience. You went through prototyping exercises that helped to establish a basic user experience for the customer management application example. This prototype is used as the basis for the mobile data services design, starting with the model for the application. The customer class represents a company with which a fictitious company does business and must contain basic customer information, such as the customer name, website, and phone number.

```
public class Customer
{
  public Customer()
  {
    ID = "0";
    Name = string.Empty;
    Website = string.Empty;
    PrimaryAddress = new Address();
    Addresses = new List<Address>();
    Contacts = new List<Contact>();
    Orders = new List<Order>();
  }
```

```
    public string ID { get; set; }
    public string Name { get; set; }
    public string Website { get; set; }
    public string PrimaryPhone { get; set; }
    public Address PrimaryAddress { get; set; }
    public List<Address> Addresses { get; set; }
    public List<Contact> Contacts { get; set; }
    public List<Order> Orders { get; set; }
}
```

You want to use the application to manage customers but also need the ability to process orders for the customers. So, you need to include company contact, address, and order information as well. Because each of these new entities represents a one-to-many relationship with the customer class, add three new lists to define these associations.

```
public class Customer
{
    .
    .
    .

    public string ID { get; set; }
    public string Name { get; set; }
    public string Website { get; set; }
    public string PrimaryPhone { get; set; }
    public Address PrimaryAddress { get; set; }
    public List<Address> Addresses { get; set; }
    public List<Contact> Contacts { get; set; }
    public List<Order> Orders { get; set; }
}
```

Until now, you've been following standard object-oriented design principles in defining the simple customer model, and this model can serve you well in most cases. But this class has the potential to become heavy in a data management sense. A customer may have dozens of addresses, hundreds of contacts, and thousands of orders over time. If you were to take a coarse-grained approach to populating each customer with a full complement of these associated items, they would quickly grow to a size that could overwhelm the storage, bandwidth, and processing resources of a mobile device. Fortunately, you can apply a few simple principles to optimize the customer services for mobile usage.

Optimizing for Mobile Usage

The existing customer class has all the elements needed for the customer management example. You can easily use this class to both list the customers and display detailed information to the users. But you need to be careful about how much information you provide and at what time you provide it. This is where the outside-in approach to services design comes into practice.

You want to display a list of customers, which includes the customer name, website, and location information, (that is, city and state). The first two elements are present in the base customer class, but the location information is embedded in the address class:

```
public class Address
{
public string ID { get; set; }
public string Description { get; set; }
```

```
public string Street1 { get; set; }
public string Street2 { get; set; }
public string City { get; set; }
public string State { get; set; }
public string Zip { get; set; }
}
```

To display city and state information on the customer list, populate the Addresses collection on the company object, and apply some logic to determine which address contains the city and state information you want. Because a company may have dozens — perhaps hundreds — of addresses, populating the entire list when you need only a single city and state for the list is unnecessary. When multiplied across potentially thousands of customers in a single list, including unnecessary information can create a large collection of company objects that can quickly consume the bandwidth of a mobile connection and overwhelm the resources on a mobile device.

To ensure efficient management of device resources, you should design your services to allow for lightly loaded lists. To accomplish this, add a `PrimaryAddress` property to the base customer class:

```
public class Customer
{
  .
  .
  .

  public string ID { get; set; }
  public string Name { get; set; }
  public string Website { get; set; }
  public string PrimaryPhone { get; set; }
  public Address PrimaryAddress { get; set; }
  public List<Address> Addresses { get; set; }
  public List<Contact> Contacts { get; set; }
  public List<Order> Orders { get; set; }
}
```

The addition of this property enables you to include a single primary address as a part of each customer in the list, while leaving the addresses uninitialized when returning a collection of customer objects from the service. This can ensure only the information necessary to render the mobile application view (in this case, the customer list) is available, while reserving delivery of the details until a particular customer's data is requested.

You should design all your model classes in the same manner. Use the prototype screens you've designed as your guide, and make sure the base object contains all the data elements needed for the view in question — but no more. After you design your model with these rules in mind, building out your services becomes simple.

CREATING RESOURCE ENDPOINTS

Now that you've designed your model classes, you're ready to start building resource endpoints. The first thing you need to do is create a data store from which to deliver the customer information. Use a simple XML data store for this example, and use LINQ to Objects to deliver results to both the REST and SOAP services. Start with a customer XML that matches the serialized customer model object, as shown in Listing 7-1.

LISTING 7-1: The Customers.xml file

Available for download on Wrox.com

```
<?xml version="1.0" encoding="utf-8"?>
<ArrayOfCompany xmlns:xsi="http://www.w3.org/2001/XMLSchema-instance"
 xmlns:xsd="http://www.w3.org/2001/XMLSchema">
  <Company>
    <ID>1</ID>
    <Name>Stein Mart, Inc.</Name>
    <Website>http://www.steinmart.com</Website>
    <PrimaryPhone>904-346-1500</PrimaryPhone>
    <PrimaryAddress>
      <ID>1-a1</ID>
      <Description>World Headquarters</Description>
      <Street1>1200 Riverplace Blvd.</Street1>
      <City>Jacksonville</City>
      <State>FL</State>
      <Zip>32207</Zip>
    </PrimaryAddress>
    <Addresses>
      <Address>
        <ID>1-a1</ID>
        <Description>World Headquarters</Description>
        <Street1>1200 Riverplace Blvd.</Street1>
        <City>Jacksonville</City>
        <State>FL</State>
        <Zip>32207</Zip>
      </Address>
    </Addresses>
    <Contacts />
    <Orders />
  </Company>
  .
  .
  .
</ArrayOfCompany>
```

Found in the CustomerManagement.Data/Xml/Customers.xml file of the download

To simplify the serialization and deserialization of the model objects in the XML data store, use the `System.Xml.Serialization.XmlSerializer` *class in both the data store and service endpoints. Because this serializer is supported in Mono, it can be used to hydrate object graphs seamlessly on multiple mobile platforms.*

To enable LINQ on the list of customer objects, you need to write a method to deserialize the file to create the collection. The `GetCustomerList()` method can serve this function, as shown in Listing 7-2.

LISTING 7-2: The GetCustomerList() method

Available for download on Wrox.com

```
static List<Customer> GetCustomerList()
{
  string dataFilePath = Path.Combine(AppPath,
                        Path.Combine("Xml", "Customers.xml"));

  var loadedData = XDocument.Load(dataFilePath);
  using (var reader = loadedData.Root.CreateReader())
  {
    List<Customer> list = (List<Customer>)new
      XmlSerializer(typeof(List<Customer>)).Deserialize(reader);
    list.Sort((a, b) => a.Name.CompareTo(b.Name));
    return list;
  }
}
```

Found in the CustomerManagement.Data/XmlDataStore.cs file of the download

Now use the `GetCustomerList()` method to expose a new data access method to enable display of the full list of customers, as shown in Listing 7-3.

LISTING 7-3: The GetCustomers() method

Available for download on Wrox.com

```
public static List<Customer> GetCustomers()
 {
     return GetCustomerList();
 }
```

Found in the CustomerManagement.Data/XmlDataStore.cs file of the download

Finally, you can expose the `GetCustomers()` method through a new RESTful service that can deliver the customer list to your application. The `GetCustomers` service is shown in Listing 7-4.

The remaining service examples in this chapter demonstrate deployment of REST services using WCF. Because the services methods simply pass through to the data store for processing, you can extend your data methods to use SOAP by adding the method signature to your `IService` *interface and implementing them in your* `Service.cs` *code file following WCF/SOAP best practices. SOAP service examples are provided in the* `CustomerMangement.SOAP` *project in the download.*

LISTING 7-4: The GetCustomers() REST service

Available for download on Wrox.com

```
 [XmlSerializerFormat]
[WebGet(UriTemplate = "customers.xml")]
public List<Customer> GetCustomers()
{
  return XmlDataStore.GetCustomers();
}
```

Found in the CustomerManagement.DataServices/CustomerManagement.REST/Service.cs file of the download

The `WebGet` attribute in WCF uses the `DataContractSerializer` by default. The `DataContractSerializer` creates additional attributes and extended element tags in the XML that are not easily handled across mobile devices. To ensure the simpler `XmlSerializer` is used instead, you must tag each service method with the `XmlSerializerFormat` attribute.

Building Indexed Lists

Now you've successfully created a simple service to return customer information in a collection, but you still are returning everything in the customer store by default. As long as the customer list remains small, this may work just fine, but as the business grows, you need to add more customers, with many orders that will be managed in the data store. You need to be judicious about the use of device and network resources, so build some automatic filtering into your services.

Start from the customer list view in the application. But rather than just delivering the information necessary to display on the screen, include additional information that can be used on the device to search the list and filter results for consumption. To do this, refactor the `GetCustomers()` method on the data store to return only the properties you need to index and search the list. In this case, that includes the customer ID, name, primary phone number, and primary address. Listing 7-5 shows the refactored `GetCustomers()` method.

LISTING 7-5: A refactored GetCustomers() method

Available for download on Wrox.com

```
public static List<Customer> GetCustomers(string filter)
{
  return (from item in GetCustomerList()
          where
          item.Name
              .Contains(string.IsNullOrWhiteSpace(filter) ?
                        filter : item.Name) ||
          item.PrimaryAddress.City
              .Contains(string.IsNullOrWhiteSpace(filter) ? filter :
          item.PrimaryAddress.City) ||
          item.PrimaryAddress.State
              .Contains(string.IsNullOrWhiteSpace(filter) ? filter :
          item.PrimaryAddress.State) ||
```

```
            item.PrimaryAddress.Zip
                .Contains(string.IsNullOrWhiteSpace(filter) ? filter :
                          item.PrimaryAddress.Zip)
            select new Customer()
            {
              ID = item.ID,
              Name = item.Name,
              PrimaryAddress = item.PrimaryAddress,
              PrimaryPhone = item.PrimaryPhone
            }).ToList();
}
```

Found in the CustomerManagement.Data/XmlDataStore.cs file of the download

This new and improved `GetCustomers()` method uses a simple LINQ to Objects query to set only the default values you need to display and index the list on the device. This results in a decreased payload over the wire when the data is delivered through the service. Listing 7-6 shows this lightweight output.

LISTING 7-6: A lightweight Customer list

```
<ArrayOfCompany xmlns:xsi="http://www.w3.org/2001/XMLSchema-instance"
 xmlns:xsd="http://www.w3.org/2001/XMLSchema">
  <Company>
    <ID>1</ID>
    <Name>Stein Mart, Inc.</Name>
    <PrimaryPhone>904-346-1500</PrimaryPhone>
    <PrimaryAddress>
      <ID>1-a1</ID>
      <Description>World Headquarters</Description>
      <Street1>1200 Riverplace Blvd.</Street1>
      <City>Jacksonville</City>
      <State>FL</State>
      <Zip>32207</Zip>
    </PrimaryAddress>
  </Company>
  <Company>
    <ID>2</ID>
    <Name>Bgc Partners, Inc.</Name>
    <PrimaryPhone>212-938-5000</PrimaryPhone>
    <PrimaryAddress>
      <ID>2-a1</ID>
      <Description>World Headquarters</Description>
      <Street1>499 Park Ave.</Street1>
      <City>New York</City>
      <State>NY</State>
      <Zip>10022</Zip>
    </PrimaryAddress>
  </Company>
  .
  .
  .
</ArrayOfCompany>
```

Retrieving Detail Objects

Now that you have created a lightweight customer list, you need a way to return the full details of a customer at the appropriate point in the application workflow. You need the ability to view, add, and edit customer detail information but leave order processing for a separate workflow path. As such, you can design the data method and endpoints accordingly.

The code in Listing 7-7 shows the `GetCustomer()` data method. The data is organized so that the first address in the Addresses collection is always the default address. You can take that address and set the `PrimaryAddress` property, if it is not already set, before returning the customer to the service.

LISTING 7-7: The GetCustomer method

Available for download on Wrox.com

```
public static Customer GetCustomer(string customer)
{
  Customer retval = GetCustomerList().Where(obj => obj.ID ==
                    customer).FirstOrDefault();
  if (retval.Addresses.Count > 0 && retval.PrimaryAddress == null)
  {
    retval.PrimaryAddress = new Address()
    {
      ID = retval.Addresses[0].ID,
      Description = retval.Addresses[0].Description,
      Street1 = retval.Addresses[0].Street1,
      Street2 = retval.Addresses[0].Street2,
      City = retval.Addresses[0].City,
      State = retval.Addresses[0].State,
      Zip = retval.Addresses[0].Zip
    };
  }
  return retval;
}
```

Found in the CustomerManagement.Data/XmlDataStore.cs file of the download

Now you can follow the same technique to expose the customer detail information in your service, as shown in Listing 7-8.

LISTING 7-8: The GetCustomer REST service

Available for download on Wrox.com

```
[XmlSerializerFormat]
[WebGet(UriTemplate = "customers/{customer}.xml")]
public Customer GetCustomer(string customer)
{
  return XmlDataStore.GetCompany(customer);
}
```

Found in the CustomerManagement.DataServices/CustomerManagement.REST/Service.cs file of the download

You can apply the same technique to all the indexed lists and detail retrieval methods in your application. Simply use your user experience prototype as the guide, and return only the information necessary at the time it is needed. This lightly loaded approach can ensure you manage device resources efficiently, and minimize the potential for poor application performance due to resource and bandwidth limitations.

You can now add data methods. Listing 7-9 shows the data retrieval method.

LISTING 7-9: XML data store retrieval methods

Available for download on Wrox.com

```
public class XmlDataStore
{
    .
    .
    .
    public static List<Customer> GetCustomers()
    {
      return GetCustomerList();
    }

  public static List<Product> GetProducts()
  {
    return GetProductList();
  }

  public static Product GetProduct(string productId)
  {
    return GetProductList().Where(obj => obj.ID == productId)
                           .FirstOrDefault();
  }

  public static List<Order> GetCustomerOrders(string customer)
  {
    return (from item in GetOrderList()
            where item.Customer.ID == customer
            select new Order()
            {
                ID = item.ID,
                PurchaseOrder = item.PurchaseOrder,
                Customer = item.Customer
            }).ToList();
  }

  public static List<Order> GetCustomerOrder(string customer, string orderId)
  {
    return (from item in GetOrderList()
            where item.Customer.ID == customer && item.ID == orderId
            select new Order()
            {
                ID = item.ID,
                PurchaseOrder = item.PurchaseOrder,
                Customer = item.Customer,
```

continues

LISTING 7-9 *(continued)*

```
                Items = item.Items
            }).ToList();
    }

    public static Customer GetCustomer(string customer)
    {
      Customer retval = GetCustomerList()
                        .Where(obj => obj.ID == customer)
                        .FirstOrDefault();
      if (retval.Addresses.Count > 0 && retval.PrimaryAddress == null)
      {
        retval.PrimaryAddress = new Address()
        {
          ID = retval.Addresses[0].ID,
          Description = retval.Addresses[0].Description,
          Street1 = retval.Addresses[0].Street1,
          Street2 = retval.Addresses[0].Street2,
          City = retval.Addresses[0].City,
          State = retval.Addresses[0].State,
          Zip = retval.Addresses[0].Zip
        };
      }
      return retval;
    }

    public static List<Contact> GetContacts(string customer)
    {
      return GetCustomerList()
        .Where(obj => obj.ID ==   customer).FirstOrDefault().Contacts;
    }

    public static Contact GetContact(string customer, string contact)
    {
      Contact retval = GetContacts(customer)
        .Where(obj => obj.ID == contact).FirstOrDefault();
      return retval;
    }
      .
      .
      .
}
```

Found in the CustomerManagement.Data/XmlDataStore.cs file of the download

Now that your data retrieval method is complete, you can add service endpoints to support retrieval of company contacts, products, and orders. Listing 7-10 shows the completed services.

LISTING 7-10: Data retrieval REST services

Available for download on Wrox.com

```
public class Service
{
  #region XML Services
```

```
    // GET Methods
    [XmlSerializerFormat]
    [WebGet(UriTemplate = "customers.xml")]
    public List<Customer> GetCustomers()
    {
      return XmlDataStore.GetCustomers();
    }

    [XmlSerializerFormat]
    [WebGet(UriTemplate = "products.xml")]
    public List<Product> GetProducts()
    {
      return XmlDataStore.GetProducts();
    }

    [XmlSerializerFormat]
    [WebGet(UriTemplate = "orders/{customer}.xml")]
    public List<Order> GetCompanyOrders(string customer)
    {
      return XmlDataStore.GetCustomerOrders(customer);
    }

    [XmlSerializerFormat]
    [WebGet(UriTemplate = "customers/{customer}.xml")]
    public Customer GetCustomer(string customer)
    {
      return XmlDataStore.GetCustomer(customer);
    }

    [XmlSerializerFormat]
    [WebGet(UriTemplate = "customers/{customer}/contacts.xml",
     ResponseFormat =   WebMessageFormat.Xml)]
    public List<Contact> GetContacts(string customer)
    {
      return XmlDataStore.GetContacts(customer);
    }

    [XmlSerializerFormat]
    [WebGet(UriTemplate = "customers/{customer}/{contact}.xml")]
    public Contact GetContact(string customer, string contact)
    {
      return XmlDataStore.GetContact(customer, contact);
    }

      .
      .
      .
}
```

Found in the CustomerManagement.DataServices/CustomerManagement.REST/Service.cs file of the download

Enabling Transactions

Now that you fleshed out the retrieval services, you need to provide for a way to add, update, and delete the various model objects that enable those transactions. The first thing you need is a way to modify the data in the data store and persist it to durable storage. Following the simple XML serialization pattern, create a save method for each data file that supports transactions. Listing 7-11 shows the method for saving customers after an update to the collection.

LISTING 7-11: The SaveCustomers() method

Available for download on Wrox.com

```
static void SaveCustomers(List<Customer> customers)
{
  string dataFilePath = Path.Combine(AppPath,
                        Path.Combine("Xml", "Customers.xml"));
  using (StreamWriter writer = new StreamWriter(dataFilePath))
  {
    var serializer = new XmlSerializer(typeof(List<Customer>));
    serializer.Serialize(writer, customers);
  }
}
```

Found in the CustomerManagement.Data/XmlDataStore.cs file of the download

Again, use the `System.Xml.Serialization.XmlSerializer` class to manage the persistence, keeping the formatting consistent from the data store out to the device. This save method can be used by any data transaction methods that require a change to the persisted store, such as the `CreateCustomer()` method shown in Listing 7-12.

LISTING 7-12: The CreateCustomer() method

Available for download on Wrox.com

```
public static Customer CreateCustomer(Customer instance)
{
  List<Customer> companies = GetCustomerList();

  // Set ID's
  string ID = (companies.Max(a => Convert.ToInt32(a.ID)) + 1).ToString();
  instance.ID = ID;
  instance.PrimaryAddress.ID = string.Format("{0}-a1", ID);

  companies.Add(instance);
  SaveCustomers(companies);
  return instance;
}
```

Found in the CustomerManagement.Data/XmlDataStore.cs file of the download

You also use the same save method when processing a customer update, as shown in Listing 7-13.

Available for download on Wrox.com

LISTING 7-13: The UpdateCustomer() method

```
public static Customer UpdateCustomer(Customer instance)
{
  List<Customer> companies = GetCustomerList();
  if (companies.Where(obj => obj.ID == instance.ID).Count() != 0)
    companies.Remove(companies.First(obj => obj.ID == instance.ID));
  companies.Add(instance);
  SaveCustomers(companies);
  return instance;
}
```

Found in the CustomerManagement.Data/XmlDataStore.cs file of the download

The same method is used for a customer deletion, as shown in Listing 7-14.

Available for download on Wrox.com

LISTING 7-14: The DeleteCustomer() method

```
public static void DeleteCustomer(string customer)
{
  List<Customer> companies = GetCustomerList();
  companies.Remove(companies.First(obj => obj.ID == customer));
  SaveCustomers(companies);
}
```

Found in the CustomerManagement.Data/XmlDataStore.cs file of the download

To expose your new data transaction methods through your RESTful service layer, simply add the methods to your service accordingly, as shown in Listing 7-15.

Available for download on Wrox.com

LISTING 7-15: Company transaction REST services

```
using System;
using System.Collections.Generic;
using System.IO;
using System.Linq;
using System.ServiceModel;
using System.ServiceModel.Activation;
using System.ServiceModel.Web;
using System.Text;
using System.Xml.Serialization;
using System.Web;
```

continues

LISTING 7-15 *(continued)*

```
using CustomerManagement.Data;
using CustomerManagement.Shared.Model;

namespace CustomerManagement.REST
{
  [ServiceContract]
  [AspNetCompatibilityRequirements(
     RequirementsMode =
       AspNetCompatibilityRequirementsMode.Allowed)]
  [ServiceBehavior(
     InstanceContextMode =
      InstanceContextMode.PerCall)]
  public class Service
  {
      #region XML Services
     .
     .
     .
    [XmlSerializerFormat]
    [WebInvoke(UriTemplate = "customers/customer.xml",
     Method = "POST",
     RequestFormat = WebMessageFormat.Xml,
     ResponseFormat = WebMessageFormat.Xml)]
    public Customer CreateCompany(Customer instance)
    {
      return XmlDataStore.CreateCustomer(instance);
    }
     .
     .
     .
    [XmlSerializerFormat]
    [WebInvoke(UriTemplate = "customers/customer.xml",
     Method = "PUT",
     RequestFormat = WebMessageFormat.Xml,
     ResponseFormat = WebMessageFormat.Xml)]
    public Customer UpdateCompany(Customer instance)
    {
    return XmlDataStore.UpdateCustomer(instance);
    }
     .
     .
     .
    [WebInvoke(UriTemplate = "customers/{customer}", Method = "DELETE")]
    public void DeleteCompany(string customer)
    {
      XmlDataStore.DeleteCustomer(customer);
    }
     .
     .
     .
  }
}
```

Found in the CustomerManagement.DataServices/CustomerManagement.REST/Service.cs file of the download

You are now ready to add transaction data methods and endpoints for the remaining entities in your application. Because products are not editable in this application, we will add transaction support for contacts and orders only. Listing 7-16 shows the completed transaction methods.

LISTING 7-16: Data store transaction methods

Available for download on Wrox.com

```
namespace CustomerManagement.Data
{
  public class XmlDataStore
  {
      .
      .
      .
      // Create Methods
      public static Customer CreateCustomer(Customer instance)
      {
        List<Customer> companies = GetCustomerList();

        // Set ID's
        string ID = (companies.Max(a => Convert.ToInt32(a.ID)) + 1).ToString();
        instance.ID = ID;
        instance.PrimaryAddress.ID = string.Format("{0}-a1", ID);

        companies.Add(instance);
        SaveCustomers(companies);
        return instance;
      }

      public static Contact CreateContact(string customer, Contact instance)
      {
        List<Contact> contacts = GetContacts(customer);

        // Set ID
        string ID = (contacts.Count + 1).ToString();
        instance.ID = string.Format("{0}-c{1}", customer, ID);

        contacts.Add(instance);
        SaveContacts(customer, contacts);
        return instance;
      }

      public static Order CreateOrder(Order instance)
      {
        List<Order> orders = GetOrderList();

        // Set ID
        string ID = (int.Parse(orders.Max(a => a.ID)) + 1).ToString();
        instance.ID = ID;

        orders.Add(instance);
        SaveOrders(orders);
        return instance;
      }
```

continues

LISTING 7-16 *(continued)*

```
// Update Methods
public static Customer UpdateCustomer(Customer instance)
{
  List<Customer> companies = GetCustomerList();
  if (companies.Where(obj => obj.ID == instance.ID).Count() != 0)
      companies.Remove(companies.First(obj => obj.ID == instance.ID));
  companies.Add(instance);
  SaveCustomers(companies);
  return instance;
}

public static Contact UpdateContact(string customer, Contact instance)
{
  List<Contact> contacts = GetContacts(customer);
  contacts.Remove(contacts.First(obj => obj.ID == instance.ID));
  contacts.Add(instance);
  SaveContacts(customer, contacts);
  return instance;
}

public static Order UpdateOrder(Order instance)
{
  List<Order> orders = GetOrderList();
  orders.Remove(orders.First(obj => obj.ID == instance.ID));
  orders.Add(instance);
  SaveOrders(orders);
  return instance;
}

// Delete Methods
public static void DeleteCustomer(string customer)
{
  List<Customer> companies = GetCustomerList();
  companies.Remove(companies.First(obj => obj.ID == customer));
  SaveCustomers(companies);
}

public static void DeleteContact(string customer, string contact)
{
  List<Contact> contacts = GetContacts(customer);
  contacts.Remove(contacts.First(obj => obj.ID == contact));
  SaveContacts(customer, contacts);
}

public static void DeleteOrder(string order)
{
  List<Order> orders = GetOrderList();
  orders.Remove(orders.First(obj => obj.ID == order));
  SaveOrders(orders);
```

```
            }
           .
           .
           .
        }
    }
```

Found in the CustomerManagement.Data/XmlDataStore.cs file of the download

Listing 7-17 shows the completed REST services for these transactions.

Available for download on Wrox.com

LISTING 7-17: Data transaction REST services

```
namespace CustomerManagement.REST
{
  [ServiceContract]
  [AspNetCompatibilityRequirements(
    RequirementsMode =
      AspNetCompatibilityRequirementsMode.Allowed)]
  [ServiceBehavior(
    InstanceContextMode =
      InstanceContextMode.PerCall)]
  public class Service
  {
      #region XML Services
     .
     .
     .
    // POST Methods
    [XmlSerializerFormat]
    [WebInvoke(UriTemplate = "customers/customer.xml",
     Method = "POST",
     RequestFormat = WebMessageFormat.Xml,
     ResponseFormat = WebMessageFormat.Xml)]
    public Customer CreateCustomer(Customer instance)
    {
      return XmlDataStore.CreateCustomer(instance);
    }

    [XmlSerializerFormat]
    [WebInvoke(UriTemplate = "customers/{customer}/contact.xml",
     Method = "POST",
     RequestFormat = WebMessageFormat.Xml,
     ResponseFormat = WebMessageFormat.Xml)]
    public Contact CreateContact(string customer, Contact instance)
    {
      return XmlDataStore.CreateContact(customer, instance);
    }
```

continues

LISTING 7-17 *(continued)*

```
[XmlSerializerFormat]
[WebInvoke(UriTemplate = "orders.xml",
 Method = "POST",
 RequestFormat = WebMessageFormat.Xml,
 ResponseFormat = WebMessageFormat.Xml)]
public Order CreateOrder(Order instance)
{
  return XmlDataStore.CreateOrder(instance);
}

// PUT Methods
[XmlSerializerFormat]
[WebInvoke(UriTemplate = "customers/customer.xml",
 Method = "PUT",
 RequestFormat = WebMessageFormat.Xml,
 ResponseFormat = WebMessageFormat.Xml)]
public Customer UpdateCompany(Customer instance)
{
  return XmlDataStore.UpdateCustomer(instance);
}

[XmlSerializerFormat]
[WebInvoke(UriTemplate = "customers/{customer}/contact.xml",
 Method = "PUT",
 RequestFormat = WebMessageFormat.Xml,
 ResponseFormat = WebMessageFormat.Xml)]
public Contact UpdateContact(string customer, Contact instance)
{
  return XmlDataStore.UpdateContact(customer, instance);
}

[XmlSerializerFormat]
[WebInvoke(UriTemplate = "orders.xml",
 Method = "PUT",
 RequestFormat = WebMessageFormat.Xml,
 ResponseFormat = WebMessageFormat.Xml)]
public Order UpdateOrder(Order instance)
{
  return XmlDataStore.UpdateOrder(instance);
}

    #endregion
  .
  .
  .
// DELETE Methods
[WebInvoke(UriTemplate = "customers/{customer}",
 Method = "DELETE")]
public void DeleteCompany(string customer)
{
  XmlDataStore.DeleteCustomer(customer);
}
```

```
        [WebInvoke(UriTemplate = "customers/{customer}/{contact}",
         Method = "DELETE")]
        public void DeleteContact(string customer, string contact)
        {
          XmlDataStore.DeleteContact(customer, contact);
        }

        [WebInvoke(UriTemplate = "orders/{order}",
         Method = "DELETE")]
        public void DeleteOrder(string order)
        {
          XmlDataStore.DeleteOrder(order);
        }
        }
}
```

Found in the CustomerManagement.DataServices/CustomerManagement.REST/Service.cs file of the download

Creating JSON Endpoints

XML has been the de facto standard format for web services for many years; but, with the maturity of web technologies such as AJAX and JavaScript Object Notation (JSON), formatting has become increasingly popular. Luckily, WCF makes extending your RESTful services to include JSON output a breeze.

Organizations that have adopted REST as a services architecture often provide developers a choice when requesting data from the services layer. XML often integrates more seamlessly into applications that already use XML data, via SOAP services, or other methods. Web applications with significant logic in JavaScript are often more suited to JSON delivery of information.

Where mobile applications are concerned, XML's verbosity can result in increased bandwidth performance issues, but JSON formatting results in a much more compact data stream — especially where large list retrieval is necessary.

To extend your existing services to deliver JSON-formatted output, simply expose parallel endpoints using a distinguishing route in the endpoint definition. Listing 7-18 uses the file extension technique, (that is, `.xml` for XML and `.json` for JSON formatting).

LISTING 7-18: REST services using JSON formatting

Available for download on Wrox.com

```
namespace CustomerManagement.REST
{
  [ServiceContract]
  [AspNetCompatibilityRequirements(
     RequirementsMode =
       AspNetCompatibilityRequirementsMode.Allowed)]
  [ServiceBehavior(InstanceContextMode =
```

continues

LISTING 7-18 *(continued)*

```
        InstanceContextMode.PerCall)]
    public class Service
    {
      .
      .
      .
  #region JSON Services

        // GET Methods
        [WebGet(UriTemplate = "customers.json?filter={filter}",
         ResponseFormat = WebMessageFormat.Json)]
        public List<Customer> GetCustomersJson(string filter)
        {
          return XmlDataStore.GetCustomers(filter);
        }

        [WebGet(UriTemplate = "products.json",
         ResponseFormat = WebMessageFormat.Json)]
        public List<Product> GetProductsJson()
        {
          return XmlDataStore.GetProducts();
        }

        [WebGet(UriTemplate = "orders/{customer}.json",
         ResponseFormat = WebMessageFormat.Json)]
        public List<Order> GetCompanyOrdersJson(string customer)
        {
          return XmlDataStore.GetCustomerOrders(customer);
        }

        [WebGet(UriTemplate = "orders/{customer}/{order}.json",
         ResponseFormat = WebMessageFormat.Json)]
        public List<Order> GetCompanyOrderJson(string customer, string order)
        {
          return XmlDataStore.GetCompanyOrder(customer, order);
        }

        [WebGet(UriTemplate = "customers/{customer}.json",
         ResponseFormat = WebMessageFormat.Json)]
        public Customer GetCompanyJson(string customer)
        {
          return XmlDataStore.GetCustomer(customer);
        }

        [WebGet(UriTemplate = "customers/{customer}/contacts.json",
         ResponseFormat = WebMessageFormat.Json)]
        public List<Contact> GetContactsJson(string customer)
        {
          return XmlDataStore.GetContacts(customer);
        }

        [WebGet(UriTemplate = "customers/{customer}/{contact}.json",
```

```
 ResponseFormat = WebMessageFormat.Json)]
public Contact GetContactJson(string customer, string contact)
{
  return XmlDataStore.GetContact(customer, contact);
}

// POST Methods
[WebInvoke(UriTemplate = "customers/customer.json",
 Method = "POST",
 RequestFormat = WebMessageFormat.Json,
 ResponseFormat = WebMessageFormat.Json)]
public Customer CreateCompanyJson(Customer instance)
{
  return XmlDataStore.CreateCustomer(instance);
}

[WebInvoke(UriTemplate = "customers/{customer}/contact.json",
 Method = "POST",
 RequestFormat = WebMessageFormat.Json,
 ResponseFormat = WebMessageFormat.Json)]
public Contact CreateContactJson(string customer, Contact instance)
{
  return XmlDataStore.CreateContact(customer, instance);
}

[WebInvoke(UriTemplate = "orders.json",
 Method = "POST",
 RequestFormat = WebMessageFormat.Json,
 ResponseFormat = WebMessageFormat.Json)]
public Order CreateOrderJson(Order instance)
{
  return XmlDataStore.CreateOrder(instance);
}

// PUT Methods
[WebInvoke(UriTemplate = "customers/customer.json",
 Method = "PUT",
 RequestFormat = WebMessageFormat.Json,
 ResponseFormat = WebMessageFormat.Json)]
public Customer UpdateCompanyJson(Customer instance)
{
  return XmlDataStore.UpdateCustomer(instance);
}

[WebInvoke(UriTemplate = "customers/{customer}/contact.json",
 Method = "PUT",
 RequestFormat = WebMessageFormat.Json,
 ResponseFormat = WebMessageFormat.Json)]
public Contact UpdateContactJson(string customer, Contact instance)
{
  return XmlDataStore.UpdateContact(customer, instance);
}
```

continues

LISTING 7-18 *(continued)*

```
        [WebInvoke(UriTemplate = "orders.json",
         Method = "PUT",
         RequestFormat = WebMessageFormat.Json,
         ResponseFormat = WebMessageFormat.Json)]
        public Order UpdateOrderJson(Order instance)
        {
          return XmlDataStore.UpdateOrder(instance);
        }

        #endregion
      .
      .
      .
    }
}
```

Found in the CustomerManagement.DataServices/CustomerManagement.REST/Service.cs file of the download

USING ADVANCED TECHNIQUES

To this point, you've built a solid foundation of services to support the mobile application, but some additional techniques can help manage the bandwidth and resource constraints inherent to mobile devices and networks. In this section you explore some additional enhancements to your services to help support mobile users. The section ends with a discussion of ways in which enterprises can adopt a RESTful approach to deliver information to their users, customers, and beyond.

Specifying Data Elements in the Request

You've created services for a customer management application, and the output of these services is custom-made for the application. But what if you need to develop another application that requires a different view of the customers for whom you have built services?

One successful technique to tailor the data delivered in varied use cases is to specify the elements you require as a part of the request. Most RESTful routing engines, including the routing service in WCF, support inclusion of query parameters in the endpoint. By creating a parameter that specifies the data elements to show, the consumers of your services can customize the output to match their application needs.

For example, if you want to make a request for an XML customer list, the only option is to retrieve the default presentation at the `customers.xml` endpoint.

```
GET http://localhost/MXDemo/customers.xml
```

But if you extend the endpoint to accept a parameter specifying the elements to include in the response, you can process accordingly in the data retrieval logic of your data store.

```
GET http://localhost/MXDemo/customers.xml?show=id,name,website
```

Listing 7-19 shows an implementation of the data retrieval method in the data store.

Available for download on Wrox.com

LISTING 7-19: Data retrieval method supporting custom output

```
namespace CustomerManagement.Data
{
  public class XmlDataStore
  {
   .
   .
   .
      public static List<Customer> GetCustomers(string[] show)
      {
        return (from item in GetCustomerList()
                select new Customer()
                {
                  ID = show.Contains("id") ? item.ID : null,
                  Name = show.Contains("name") ?
                                   item.Name : null,
                  PrimaryAddress = show.Contains("primaryaddress") ?
                                   item.PrimaryAddress : null,
                  PrimaryPhone = show.Contains("primaryphone") ?
                                   item.PrimaryPhone : null,
                  Website = show.Contains("website") ?
                                   item.Website : null,
                  Addresses = show.Contains("addresses") ?
                                   item.Addresses : null,
                  Contacts = show.Contains("contacts") ?
                                   item.Contacts : null,
                  Orders = show.Contains("orders") ?
                                   item.Orders : null,
                }).ToList();
      }
```

Found in the CustomerManagement.Data/XmlDataStore.cs file of the download

Listing 7-20 shows the modified customer list endpoint in the REST service.

Available for download on Wrox.com

LISTING 7-20: REST service supporting custom output

```
namespace CustomerManagement.REST
{
  [ServiceContract]
  [AspNetCompatibilityRequirements(
     RequirementsMode =
       AspNetCompatibilityRequirementsMode.Allowed)]
  [ServiceBehavior(
     InstanceContextMode = InstanceContextMode.PerCall)]
  public class Service
  {
    #region XML Services
```

continues

LISTING 7-20 *(continued)*

```
        .
        .
        .
        [XmlSerializerFormat]
        [WebGet(UriTemplate = "customers.xml?show={show}")]
        public List<Customer> GetCustomers(string show)
        {
          return show == null ?
              XmlDataStore.GetCustomers() :
              XmlDataStore.GetCustomers(show.Split(char.Parse(",")));
        }
        .
        .
        .
    }
}
```

Found in the CustomerManagement.DataServices/CustomerManagement.REST/Service.cs file of the download

Listing 7-21 shows the results of this customized request.

LISTING 7-21: A customized Company list

```
<ArrayOfCompany xmlns:xsi="http://www.w3.org/2001/XMLSchema-instance"
 xmlns:xsd="http://www.w3.org/2001/XMLSchema">
  <Company>
    <ID>1</ID>
    <Name>Stein Mart, Inc.</Name>
    <Website>http://www.steinmart.com</Website>
  </Company>
  <Company>
    <ID>2</ID>
    <Name>Bgc Partners, Inc.</Name>
    <Website>http://www.bgcpartners.com</Website>
  </Company>
  .
  .
  .
</ArrayOfCompany>
```

Building Pagination into Your Services

Enterprise applications often deal with large collections of data that require paging of information to make it easier for the user to consume. Paging in mobile applications can also provide the added benefit of limiting the data set returned to better manage device resources. Both these are compelling reasons to build pagination into your data services.

To extend the customer list endpoint to provide paged information, you need to specify the page number you want to receive, and optionally the number of items on each page.

```
GET http://localhost/MXDemo/customers.xml?page=1&items=5
```

Listing 7-22 shows the paged implementation for retrieval from the data store.

Available for download on Wrox.com

LISTING 7-22: Data retrieval method with pagination

```
namespace CustomerManagement.Data
{
  public class XmlDataStore
  {
    .
    .
    .

    public static List<Customer> GetCustomers(int page, int items)
    {
      return (from item in GetCustomerList()
              select new Customer()
              {
                ID = item.ID,
                Name = item.Name,
                PrimaryAddress = item.PrimaryAddress,
                PrimaryPhone = item.PrimaryPhone
              }).Skip((page - 1) * items).Take(items).ToList();
    }
    .
    .
    .
  }
}
```

Found in the CustomerManagement.Data/XmlDataStore.cs file of the download

Listing 7-23 shows the paged customer list endpoint in the REST service.

Available for download on Wrox.com

LISTING 7-23: REST service with pagination

```
namespace CustomerManagement.REST
{
  [ServiceContract]
  [AspNetCompatibilityRequirements(RequirementsMode =
   AspNetCompatibilityRequirementsMode.Allowed)]
  [ServiceBehavior(InstanceContextMode = InstanceContextMode.PerCall)]
  public class Service
  {
    #region XML Services
    .
    .
    .

    [XmlSerializerFormat]
    [WebGet(UriTemplate =
     "customers.xml?show={show}&page={page}&items={items}")]
```

continues

LISTING 7-23 *(continued)*

```
        public List<Company> GetCustomers(string show, int page, int items)
        {
          return show == null ?
              XmlDataStore.GetCustomers(page == 0 ? 1 :
                                        page, items == 0 ? 5 :
                                        items) :
              XmlDataStore.GetCustomers(show.Split(char.Parse(",")),
                                        page == 0 ? 1 : page,
                                        items == 0 ? 10 : items);
        }
        .
        .
        .
      }
}
```

Found in the CustomerManagement.DataServices/CustomerManagement.REST/Service.cs file of the download

Filtering Results on the Server

Navigating and consuming large lists can be cumbersome, especially in a mobile application where the form-factor and interaction paradigms can be limited compared to a desktop or web application. Because of this, mobile applications often provide a means for filtering a large list of information using a data-filtering scheme. However, complex searches that involve selection of specific fields and explicit AND/OR logic can be difficult to use on a mobile device. As a result, most devices use a simple, text-based search field that applies the term to all relevant fields in the data set.

To support this method of filtering in your services, simply add a single filter parameter to your endpoint. Whatever term you provide will be applied to all the fields you specify as searchable. For example, to return only customers who have a primary address in the state of New York, use a filter on the endpoint.

```
GET http://localhost/MXDemo/customers.xml?filter=NY
```

If you want to narrow the results to a specific ZIP code, simply provide the proper filter term.

```
GET http://localhost/MXDemo/customers.xml?filter=10022
```

If you want to return customers with the term *communication* in their name, modify your filter accordingly.

```
GET http://localhost/MXDemo/customers.xml?filter=communication
```

The code in Listing 7-24 shows the simple filtering code in the data store.

Available for download on Wrox.com

LISTING 7-24: Data retrieval method with simple filtering

```
namespace CustomerManagement.Data
{
  public class XmlDataStore
```

```
    {
      .
      .
      .
      public static List<Customer> GetCustomers(string filter)
      {
        bool test = string.IsNullOrWhiteSpace(filter);
        return (from item in GetCustomerList()
                where
                  item.Name
                      .Contains(!string.IsNullOrWhiteSpace(filter) ?
                               filter : item.Name) ||
                  item.PrimaryAddress.City
                      .Contains(!string.IsNullOrWhiteSpace(filter) ?
                               filter : item.PrimaryAddress.City) ||
                  item.PrimaryAddress.State
                      .Contains(!string.IsNullOrWhiteSpace(filter) ?
                               filter : item.PrimaryAddress.State) ||
                  item.PrimaryAddress.Zip
                      .Contains(!string.IsNullOrWhiteSpace(filter) ?
                               filter : item.PrimaryAddress.Zip)
                select new Customer()
                {
                  ID = item.ID,
                  Name = item.Name,
                  Website = item.Website
                }).ToList();
      }
      .
      .
      .
    }
  }
```

Found in the CustomerManagement.Data/XmlDataStore.cs file of the download

Listing 7-25 shows the filtered customer endpoint in the REST service.

LISTING 7-25: REST service with simple filtering

Available for download on Wrox.com

```
namespace CustomerManagement.REST
{
  [ServiceContract]
  [AspNetCompatibilityRequirements(RequirementsMode =
   AspNetCompatibilityRequirementsMode.Allowed)]
  [ServiceBehavior(InstanceContextMode = InstanceContextMode.PerCall)]
  public class Service
  {
    #region XML Services
    .
    .
    .
```

continues

LISTING 7-25 *(continued)*

```
        [XmlSerializerFormat]
        [WebGet(UriTemplate =
               "customers.xml?
                filter={filter}&show={show}
                &page={page}&items={items}")]
        public List<Customer> GetCustomers(string filter,
                                           string show,
                                           int page,
                                           int items)
        {
          return show == null ?
                 page == 0 && items == 0 ?
              XmlDataStore.GetCustomers(filter) :
              XmlDataStore.GetCustomers(filter, page, items) :
              XmlDataStore.GetCustomers(filter,
                           show.Split(char.Parse(",")), page, items);
        }
        .
        .
        .
      }
    }
```

Found in the CustomerManagement.DataServices/CustomerManagement.REST/Service.cs file of the download

SUMMARY

In this chapter you learned how to optimize and build your web services for mobile applications. The chapter discussed both SOAP and RESTful techniques, and you learned to make your services mirror your application design to best provide data to your application. Finally, you applied techniques to further specify the information needed and to limit the volume of data returned to your mobile application in accordance with mobile application best practices. In the next chapter you learn how to consume these services to populate your mobile application with the information critical to your users.

Consuming Data Services

WHAT'S IN THIS CHAPTER?

- Initiating web transactions
- Working disconnected
- Exploring device resource considerations

The previous chapter showed you how to create REST and SOAP services to provide web-based data functionality. From retrieving data (GETs) to saving data (PUTs and POSTs) to deleting it (DELETEs), you perform the functions by consuming these data services.

This chapter provides you with a detailed introduction to RESTful consumption of data services and explains how to ensure that the data your mobile application requires to run correctly is available, even when your network connection isn't available. The chapter also discusses device resource considerations to keep in mind when devising a caching scheme for storing data locally.

INITIATING RESTFUL TRANSACTIONS

The RESTful services described in the previous chapter present the opportunity for an application to interact with centralized data and functionality that resides on the server. You can call these services from the mobile applications (that is, the consumers of the services) via RESTful web transactions.

These RESTful transactions support each data entity (or business object) to be operated upon in multiple ways via a single Uniform Resource Identifier (URI), aka a RESTful interface. You can accomplish this through the use of HTTP Request Methods or RESTful verbs. There are several RESTful verbs that specifically focus on basic data interactions. Table 8-1 summarizes the verbs covered in this chapter.

TABLE 8-1: RESTful Verbs

UTILITY	DESCRIPTION
GET	Requests information from the RESTful service, such as an object or list
DELETE	Requests the RESTful service to remove a particular object
POST	Submits a new object to the RESTful service; also refers generically to submitting information to the service
PUT	Submits an updated object to the RESTful service

In simple terms, GETs are about obtaining information from the server and POSTs, PUTs, and DELETEs are about sending information back to the server. All these commands can operate on the same URI, and the actual operation performed is dependent on the type of verb used when calling the RESTful service.

This chapter uses many samples, and to keep them as simple as possible, much of the potentially repetitious code has been extracted into reusable methods to enable you to focus on the web transactions. Table 8-2 summarizes the `WebHelpers` methods used in this chapter's samples.

TABLE 8-2: WebHelpers Methods

UTILITY	DESCRIPTION
`ByteArrayToStr`	Converts a `byte[]` to a `string`
`DeserializeJson<T>`	Deserializes a JSON `string` or `byte[]` into an `object` of type T
`DeserializeXml<T>`	Deserializes an XML `string` or `byte[]` into an `object` of type T
`DirectoryName`	Returns the expected directory name of a given file path `string`
`ReadFromFile<T>`	Reads the contents from a file, deserializes them, and returns an `object` of type T
`StreamToByteArray`	Converts a `stream` into a `byte[]`
`StreamToString`	Converts a `stream` into a `string`
`StrToByteArray`	Converts a `string` into a `byte[]`
`WriteToFile<T>`	Serializes an `object` of type T and then writes contents to a file
`XmlSerializeObjectToBytes`	Serializes an `object` to XML and then converts results to a `byte[]`

Each of these methods simplifies the code samples so you can focus on the concepts presented by each sample. These methods are not the only ways to abstract and generalize repetitious code, but they serve as a starting point for your development efforts. Listing 8-1 contains the code implementation for the `WebHelpers` class whose methods appear in this chapter's samples.

Available for download on Wrox.com

LISTING 8-1: WebHelpers class implementation

```
// helpful utilities for processing web calls.
public class WebHelpers
{
  // Serializes an object into a byte array
  public static byte[] XmlSerializeObjectToBytes(object obj)
  {
    byte[] byteData = null;

    MemoryStream stream = new MemoryStream();

    XmlSerializer ser = new XmlSerializer(obj.GetType());
    XmlWriter writer = null;
    try
    {
      writer = XmlWriter.Create(stream, new XmlWriterSettings()
      {
        Encoding = Encoding.UTF8
      });

      ser.Serialize(stream, obj);
      byteData = stream.ToArray();
    }
    finally
    {
      if (writer != null)
        writer.Close();
    }

    return byteData;
  }

  // Converts a string to a byte array
  public static byte[] StrToByteArray(string str)
  {
    System.Text.UTF8Encoding encoding = new System.Text.UTF8Encoding();
    return encoding.GetBytes(str);
  }

  // Converts a byte array to a string
  public static string ByteArrayToStr(byte[] byteData)
  {
    try
    {
      Encoding enc = Encoding.GetEncoding("utf-8");
      return enc.GetString(byteData, 0, byteData.Length);
    }
    catch
```

continues

LISTING 8-1 *(continued)*

```
    {
      // swallow exception if cannot convert to UTF8 string.
    }

    return null;
  }

  // Converts a stream into a byte array
  public static byte[] StreamToByteArray(Stream stream)
  {
    byte[] buffer = new byte[32768];
    using (MemoryStream ms = new MemoryStream())
    {
      while (true)
      {
        int read = stream.Read(buffer, 0, buffer.Length);
        if (read <= 0)
          return ms.ToArray();
        ms.Write(buffer, 0, read);
      }
    }
  }

  // Converts a stream into a string
  public static string StreamToString(Stream stream)
  {
    byte[] responseBytes = WebHelpers.StreamToByteArray(stream);
    return WebHelpers.ByteArrayToStr(responseBytes);
  }

  // XML deserialize to object
  public static T DeserializeXml<T>(Stream stream)
  {
    return (T)new XmlSerializer(typeof(T)).Deserialize(stream);
  }
  // XML deserialize to object
  public static T DeserializeXml<T>(string value)
  {
    return (T)new XmlSerializer(typeof(T)).Deserialize(new StringReader(value));
  }

  // JSON deserialize to object
  public static T DeserializeJson<T>(Stream stream)
  {
    // Uses NewtonSoft.Json http://james.newtonking.com/projects/json-net.aspx
    return JsonConvert.DeserializeObject<T>(WebHelpers.StreamToString(stream));
  }

  // JSON deserialize to object
  public static T DeserializeJson<T>(string value)
  {
    // Uses NewtonSoft.Json (http://james.newtonking.com/projects/json-net.aspx)
```

```
      return JsonConvert.DeserializeObject<T>(value);
    }

    public static void WriteToFile<T>(T obj, string filename)
    {
      byte[] bytes = WebHelpers.XmlSerializeObjectToBytes(obj);
      string path = DirectoryName(filename);
      if (!Directory.Exists(path)) Directory.CreateDirectory(path);

      File.WriteAllBytes(filename, bytes);
    }
    public static T ReadFromFile<T>(string filename)
    {
      if (!File.Exists(filename)) return default(T);
      return DeserializeXml<T>(File.ReadAllText(filename));
    }

    public static string DirectoryName(string filename)
    {
      if (string.IsNullOrEmpty(filename))
        return string.Empty;

      int idx = filename.LastIndexOf(System.IO.Path.DirectorySeparatorChar);

      if (idx > 0)
        return filename.Remove(idx);

      return string.Empty;
    }
  }
```

Found in the CustomerManagement.DataServices/CustomerManagement.Samples/ WebHelpers.cs file of the download

Performing RESTful GETs

You can use RESTful GET transactions to obtain information from the RESTful server so your mobile application can use them.

The following samples in this section illustrate how to consume RESTful Services starting with some simple GETs and expanding into more complex scenarios. Although these examples work for MonoCross applications, they are more general in nature, and you can use them to consume RESTful services in any C# application.

Listing 8-2 contains an implementation of a simple RESTful GET call.

Available for download on Wrox.com

LISTING 8-2: Simple GET implementation

```
/// Simple Synchronous GET call to make request and return the results in a string
public static string SimpleGet()
```

continues

LISTING 8-2 *(continued)*

```
{
  string uri = "http://localhost/MxDemo/products.xml";

  HttpWebRequest request = (HttpWebRequest)WebRequest.Create(uri);
  HttpWebResponse response = (HttpWebResponse)request.GetResponse();

  if (response.StatusCode != HttpStatusCode.OK) return null;

  return WebHelpers.StreamToString(response.GetResponseStream());
}
```

Found in the CustomerManagement.DataServices/CustomerManagement.Samples/ RESTfulGet.cs file of the download

As you can see, you can initiate a simple GET call to obtain a list of products from the RESTful server with just a few short lines of code. It's simple; you specify the URI to call, make the request to the URI, obtain the response, and return it back to the calling function.

Listing 8-3 shows the Product list output in XML.

LISTING 8-3: GET call results in XML format

```
<?xml version="1.0" encoding="utf-8"?>
<ArrayOfProduct xmlns:xsd="http://www.w3.org/2001/XMLSchema"
 xmlns:xsi="http://www.w3.org/2001/XMLSchema-instance">
  <Product>
    <ID>1000</ID>
    <Description>This is a basic Widget.</Description>
    <Price>100.00</Price>
  </Product>
</ArrayOfProduct>
```

Sample GET response represented in XML format

Now, if your data format is in JSON rather than XML, then the same GET method works with a simple change to the URI, as shown in Listing 8-4.

Available for download on Wrox.com

LISTING 8-4: Simple JSON GET implementation

```
// Simple Synchronous GET call to make request
// and return the results in a JSON string
public static string SimpleGetJson()
{
```

```
    string uri = "http://localhost/MxDemo/products.json";

    HttpWebRequest request = (HttpWebRequest)WebRequest.Create(uri);
    HttpWebResponse response = (HttpWebResponse)request.GetResponse();

    if (response.StatusCode != HttpStatusCode.OK) return null;

    return WebHelpers.StreamToString(response.GetResponseStream());
}
```

Found in the CustomerManagement.DataServices/CustomerManagement.Samples/ RESTfulGet.cs file of the download

Listing 8-5 shows that the results returned are now in JSON format.

LISTING 8-5: GET Call Results in JSON Format


```
[
  {  "Description":"This is a basic Widget."
   , "ID":"1000"
   , "Manufacturer":null
   , "Price":100.00
  }
]
```


Sample GET response represented in JSON format

You can change the URI to accommodate more than just whether the format is XML or JSON. You can use the URI to accommodate more complex RESTful endpoints that contain parameters in the URI Path or the URI Query. Following are just a few of the possible more complex URIs:

```
http://localhost/MxDemo/customers/7.xml
http://localhost/MxDemo/orders/1/10002.json
http://localhost/MxDemo/customers.xml?filter=Altera&page=0&items=0
```

Listing 8-6 shows an implementation of a GET that uses parameters in the URI.

LISTING 8-6: Simple GET with Parameter Implementation

Available for download on Wrox.com

```
// Simple Synchronous GET call to make request with a parameter
// and return the results in an XML string
public static string SimpleGetWithParameters(string customerId)
{
  string uri
    = string.Format("http://localhost/MxDemo/customers/{0}.xml", customerId);
```

continues

LISTING 8-6 *(continued)*

```
    HttpWebRequest request = (HttpWebRequest)WebRequest.Create(uri);
    HttpWebResponse response = (HttpWebResponse)request.GetResponse();

    if (response.StatusCode != HttpStatusCode.OK) return null;

    return WebHelpers.StreamToString(response.GetResponseStream());
  }
```

Found in the CustomerManagement.DataServices/CustomerManagement.Samples/ RESTfulGet.cs file of the download

It's easy to see how with just a few changes you can create methods to support any number of URIs, both with and without parameters.

Although creating a method to make a call to a specific URI works, you can certainly do better by creating a generalized GET method whose purpose is to return string results for any URI provided to it. And, you can add a little more exception handling to make the method more robust. If you want to use the URI object from .NET in place of a string, then the implementation would look a little different.

Listing 8-7 contains the implementation of these generalized GET methods.

Available for download on Wrox.com

LISTING 8-7: Generalized GET methods

```
// Generalized GET
public static string Get(string uri)
{
  if (string.IsNullOrEmpty(uri)) return null;
  if (!Uri.IsWellFormedUriString(uri, UriKind.RelativeOrAbsolute))
    return null;  // or log and/or throw an exception...

  HttpWebResponse response = null;
  try
  {
    HttpWebRequest request = (HttpWebRequest)WebRequest.Create(uri);
    response = (HttpWebResponse)request.GetResponse();

    if (response.StatusCode != HttpStatusCode.OK) return null;

    return WebHelpers.StreamToString(response.GetResponseStream());
  }
  catch (Exception exc)
  {
    Console.WriteLine("Error in getting data for URI " + uri);
    Console.WriteLine(exc.Message);
    return null;
  }
```

```
        finally
        {
          if (response != null)
            response.Close();
        }
      }

      // Generalized GET with URI Object
      public static string Get(Uri uri)
      {
        HttpWebResponse response = null;
        try
        {
          HttpWebRequest request = (HttpWebRequest)WebRequest.Create(uri);
          response = (HttpWebResponse)request.GetResponse();

          if (response.StatusCode != HttpStatusCode.OK) return null;

          return WebHelpers.StreamToString(response.GetResponseStream());
        }
        catch (Exception exc)
        {
          Console.WriteLine("Error in getting data for URI " + uri.OriginalString);
          Console.WriteLine(exc.Message);
          return null;
        }
        finally
        {
          if (response != null)
            response.Close();
        }
      }
```

Found in the CustomerManagement.DataServices/CustomerManagement.Samples/ RESTfulGet.cs file of the download

With such generalized GET methods, you can simplify your mobile application's RESTful service calls to a single line of code per call, as shown in the sample GET calls in Listing 8-8.

LISTING 8-8: Generalized GET sample usage

Available for download on Wrox.com

```
// Generalized GET method Usage Samples
public void GetMethodCalls()
{
  // calling Get method with String URI
  string results1 = RESTfulGet.Get("http://localhost/MxDemo/customers/7.xml");
  string results2 = RESTfulGet.Get("http://localhost/MxDemo/customers/7.json");
  string results3
    = RESTfulGet.Get("http://localhost/MxDemo/customers/7/contacts.xml");
```

continues

LISTING 8-8 *(continued)*

```
    string results4 = RESTfulGet.Get("http://localhost/MxDemo/orders/1/10002.xml");

    // calling Get method with URI object
    Uri uri1 = new Uri("http://localhost/MxDemo/customers/7.xml");
    string uriResults1 = RESTfulGet.Get(uri1);

    Uri uri2 = new Uri("http://localhost/MxDemo/customers/7.json");
    string uriResults2 = RESTfulGet.Get(uri2);

    Uri uri3 = new Uri("http://localhost/MxDemo/customers/7/contacts.xml");
    string uriResults3 = RESTfulGet.Get(uri3);

    Uri uri4 = new Uri("http://localhost/MxDemo/orders/1/10002.xml");
    string uriResults4 = RESTfulGet.Get(uri4);
}
```

Found in the CustomerManagement.DataServices/CustomerManagement.Samples/ RESTfulGet.cs file of the download

You considered a few basic approaches with the RESTful web service calls to obtain information from the server, but so far all the methods returned the results of the service call in the form of a string. The string, presumably, is to be operated on in some fashion, whether it is to write the output to a file, process an XML result via XSLT, or convert the string into a usable object, a process known as deserialization.

To deserialize the string into an object, you need to know the format of the string in question. That format is generally either XML or JSON; although, it could be in other formats as well. It's a simple matter to create a generic GET method that can both retrieve the data for the given URI string and return a fully populated object. Listing 8-9 contains a generic method that performs both of these tasks.

LISTING 8-9: Generic GET implementation

Available for download on Wrox.com

```
public static T Get<T>(string uriString)
{
  if (string.IsNullOrEmpty(uriString)) return default(T);
  if (!Uri.IsWellFormedUriString(uriString, UriKind.RelativeOrAbsolute))
    return default(T);  // or log and/or throw an exception...

  Uri uri = new Uri(uriString);

  HttpWebResponse response = null;
  try
  {
    HttpWebRequest request = (HttpWebRequest)WebRequest.Create(uri);
    response = (HttpWebResponse)request.GetResponse();
```

```
        if (response.StatusCode != HttpStatusCode.OK)
          return default(T);  // or error message...

        string path = uri.GetLeftPart(UriPartial.Path);
        Stream stream = response.GetResponseStream();

        // XML deserialization
        if (path.EndsWith("xml", StringComparison.InvariantCultureIgnoreCase))
          return WebHelpers.DeserializeXml<T>(stream);
        // JSON deserialization
        else if (path.EndsWith("json", StringComparison.InvariantCultureIgnoreCase))
          return WebHelpers.DeserializeJson<T>(stream);
        else
          return default(T);
      }
      catch (Exception exc)
      {
        Console.WriteLine("Error in getting data for URI " + uriString);
        Console.WriteLine(exc.Message);
        return default(T);
      }
      finally
      {
        if (response != null)
          response.Close();
      }
    }
```

Found in the CustomerManagement.DataServices/CustomerManagement.Samples/ RESTfulGet.cs file of the download

The `JsonConvert` class referred to in the Listing 8-9 is from the set of JSON.NET tools available at `http://james.newtonking.com/projects/json-net.aspx`, but you can certainly replace it with other JSON tools, if you prefer a different tool.

You can see from the listing, we have added basic validation and some simple exception handling to the RESTful GET call. Usage of this particular method is as simple as specifying the URI being called and the generic type being returned. Listing 8-10 shows some sample usage of this method.

LISTING 8-10: Generic GET method usage samples

Available for download on Wrox.com

```
// Generic GET Method Calls
public void GetMethodCallsGeneric()
{
  string uri1 = "http://localhost/MxDemo/products.xml";
  List<Product> listProd = RESTfulGet.Get<List<Product>>(uri1);

  string uri2 = "http://localhost/MxDemo/customers/7.xml";
  Company company = RESTfulGet.Get<Company>(uri2);
```

continues

LISTING 8-10 *(continued)*

```
    string uri3 = "http://localhost/MxDemo/orders/1.xml";
    List<Order> listOrder = RESTfulGet.Get<List<Order>>(uri3);

    string uri4 = "http://localhost/MxDemo/customers/7/contacts.xml";
    List<Contact> listContact = RESTfulGet.Get<List<Contact>>(uri4);

    string uri5 = "http://localhost/MxDemo/products.json";
    List<Product> listProd2 = RESTfulGet.Get<List<Product>>(uri5);

    string uri6 = "http://localhost/MxDemo/customers/7.json";
    Company company2 = RESTfulGet.Get<Company>(uri6);

    string uri7 = "http://localhost/MxDemo/orders/1.json";
    List<Order> listOrder2 = RESTfulGet.Get<List<Order>>(uri7);

    string uri8 = "http://localhost/MxDemo/customers/7/contacts.json";
    List<Contact> listContact2 = RESTfulGet.Get<List<Contact>>(uri8);
  }
```

Found in the CustomerManagement.DataServices/CustomerManagement.Samples/ RESTfulGet.cs file of the download

Synchronous methods to access RESTful data from a web service, such as those presented in Listing 8-10 are fairly straightforward, but they do have drawbacks. Synchronous methods block the primary processing while the RESTful calls are made rather than yielding the process to the primary thread. Asynchronous method calls, on the other hand, are slightly more complex to write, but they have the advantage of yielding the processing to a primary thread while the RESTful GET is performed.

You can think of it this way: suppose for a moment that you're talking to someone on the telephone and she needs to take care of something quickly. She can either put you on hold while she does whatever it is (that is, synchronous) and make you wait on the line until she completes the task, or she can call you back when the task has been completed (that is, asynchronous).

Listing 8-11 shows a sample class that illustrates how an asynchronous RESTful GET can be written.

LISTING 8-11: Asynchronous GET implementation

Available for download on Wrox.com

```
public class RESTfulGetAsynch
{
  private ManualResetEvent allDone;

  const int DefaultTimeout = 60 * 1000;  // default a 60 second timeout.

  public string Get(string uriString)
  {
    if (string.IsNullOrEmpty(uriString)) return null;
```

```
    if (!Uri.IsWellFormedUriString(uriString, UriKind.RelativeOrAbsolute))
      return null;  // or log and/or throw an exception...

    return GetAsynch(new Uri(uriString));
  }

  public string Get(Uri uri)
  {
    return GetAsynch(uri);
  }

  private string GetAsynch(Uri uri)
  {
    HttpWebRequest request = (HttpWebRequest)WebRequest.Create(uri);
    allDone = new ManualResetEvent(false);

    RequestState state = new RequestState()
    {
      Request = request,
      Uri = uri
    };

    // Start the asynchronous request.
    IAsyncResult result
      = request.BeginGetResponse(new AsyncCallback(ResponseCallback), state);
    if (!allDone.WaitOne(DefaultTimeout))
    {
      Console.WriteLine("Call to {0} timed out", state.Uri);
      return null;
    }

    if (!string.IsNullOrEmpty(state.ResponseString))
      return state.ResponseString;
    else
      return null;
  }

  private void ResponseCallback(IAsyncResult result)
  {
    // Get and fill the RequestState
    RequestState state = (RequestState)result.AsyncState;
    try
    {
      HttpWebRequest request = state.Request;

      // End the Asynchronous response and get the actual response object
      state.Response = (HttpWebResponse)request.EndGetResponse(result);

      state.Expiration = state.Response.Headers["Expires"].TryParseDateTimeUtc();
      state.StatusCode = state.Response.StatusCode;

      if (state.StatusCode != HttpStatusCode.OK)
      {
        Console.WriteLine("GET {0} had status {1}", state.Uri, state.StatusCode);
        return;
```

continues

LISTING 8-11 *(continued)*

```
        }

        state.ResponseString
          = WebHelpers.StreamToString(state.Response.GetResponseStream());
      }
      catch (Exception ex)
      {
        // capture relevant details about the request
        ex.Data.Add("Uri", state.Request.RequestUri);
        ex.Data.Add("Verb", state.Request.Method);

        if (ex is WebException)
        {
          HttpWebResponse response = (HttpWebResponse)((WebException)ex).Response;
          state.StatusCode = response.StatusCode;
          ex.Data.Add("StatusDescription", response.StatusDescription);
          ex.Data.Add("StatusCode", state.StatusCode);
        }
        else
          state.StatusCode = (HttpStatusCode)(-1);

        state.ErrorMessage = string.Format("GET {0} ", state.Request.RequestUri );
        state.ErrorMessage += string.Format("had Exception {1}", ex.Message);
        state.Exception = ex;
        state.Expiration = DateTime.UtcNow;

        // Log exception
      }
      finally
      {
        if (state.Response != null)
          state.Response.Close();
        state.Request = null;

        allDone.Set();
      }
    }

    public class RequestState
    {
      public Uri Uri { get; set; }
      public HttpWebRequest Request { get; set; }
      public HttpWebResponse Response { get; set; }
      public string ResponseString { get; set; }
      public DateTime Expiration { get; set; }
      public HttpStatusCode StatusCode { get; set; }
      public Exception Exception { get; set; }
      public string ErrorMessage { get; set; }
    }
  }
```

Found in the CustomerManagement.DataServices/CustomerManagement.Samples/ RESTfulGetAsynch.cs file of the download

Performing PUTs, POSTs, and DELETEs

Obtaining data from a server with a RESTful GET is only part of what clients need to consume a web service. Although getting the data from the server is important, you also need to consider how to send updates back to the RESTful server, whether those updates are to add a new invoice, to update a customer, or even to delete an address that is no longer needed.

You can send changes to the RESTful server with a `WebRequest`, just like the GET calls presented earlier, but you have the added steps of sending the new or updated information to the server (in the case of PUTs and POSTs) or simply requesting the removal of information (in the case of DELETEs).

Just like GETs, you can perform PUTs and POSTs either synchronously or asynchronously. Listing 8-12 shows an example of a synchronous post that you can use to submit web requests for both POSTs and PUTs.

LISTING 8-12: RESTful PUT/POST implementation

Available for download on Wrox.com

```
// Post information to server, POSTs and PUTs can use this method by specifying verb
public static PostReturn
  Post(Uri uri, byte[] postBytes, string contentType, string verb)
{
  // Create the request object
  HttpWebRequest request = (HttpWebRequest)WebRequest.Create(uri);

  // Set values for the request back
  request.Method = verb;
  request.ContentType = contentType;
  request.ContentLength = postBytes.Length;

  Stream postStream = null;

  HttpWebResponse response = null;
  Stream streamResponse = null;
  StreamReader streamRead = null;
  try
  {
    // obtain request stream from server to stream data to server
    postStream = request.GetRequestStream();
    postStream.Write(postBytes, 0, postBytes.Length);
    postStream.Close();

    response = (HttpWebResponse)request.GetResponse();

    PostReturn postReturn = new PostReturn()
      {
        StatusCode = response.StatusCode,
        Method = verb,
        Uri = uri
      };

    if (response.StatusCode != HttpStatusCode.OK)
```

continues

LISTING 8-12 *(continued)*

```
        {
          Console.WriteLine("{0}", verb, uri, response.StatusCode);
          postReturn.ResponseString = null;
          return postReturn;
        }

        // return response from server if any
        postReturn.ResponseString = WebHelpers.StreamToString(response.GetResponseStream());
        return postReturn;
      }
      catch (Exception ex)
      {
        ex.Data.Add("Uri", request.RequestUri);
        ex.Data.Add("Verb", request.Method);
        ex.Data.Add("ContentType", request.ContentType);
        ex.Data.Add("ContentLength", request.ContentLength);

        if (ex is WebException)
        {
          HttpWebResponse webResponse = (HttpWebResponse)((WebException)ex).Response;
          ex.Data.Add("StatusDescription", webResponse.StatusDescription);
          ex.Data.Add("StatusCode", webResponse.StatusCode);
        }

        Console.WriteLine("Error in getting data for URI " + uri);
        Console.WriteLine(ex.Message);
        // log exception data if desired...
        return null;
      }
      finally
      {
        if (postStream != null) postStream.Close();
        if (streamResponse != null) streamResponse.Close();
        if (streamRead != null) streamRead.Close();
        if (response != null) response.Close();
      }
    }
```

Found in the CustomerManagement.DataServices/CustomerManagement.Samples/ RESTfulPost.cs file of the download

You can use this example as-is to submit POSTs and PUTs to the RESTful web service. It simply takes in a URI and a byte array of a serialized object to POST.

Possible enhancements to this method include creating overloads that take in the object and serialize them to a byte array prior to posting, or even make the method call generic to allow for the return from the POST to be deserialized into an object.

This example doesn't just POST or PUT the data to the server; it also accepts a response back from the server. By convention, this response is the current state of the object after the server completes the POST or PUT. Listing 8-12 includes an object to contain the response from the POST calls to your server so that your mobile application can process them.

The `PostReturn` object is a simple Data Transfer Object that contains some basic information about the call and its results. The sample code simply uses this information to report on the status or to provide a string for deserializing returned objects for caching. If you need to track more properties for your application, simply add them to the `PostReturn` class. Listing 8-13 shows the implementation of the `PostReturn` class.

LISTING 8-13: PostReturn implementation

Available for download on Wrox.com

```
public class PostReturn
{
  public HttpStatusCode StatusCode { get; set; }
  public string ResponseString { get; set; }
  public Uri Uri { get; set; }
  public string Method { get; set; }
}
```

Found in the CustomerManagement.DataServices/CustomerManagement.Samples/PostReturn.cs file of the download

Using the `RESTfulPost` class is as simple as generating or obtaining an object, changing some property, and then sending the changes to the server via a single method call. Listing 8-14 shows a sample usage of the RESTfulPost class and `GenerateCompany` method, which you can use in this and future examples.

LISTING 8-14: RESTful PUT/POST usage example

Available for download on Wrox.com

```
public static string PostCompany()
{
  // get a new company record.
  Company company = GenerateCompany();

  // XML Seralize the company to a byte array for posting to server
  byte[] postBytes = WebHelpers.XmlSerializeObjectToBytes(company);

  // Create new URI
  Uri uri = new Uri("http://localhost/MxDemo/customers/company.xml");

  // post to server and return results if any.
  PostReturn results = Post(uri, postBytes, "application/xml", "POST");
  return results.ResponseString;
}

public static string PutCompany()
{
  // Obtain an existing company records
  Company company
```

continues

LISTING 8-14 *(continued)*

```
    = RESTfulGet.Get<Company>("http://localhost/MxDemo/customers/7.xml");

  // Make a change to the company record
  company.Name += " - Test Name Change";
  company.PrimaryPhone = "952-555-1212";

  // XML Seralize the company to a byte array for posting to server
  byte[] putBytes = WebHelpers.XmlSerializeObjectToBytes(company);

  // Create new URI
  Uri uri = new Uri("http://localhost/MxDemo/customers/company.xml");

  // post to server and return results if any.
  PostReturn results = Post(uri, putBytes, "application/xml", "PUT");
  return results.ResponseString;
}

public static Company GenerateCompany()
{
  Company company = new Company()
  {
    ID = "99",
    Name = "Tri Marine International, Inc.2",
    Website = "http://www.trimarinegroup.com",
    PrimaryPhone = "425-688-1288",
    PrimaryAddress = new Address()
    {
      ID = "99-a1",
      Description = "World Headquarters",
      Street1 = "10500 N.E. 8th St.",
      Street2 = "Ste. 1888",
      City = "Bellevue",
      State = "WA",
      Zip = "98004"
    },
    Addresses = new List<Address>()
    {
      new Address()
      {
        ID="99-a1",
        Description="World Headquarters",
        Street1="10500 N.E. 8th St.",
        Street2="Ste. 1888",
        City="Bellevue",
        State="WA",
        Zip="98004"
      }
    },
    Contacts = new List<Contact>()
    {
      new Contact()
      {
        ID="99-c1",
```

```
          FirstName="Renato",
          LastName="Curto",
          Title="Chairman and CEO",
          Email="renato.curto@trimarinegroup.com",
          OfficePhone="425-688-1288",
        },
        new Contact()
        {
          ID="99-c2",
          FirstName="Steve",
          LastName="Farno",
          Title="CFO",
          Email="steve.farno@trimarinegroup.com",
          OfficePhone="425-688-1288"
        }
      }
    };
    return company;
  }
```

Found in the CustomerManagement.DataServices/CustomerManagement.Samples/ RESTfulPost.cs file of the download

Just like the GET calls, you can perform the POSTs and PUTs both synchronously, as in the previous example, or asynchronously, as shown in Listing 8-15, which contains an asynchronous method for POSTing or PUTing data to a server.

LISTING 8-15: Asynchronous RESTful PUT/POST implementation

Available for download on Wrox.com

```
public class RESTfulPostAsynch
{
  private ManualResetEvent allDone = new ManualResetEvent(false);
  const int DefaultTimeout = 60 * 1000;

  private PostReturn Post(Uri uri, byte[] postBytes, string contentType, string verb)
  {
    RequestState state = new RequestState()
    {
      PostBytes = postBytes
    };

    HttpWebRequest request = (HttpWebRequest)WebRequest.Create(uri);

    request.Method = verb;
    request.ContentType = contentType;
    request.ContentLength = postBytes.Length;
    request.KeepAlive = false;

    state.Request = request;
```

continues

LISTING 8-15 *(continued)*

```
    // Start the asynchronous request.
    IAsyncResult result
      = request.BeginGetRequestStream(new AsyncCallback(RequestCallback), state);

    if (!allDone.WaitOne(DefaultTimeout))
    {
      Console.WriteLine("Call to {0} timed out", state.Uri);
      return null;
    }

    // return response from server if any
    PostReturn postReturn = new PostReturn()
    {
      StatusCode = state.StatusCode,
      ResponseString = state.ResponseString,
      Method = verb,
      Uri = uri
    };

    return postReturn;
  }

  private void RequestCallback(IAsyncResult asynchronousResult)
  {
    // Get and fill the RequestState
    RequestState state = (RequestState)asynchronousResult.AsyncState;
    HttpWebRequest request = state.Request;

    // End the operation
    Stream postStream = request.EndGetRequestStream(asynchronousResult);

    // Write to the request stream.
    postStream.Write(state.PostBytes, 0, state.PostBytes.Length);
    postStream.Close();

    // Start the asynchronous operation to get the response
    IAsyncResult result
      = request.BeginGetResponse(new AsyncCallback(ResponseCallback), state);
  }

  private void ResponseCallback(IAsyncResult result)
  {
    // Get and fill the RequestState
    RequestState state = (RequestState)result.AsyncState;
    try
    {
      HttpWebRequest request = state.Request;

      // End the Asynchronous response and get the actual response object
      state.Response = (HttpWebResponse)request.EndGetResponse(result);

      state.StatusCode = state.Response.StatusCode;
```

```
    if (state.StatusCode != HttpStatusCode.OK)
    {
      Console.WriteLine("{0} {1} had status {2}"
         , state.Request.Method, state.Uri, state.StatusCode);
      return;
    }

    state.ResponseString
      = WebHelpers.StreamToString(state.Response.GetResponseStream());
  }
  catch (Exception ex)
  {
    // capture relevant details about the request
    ex.Data.Add("Uri", state.Request.RequestUri);
    ex.Data.Add("Verb", state.Request.Method);

    if (ex is WebException)
    {
      HttpWebResponse response = (HttpWebResponse)((WebException)ex).Response;
      state.StatusCode = response.StatusCode;
      ex.Data.Add("StatusDescription", response.StatusDescription);
      ex.Data.Add("StatusCode", state.StatusCode);
    }
    else
      state.StatusCode = (HttpStatusCode)(-1);

    state.ErrorMessage = string.Format("{0} {1} "
                            , state.Request.Method, state.Request.RequestUri);
    state.ErrorMessage += string.Format("had Exception {0}", ex.Message);
    state.Exception = ex;
    state.Expiration = DateTime.UtcNow;

    // Log exception
  }
  finally
  {
    if (state.Response != null)
      state.Response.Close();
    state.Request = null;

    allDone.Set();
  }
}

public class RequestState
{
  public Uri Uri { get; set; }
  public HttpWebRequest Request { get; set; }
  public HttpWebResponse Response { get; set; }
  public string ResponseString { get; set; }
  public DateTime Expiration { get; set; }
  public HttpStatusCode StatusCode { get; set; }
  public Exception Exception { get; set; }
  public string ErrorMessage { get; set; }
  public byte[] PostBytes { get; set; }
```

continues

LISTING 8-15 *(continued)*

```
    }

    public static string PostCompanyAsynch()
    {
      // get a new company record.
      Company company = RESTfulPost.GenerateCompany();

      // XML Seralize the company to a byte array for posting to server
      byte[] postBytes = WebHelpers.XmlSerializeObjectToBytes(company);

      // Create new URI
      Uri uri = new Uri("http://localhost/MxDemo/customers/company.xml");

      // post to server and return results if any.
      RESTfulPostAsynch restfulPostAsynch = new RESTfulPostAsynch();

      PostReturn results
        = restfulPostAsynch.Post(uri, postBytes, "application/xml", "POST");
      return results.ResponseString;
    }

    public static string PutCompanyAsynch()
    {
      // Obtain an existing company records
      Company company
        = RESTfulGet.Get<Company>("http://localhost/MxDemo/customers/7.xml");

      // Make a change to the company record
      company.Name += " - Test Name Change";
      company.PrimaryPhone = "952-555-1212";

      // XML Seralize the company to a byte array for posting to server
      byte[] putBytes = WebHelpers.XmlSerializeObjectToBytes(company);

      // Create new URI
      Uri uri = new Uri("http://localhost/MxDemo/customers/company.xml");

      // post to server and return results if any.
      RESTfulPostAsynch restfulPostAsynch = new RESTfulPostAsynch();

      PostReturn results
        = restfulPostAsynch.Post(uri, putBytes, "application/xml", "PUT");
      return results.ResponseString;
    }

  }
```

Found in the CustomerManagement.DataServices/CustomerManagement.Samples/ RESTfulPostAsynch.cs file of the download

The last request method in this chapter is the RESTful DELETE. DELETEs are self-explanatory in that their purpose is to remove information that is no longer required. They are simpler to implement than GETs and POSTs because they neither send nor receive object information from the RESTful server.

All that you need to send a delete is the URI along with the HTTP verb of DELETE, as shown in the sample DELETE in Listing 8-16.

Available for download on Wrox.com

LISTING 8-16: Synchronous RESTful DELETE implementation

```
public static void Delete(Uri uri)
{
  // Create the request object
  HttpWebRequest request = (HttpWebRequest)WebRequest.Create(uri);

  // Set values for the request back
  request.Method = "DELETE";

  HttpWebResponse response = null;
  try
  {
    response = (HttpWebResponse)request.GetResponse();

    if (response.StatusCode != HttpStatusCode.OK)
      Console.WriteLine("{0} {1} returned status {2}"
                        , request.Method, uri, response.StatusCode);
  }
  catch (Exception ex)
  {
    ex.Data.Add("Uri", request.RequestUri);
    ex.Data.Add("Verb", request.Method);

    if (ex is WebException)
    {
      HttpWebResponse webResponse = (HttpWebResponse)((WebException)ex).Response;
      ex.Data.Add("StatusDescription", webResponse.StatusDescription);
      ex.Data.Add("StatusCode", webResponse.StatusCode);
    }

    Console.WriteLine("Error in deleting uri " + uri);
    Console.WriteLine(ex.Message);
    // log exception data if desired...
    return;
  }
  finally
  {
    if (response != null) response.Close();
  }
}
```

Found in the CustomerManagement.DataServices/CustomerManagement.Samples/ RESTfulDelete.cs file of the download

Use of the synchronous RESTful DELETE is as simple as creating the proper URI and calling the delete method, as shown in Listing 8-17.

LISTING 8-17: Synchronous RESTful DELETE usage sample

Available for download on Wrox.com

```
public static void DeleteCompany()
{
  Uri uri = new Uri("http://localhost/MxDemo/customers/9");
  RESTfulDelete.Delete(uri);
}
```

Found in the CustomerManagement.DataServices/CustomerManagement.Samples/ RESTfulDelete.cs file of the download

You can also asynchronously perform RESTful DELETEs, as shown in Listing 8-18.

LISTING 8-18: Asynchronous RESTful DELETE implementation

Available for download on Wrox.com

```
public class RESTfulDeleteAsynch
{
  private ManualResetEvent allDone;

  const int DefaultTimeout = 60 * 1000;  // default a 60 second timeout.

  private void Delete(Uri uri)
  {
    HttpWebRequest request = (HttpWebRequest)WebRequest.Create(uri);
    allDone = new ManualResetEvent(false);

    request.Method = "DELETE";

    RequestState state = new RequestState()
    {
      Request = request,
      Uri = uri
    };

    // Start the asynchronous request.
    IAsyncResult result
      = request.BeginGetResponse(new AsyncCallback(ResponseCallback), state);

    if (!allDone.WaitOne(DefaultTimeout))
    {
      Console.WriteLine("Delete {0} timed out", state.Uri);
      return;
    }

    return;
  }
```

```
private void ResponseCallback(IAsyncResult result)
{
  // Get and fill the RequestState
  RequestState state = (RequestState)result.AsyncState;
  try
  {
    HttpWebRequest request = state.Request;

    // End the Asynchronous response and get the actual response object
    state.Response = (HttpWebResponse)request.EndGetResponse(result);

    state.StatusCode = state.Response.StatusCode;

    if (state.StatusCode != HttpStatusCode.OK)
      Console.WriteLine("DELETE {0} had status {1}", state.Uri, state.StatusCode);

    return;
  }
  catch (Exception ex)
  {
    // capture relevant details about the request
    ex.Data.Add("Uri", state.Request.RequestUri);
    ex.Data.Add("Verb", state.Request.Method);

    if (ex is WebException)
    {
      HttpWebResponse response = (HttpWebResponse)((WebException)ex).Response;
      state.StatusCode = response.StatusCode;
      ex.Data.Add("StatusDescription", response.StatusDescription);
      ex.Data.Add("StatusCode", state.StatusCode);
    }
    else
      state.StatusCode = (HttpStatusCode)(-1);

    state.ErrorMessage = string.Format("DELETE {0} ", state.Request.RequestUri);
    state.ErrorMessage += string.Format("had Exception {0}", ex.Message);
    state.Exception = ex;

    // Log exception
  }
  finally
  {
    if (state.Response != null)
      state.Response.Close();
    state.Request = null;

    allDone.Set();
  }
}

public class RequestState
{
  public Uri Uri { get; set; }
  public HttpWebRequest Request { get; set; }
```

continues

LISTING 8-18 *(continued)*

```
        public HttpWebResponse Response { get; set; }
        public HttpStatusCode StatusCode { get; set; }
        public Exception Exception { get; set; }
        public string ErrorMessage { get; set; }
    }

}
```

Found in the CustomerManagement.DataServices/CustomerManagement.Samples/ RESTfulDeleteAsynch.cs file of the download

You can use the `RESTfulPost` class methods to perform the DELETE. This works but is more expensive because you serialize an object to be posted to the server. Depending on your RESTful service requirements, this may be necessary, for instance, in the case in which the service needs to inspect the object to confirm whether a delete is allowed.

In the preceding examples and discussion, you learned a lot about RESTful calls to the server so that your mobile application can have the data it needs to operate. All these examples carry the assumption that your mobile application is connected to the server and can carry out these calls. But connectivity isn't guaranteed, and your application needs to be prepared for those times when connectivity isn't available. The next section describes how to manage your data and corresponding interactions in a disconnected setting.

WORKING DISCONNECTED

Although the previous examples describe in detail how to make RESTful web requests to retrieve, update, and delete information, they all carry the same assumption: The user is connected to the network and has all Intranet/Internet access and connectivity needed for the application to run as designed. Whether the application is on a desktop connected to a LAN or a laptop connected via wireless at a local coffee shop, there's an assumption that the connection will be available when and how it's needed.

However, that assumption of connectedness is just that, an assumption; one that you shouldn't rely upon to a great extent. You could rewrite an old adage to reflect this notion. "All mobile users will be connected some of the time and some mobile users will be connected all of the time, but not all mobile users will be connected all the time."

Because connection cannot be guaranteed all the time, a mobile application developer has a couple options. One is for the application to simply not function completely when connections are not available. The other option is to write the application so that it can adequately function even when disconnected. The next section begins the discussion on when and how to cache data on the mobile applications.

Caching Data

Assume that the major need for connectedness is that the mobile applications use data obtained from a server, and specifically in these examples, a RESTful server. For a mobile application to function adequately when disconnected, it needs to have its data available for the user when and where the user needs it. After all, that's what mobile applications are for, right?

To meet this need, the mobile applications need to cache the data on the device so it's there when the user needs it, even if the connection isn't. Ultimately, consider two forms of caching for mobile applications: Volatile Cache and Persistent Cache, which are both detailed in Table 8-3.

TABLE 8-3: Mobile Device Cache Variants

CACHE TYPE	DESCRIPTION
Volatile Cache	Cache is maintained in the device's memory. It provides quicker access to the cached data at the expense of not persisting between application and/or device restarts.
Persistent Cache	Cache is maintained in the device's physical storage. It maintains the cached data between application and/or device sessions but doesn't perform as well.
No Cache	Cache is not maintained. This option is included to call attention to the idea that not all data should be cached.

Volatile Cache is stored in the memory of the device and persists cached data only while the mobile application runs and doesn't persist between application or device restarts. *Persistent Cache*, on the other hand, maintains cached data on the physical storage of the device so that it remains available between application sessions and device restarts. Although *No Cache* isn't actually a caching type per se, it is a necessary consideration because there are cases in which certain data does not need to be cached and indeed must be deliberately excluded from caching, depending on the mobile application's business constraints.

Standardizing Cache Interface

Because you can cache data on the device in many ways, standardize all the caching mechanisms with a common interface. This allows for changing out the caching mechanism by platform or by application while minimizing any impact to the business logic, especially if you program to the cache interface rather than any particular implementation.

For example, you most likely need to implement a file-system persistent cache differently on an iOS Touch platform than you would on an Android or Windows Phone 7 platform. This is because they each have unique requirements for storing files used by the application.

Caching Mobile Data In-Memory

Recall that one type of cache is Volatile Cache. It hangs around in memory for as long as the application is running. When the application stops, this type of memory goes away and needs to be re-created when the application restarts.

The primary advantage of Volatile Cache is that it is faster to retrieve data than other methods because the objects are currently instantiated and the cache simply returns a reference to the object.

Of course, this means that the objects in the volatile cache are actually consuming memory. This is not a problem for applications running on platforms with a lot of memory available. However, that doesn't apply to most mobile devices, where utilization and consumption of memory needs to be closely watched to prevent adverse impacts on the application, such as the operating system shutting down the application for using too much memory.

Listing 8-19 displays one possible implementation of a Volatile Cache.

Available for download on Wrox.com

LISTING 8-19: Volatile Cache implementation

```
public class VolatileCache
{
  Dictionary<string, Customer> _cache = new Dictionary<string, Customer>();

  public void Store(string key, Customer customer)
  {
    if (string.IsNullOrEmpty(key))
      throw new ArgumentNullException("key");

    _cache[key] = customer;
  }

  public Customer Fetch(string key)
  {
    if (string.IsNullOrEmpty(key))
      throw new ArgumentNullException("key");

    if (!_cache.ContainsKey(key))
      return null;

    return _cache[key];
  }

  public void Clear(string key)
  {
    if (string.IsNullOrEmpty(key))
      throw new ArgumentNullException("key");

    if (_cache.ContainsKey(key))
      _cache.Remove(key);
  }

  public void ClearCache()
  {
    _cache = new Dictionary<string, Customer>();
  }
}
```

Found in the CustomerManagement.DataServices/CustomerManagement.Samples/cache.cs file of the download

You can implement a volatile cache in many ways besides the one shown. For example, you could use a `List<Customer>` instead of a `Dictionary<string, Customer>` as the data type of the cache storage object in memory. Or you could use a custom cache key object in place of a string. Or... you get the idea.

Usage of the `VolatileCache` class is straightforward, as shown in Listing 8-20.

Available for download on Wrox.com

LISTING 8-20: Volatile Cache usage

```
public static void VolatileCacheSample()
{
  VolatileCache cache = new VolatileCache();
  Customer customer = RESTfulPost.GenerateCompany();

  // key could be any unique string like customer ID, or even the URL,
  // just so long as it is unique
  string key = customer.ID;

  // put item into cache directly
  cache.Store(key, customer);

  // get item from cache
  Customer customer2 = cache.Fetch(key);

  // remove item from cache
  cache.Clear(key);

  // clear entire cache
  cache.ClearCache();
}
```

Found in the CustomerManagement.DataServices/CustomerManagement.Samples/cache.cs file of the download

Caching Mobile Data Persistently

Storing data in volatile cache is all well and good until you actually have to restart the application, and then all the data in the volatile cache goes away in a puff of binary smoke. This can leave the mobile application without the data it needs to function properly, especially if the fickle network connection happens to be unavailable at the same time.

This leaves your applications with a need for a more durable cache storage mechanism, a persistent cache. You can implement the persistent cache in several different ways. You can write it as a simple file storage writing and reading class, which contains its own variations per platform. You can add it to a volatile cache implementation to save the cached data for later restoration after an application restart. You can even write it as a front end to a mobile device data storage database application, such as SQLite, or even a mobile database that you developed.

Listing 8-21 displays one possible implementation of a persistent cache using a simple file storage approach.

Available for download on Wrox.com

LISTING 8-21: Persistent Cache implementation

```
public class PersistentCache
{
  private static string
    RootPath = Environment.GetFolderPath(Environment.SpecialFolder.Personal);
  private static string CachePath = Path.Combine(RootPath, "MobileCache");

  private string FileName(string key)
  {
    // file path is {CachePath}\{type}\{key}
    return Path.Combine(CachePath, "Customer", key);
  }

  public void Store(string key, Customer item)
  {
    if (string.IsNullOrEmpty(key))
      throw new ArgumentNullException("key");

    WebHelpers.WriteToFile<Customer>(item, FileName(key));
  }

  public Customer Fetch(string key)
  {
    if (string.IsNullOrEmpty(key))
      throw new ArgumentNullException("key");

    return WebHelpers.ReadFromFile<Customer>(FileName(key));
  }

  public void Clear(string key)
  {
    if (string.IsNullOrEmpty(key))
      throw new ArgumentNullException("key");

    File.Delete(FileName(key));
  }

  public void ClearCache()
  {
    string path = WebHelpers.DirectoryName(FileName(string.Empty));

    if (Directory.Exists(path))
      Directory.Delete(path, true);
  }
}
```

Found in the CustomerManagement.DataServices/CustomerManagement.Samples/cache.cs file of the download

Usage of the persistent cache sample is the same as the volatile cache usage with the simple replacement of the `cache` variable to a new `PersistentCache` object rather than a `VolatileCache` object, as shown in Listing 8-22.

LISTING 8-22: Persistent Cache usage

```
public static void PersistentCacheSample()
{
  PersistentCache cache = new PersistentCache();
  Customer customer = RESTfulPost.GenerateCompany();

  // key could be any unique string like customer ID, or even the URL,
  // just so long as it is unique
  string key = customer.ID;

  // put item into cache directly
  cache.Store(key, customer);

  // get item from cache
  Customer customer2 = cache.Fetch(key);

  // remove item from cache
  cache.Clear(key);

  // clear entire cache
  cache.ClearCache();
}
```

Found in the CustomerManagement.DataServices/CustomerManagement.Samples/cache.cs file of the download

Securing Mobile Data (Encryption)

When you cache data onto a file system so it can persist between application sessions, you need to consider the value of the data and what you should do to protect it.

If you need to store sensitive enterprise data, you need to manage two different basic threats to that data. The first threat you need to manage is to prevent unauthorized access to the data (that is, prevent theft of the data). The second is to prevent unauthorized changes to the data (that is, prevent tampering with the data).

You can handle both of these objectives via encryption. If your mobile device hardware supports it, you can encrypt the data stored at a file-system level. Or, when you write your persistent cache objects, you can encrypt the files when they are written to the file system and decrypt them when they are needed. This adds to the overhead of the caching, but the trade-off is better protection of the data.

The stronger encryption/decryption algorithms (such as AES-256) utilize a combination of a key and salt to make cracking the encryption considerably more difficult. This however leads to an inescapable question of where to store the key and salt so they can be used for encryption.

You could store the data on the RESTful server and give it to the application only when an HTTPS call can be safely made. But wait, that defeats the purpose of caching the data in the first place because there is little value in caching data that you can access only while connected.

Or, you could store the key and salt on the device so it's available for decrypting the cached data. Then, however, you run into the problem of how to protect the key and salt. You can't store it in plain text because that's like giving the keys to the kingdom to anyone who can find the file. So what do you do? One solution is to use a second level of encryption to protect the key and salt and base the secondary key and salt on device-level information (such as a device hardware ID) combined with a known user ID or password/PIN that the user must enter.

Another consideration to protect the data is that you may have multiple users of the same mobile device. Normally, you would expect just one user, but suppose a few sales reps meet at a convention for coffee (or drinks; they are sales reps after all). One rep needs to confirm that a particular sale was fulfilled. Having a single primary key for the application is no longer sufficient if you need to isolate one user's set of data from another's. It's also worthwhile to provide each user with a separate and distinct encryption key and salt so that if one of the users' information is compromised, the other users' information is still protected.

Not Caching Mobile Data

This chapter covers a lot about caching data so it's available whenever and wherever you need it. So, it would seem a logical thought that you would need to cache everything on the device all the time. Who wouldn't want to have all their data at their fingertips regardless of whether their device is connected? Sounds like the best of all possible worlds, doesn't it?

Not so fast. You see, there are many times in which it doesn't make sense to cache data on the device, or rather, where it makes sense to NOT cache the data.

First, there are obvious device limitations in terms of memory and storage space that you need to manage. We cover those limitations later in this chapter.

Secondly, the data might be of such a sensitive and classified nature that the risk is too high to cache the data even if it's protected by encryption. This might include the information that poses a competitive risk, such as customer account information or sales data, perhaps. It might also include financial information that might have legal or regulatory compliance requirements.

In the medical industry, for example, patient information is sacrosanct. With the Health Insurance Portability and Accountability Act (HIPAA) requirements, only those people who need to know a person's health information are allowed to know it. Failing to meet this requirement can come at a serious cost in the form of fines and lawsuits to any company storing this information inappropriately. Some hospitals forbid the storage of patient information on any mobile device allowed on their premises, regardless of how well the data may be encrypted.

You need to carefully consider the type of information you want to cache and take into account any business and legal ramifications before caching data on mobile devices.

Queuing Data to Server

This chapter provided much discussion around how and when to cache data so mobile applications can have data when and where it is needed. However, having the data available is only part of what is required for mobile applications to run when disconnected.

The other part is how to save the data and post changes back the server, whether it's adding a new company object, changing the price of a product, or removing an order that is no longer required. There needs to be a way to send the information back to the RESTful server.

Yes, this is what RESTful POSTs and PUTs are for. However, if your network connection is not active, then you still need a means to store any changes on a mobile device until a network connection is available for them to be POSTed to the server.

You can accomplish this in C# by using a `Queue<T>` to hold the data and then process each item on the `Queue<T>` while the connections are active. When connections aren't active, the queue processing should halt until the connection resumes.

You can retrigger the queue processing in several ways. You can use a `System.Timer` and regularly trigger the queue processing. Although the `System.Timer` approach works well, it has the drawback of its associated overhead. If your application is queuing only one or two data types, then you'd have one or two system timers running, but if you are queuing a couple dozen objects, you would then have a couple dozen `Timer` threads running, which would be a drain on the application's performance (and on the device's battery) due to the extra processing. Of course, you could also create a scenario in which you could manage all the queues from a single thread, which would also work.

It's worth considering a simpler option of starting the queue processing every time a new item is added to the queue and also when the mobile application restarts. These approaches are simple to implement and work quite well, even in an enterprise production setting. The trade-off with this approach is that while there is less overhead, there's also a potential for the posting to wait a longer time for the next data change or application restart. But remember, when talking about disconnected data, you cannot predict when the connection will return, so that might not be as big a drawback as it would seem otherwise. Take into account how reliable your connectivity is and consider adding an event handler that executes when the network reconnects.

The following samples of the `CustomerQueue` trigger the queue processing when a new item is added and provide a method to call when the application restarts. Listing 8-23 displays the implementation of the `CustomerQueue` class.

LISTING 8-23: CustomerQueue implementation

Available for download on Wrox.com

```
public class CustomerQueue
{
  Queue<Customer> _queue = new Queue<Customer>();
  private object _lock = new object();

  // set up events for response.
```

continues

LISTING 8-23 *(continued)*

```
    public delegate void PostComplete(PostReturn postReturn);
    public event PostComplete OnPostComplete;

    public bool Enabled { get; set; }

    public void PostItem(Customer customer)
    {
      lock (_lock)
      {
        _queue.Enqueue(customer);
      }
      ProcessQueue();
    }

    // process queue
    public void ProcessQueue()
    {
      // ProcessQueue queue items and only serialize queue when there
      // is an error and the processing is halted.
      HttpStatusCode statusCode;
      bool exitLoop = false;

      // if not enabled, then serialize the queue and return
      if (!Enabled)
      {
        SerializeQueue();
        return;
      }

      lock (_lock)
      {
        int qCount = _queue.Count;
        if (qCount <= 0) return;

        while (_queue.Count > 0 && !exitLoop)
        {
          Customer nextCustomer = _queue.Peek();

          if (nextCustomer == null)
          {
            _queue.Dequeue();
            continue;
          }

          try
          {
            statusCode = PostRequest(nextCustomer);

            if (statusCode == HttpStatusCode.OK)
            {
              // post was successful, remove customer from queue
              _queue.Dequeue();
            }
```

```
          else
          {
            // post not successful.
            Console.WriteLine("POST Customer returned status {0}", statusCode);
            _queue.Dequeue();
          }

        }
        catch (Exception exc)
        {
          // Log exception
          Console.WriteLine("Customer Post encountered exception {0}", exc.Message);
        }
      }
      SerializeQueue();
    }
  }


  private HttpStatusCode PostRequest(Customer customer)
  {
    byte[] postBytes = WebHelpers.XmlSerializeObjectToBytes(customer);

    Uri uri = new Uri("http://localhost/MxDemo/customers/customer.xml");
    PostReturn postReturn
      = RESTfulPost.Post(uri, postBytes, "application/xml", "POST");

    // handle post return as needed. XML used for example
    Customer customerReturn = null;
    if (!string.IsNullOrEmpty(postReturn.ResponseString))
      customerReturn = WebHelpers.DeserializeXml<Customer>(postReturn.ResponseString);

    // post return to the post complete event
    if (OnPostComplete != null)
      OnPostComplete(postReturn);

    return postReturn.StatusCode;
  }

  private readonly string QueueFileName
    = Path.Combine(Environment.GetFolderPath(Environment.SpecialFolder.Personal),
                                              "Queue", "Customer_queue.xml");

  // serialize queue, convert to List for Serialization
  public void SerializeQueue()
  {
    lock (_lock)
    {
      if (_queue.Count > 0)
        WebHelpers.WriteToFile<List<Customer>>(_queue.ToList(), QueueFileName);
      else
        File.Delete(QueueFileName);
    }
  }
```

continues

LISTING 8-23 *(continued)*

```
    // deserialize queue,
    public void DeserializeQueue()
    {
      lock (_lock)
      {
        List<Customer> queuelist
          = WebHelpers.ReadFromFile<List<Customer>>(QueueFileName);

        if (queuelist == null)
          return;

        queuelist.ForEach(_queue.Enqueue);
      }
    }

    // remove queue file,
    public void DeleteQueue()
    {
      lock (_lock)
      {
        File.Delete(QueueFileName);
      }
    }
  }
```

Found in the CustomerManagement.DataServices/CustomerManagement.Samples/queue.cs file of the download

The `CustomerQueue` class is responsible for storing objects until they get POSTed. To preserve the data between application sessions and reboots, the items on the queue are serialized to the file system, so they're available for deserialization when needed. Also, there are controls to allow the consuming methods to determine when the queue processing is allowed.

Depending on the response returned from the server, sometimes the item is removed from the queue. For successful postings, the item is removed to make room for any subsequent items to be POSTed next. If there is an error connecting to the server, it doesn't remove the item from the queue but does halt the queue processing, so the system doesn't continually retry to post data when the servers are unavailable, for example. The remaining errors assume that the posting was rejected by the RESTful server and thus get removed. All POST attempts call the `OnPostComplete` event so that any calling application can respond as needed.

Listing 8-24 shows a sample method for how to use the `CustomerQueue` class and process the response from the server.

LISTING 8-24: Sample usage of the CustomerQueue class

Available for download on Wrox.com

```
public class QueueSample
{
  public static void PostQueueSample()
  {
```

```
        // create new customer Queue
        CustomerQueue queue = new CustomerQueue();

        // subscribe to Post Complete event.
        queue.OnPostComplete += new CustomerQueue.PostComplete(queue_OnPostComplete);

        // obtain customer object
        Customer customer
          = RESTfulGet.Get<Customer>("http://localhost/MxDemo/customers/1.xml");

        // make a simple change
        customer.Name += " - Test";

        // post change to customer object
        queue.PostItem(customer);

        // start queue processing
        queue.ProcessQueue();
      }

      static void queue_OnPostComplete(PostReturn postReturn)  {
        Console.WriteLine("{0} to {1}", postReturn.Method, postReturn.Uri.AbsoluteUri);
        Console.WriteLine("returned status {0}", postReturn.StatusCode);
        Console.WriteLine("With the following results:");
        Console.WriteLine(postReturn.ResponseString);
      }
    }
```

Found in the CustomerManagement.DataServices/CustomerManagement.Samples/queue.cs file of the download

DEVICE RESOURCE CONSIDERATIONS

This chapter covered a lot about making RESTful calls and keeping the data cached so that the applications can work properly even while disconnected from the network and servers. So, all you need to do is simply download and cache every object that you might possibly need so that all the data for every conceivable need is at your fingertips at all possible times, right?

Definitely not!

Today's mobile devices have problems similar to the original personal computers in that their resources are limited. Resources such as memory and network bandwidth are certainly more constrained on mobile devices than the modern PCs.

Mobile devices, whether iPads or Androids, monitor memory usage closely. Even when your application is well behaved in terms of memory consumption, the OS closes your application if it's been idle and the device thinks the memory your application is using is needed elsewhere. Of course, if your application consumes too much memory, the devices won't think twice before closing your application.

Depending on where your mobile device is, the wireless connection may be sketchy at best, and the edge bandwidth on 3G isn't always the fastest. So you need to minimize the size and quantity of objects you download and ensure the objects that you do download contain only those fields and properties essential for the applications to function. Downloading data that you don't need only consumes excess memory and slows down the performance of the network calls.

Managing Memory/File System Consumption

Each mobile device has its own set of memory specifications, and instead of delving into the specifics of each device, in this section we review some principles for managing memory. These are principles you've heard before, of course, but they are still worth mentioning.

- Keep your objects as small as possible. Include only the details you need, not those that you might need at a later date.
- Add details to your objects only when they are needed.
- Create the objects only when you need them, and then allow them to go out of scope as soon as you finish with them.
- Restrict the scope of variables to the smallest scope possible. Use local variables rather than class variables, especially if the object is going to be around for awhile.
- Be extra vigilant about memory leaks.

Managing Network Bandwidth

Although there is little your application can do to improve the performance of the network connections, consider a few ideas about how you can use that scarce network bandwidth.

Two primary strategies for managing the network bandwidth are to simply reduce the size and the frequency of the download. The smaller the payload of the service call, the less time it takes to complete. So, limit your lists of objects to only those items needed to present the list in the application, and reserve more detailed information for the individual objects in their separate calls.

In addition, you should limit the size of the lists to only what you need for the application to function. This could include filtering search result sets on the server or just sending one page of results at a time.

If an application requires a large set of data, then focus on shrinking the data to as small as possible. Although XML is useful, perhaps you can consider using pipe-delimited strings instead of XML records. (Yes, that's rather old school, but it *is* smaller.)

Another option is to use the compression utilities built into the `WebRequest` calls. `WebRequest` calls can support `GZIP` and `Deflate` compression using the `AutomaticDecompression` property. These compression types are expressed in the `enum DecompressionMethods`.

Often the most effective means to reduce network consumption is simply to exclude details that are not absolutely essential to the function of the application. If you're in doubt about including a particular data item in your service call, just remember the YAGNI principle: You Aren't Going To Need It. Okay, so you might, but be certain to establish the clear need for an item before burdening your application with it.

SUMMARY

In this chapter, you learned how to make RESTful calls from your mobile applications and how to obtain data, modify it, and send the changes back to the RESTful servers. In addition, you learned how to cache the data so that it's available even if the network connection to the server is unavailable so that your mobile applications can still function correctly even while disconnected.

In the next chapter, you learn more about how to code for device-specific functions, such as audio, camera, and geo-location.

9 Accessing the Device

WHAT'S IN THIS CHAPTER:

- Understanding the common hardware on the devices
- Using input sensors
- Playing multimedia files within applications

Smartphones and tablets include a lot of sensors and information. You can enhance the capabilities of today's applications to include a personalized experience. Today's devices can detect where users are, their velocity of travel, and the contact closest to their current location. The devices include multiple types of messaging tools such as voicemail, text messaging (SMS/MMS), instant messengers such as Skype, video conferencing with FaceTime, and raw TCP/IP communication using WiFi or cellular data networks. Application developers can count on their users having sophisticated hardware in their hands. This chapter explores how to access and use the ever-advancing hardware and software capabilities of today's smartphones.

The mobile application ecosystems have produced many creative apps today. Dropbox and a dozen other cloud storage services have created applications for viewing, editing, and syncing your documents between PCs and mobile computing devices. Services such as Evernote have sprung up to give users seamless integration of digital artifacts from brainstorming to note-taking sessions. Urbanspoon and other information delivery apps leverage location data to present prefiltered data based on location. Dragon Dictation and other voice recognition applications use a user's contacts to more accurately interpret speech, create messages, and initiate voice or text communications using the device's SMS or call functionality. And, with Nintendo being overtaken by both Android and iOS as the most popular gaming platforms, it's evident that accelerometers and multitouch touch screens demonstrate that user input is not limited to touching and typing. The opportunity to innovate with these new user-input capabilities appears limitless.

Many of today's devices come with touch-screen interfaces. Failing to include a touch screen has quickly become a huge detriment to gaining market share. However, eliminating the keyboard in lieu of a software keyboard remains a differentiator among mobile users; some users seek to buy a device with a physical keyboard, whereas others prefer devices with no hard keyboard.

Although keyboard input preferences differ among users, they all want quick and intuitive interactions. When designing user input strategies, one of the driving questions should be, "How can I eliminate clicks and text entry?" Developers can leverage the audio, video, geo-location, and messaging capabilities, along with Personal Information Manager (PIM) information to accelerate interaction with the device.

Beyond creating new ways to interact with applications, the enhanced capabilities of modern model devices give application developers more options for in-app content and accessibility. Applications can use built-in speakers to play instructional audio. You can use the built-in cameras to capture videos and still images, which you can then manipulate in the application or send to servers for off-device utilization or messaging. You can use the accelerometer for clever device simulations such as mimicking a virtual medical device's reaction to the hand motions of a surgeon. The sensory input isn't just for gaming and virtual device simulation. You can use it for simple tasks such as controlling the scroll speed as the user reads lengthy text.

Geo-location is probably the most used of the modern user input sensors. A large percentage of popular applications use the GPS chip available in all cell-enabled mobile devices today. In social media apps, it provides a mechanism for users to share their location without having to key in the information. For retail stores, it enables customers to easily locate the nearest store and to get directions to the store from their current location, as well as providing store information such as hours of operation and contact information such as phone numbers and web addresses. For enterprise applications, the most common use has been to assist with customer lookup or digitally record the location of tasks performed within the application. With the race currently raging among different smartphone and tablet hardware manufacturers, it's generally safe to assume that any well-received input sensors introduced into one platform will soon find their way into devices on all the platforms.

UTILIZING DEVICE AUDIO AND VIDEO PLAYBACK CAPABILITIES

The initial uses of the audio and video capabilities have been playing music and capturing home video. Skype was the first to create a cross-platform video conferencing network that iOS, Android, and personal computers can use to participate. The Skype mobile applications demonstrate the capability of mobile devices to capture video and stream it in real time. That capability has been leveraged by many apps to capture and share videos — YouTube and Facebook are some of the most popular apps for video sharing. The camera has also been used in medical applications to capture video, manipulate it using complex algorithms, and display the altered video stream to help doctors analyze their patients' medical conditions.

WebEx and others have created networks through which participants can share screens and feed the handset's audio into a conference bridge. Line-of-business applications have included record-a-note features in which audio messages could be recorded, allowing feedback to be sent with less physical interaction on the mobile device.

Perhaps the most interesting approaches have been applications in which users can record audio and video that they can review to make shopping decisions or analyze performance. One app allows users to take a photo of themselves and then apply different apparel graphics over their image. This helps potential customers get a better virtual sense of how the product might look on them. Another, a sales coaching application, uses the audio functionality to capture practice sessions. The users record their best sales pitch and play it back to self-analyze their performance.

Capturing Audio

The audio capture code needs to reside in the individual view classes within your container projects. Each audio interface is particular to the platform and usually includes a user control onscreen that initiates the audio capture. For the purposes of demonstration, the following is a piece of code for capturing audio from each platform and storing it to an object or file that the controller and model code bases can work with.

iOS

iOS provides access to the device's microphone using the `MonoTouch.AVFoundation.AVAudioRecorder` object. The `AVAudioRecorder` can record for a specific duration or until the user stops it. The user then can pause and resume the recording as necessary. The object also reports input audio level data that the application can use.

Listing 9-1 shows a basic object you can use to record audio on an iOS device.

Available for download on Wrox.com

LISTING 9-1: Accessing the mic on iOS

```
using System;
using MonoTouch.AVFoundation;
using MonoTouch.Foundation;
using MonoTouch.AudioToolbox;
using System.IO;

namespace DeviceAccess
{
  class MicAccess
  {
    public MicAccess()
    {
      _mic = new AVAudioRecorder();
    }

    public void StartRecordingFroMic(string FilePath)
    {
      // set some default values for recording settings
      NSObject[] keys = new NSObject[]
            {
                AVAudioSettings.AVSampleRateKey,
                AVAudioSettings.AVFormatIDKey,
                AVAudioSettings.AVNumberOfChannelsKey,
                AVAudioSettings.AVEncoderAudioQualityKey,
```

continues

LISTING 9-1 *(continued)*

```
            };
        NSObject[] values = new NSObject[]
            {
                NSNumber.FromFloat(44100.0f),
                NSNumber.FromInt32((int)AudioFileType.WAVE),
                NSNumber.FromInt32(1),
                NSNumber.FromInt32((int)AVAudioQuality.Max),
            };
        NSDictionary settings = NSDictionary.FromObjectsAndKeys(values, keys);

        // define a filename and location for the output file
        string fileName = FilePath;
        string path =
          Path.Combine(Environment.GetFolderPath(Environment.SpecialFolder.Personal), fileName);
        outputFileUrl = NSUrl.FromFilename(path);

        // pass the configured url to the AVAudioRecorder object
        NSError error = new NSError();
        _mic = AVAudioRecorder.ToUrl(outputFileUrl, settings, out error);

        if (error != null)
        {
          // prepare and start recording
          _mic.PrepareToRecord();
          _mic.Record();
        }
        else
        {
          throw new Exception("Error loading mic: " + error.ToString());
        }
      }

      public void StopRecording()
      {
        _mic.Stop();

        // prepare object for GC by calling dispose
        _mic.FinishedRecording += delegate
        {
          _mic.Dispose();
          _mic = null;
        };
      }

      AVAudioRecorder _mic;
      private NSUrl outputFileUrl;
    }
  }
```

Found in the DeviceAccess/DeviceAccess.MT/MicAccess.cs file of the download

You can find API documentation at `http://developer.apple.com/library/ios/#DOCUMENTATION/AVFoundation/Reference/AVAudioRecorder_ClassReference/Reference/Reference.html`.

Android

The Android SDK provides access to the device's microphone using the `Android.Media.MediaRecorder` object. The object is configured with an audio source, audio file format, and audio file location. Much like the `AVAudioRecorder` object in iOS, Android's `MediaRecorder` object should be released as soon as the resource is no longer needed.

Listing 9-2 shows the same basic audio object written to work on the Android OS.

LISTING 9-2: Accessing the mic on Android

```
using Android.Media;

namespace DeviceAccess
{
  class MicAccess
  {
    public void StartRecordingFroMic(string FileName)
    {
      // set some default values for recording settings
      _mic.SetAudioSource(AudioSource.Mic);
      _mic.SetOutputFormat(OutputFormat.Default);
      _mic.SetAudioEncoder(AudioEncoder.Default);

      // define a filename and location for the output file
      _mic.SetOutputFile(FileName);

      // prepare and start recording
      _mic.Prepare();
      _mic.Start();
    }

    public void StopRecording()
    {
      // stop recording
      _mic.Stop();

      // prepare object for GC by calling dispose
      _mic.Release();
      _mic = null;
    }

    public MicAccess()
    {
      _mic = new MediaRecorder();
    }
    MediaRecorder _mic;
  }
}
```

Found in the DeviceAccess/DeviceAccess.MD/MicAccess.cs file of the download

You can find API documentation at `http://developer.android.com/guide/topics/media/audio-capture.html`.

Windows Phone 7

Windows Phone 7 provides access to the device's microphone through the `Microsoft.Xna.Framework.Audio.Microphone` object. Setting up a `Microphone` object correctly includes calling `FrameworkDispatcher.Update()` to manually dispatch messages in the XNA Framework update message queue. You can do this on a timer loop or hand it off to an object implementing the `IApplicationService` interface with a `DispatcherTimer` and a `Tick` event handler.

Listing 9-3 shows the same basic audio object written to work on Windows Phone 7 devices.

LISTING 9-3: Accessing the mic on Windows Phone 7

Available for download on Wrox.com

```
using System;
using System.IO;
using Microsoft.Xna.Framework.Audio;

namespace DeviceAccess
{
  public class MicAccess
  {
    public void StartRecordingFroMic(string FilePath)
    {
      // close memory steam if left open
      if (_memoryStream != null)
      {
        _memoryStream.Close();
      }

      // start a new memory stream
      _memoryStream = new MemoryStream();

      // start recording
      _mic.Start();
    }

    public void StopRecording()
    {
      // stop recording
      if (_mic.State != MicrophoneState.Stopped)
      {
        _mic.Stop();
      }

      // reset memory buffer
      _memoryStream.Position = 0;
    }

    void ProcessingBuffer(object sender, EventArgs e)
    {

      // read in read values
```

```
          byte[] buffer = new byte[4096];
          int bytesRead = _mic.GetData(buffer, 0, buffer.Length);

          // write and read mic buffer contents
          while (bytesRead > 0)
          {
            _memoryStream.Write(buffer, 0, bytesRead);
            bytesRead = _mic.GetData(buffer, 0, buffer.Length);
          }
        }

        public MicAccess()
        {
          _mic.BufferReady += ProcessingBuffer;
        }
        MemoryStream _memoryStream;
        Microphone _mic = Microphone.Default;
      }
    }
```

Found in the DeviceAccess/DeviceAccess.WP/MicAccess.cs file of the download

You can find API documentation at `http://msdn.microsoft.com/en-us/library/microsoft.xna.framework.audio.microphone.aspx`.

Playing Audio

Playing audio can be something an app does for several different reasons. An audible indicator can provide feedback for an invalid character, a successful touch event, or completion of a long data load. You can use audio for instructional purposes or as part of an on-screen product demonstration.

Playing sounds on the different platforms requires unique data calls. Because of this, the code must reside in the individual view classes implemented in each container. Listings 9-4, 9-5, and 9-6 provide some sample classes to help illustrate how each platform plays sounds.

iOS

You can play audio files from memory or via streaming using the `MonoTouch.AVFoundation.AVAudioPlayer` object. Apple provides APIs for playing sounds of any duration. You can loop the sound or merge it with several sounds. The API also includes data feedback for playback-level metering.

Listing 9-4 shows a basic audio object you can use to play sounds on iOS devices.

LISTING 9-4: Playing audio on iOS

Available for download on Wrox.com

```
using System;
using MonoTouch.Foundation;
using MonoTouch.AVFoundation;
```

continues

LISTING 9-4 *(continued)*

```
namespace DeviceAccess
{
  public class AudioAccess
  {
    public void StartAudioPlayback(string AudioFilePath)
    {
      NSError error = null;
      NSUrl audioFileUrl = NSUrl.FromFilename(AudioFilePath);
      _player = AVAudioPlayer.FromUrl(audioFileUrl, out error);
      if (_player != null)
      {
        _player.PrepareToPlay();
        _player.Play();
      }
      else
      {
        throw new Exception("Could not load Accelerometer sensor");
      }
    }

    public void StopAudioPlayback()
    {
      if (_player != null)
      {
        _player.Stop();
        _player.Dispose();
        _player = null;
      }
    }

    AVAudioPlayer Player
    {
      get
      {
        return _player;
      }
      set
      {
        _player = value;
      }
    }
    AVAudioPlayer _player;
  }
}
```

Found in the DeviceAccess/DeviceAccess.MT/AudioAccess.cs file of the download

You can find more information about the API at `http://developer.apple.com/library/IOS/#documentation/AVFoundation/Reference/AVAudioPlayerClassReference/Reference/Reference.html`.

Android

The Android OS SDK provides the `MediaManager` object to play sounds and videos from a variety of sources. You can use the `Android.Media.MediaPlayer` to view and manage the state machine, which is used for audio/video playback. If an error state occurs while playing the audio source, you need to either call the `MediaManager.Reset()` method or create a new `MediaManager` instance.

Listing 9-5 shows a basic audio object you can use to play sounds on an Android device.

LISTING 9-5: Playing audio on Android

Available for download on Wrox.com

```
using System;
using System.IO;
using Android.Media;

namespace DeviceAccess
{
  public class AudioAccess
  {
    public void StartAudioPlayback(string AudioFilePath)
    {
      // first stop any active audio on MediaPlayer instance
      if (_player != null) { StopAudioPlayback(); }

      _player = new MediaPlayer();
      if (_player != null)
      {
        _player.SetDataSource(AudioFilePath);
        _player.Prepare();
        _player.Start();
      }
      else
      {
        throw new Exception("Could not load MediaPlayer");
      }
    }

    public void StopAudioPlayback()
    {
      if (_player != null)
      {
        if (_player.IsPlaying)
        {
          _player.Stop();
        }

        _player.Release();
        _player = null;
      }
    }

    public void MultiMediaPlayer(String path, String fileName)
```

continues

LISTING 9-5 *(continued)*

```
      {
        //set up MediaPlayer
        MediaPlayer mp = new MediaPlayer();

        try
        {
          mp.SetDataSource(Path.Combine(path, fileName));
        }
        catch (Exception e)
        {
          Console.WriteLine("");
        }
        try
        {
          mp.Prepare();
        }
        catch (Exception e)
        {
          Console.WriteLine(e);
        }
        mp.Start();
      }

      MediaPlayer _player;
    }
  }
```

Found in the DeviceAccess/DeviceAccess.MD/AudioAccess.cs file of the download

You can find more information about the API at `http://developer.android.com/reference/android/media/MediaPlayer.html`.

Windows Phone 7

Windows Phone 7 can easily play sounds using the `Microsoft.Xna.Framework.Audio.SoundEffect` object. You can pass the audio source into the object using either a stream or a file path.

Listing 9-6 shows a snippet of code that can play a sound file on a Windows Phone 7 device.

Available for download on Wrox.com

LISTING 9-6: Playing audio on Windows Phone 7

```
using System.IO;
using Microsoft.Xna.Framework;
using Microsoft.Xna.Framework.Audio;

namespace DeviceAccess
{
  public static class AudioAccess
```

```
    {
      public static void StartAudioPlayback(string AudioFilePath)
      {
        Stream stream = TitleContainer.OpenStream(AudioFilePath);
        SoundEffect effect = SoundEffect.FromStream(stream);
        FrameworkDispatcher.Update();
        effect.Play();
      }
    }
}
```

Found in the DeviceAccess/DeviceAccess.WP/AudioAccess.cs file of the download

You can find more information about the API at `http://msdn.microsoft.com/en-us/library/microsoft.xna.framework.audio.soundeffect.aspx`.

Capturing Video

The camera functionality in today's smartphones makes them powerful for documenting events and presenting instructional content. A captured video can provide facial recognition, capture an image to better explain the layout of a physical space, or facilitate communication in countless other fashions. A picture *can* be worth a thousand words. Video capture is most popular in communication applications, but its uses are just starting to manifest themselves.

Following are some sample classes to provide a basic understanding for how video capture occurs on each platform.

iOS

The `AVCaptureSession` object can facilitate video capture. The `MonoTouch.AVFoundation.AVCaptureSession` object handles the flow of data from the audio and video inputs of the iOS device. You can use the `SessionPreset` property to customize the bit rate and quality levels. The `StartRunning()` and `StopRunning()` methods control the flow of data.

Listing 9-7 shows a simple object with the `AVCaptureSession` object configured and receiving video.

LISTING 9-7: Capturing video on iOS

Available for download on Wrox.com

```
using System;
using System.Collections.Generic;
using System.Linq;
using System.Text;
using MonoTouch.AVFoundation;
using MonoTouch.CoreMedia;
using MonoTouch.UIKit;
using MonoTouch.Foundation;
using MonoTouch.CoreVideo;

namespace DeviceAccess
```

continues

LISTING 9-7 *(continued)*

```
{
  class VideoRecorder
  {
    public void RecordVideoToPath(UIViewController ViewController, string VideoPath)
    {
      // set up capture device
      AVCaptureDevice videoRecordingDevice =
        AVCaptureDevice.DefaultDeviceWithMediaType(AVMediaType.Video);
      NSError error;
      AVCaptureDeviceInput videoInput = new
        AVCaptureDeviceInput(videoRecordingDevice, out error);

      // create and assign a capture session
      AVCaptureSession captureSession = new AVCaptureSession();
      captureSession.SessionPreset = AVCaptureSession.Preset1280x720;
      captureSession.AddInput(videoInput);

      // Create capture device output
      AVCaptureVideoDataOutput videoOutput = new AVCaptureVideoDataOutput();
      captureSession.AddOutput(videoOutput);
      videoOutput.VideoSettings.PixelFormat = CVPixelFormatType.CV32BGRA;
      videoOutput.MinFrameDuration = new CMTime(1, 30);
      videoOutput.SetSampleBufferDelegatequeue(captureVideoDelegate,
        System.IntPtr.Zero);

      // create a delegate class for handling capture
      captureVideoDelegate = new CaptureVideoDelegate(ViewController);

      // Start capture session
      captureSession.StartRunning();
    }
    CaptureVideoDelegate captureVideoDelegate;

    public class CaptureVideoDelegate : AVCaptureVideoDataOutputSampleBufferDelegate
    {
      private UIViewController _viewController;

      public CaptureVideoDelegate(UIViewController viewController)
      {
        _viewController = viewController;
      }

      public override void DidOutputSampleBuffer(AVCaptureOutput output,
        CMSampleBuffer buffer, AVCaptureConnection con)
      {
        //  Implement
        //  - see: http://go-
        //mono.com/docs/index.aspx?link=T%3aMonoTouch.Foundation.ModelAttribute
        //
      }
```

```
      }
    }
  }
```

Found in the DeviceAccess/DeviceAccess.MT/VideoRecorder.cs.cs file of the download

You can find more information about the API at `http://developer.apple.com/library/ios/#DOCUMENTATION/AVFoundation/Reference/AVCaptureSession_Class/Reference/Reference.html`.

Android

You can achieve video capture on Android devices using the same `MediaRecorder` object used for playing audio. By deviating just a bit from the original `AudioAndMicAccess` sample class in Listing 9-2, it is easy to include video recording. Recoding video requires many of the same configuration options, with a few additions, to be set on the `Android.Media.MediaRecorder` object.

Listing 9-8 provides the code necessary to capture video on Android devices.

LISTING 9-8: Capturing video on Android

Available for download on Wrox.com

```
using System;
using Android.App;
using Android.OS;
using Android.Views;
using Android.Media;

namespace DeviceAccess
{

  public class RecordVideo
  {
    public void RecordVideoToPath(SurfaceView Sv, string VideoPath)
    {
      // set up and configure recorder
      _mediaRecorder = new MediaRecorder();

      // set the input source
      _mediaRecorder.SetAudioSource(Android.Media.AudioSource.Mic);
      _mediaRecorder.SetVideoSource(Android.Media.VideoSource.Camera);

      // set encoding values
      _mediaRecorder.SetAudioEncoder(Android.Media.AudioEncoder.Default);
      _mediaRecorder.SetVideoEncoder(Android.Media.VideoEncoder.Default);

      // set the desirable preview display
      _mediaRecorder.SetPreviewDisplay(Sv.Holder.Surface);

      // set output file locationa and format
      _mediaRecorder.SetOutputFormat(Android.Media.OutputFormat.Default);
```

continues

LISTING 9-8 *(continued)*

```
      _mediaRecorder.SetOutputFile(VideoPath);

      _mediaRecorder.Prepare();

    }

    public void StopRecording()
    {
      if (_mediaRecorder != null)
      {
        _mediaRecorder.Stop();
        _mediaRecorder.Release();
        _mediaRecorder = null;
      }
    }

    MediaRecorder _mediaRecorder;
  }}
```

Found in the DeviceAccess/DeviceAccess.MD/VideoRecorder.cs file of the download

You can find more information about the API at `http://developer.android.com/reference/android/media/MediaRecorder.html`.

Windows Phone 7

Video capture is achieved on Windows Phone devices using the `FileSink` object. Providing an `IsolatedStorageFileStream` object from the start is required to store the recorded video, as shown in Listing 9-9.

LISTING 9-9: Capturing video on Windows Phone 7

Available for download on Wrox.com

```
using System;
using System.Windows;
using System.Windows.Media;
using System.Windows.Shapes;
using System.IO.IsolatedStorage;

namespace DeviceAccess
{
  public class VideoAccess
  {
    // Source and device for capturing video.
    CaptureSource captureSource;
    VideoCaptureDevice videoCaptureDevice;

    // File details for storing the recording.
    IsolatedStorageFileStream isoVideoFile;
    FileSink fileSink;
```

```
// Viewfinder for capturing video.
VideoBrush videoRecorderBrush;

public void StartRecording(Rectangle viewfinderRectangle, string filePath)
{
  InitializeVideoRecorder(viewfinderRectangle);

  // Connect fileSink to captureSource.
  if (captureSource.VideoCaptureDevice != null
      && captureSource.State == CaptureState.Started)
  {
    captureSource.Stop();

    // Connect the input and output of fileSink.
    fileSink.CaptureSource = captureSource;
    fileSink.IsolatedStorageFileName = filePath;
  }

  // Begin recording.
  if (captureSource.VideoCaptureDevice != null
      && captureSource.State == CaptureState.Stopped)
  {
    captureSource.Start();
  }
}

public void StopRecording()
{
  if (captureSource != null)
  {
    // Stop captureSource if it is running.
    if (captureSource.VideoCaptureDevice != null
        && captureSource.State == CaptureState.Started)
    {
      captureSource.Stop();
    }

    // Remove the event handlers for captureSource and the shutter button.
    captureSource.CaptureFailed -= OnCaptureFailed;

    // Remove the video recording objects.
    captureSource = null;
    videoCaptureDevice = null;
    fileSink = null;
    videoRecorderBrush = null;
  }
}

void InitializeVideoRecorder(Rectangle viewfinderRectangle)
{
  if (captureSource == null)
  {
    // Create the VideoRecorder objects.
    captureSource = new CaptureSource();
    fileSink = new FileSink();
```

continues

LISTING 9-9 *(continued)*

```
            videoCaptureDevice = CaptureDeviceConfiguration.GetDefaultVideoCaptureDevice();

            // Add eventhandlers for captureSource.
            captureSource.CaptureFailed += new
    EventHandler<ExceptionRoutedEventArgs>(OnCaptureFailed);

            // Initialize the camera if it exists on the device.
            if (videoCaptureDevice != null)
            {
              // Create the VideoBrush for the viewfinder.
              videoRecorderBrush = new VideoBrush();
              videoRecorderBrush.SetSource(captureSource);

              // Display the viewfinder image on the rectangle.
              viewfinderRectangle.Fill = videoRecorderBrush;

              // Start video capture and display it on the viewfinder.
              captureSource.Start();
            }
            else
            {
              // A camera is not supported on this device
            }
          }
        }

        void OnCaptureFailed(object sender, ExceptionRoutedEventArgs e)
        {
        }
      }
    }
    }
```

Found in the DeviceAccess/DeviceAccess.WP/VideoAccess.cs.cs file of the download

You can find more information about the API at `http://msdn.microsoft.com/library/system.windows.media.filesink.aspx`

Playing Video

Displaying video on a smartphone can be a great tool for sales presentations, self-service product demo applications, collaboration applications, and instructional applications. The lower resolution screens make packaging video less memory-intensive because they don't typically need to display videos in 1080p quality. With the storage space these devices are starting to come bundled with, storing multiple 1080p videos is still a possibility.

iOS

Playing videos within an iOS app is simple. The `MonoTouch.MediaPlayer.MPMoviePlayerController` object takes an `NSUrl` object. With a simple URL or file path, you can instantiate the

MPMoviePlayerController object, and a simple call to a Play() method can initialize video playback.

This is a simple code snippet. You need to add the object to a view and its frame set:

```
using MonoTouch.MediaPlayer;

var videoPlayer = new MPMoviePlayerController(new NSUrl("myVideo.m4v"));
videoPlayer.Play ();
```

You can find more information about the API at http://developer.apple.com/library/IOs/#documentation/MediaPlayer/Reference/MPMoviePlayerController_Class/Reference/Reference.html.

Android

You can also use the versatile Android.Media.MediaPlayer object to view video playback and manage its state machine. If an error state occurs while playing the video source, you need to either call the MediaManager.Reset() method or create a new MediaManager instance, just as you did for playing audio files.

Listing 9-10 shows a method you can use to play videos on an Android device.

LISTING 9-10: Playing video on Android

Available for download on Wrox.com

```
using Android.Views;
using Android.Media;

namespace DeviceAccess
{
  class VideoPlayer
  {
    public void StartVideoPlayback(SurfaceView surface, string FilePath)
    {
      if (_player != null)
      {
        StopVideoPlayback();
      }
      _player = new MediaPlayer();

      ISurfaceHolder holder = surface.Holder;
      holder.SetType(Android.Views.SurfaceType.PushBuffers);
      holder.SetFixedSize(400, 300);

      _player.SetDisplay(holder);
      _player.SetDataSource(FilePath);
      _player.Prepare();
      _player.Start();
    }

    public void StopVideoPlayback()
    {
```

continues

LISTING 9-10 *(continued)*

```
        if (_player != null)
        {
          if (_player.IsPlaying)
          {
            _player.Stop();
          }

          _player.Release();
          _player = null;
        }
      }
      MediaPlayer _player;
    }
  }
```

Found in the DeviceAccess/DeviceAccess.MD/VideoPlayer.cs file of the download

You can find more information about the API at `http://developer.android.com/reference/android/media/MediaPlayer.html`.

Windows Phone 7

Playing videos within a Windows Phone application is easy. The `MediaPlayerLauncher` object takes just a few parameters. You can play the video from isolated storage or from the application's directory, which is bundled with the `.xap` file. Listing 9-11 provides the code necessary.

LISTING 9-11: Playing video on Windows Phone 7

Available for download on Wrox.com

```
using System;
using Microsoft.Phone.Tasks;

namespace DeviceAccess
{
  public class VideoPlayer
  {
    public void StartAudioPlayback(string AudioFilePath)
    {
      MediaPlayerLauncher objMediaPlayerLauncher = new MediaPlayerLauncher();
      objMediaPlayerLauncher.Media = new Uri(AudioFilePath, UriKind.Relative);
      objMediaPlayerLauncher.Location = MediaLocationType.Install;
      objMediaPlayerLauncher.Controls = MediaPlaybackControls.Pause |
        MediaPlaybackControls.Stop | MediaPlaybackControls.All;
      objMediaPlayerLauncher.Orientation = MediaPlayerOrientation.Landscape;
      objMediaPlayerLauncher.Show();
    }
  }
}
```

Found in the DeviceAccess/DeviceAccess.WP/VideoPlayer.cs file of the download

CONTACTS AND CALENDAR

The root of today's smartphone is the Personal Information Manager (PIM). These electronic PIMs came in the form of Apple's Newton, the HP Jornada line, and of course the PalmPilot. These devices specialized in contact, task, and calendar management.

The iPhone, Android, and Windows Phone 7 devices all come with build-in PIM software. Each of the devices offers a different level of access to the contacts and calendar events stored on the device.

Accessing Contacts

To access the contacts on the devices, some of the platforms require special provisioning to be compiled into the application at build time. The process and level of access is different between the platforms, but ultimately some degree of access is available on all three platforms.

iOS

The `ABAddressBook` object provides access to the device's contact list. Each contact has a list of numbers, consisting of a label (that is, home, work, iPhone, fax, and so on). Getting contact info from an iOS device is as simple as looping through the `ABPerson` contained in the `Contacts` of a `iPhoneAddressBook`, as illustrated in the following code:

```
ABAddressBook iPhoneAddressBook = new ABAddressBook();
ABPerson[] Contacts = iPhoneAddressBook.GetPeople();

foreach (ABPerson item in Contacts)
{
    ABMultiValue<NSDictionary> Contact  = item.GetPhones();
    foreach (ABMultiValueEntry<NSDictionary> cont in Contact)
    {
        // a label containing text describing the number
        // the phone number value

    }
}
```

Android

In Android 2.0, the storage mechanism for storing contacts was transitioned to the `Android.Provider.ContactsContract` object. The process includes a generic table for storing all contact information. Each row has a data kind that determines the values each of the columns hold.

Each row in the contact table represents data aggregated from one or more raw contact data elements. These `RawContacts` objects are aggregated by the API and presented in the contacts table. The `Contacts` API retrieves contacts using a lookup key or each contact.

Before you can access contact records in an application, you must add the following permissions to the `AndroidManifest.xml` file:

```
<uses-permission android:name="android.permission.READ_CONTACTS" />
```

Listing 9-12 shows how to access the contact on an Android device.

LISTING 9-12: Looking up contacts on Android

Available for download on Wrox.com

```
using System;
using Android.App;
using Android.Content;
using Android.Provider;
using Android.Database;

namespace DeviceAccess
{
  class ContactsAccess : Activity
  {
    public IntPtr LookupContactByName(string name, ContentResolver cr)
    {
      IntPtr handle = IntPtr.Zero;

      ICursor cur = cr.Query(ContactsContract.Contacts.ContentUri,
                                         null, null, null, null);
      if (cur.Count > 0)
      {
        while (cur.MoveToNext())
        {
          int lookupColumn =
            cur.GetColumnIndex(ContactsContract.ContactsColumnsConsts.LookupKey);
          int columnIndex = cur.GetColumnIndex(lookupColumn.ToString());
          String id = cur.GetString(columnIndex);

          string displayNameColumn =
            ContactsContract.ContactsColumnsConsts.DisplayName.ToString();
          string displayNameColumnIndex =
            cur.GetColumnIndex(displayNameColumn).ToString();
          String displayName =
            cur.GetString(cur.GetColumnIndex(displayNameColumnIndex));
          if (displayName.Contains(name))
          {

            handle = cur.Handle;
          }
        }
      }
      return handle;
    }
  }
}
```

Found in the DeviceAccess/DeviceAccess.MD/ContactsAccess.cs file of the download

For more information about the API, go to `http://developer.android.com/resources/articles/contacts.html`.

Windows Phone 7

The Windows Phone platform provides read-only access to contacts, combining the contact list from all the accounts configured on the account. The list is available in the API through the `Microsoft.`

Phone.UserData.Contacts class. Using the Contacts class, perform an asynchronous search and work with the results in the event handler.

Listing 9-13 shows how to access the contacts on a Windows Phone device.

LISTING 9-13: Looking up contacts on Windows Phone 7

Available for download on Wrox.com

```
using System;
using Microsoft.Phone.UserData;
using System.Collections.Generic;
using System.Threading;

namespace DeviceAccess
{
  public class ContactsAccess
  {
    public List<string> LookupContactName(string Name)
    {
      // create a contact object and it's search handler
      Contacts cons = new Contacts();
      cons.SearchCompleted += new
            EventHandler<ContactsSearchEventArgs>(Contacts_SearchCompleted);

      // start the search
      cons.SearchAsync(Name, FilterKind.None, string.Empty);

      // block on the search until the async result return
      List<string> results;
      lock (_locker)
      {
        while (name == null)
        {
          Monitor.Pulse(_locker);
        }

        results = name;
        name = null;
      }
      return results;
    }
    static readonly object _locker = new object();
    List<string> name = null;

    void Contacts_SearchCompleted(object sender, ContactsSearchEventArgs e)
    {
      lock (_locker)
      {
        // reset list
        name = new List<string>();

        // build new result list
        if (e.Results != null)
        {
          var en = e.Results.GetEnumerator();
```

continues

LISTING 9-13 *(continued)*

```
                while (en.MoveNext())
                {
                  name.Add(en.Current.DisplayName);
                }
              }
              Monitor.Pulse(_locker);
            }
          }
        }
      }
```

Found in the DeviceAccess/DeviceAccess.WP/ContactsAccess.cs file of the download

For more information about the API, go to `http://msdn.microsoft.com/en-us/library/hh286414`.

MESSAGING AND COMMUNICATION

Receiving phones call while away from home might have been the root problem cell phones solved. And, the Blackberry solved the problem of receiving e-mails while away from the office. Today's smartphones keep you connected across a multitude of mediums. Facebook, Twitter, e-mail, and SMS all have their place as communication tools. Ultimately voice communication continues to hold a strong position in the communication tool hierarchy.

Initiating a Voice Call

For applications attempting to hook into the devices' phone capabilities, the API for initiating a phone call is easy. In Android, the user still needs to confirm the action before an application can initiate a phone call. For iOS the API provides the option for a user confirmation first. Windows Phone dials immediately.

iOS

Kicking off a data call from inside iOS is simple. Using iOS applications, you can take advantage of deep linking as a simple COM communication style. The operating system can marshal navigation requests to other applications based on registering applications with URI protocols. The built-in phone application in iOS uses the `tel` protocol, so a URI starting with "`tel://`" routes to the phone application for handling.

Listing 9-14 shows how to initiate a phone call on an iOS device.

Available for download on Wrox.com

LISTING 9-14: Initiating a phone call on cell-enabled iOS devices

```
using MonoTouch.Foundation;
using MonoTouch.UIKit;

namespace DeviceAccess
```

```
{
  class PhoneAccess
  {
    public bool DialNumber(string PhoneNumber, bool DisplayWarning)
    {
      bool successfulDialing = false;

      // Kick off dialing using iOS's deep linking
      NSUrl url = new NSUrl("tel:" + PhoneNumber);
      if (UIApplication.SharedApplication.OpenUrl(url))
      {
        successfulDialing = true;
      }
      else if (DisplayWarning)
      {
        UIAlertView av =
            new UIAlertView("Dialing Failed", "Dialing not supported",
              null, "OK", null);
        av.Show();
      }

      return successfulDialing;
    }
  }
}
```

Found in the DeviceAccess/DeviceAccess.MT/PhoneAccess.cs file of the download

Android

Displaying a confirmation dialog that initiates a phone call is as simple as starting an activity with an `Intent` of `Intent.ActionDial` and a phone number wrapped in a `Uri`:

```
string uri = string.Format("tel:{0}", "612-555-1212");
Android.Net.Uri phoneNumber = Android.Net.Uri.Parse(uri);
StartActivity(new Intent(Intent.ActionDial, phoneNumber));
```

Windows Phone 7

Initiating phone calls from within a Windows Phone application is just as easy as initiating a call with an iOS. The mechanics are different, but the resulting lines of code are similar.

The Windows Phone SDK provides Tasks for the application to initiate, which are available in the `Microsoft.Phone.Tasks` namespace. You set up the `PhoneCallTask` by initiating its no argument constructor and assigning the `PhoneNumber` property a string. This starts the phone application in the background and displays a confirmation dialog only when the `Show()` method is called. When the method is called, the user must interact with a dialog box to initiate the phone call.

Listing 9-15 shows how to initiate a phone call on a device running Windows Phone 7.

LISTING 9-15: Initiating a phone call on Windows Phone 7 devices

Available for download on Wrox.com

```
using Microsoft.Phone.Tasks;

namespace DeviceAccess
{
  class PhoneAccess
  {
    public void DialNumber(string PhoneNumber)
    {
      PhoneCallTask task = new PhoneCallTask();
      task.PhoneNumber = "651-555-1212";
      task.Show();
    }
  }
}
```

Found in the DeviceAccess/DeviceAccess.WP/PhoneAccess.cs file of the download

For more information about the API, go to `http://msdn.microsoft.com/en-us/library/hh286414`.

GEO-LOCATION

The GPS chip is, by far, the piece of hardware used most frequently by smartphone apps. Store locators and turn-by-turn navigation apps were the first to arrive on the scene. Applications such as iHeartRadio and other content providers use the GPS chip to filter advertising based on the end user's location. A recent legal controversy has centered on whether in-app advertisement can be delivered based on the user's immediate location. This would allow the local bakery to request their ads be displayed only on devices within a few block radius. The hope is that customers in the vicinity would receive notification of the deals at a time when they could immediately take advantage of them. Store applications have even tried using the GPS functionally to reward shopper loyalty based on number of "check-ins." In the end, users dictate the level of privacy they wish through user feedback.

Getting GPS Location Information

You can retrieve location information in several ways, but it's generally best to set up a GPS listener in your application code and then reference the listener's cached data values when the view needs to display them.

iOS

GPS information is available to iOS applications using the `MonoTouch.CoreLocation.CLLocationManager` class. The application must instantiate the `CLLocationManager` and assign it a delegate to monitor and store data points broadcast through the event.

Listing 9-16 shows how to get heading information from the onboard GPS.

Available for download on Wrox.com

LISTING 9-16: Getting location information on an iOS device

```
using System.Threading;
using MonoTouch.CoreLocation;

namespace DeviceAccess
{
  public class GpsAccess
  {
    public string ReturnHeading()
    {
      if (_lm != null)
      {
        _lm = new CLLocationManager();
        _lm.UpdatedHeading += HeadingUpdateDelegate;
        _lm.StartUpdatingHeading();
      }

      // block on the search until the async result return
      string result;
      lock (_locker)
      {
        while (location == null)
        {
          Monitor.Pulse(_locker);
        }

        result = location;
        location = null;
      }
      return result;
    }

    void CompassCancel()
    {
      if (_lm != null)
      {
        _lm.StopUpdatingHeading();
        _lm.Dispose();
        _lm = null;
      }
    }
    static CLLocationManager _lm;

    private void HeadingUpdateDelegate(object sender, CLHeadingUpdatedEventArgs e)
    {
      lock (_locker)
      {
        // build new result list
        if (_lm != null && _lm.Heading != null)
        {
          location = _lm.Heading.MagneticHeading.ToString();
        }
        Monitor.Pulse(_locker);
```

continues

LISTING 9-16 *(continued)*

```
      }
    }
    static readonly object _locker = new object();
    string location = null;
  }
}
```

Found in the DeviceAccess/DeviceAccess.MT/GpsAccess.cs file of the download

For more information about the API, go to `http://developer.apple.com/library/mac/#documentation/CoreLocation/Reference/CLLocationManager_Class/CLLocationManager/CLLocationManager.html`.

Android

The Android SDK provides access to device sensors through the `SensorManager` class. The `Android.Hardware.SensorManager` class can listen to a type of sensor or all the sensors by calling the `GetDefaultSensor(`*SensorType*`)` method on a `SensorManager` object. The `SensorManager` requires a registered listener before the application can receive the sensor's data. For the compass functionality, you must set up a listener for the `SensorType.Proximity` type. The listener is provided information in the `Value` property of the `SensorEvent`. Listing 9-17 displays how to set up a listener and read the heading out.

Available for download on Wrox.com

LISTING 9-17: Getting location information on an Android device

```
using System;
using System.Threading;
using Android.Content;
using Android.Hardware;

namespace DeviceAccess
{
  public class CompassSensor : ISensorEventListener
  {
    protected string ReturnHeading()
    {
      SensorManager sm = _context.GetSystemService(Context.SensorService)
        as SensorManager;

      Sensor sensor = sm.GetDefaultSensor(SensorType.Orientation);
      if (sensor != null)
      {
        sm.RegisterListener(this, sensor, SensorDelay.Ui);
      }

      // block on the search until the async result return
```

```
        string heading;
        lock (_locker)
        {
          while (location == null)
          {
            Monitor.Pulse(_locker);
          }

          heading = location;
          location = null;
        }
        return heading;
      }

      protected void CompassCancel()
      {
        SensorManager sm = _context.GetSystemService(Context.SensorService)
          as SensorManager;
        Sensor sensor = sm.GetDefaultSensor(SensorType.Orientation);
        sm.UnregisterListener(this, sensor);
      }

      public void OnSensorChanged(SensorEvent e)
      {
        if (e.Sensor.Type == SensorType.Proximity)
        {
          lock (_locker)
          {

            location = e.ToString();
            Monitor.Pulse(_locker);
          }
        }
      }
      static readonly object _locker = new object();
      string location = null;

      Context _context;


      public void OnAccuracyChanged(Sensor sensor, int accuracy)
      {
        return;
      }

      public IntPtr Handle
      {
        get { throw new NotImplementedException(); }
      }
    }
  }
```

Found in the DeviceAccess/DeviceAccess.MD/GpsAccess.cs file of the download

You can find more information about the API at `http://developer.android.com/reference/android/hardware/SensorManager.html`.

Windows Phone 7

The Window Phone SDK provides access to the `Compass` class. You can configure the `Microsoft.Devices.Sensors.Compass` class for different intervals, depending on the latency requirements of the application. An event handler provides the compass readings. The `SensorReadingEventArgs` object includes properties such as the `TrueHeading`. Listing 9-18 shows how to set up the event hander and receive compass readings.

LISTING 9-18: Getting location information on a Windows Phone 7 device

Available for download on Wrox.com

```
using System;
using System.Threading;
using Microsoft.Devices.Sensors;

namespace DeviceAccess
{
  public class GpsAccess
  {
    static Compass _compass;

    public string ReturnHeading()
    {
      if (!Compass.IsSupported)
      {
        throw new Exception("Could not load Compass");
      }
      if (_compass == null)
      {
        _compass = new Compass();
        _compass.TimeBetweenUpdates = TimeSpan.FromMilliseconds(100);
        _compass.CurrentValueChanged += new
         EventHandler<SensorReadingEventArgs<CompassReading>>(_compass_CurrentValueChanged);
        try
        {
          _compass.Start();
        }
        catch (InvalidOperationException e)
        {
          if (_compass != null)
          {
            _compass.Dispose();
            _compass = null;
          }

          throw new Exception("Could not initiate compass readings", e);
        }
      }

      string trueHeading = null;
      if (_compass != null)
      {
```

```
            // block on the search until the async result return
            lock (_locker)
            {
              while (_trueHeading == null)
              {
                Monitor.Pulse(_locker);
              }

              trueHeading = _trueHeading;
              _trueHeading = null;
            }
          }
          return trueHeading;
        }
        static readonly object _locker = new object();
        string _trueHeading = null;

        void _compass_CurrentValueChanged(object sender,
          SensorReadingEventArgs<CompassReading> e)
        {
          lock (_locker)
          {

            _trueHeading = e.SensorReading.TrueHeading.ToString();
            Monitor.Pulse(_locker);
          }
        }

        void CompassCancel()
        {
          if (_compass != null)
          {
            _compass.Stop();
            _compass.Dispose();
            _compass = null;
          }
        }
      }
    }
```

Found in the DeviceAccess/DeviceAccess.WP/GpsAccess.cs file of the download

For more information about the API, go to `http://msdn.microsoft.com/en-us/library/microsoft.devices.sensors.compass`.

ACCELEROMETER

The accelerometer is popular in gaming applications. You can easily use it to control navigation on the screen, but to date, it has been most successfully implemented in games in which screen navigation is continuous. Reading applications use the sensor to control scrolling speeds. In addition, the accelerometer is useful in applications that use a "shake" movement to kick off a data refresh or initiate a particular workflow, such as refreshing the screen to default values.

Getting X, Y, and Z

For the most part, the accelerometer APIs on each of the platforms provide the same information. It's all about the X, Y, and Z values. Once the values are retrieved, it's up to the application developer to make the application respond creatively.

iOS

Accelerometer information is available on iOS devices using the `MonoTouch.UIKit.UIAccelerometer` class. The `UIAccelerometer` object can provide X, Y, and Z value updates based on a specified interval. When an update delegate is assigned, it is provided the XYZ information in the `UIAccelerometerEventArgs` object passed to it.

Listing 9-19 shows how to get accelerometer information from an iOS device.

Available for download on Wrox.com

LISTING 9-19: Getting accelerometer information on an iOS device

```
using MonoTouch.UIKit;
using System.Threading;

namespace DeviceAccess
{
  public class AccelerometerAccess
  {
    public string ReturnXyz()
    {
      if (UIAccelerometer.SharedAccelerometer != null)
      {
        UIAccelerometer.SharedAccelerometer.UpdateInterval = 0.05;
        UIAccelerometer.SharedAccelerometer.Acceleration += XyzUpdateDelegate;
      }

      // block on the search until the async result return
      string result;
      lock (_locker)
      {
        while (_xyz == null)
        {
          Monitor.Pulse(_locker);
        }

        result = _xyz;
        _xyz = null;
      }
      return result;
    }
    static readonly object _locker = new object();
    string _xyz = null;

    private void XyzUpdateDelegate(object sender, UIAccelerometerEventArgs e)
    {
      lock (_locker)
      {
```

```
            _xyz =
                string.Format("{0:0.00}, {1:0.00}, {2:0.00})",
                  e.Acceleration.X, e.Acceleration.Y, e.Acceleration.Z);

            Monitor.Pulse(_locker);
          }
        }

        void AccelerometerCancel()
        {
          UIAccelerometer.SharedAccelerometer.UpdateInterval = 0.0;
        }

      }
    }
```

Found in the DeviceAccess/DeviceAccess.MT/AccelerometerAccess.cs file of the download

You can find more information about the API at `http://iosapi.xamarin.com/index.aspx?link=C%3AMonoTouch.UIKit.UIAccelerometer`.

Android

The Android SDK provides access to the device's accelerometer information using the same `SensorManager` class as the GPS. The `Android.Hardware.SensorManager` class can listen to accelerometer information by calling the `GetDefaultSensor(`*`SensorType`*`)` method and passing it the `SensorType.Accelerometer` value. Once the sensor is retrieved, set up a listener to read in and evaluate the Value property of the `SensorEvent`. Listing 9-20 contains a class that registers and unregisters a listener from the accelerometer sensor.

LISTING 9-20: Getting accelerometer information on an Android device

Available for download on Wrox.com

```
using System;
using Android.Content;
using Android.Hardware;

namespace DeviceAccess
{
  class AccelerometerSensor : ISensorEventListener
  {
    Context _context;

    protected void AccelerometerStart()
    {
      SensorManager sm = _context.GetSystemService(Context.SensorService)
as SensorManager;
      Sensor sensor = sm.GetDefaultSensor(SensorType.Accelerometer);
      if (sensor != null)
      {
        sm.RegisterListener(this, sensor, SensorDelay.Ui);
      }
```

continues

LISTING 9-20 *(continued)*

```
        else
        {
          throw new Exception("Could not load Accelerometer sensor");
        }
      }

      void AccelerometerCancel()
      {
        SensorManager sm = _context.GetSystemService(Context.SensorService)
          as SensorManager;
        Sensor sensor = sm.GetDefaultSensor(SensorType.Accelerometer);
        sm.UnregisterListener(this);
      }

      public void OnAccuracyChanged(Sensor sensor, int accuracy)
      {
      }

      public void OnSensorChanged(SensorEvent e)
      {
        string js = string.Empty;
        switch (e.Sensor.Type)
        {
          case SensorType.Accelerometer:
            js = string.Format(
              "javascript:accelerometer.onAccelerometerSuccess({0:0.00})",
                e.Values[0], e.Values[1], e.Values[2]);
            break;
        }
        if (js.Length > 0)
        {

        }
      }

      public IntPtr Handle
      {
        get { throw new NotImplementedException(); }
      }
    }
  }
```

Found in the DeviceAccess/DeviceAccess.MD/AccelerometerAccess.cs file of the download

For more information about the API, go to `http://developer.android.com/reference/android/hardware/SensorManager.html`.

Windows Phone 7

The Window Phone SDK provides access to the accelerometer information using the `Accelerometer` class, as shown in Listing 9-21. The `Microsoft.Devices.Sensors.Accelerometer` class provides an event that a handler can be wired to and be provided with the accelerometer's readings. The same `SensorReadingEventArgs` object used with GPS data includes properties for the accelerometer's X, Y, and Z values.

LISTING 9-21: Getting accelerometer information on a Windows Phone 7 device

Available for download on Wrox.com

```
using System;
using System.Threading;
using Microsoft.Devices.Sensors;

namespace DeviceAccess
{
  public class AccelerometerAccess
  {
    Accelerometer _accelerometer = new Accelerometer();

    public string GetAccelerometerXyz()
    {
      if (!Accelerometer.IsSupported)
      {
        throw new Exception("Not supported on this device");
      }
      try
      {
        // Start accelerometer for detecting compass axis
        _accelerometer = new Accelerometer();
        _accelerometer.CurrentValueChanged +=
          new EventHandler<SensorReadingEventArgs<AccelerometerReading>>
                                  (_accelerometer_CurrentValueChanged);
        _accelerometer.Start();
      }
      catch (InvalidOperationException e)
      {
        throw new Exception("Error starting accelerometer", e);
      }

      string xyz = null;
      if (_accelerometer != null)
      {
        // block on the search until the async result return
        lock (_locker)
        {
          while (_xyz == null)
          {
            Monitor.Pulse(_locker);
          }

          xyz = _xyz;
          _xyz = null;
        }

      }
      return xyz;
```

continues

LISTING 9-21 *(continued)*

```
        }
        static readonly object _locker = new object();
        string _xyz = null;

        private void _accelerometer_CurrentValueChanged(object sender,
          SensorReadingEventArgs<AccelerometerReading> e)
        {
          lock (_locker)
          {
            _xyz = string.Format("{0:0.00}, {1:0.00}, {2:0.00}",
                                     e.SensorReading.Acceleration.X,
                                      e.SensorReading.Acceleration.Y,
                                       e.SensorReading.Acceleration.Z);
            Monitor.Pulse(_locker);
          }
        }

        public void AccelerometerCancel()
        {
          if (_accelerometer != null)
          {
            _accelerometer.Stop();
            _accelerometer.Dispose();
            _accelerometer = null;
          }
        }
      }
    }
```

Found in the DeviceAccess/DeviceAccess.WP/AccelerometerAccess.cs file of the download

For more information about the API, go to `http://msdn.microsoft.com/en-us/library/microsoft.devices.sensors.accelerometer`.

SUMMARY

In this chapter you dug into the assortment of APIs that exist for accessing a device's built-in hardware sensors and communication chipsets, as well as the user's PIM information stored on the device. Today's mobile apps are targeted for a user experience that blends into a user's workday and lifestyle. Smartphones and tablets are convenience and productivity devices with capabilities that only software can release. Creating the next wave of interactive software is here today. Developers are now empowered with new types of user inputs; computing systems are no longer shackled to keyboard and mouse input.

In the following chapter you learn about utility access. We discuss file storage systems and encrypting data. The discussion extends to network functionality, threading, and logging. In addition, the chapter touches on the serialization of objects to JSON or XML and how the MonoCross Utilities can simplify that effort when coding for cross-platform code portability.

10

Using MonoCross Utilities

WHAT'S IN THIS CHAPTER?

- Surveying the MonoCross Utilities
- Encrypting sensitive data
- Storing objects to the file system
- Serializing objects
- Tracking application events
- Utilizing network functions
- Multithreading MonoCross applications

Earlier chapters discussed the MonoCross framework and how to use it to design and build cross-platform applications. You learned how to create data services as well as how to consume them. Now it's time to explore the MonoCross Utilities.

The MonoCross Utilities are a collection of service functions that perform basic programming tasks using a common set of interfaces. They are cross-platform in that the same usage in your application correctly functions without the need to write custom code for each platform. This chapter introduces you to the MonoCross Utilities, delves into their interfaces, and clearly and simply shows how to use them in your applications.

The MonoCross Utilities are available for evaluation at `www.monocross.net`. See Chapter 3, "Setting Up Your Development Environment" for more information on how to download and install the MonoCross Utilities.

UNDERSTANDING MONOCROSS UTILITIES

The MonoCross Utilities are a collection of interfaces that you use to perform common application functions, such as saving files, serializing objects, making calls to RESTful web service endpoints, and so forth. When you use the MonoCross Utilities in your code, you program to the common interfaces of the utilities rather than particular platform-specific implementations.

The MonoCross Utilities are a series of interfaces that have been implemented for each mobile platform. These utilities allow you to code your application once for all platforms, rather than once for each platform. Table 10-1 summarizes the cross-platform interfaces contained within the MonoCross Utilities.

TABLE 10-1: MonoCross Utilities

UTILITY	DESCRIPTION
Encryption	Encrypts and decrypts strings, byte arrays, and streams
Logging	Manages the logging of application events
Network	Performs web service requests and provides simple and convenient access to a RESTful endpoint for GET and POST commands
Serializer	Supports the transformation of objects in memory to and from strings, byte arrays, and files
Storage	Stores and retrieves files from persistent storage and performs other file system-related tasks
Threading	Supports the background execution of methods in a direct call as well as a worker pool and an idle pool

You can access all the MonoCross Utilities from a single static class called `MonoCross.Utilities.MXDevice`. A static accessor method exists for each. For example, you can call the MonoCross File Utility functions via methods on the `MXDevice.File` interface described in the "Using File Storage" section later in this chapter.

When an application needs to interface with file storage, it makes certain assumptions about where to store and access data. On Windows, it might be in a temporary folder such as `C:\Temp`, whereas on iOS it is within an isolated application sandbox. This leads to the obvious question: How can you perform cross-platform file interactions if the root folder is different for each platform?

This is where the `MXDevice.DataPath` comes in. MonoCross uses the `DataPath` abstract property to establish the root folder for file storage interactions. When you specify a file in your application code to read or write, use the `MXDevice.DataPath` as part of the filename, instead of such things as `C:\temp` or other platform-specific notation.

If necessary, the application code can set the `MXDevice.DataPath` property; it defaults to a cross-platform value if it is not otherwise set.

You learn how to extend the `MXDevice.DataPath` property for use in the code examples in the "Using File Storage" and "Serializing Objects" sections later in this chapter. In the examples, a new property, named `RootPath`, extends the `MXDevice.DataPath` as the root folder for storing and retrieving files so that you can use the examples on any platform. Listing 10-1 displays the code that defines the `RootPath` property.

LISTING 10-1: RootPath Property

Available for download on Wrox.com

```
public static string RootPath
{
  get
  {
    // AppendPath simplifies appending subfolders to strings
    return MXDevice.DataPath.AppendPath( "MonoCross.Utilities.Samples" );
  }
}
```

Found in the CustomerManagement.DataServices/CustomerManagement.Samples/StorageSample.cs file of the download

ENCRYPTING APPLICATION INFORMATION

Applications deal in data, and sometimes these data are sensitive and/or confidential and need to be protected from prying eyes, while at the same time be readily available for those who have access permission. Whether the data is customer details in a business application or patient information in a medical application, you need to protect the data.

The MonoCross Encryption Utility provides a simple, yet effective, means to encrypt your application's data. Because many texts cover encryption as an advanced topic, you may ask why this chapter covers encryption first among all the MonoCross Utilities. The answer is that both the MonoCross File Utility and the MonoCross Serialization Utility heavily use the MonoCross Encryption Utility, so it makes sense to cover it first.

Understanding the Encryption Utility

The MonoCross Encryption Utility encrypts and decrypts `string`, `byte[]`, and `Stream` objects. A complete coverage of encryption is beyond the scope of this text, but this chapter covers how the MonoCross Encryption Utility abstracts and simplifies the encryption functionality provided by .NET for use across platforms. The utility contains several methods designed to be fully functional with just a single line of code.

The MonoCross Encryption Utility leverages .NET support for Advanced Encryption Standard (AES256). When used with sufficiently strong key and salt values, this encryption is secure enough to meet current enterprise security standards.

The MonoCross Encryption Utility supports three separate modes of encryption. The *Default Encryption* specifies application-level settings that indicate whether encryption is required as well as the default encryption key and salt. *Specific Encryption* and *No Encryption* are exceptions to the Default Encryption settings. Table 10-2 further defines these modes.

TABLE 10-2: MonoCross Encryption Utility Modes

ENCRYPTION MODE	DESCRIPTION
Default Encryption	Manages application-level encryption settings, specifying whether encryption is required — and if so, the key and salt to use.
Specific Encryption	Provides an exception to the Default Encryption settings by enabling you to use an alternative key and salt to encrypt and decrypt information.
No Encryption	Provides another exception to Default Encryption settings by ensuring that no encryption or decryption be used in that mode. You primarily use this mode within the MonoCross File and Serialization Utilities.

In code, you express these encryption modes as `enum EncryptionMode` with `Default`, `Encryption`, and `NoEncryption` values.

You can find the MonoCross Encryption Utility within the `MonoCross.Utilities.Encryption` namespace. Table 10-3 describes the available methods.

TABLE 10-3: MonoCross Encryption Utility

METHOD	DESCRIPTION
`DecryptBytes`	Decrypts a `byte[]` into a `byte[]` using the default key and salt. Method overloads support the use of specified key and salts.
`DecryptStream`	Decrypts a `stream` into a `stream` using the default key and salt. Method overloads support the use of specified key and salts.
`DecryptString`	Decrypts a `string` into a `string` using the default key and salt. Method overloads support the use of specified key and salts.
`EncryptBytes`	Encrypts a `byte[]` into a `byte[]` using the default key and salt. Method overloads support the use of specified key and salts.
`EncryptStream`	Encrypts a `stream` into a `stream` using the default key and salt. Method overloads support the use of specified key and salts.
`EncryptString`	Encrypts a `string` into a `string` using the default key and salt. Method overloads support the use of specified key and salts.
`Key`	`String` property indicating the default encryption key to use for encrypting and decrypting information.
`Required`	`Boolean` to indicate whether encryption is required for the current application instance.
`Salt`	`Byte[]` property indicating the default salt to use for encrypting and decrypting information.

Putting the Encryption Utility to Work

The MonoCross Encryption Utility abstracts and simplifies data encryption into easy-to-use functions. The utility becomes slightly more complicated when you use Specific Encryption and No Encryption modes.

Start with Default Encryption. To activate encryption for the entire application, you need to set Encryption to Required (via the `MXDevice.Encryption.Required` property) and populate an application level key and salt for performing encryption, `MXDevice.Encryption.Key` and `MXDevice.Encryption.Salt`, respectively.

Listing 10-2 shows sample methods that demonstrate how to enable and disable Default Encryption. You also use these methods in later samples in this section.

LISTING 10-2: Enable/Disable Default Encryption

Available for download on Wrox.com

```
public static void EnableEncryption()
{
  // Activate Default Encryption
  MXDevice.Encryption.Required = true;
  // This key and salt is for example purposes only. Change your own key and salt.
  MXDevice.Encryption.Key = "1lMkihr6tN4JO16LAdGJsEEdy6m+/vNqy2rYQuydBk2=";
  MXDevice.Encryption.Salt = Convert.FromBase64String( "mDE9r+ACKTqVwFc6nTdPbl==" );
}

public static void DisableEncryption()
{
  // Deactivate Default Encryption
  MXDevice.Encryption.Required = false;
  MXDevice.Encryption.Key = String.Empty;
  MXDevice.Encryption.Salt = new byte[] { };
}
```

Found in the CustomerManagement.DataServices/CustomerManagement.Samples/EncryptionSample.cs file of the download

Now that the Default Encryption is set up, it's a simple call to one of the `EncryptXXX()` or `DecryptXXX()` methods located within `MXDevice.Encryption`. Listing 10-3 demonstrates how to encrypt and decrypt a string.

LISTING 10-3: Encrypting and Decrypting Text

Available for download on Wrox.com

```
public static void TextWithDefaultEncryption()
{
  string text = "A quick little critter went to pick up litter.";

  // enable Default Encryption,
    // note this can be performed when application starts
```

continues

LISTING 10-3 *(continued)*

```
        // and only needs to be performed once.
        EnableEncryption();

      string encrypted = MXDevice.Encryption.EncryptString( text );
      string decrypted = MXDevice.Encryption.DecryptString( encrypted );
    }

    public static void TextWithSpecificEncryption()
    {
      string key = "kjWkslr4qw4UT28LAfKJsYIdy9m+/vHry3fYDuydGk2=";
      byte[] salt = Convert.FromBase64String( "lRG7r+BNLTqVcKq6pTsMfi==" );

      string text = "A quick little critter went to pick up litter.";

      // Example uses alternate key and salt properties.
      string encrypted = MXDevice.Encryption.EncryptString( text, key, salt );
      string decrypted = MXDevice.Encryption.DecryptString( encrypted, key, salt );
    }
```

Found in the CustomerManagement.DataServices/CustomerManagement.Samples/EncryptionSample.cs file of the download

USING FILE STORAGE

The MonoCross File Utility simplifies the basic tasks required for file system interactions. This includes saving to and reading from files as well as moving/copying files, creating directories, and many other file system needs.

Understanding the File Utility

The MonoCross File Utility stores and reads text, byte arrays, and streams to files. The MonoCross File Utility also integrates with the MonoCross Encryption Utility and follows the Default Encryption settings for applying encryption to file storage. For instance, your application may have the requirement to encrypt any file stored that contains data of a proprietary or sensitive nature, such as customer information, product and sales data, and so on.

You can store files as encrypted or plain text. If you use Default Encryption, the file is automatically encrypted. Otherwise, you can include a key and salt in the file read and save methods for Specific Encryption and also apply the `enum EncryptionMode.NoEncryption` where you want plain text interaction.

The MonoCross File Utility manages the application interactions with the file system via a simple, cross-platform interface. You can find the MonoCross File Utility within the `MonoCross.Utilities.Storage` namespace. Table 10-4 describes the available methods.

TABLE 10-4: MonoCross File Utility

METHOD	DESCRIPTION
`Copy`	Copies a file, either to a new file in the same directory or to a new directory.
`CopyDirectory`	Copies a directory including its subdirectory and file contents. Method overloads support overwriting at the destination directory.
`CreateDirectory`	Creates a directory at a specified location.
`Delete`	Removes a file from the file system.
`DeleteDirectory`	Removes a directory from the file system.
`DirectoryName`	Returns the name of the containing directory of a given file or directory.
`EnsureDirectoryExists`	Ensures that a directory exists for a given file or directory path. If the containing directory doesn't exist, this method creates it.
`Exists`	Returns `true` or `false` depending on whether the given file exists.
`GetDirectoryNames`	Returns a string array of directory names contained within a given directory path.
`GetFileNames`	Returns a `string[]` of filenames contained within a given directory path.
`Length`	Returns the length of a given filename.
`Move`	Changes a file's location or renames the file if moving to a different filename in the same directory.
`MoveDirectory`	Changes a directory's location along with its subdirectory and file contents.
`Read`	Reads a file into a `byte[]`. Method overloads support file decryption.
`ReadString`	Reads a file into a `string`. Method overloads support file decryption.
`Save`	Saves contents into a named file. Method overloads support multiple content types (`string`, `byte[]` and `stream`). Additional method overloads support encryption.

Putting the File Utility to Work

Using the MonoCross File Utility is simple and focuses on what you intend the code to accomplish rather than on platform-specific implementation details. It automatically handles stream management and other issues. Listing 10-4 demonstrates how to save text and byte arrays to files and read the contents into variables.

Available for download on Wrox.com

LISTING 10-4: Save and Read a File

```
public static void TextToFile()
{
  string text = "A quick little critter went to pick up litter.";
  string fileName = RootPath.AppendPath( "String.txt" );

  // Save text to file
  MXDevice.File.Save( fileName, text );

  // Read text from file
  string text1 = MXDevice.File.ReadString( fileName );
}

public static void BytesToFile()
{
  byte[] bytes = { 1,2,3,4,5,6,7,8,9,10,11,12,13,14,15,16,17,18,19,20 };
  string fileName = RootPath.AppendPath( "Bytes.txt" );

  // Save byte array to file
  MXDevice.File.Save( fileName, bytes );

  // Read byte array from file
  byte[] bytes1 = MXDevice.File.Read( fileName );
}
```

Found in the CustomerManagement.DataServices/CustomerManagement.Samples/StorageSample.cs file of the download

The previous example performs the `Save()` and `Read()` methods using the Default Encryption settings, so the files encrypt automatically, if required, with no extra coding on your part. In addition, these settings enable different environments (for example, development versus production) to have different encryption requirements without changing your file interaction code.

Now, suppose you have a situation in which you need to always store certain files as encrypted but with a different encryption key and salt from the Default Encryption settings. Simply add an alternative key and salt to the file `ReadXXX()` and `SaveXXX()` methods to support Specific Encryption. Listing 10-5 demonstrates this usage.

LISTING 10-5: Save and Read a File with Specific Encryption

```
public static void TextToFileWithSpecificEncryption()
{
  string key = "kjWkslr4qw4UT28LAfKJsYIdy9m+/vHry3fYDuydGk2=";
  byte[] salt = Convert.FromBase64String( "lRG7r+BNLTqVcKq6pTsMfi==" );

  string text = "A quick little critter went to pick up litter.";
  string fileEnc = RootPath.AppendPath( "StringWithSpecificEncryption.txt" );

  // Save text to an encrypted file, using specific Key and Salt.
```

```
    MXDevice.File.Save( fileEnc, text, key, salt );

    // Read text from encrypted file with same Key and Salt file was encrypted with.
    string text1 = MXDevice.File.ReadString( fileEnc, key, salt );
  }

  public static void BytesToFileWithSpecificEncryption()
  {
    string key = "kjWkslr4qw4UT28LAfKJsYIdy9m+/vHry3fYDuydGk2=";
    byte[] salt = Convert.FromBase64String( "lRG7r+BNLTqVcKq6pTsMfi==" );

    byte[] bytes = { 1,2,3,4,5,6,7,8,9,10,11,12,13,14,15,16,17,18,19,20 };
    string fileEnc = RootPath.AppendPath( "BytesWithSpecificEncryption.txt" );

    // Save byte array to an encrypted file.
    MXDevice.File.Save( fileEnc, bytes, key, salt );

    // Read byte array from encrypted file
    byte[] bytes1 = MXDevice.File.Read( fileEnc, key, salt );
  }
```

Found in the CustomerManagement.DataServices/CustomerManagement.Samples/StorageSample.cs file of the download

Through these examples, you can learn how the MonoCross File Utility enables encryption via Default Encryption and Specific Encryption. Consider one final encryption scenario in which you need to use Default Encryption for the application but you need to save or read a file in a plain text or unencrypted state. This could occur when your application needs to read a file from a different application that perhaps doesn't support encryption or doesn't have your application's key and salt.

You handle this situation with the No Encryption mode. Simply apply the `EncryptionMode.NoEncryption` enumeration value to the `Save()` and `Read()` method calls to ensure that the saves or reads do not use encryption. Listing 10-6 demonstrates how this is done.

Available for download on Wrox.com

LISTING 10-6: Save and Read a File with No Encryption

```
  public static void TextToFileWithNoEncryption()
  {
    string text = "A quick little critter went to pick up litter.";
    string fileEnc = RootPath.AppendPath( "StringWithNoEncryption.txt" );

    // Save text to a plain text file,
    // regardless whether the default encryption settings are active or not.
    MXDevice.File.Save( fileEnc, text, EncryptionMode.NoEncryption );

    // Read plain text from file, do not decrypt.
    string text1 = MXDevice.File.ReadString( fileEnc, EncryptionMode.NoEncryption );
  }
```

Found in the CustomerManagement.DataServices/CustomerManagement.Samples/StorageSample.cs file of the download

The previous examples show how to save and read files both with and without encryption, but the MonoCross File Utility contains additional methods for manipulating files. Listing 10-7 demonstrates how to copy, move, and delete files.

Available for download on Wrox.com

LISTING 10-7: Manipulating Files

```
public static void FileManipulation()
{
  string text = "A quick little critter went to pick up litter.";
  string fileName = RootPath.AppendPath( "StringManip.txt" );

  // Disable Default Encryption for this this sample
  EncryptionSample.DisableEncryption();

  // Save text to file
  MXDevice.File.Save( fileName, text );

  // Move file
  string fileMove = RootPath.AppendPath( "StringManipMove.txt" );
  MXDevice.File.Move( fileName, fileMove );

  // Copy file
  string fileCopy = RootPath.AppendPath( "StringManipCopy.txt" );
  MXDevice.File.Copy( fileMove, fileCopy );

  // Delete File.
  MXDevice.File.Delete( fileMove );
}
```

Found in the CustomerManagement.DataServices/CustomerManagement.Samples/StorageSample.cs file of the download

SERIALIZING OBJECTS

An application that uses objects needs to be able to share those objects with another application, a web server, or even between sessions of the same application. *Serialization* is the process of transferring objects from their in-memory representation into some other form and back again.

Understanding the Serializer Utility

The MonoCross Serializer Utility simplifies the serialization of objects and lists of objects through a common cross-platform interface. You can serialize (and deserialize) the objects into strings, byte arrays, and even to files. The `SerializationFormat` enumeration supports both XML and JSON formats within namespace `MonoCross.Utilities.Serialization`.

The MonoCross Serializer Utility internally supports both the MonoCross File and Encryption Utilities and offers encryption overloads in all the *`SerializeXXX()`* and *`DeserializeXXX()`* methods. Further, the utility uses generics to simplify the interface and avoid the overhead of casting and boxing/unboxing of objects.

You can find the MonoCross Serializer Utility within the `MonoCross.Utilities.Serialization` namespace. Table 10-5 describes the available methods.

TABLE 10-5: MonoCross Serializer Utility

METHOD	DESCRIPTION
`ContentType`	Specifies the content type associated with the specific serialization (XML or JSON) formats used (namely `application/xml` and `application/json`).
`DeserializeList`	Deserializes a `string` or `byte[]` into a `List<object>`. Method overloads support decryption as part of the deserialization.
`DeserializeListFromFile`	Deserializes the contents of a file into a `List<object>`. Method overloads support decryption as part of the deserialization.
`DeserializeObject`	Deserializes a `string` or `byte[]` into an `object`. Method overloads support decryption as part of the deserialization.
`DeserializeObjectFromFile`	Deserializes the contents of a file into an `object`. Method overloads support decryption as part of the deserialization.
`SerializeList`	Serializes a `List<object>` to a `string`. Method overloads support encryption as part of the serialization.
`SerializeListToBytes`	Serializes a `List<object>` to a `byte[]`. Method overloads support encryption as part of the serialization.
`SerializeListToFile`	Serializes a `List<object>` to a specified file. Method overloads support encryption as part of the serialization.
`SerializeObject`	Serializes an `object` to a `string`. Method overloads support encryption as part of the serialization.
`SerializeObjectToBytes`	Serializes an `object` to a `byte[]`. Method overloads support encryption as part of the serialization.
`SerializeObjectToFile`	Serializes an `object` to a specified file. Method overloads support encryption as part of the serialization.

Putting the Serializer Utility to Work

The MonoCross Serializer Utility supports your application's serialization needs with as simple an interface as possible. In most instances you need only two lines of code to perform serialization. The first line uses a generic factory method to create a serializer specific to the business object being serialized. The second line actually performs the serialization. As you can see in the following examples, after the serializer for a specific type has been created, you can use it to make multiple *`SerializeXXX()`* and *`DeserializeXXX()`* calls.

All the MonoCross Serializer Utility examples rely on the `CustomerManagement.Shared.Model.Product` class for demonstrating the serialization and deserialization of objects and lists. Listing 10-8 displays a simple `List<Product>` generation method.

LISTING 10-8: Get Product List Implementation

Available for download on Wrox.com

```
namespace CustomerManagement.Shared.Model
{

public static List<Product> GetProductList()
{
  List<Product> list = new List<Product>();

  list.Add( new Product() { ID = "1", Description = "First Sample Product" } );
  list.Add( new Product() { ID = "2", Description = "Second Sample Product" } );
  list.Add( new Product() { ID = "3", Description = "Third Sample Product" } );
  list.Add( new Product() { ID = "4", Description = "Fourth Sample Product" } );

  return list;
}
```

Found in the CustomerManagement.DataServices/CustomerManagement.Samples/SerializationSample.cs file of the download

MonoTouch and Mono for Android both support compiler linking to shrink the size of the application by removing unused functions and methods from the application classes. Using compiling with linking has the side effect of removing default public constructors from classes needed for deserialization. This error manifests itself as a "Missing default constructor" runtime error during object deserialization.

You can apply the preserve attributes to the business object to preserve these methods so that deserialization can proceed unhindered. Due to namespace differences, you need a separate attribute for MonoTouch and Mono for Android development.

The C# compiler tags in Listing 10-8 apply the `Preserve` *attribute in a cross-platform manner.*

```
#if (ANDROID)

    [Android.Runtime.Preserve( AllMembers = true )]

#elif (TOUCH)

    [MonoTouch.Foundation.Preserve (AllMembers = true)]

#endif
```

Android and Touch are arbitrary project compilation tags to indicate whether the project compiles under Mono for Android or MonoTouch, respectively.

Listing 10-9 demonstrates how to serialize a `Product` to an XML string and deserialize the string into a `Product`.

Available for download on Wrox.com

LISTING 10-9: Serialize Product to Text

```
public static void XmlSerializeObjectToText()
{
  Product product = GetProductList().First();

  // create a product serializer. Serializer defaults to XML.
  ISerializer<Product> serializer = SerializerFactory.Create<Product>();

  // Serialize object to a string.
  string sXml = serializer.SerializeObject( product );

  // deserialize the object into a product
  Product product1 = serializer.DeserializeObject( sXml );
}
```

Found in the CustomerManagement.DataServices/CustomerManagement.Samples/SerializationSample.cs file of the download

The serializer defaults to XML serialization, but it also supports JSON serialization simply by entering a `SerializationFormat` enumeration parameter to the `SerializerFactory.Create()` method.

Listing 10-10 demonstrates how to serialize a `Product` to a JSON string and deserialize the string back into a `Product`.

Available for download on Wrox.com

LISTING 10-10: Serialize Product to JSON Text

```
public static void JsonSerializeObjectToText()
{
  Product product = GetProductList().First();

  // create a JSON product serializer.
  ISerializer<Product> serializer;
  serializer = SerializerFactory.Create<Product>( SerializationFormat.JSON );

  // Serialize object to a string.
  string sJson = serializer.SerializeObject( product );

  // deserialize the object into a product
  Product product1 = serializer.DeserializeObject( sJson );
}
```

Found in the CustomerManagement.DataServices/CustomerManagement.Samples/SerializationSample.cs file of the download

You can also serialize objects and lists into `byte[]` and into files by calling the appropriate *`SerializeXXX()`* methods such as `SerializeObjectToByteArray()` and `SerializeListToFile()`.

Listing 10-11 demonstrates how to serialize a `Product` and a `List< Product>` into XML files and deserialize them again.

Available for download on Wrox.com

LISTING 10-11: Serialize Product to Files

```
public static void XmlSerializeToFile()
{
  List<Product> list = GetProductList();
  Product product = list.First();

  string fileList = RootPath.AppendPath( "SerializeList.xml" );
  string fileObject = RootPath.AppendPath( "SerializeObject.xml" );

  // create a product serializer.  Serializer defaults to XML.
  ISerializer<Product> serializer = SerializerFactory.Create<Product>();

  // Serialize to a file, using Default Encryption settings.
  serializer.SerializeListToFile( list, fileList );
  serializer.SerializeObjectToFile( product, fileObject );

  // deserialize the files into a list and product
  List<Product> list1 = serializer.DeserializeListFromFile( fileList );
  Product product1 = serializer.DeserializeObjectFromFile( fileObject );
}
```

Found in the CustomerManagement.DataServices/CustomerManagement.Samples/SerializationSample.cs file of the download

The MonoCross Serialization Utility supports Default Encryption so that the previous listing can write the objects to a file encrypted if required. The MonoCross Serialization Utility supports Specific Encryption through similar method overloads used in the File Interface and also supports the No Encryption method.

Listing 10-12 demonstrates how to serialize a `Product` and a `List<Product>` into XML files using both Specific Encryption and No Encryption and deserialize them again.

Available for download on Wrox.com

LISTING 10-12: Serialize Product to Files with Encryption

```
public static void XmlSerializeObjectToFileWithEncryption()
{
  string key = "kjWkslr4qw4UT28LAfKJsYIdy9m+/vHry3fYDuydGk2=";
  byte[] salt = Convert.FromBase64String( "lRG7r+BNLTqVcKq6pTsMfi==" );

  Product prod = GetProductList().First();
  string fileEnc = RootPath.AppendPath( "SerializeSpecificEncryption.xml" );
  string filePlain = RootPath.AppendPath( "SerializePlain.xml" );

  // create a product serializer. Serializer defaults to XML.
```

```
        ISerializer<Product> serializer = SerializerFactory.Create<Product>();

        // Serialize object to a file, using Specific Encryption settings.
        serializer.SerializeObjectToFile( prod, fileEnc, key, salt );

        // Serialize object to a file, using No Encryption settings.
        serializer.SerializeObjectToFile( prod, filePlain, EncryptionMode.NoEncryption );

        // deserialize the file into a product, using Specific Encryption settings.
        Product prod1 = serializer.DeserializeObjectFromFile(fileEnc, key, salt );

        // deserialize file into a product, using No Encryption settings.
        serializer.DeserializeObjectFromFile( filePlain, EncryptionMode.NoEncryption );
    }
```

Found in the CustomerManagement.DataServices/CustomerManagement.Samples/SerializationSample.cs file of the download

LOGGING APPLICATION EVENTS

Applications occasionally need to record internal events to describe what happens during application run time. Whether it's to record critical information before a crash, track metrics used to improve performance, or log a series of breadcrumbs to track an application's progress, you need to be able to record information and have that recording persist between application sessions.

Understanding the Log Utility

The MonoCross Log Utility provides a cross-platform approach for logging application events. It follows standard logging levels of Debug, Info, Warning, Error, and Fatal, plus it adds an additional level for tracking application metrics, called *Metrics*.

In addition, the MonoCross Log Utility supports the logging of exceptions. The exceptions display in the log file with the message, stack trace, and the `Exception.Data` collection, so you can add additional information to the Exception before logging it.

Table 10-6 shows the details of the MonoCross Log Utility.

TABLE 10-6: MonoCross Log Utility

METHOD	DESCRIPTION
`Debug`	Logs a Debugging event. Method overloads support logging exceptions as well as messages.
`Error`	Logs an Error event. Method overloads support logging exceptions as well as messages.
`Fatal`	Logs a Fatal event. Method overloads support logging exceptions as well as messages.

continues

TABLE 10-6 *(continued)*

METHOD	DESCRIPTION
`Info`	Logs an Information event. Method overloads support logging exceptions as well as messages.
`Metric`	Logs a Metric event. Method overloads support logging of messages in addition to time duration of the metric being tracked expressed in milliseconds.
`Warning`	Logs a Warning event. Method overloads support logging exceptions as well as messages.

Putting the Log Utility to Work

The MonoCross Log Utility is simple to use. Just determine the log level of the message your application is to record and then call the appropriate `MXDevice.Log` method.

Listing 10-13 demonstrates the basic usage of the Log Interface.

LISTING 10-13: Logging Sample

Available for download on Wrox.com

```
public static void SimpleLogging()
{
  MXDevice.Log.Debug( "Logging an Debug Message" );
  MXDevice.Log.Info( "Logging an Information Message" );
  MXDevice.Log.Warn( "Logging a Warning Message" );
  MXDevice.Log.Error( "Logging an Error Message" );
  MXDevice.Log.Fatal( "Logging a Fatal Message" );

  MXDevice.Log.Metric( "Logging a Metric: Time: 100 milliseconds" );
  MXDevice.Log.Metric( "Logging a Metric:", 100 );
}
```

Found in the CustomerManagement.DataServices/CustomerManagement.Samples/LoggingSample.cs file of the download

The MonoCross Log Utility also supports overloads for logging an `Exception` in addition to text messages. Each of the logging methods has overloads to log the message text and the `Exception`. As stated before, the exception logging also supports the output of the `Exception.Data` collection, so it is worthwhile to collect supporting information for the exceptions.

Listing 10-14 demonstrates how to log an exception.

LISTING 10-14: Logging Exceptions

Available for download on Wrox.com

```
public static void ExceptionLogging()
{
  Product prod = null;
```

```
    try
    {
      prod = new Product();
      throw new Exception( "Test Exception" );
    }
    catch ( Exception exc )
    {
      // Add optional Data entries to the exception.
      exc.Data.Add( "Uri", "www.monocross.net" );
      exc.Data.Add( "Object Type Name", prod.GetType().Name );

      // we can just log a message
      MXDevice.Log.Error( "An exception occurred." );

      // we can just log the exception
      MXDevice.Log.Error( exc );

      // or both
      MXDevice.Log.Error( "An exception occurred.", exc );

      // And yes, all Log levels support exception logging.
      MXDevice.Log.Info( exc );
    }
  }
```

Found in the CustomerManagement.DataServices/CustomerManagement.Samples/LoggingSample.cs file of the download

The log output is sent to `MXDevice.DataPath` in a file named in the format `YYYY_MM_DD_BasicLogger.log` (for example, `2011_07_04_BasicLogger.log`). In addition, the log file contains the date and time of the logging event, the process ID of the event, useful for tracking issues in multi-threaded applications and the log level. This file contains entries similar those in Listing 10-15.

LISTING 10-15: Sample Log File Entries

```
07-04-2011 19:53:37:0938 :10: [Debug] Logging an Debug Message
07-04-2011 19:53:37:0948 :10: [Info] Logging an Information Message
07-04-2011 19:53:37:0958 :10: [Warn] Logging a Warning Message
07-04-2011 19:53:37:0968 :10: [Error] Logging an Error Message
07-04-2011 19:53:37:0978 :10: [Fatal] Logging a Fatal Message
07-04-2011 19:53:37:0988 :10: [Metric] Logging a Metric: Time: 100 milliseconds
07-04-2011 19:53:37:1008 :10: [Metric] Logging a Metric: : Milliseconds: 100
07-04-2011 19:53:37:1128 :10: [Error] An exception occurred.
07-04-2011 19:53:37:1198 :10: [Error] Date: 7/4/2011 7:53:37 PM, [Exception]
 Error
 Message: Test Exception
 Stack:    at CustomerManagement.Samples.LoggingSample.ExceptionLogging() in
 C:\Development\monocross-net\branches\Alpha\CustomerManagement.Samples
\LoggingSample.cs:line 30
 Data: key:Uri, value:www.monocross.net; key:Object Type Name, value:Product;
07-04-2011 19:53:37:1238 :10: [Error] An exception occurred.
```

continues

LISTING 10-15 *(continued)*

```
07-04-2011 19:53:37:1248 :10: [Error] Date: 7/4/2011 7:53:37 PM, [Exception]
 Error
 Message: Test Exception
 Stack:     at CustomerManagement.Samples.LoggingSample.ExceptionLogging() in
 C:\Development\monocross-net\branches\Alpha\CustomerManagement.Samples
\LoggingSample.cs:line 30
 Data: key:Uri, value:www.monocross.net; key:Object Type Name, value:Product;
07-04-2011 19:53:37:1278 :10: [Info] Date: 7/4/2011 7:53:37 PM, [Exception]
 Info
 Message: Test Exception
 Stack:     at CustomerManagement.Samples.LoggingSample.ExceptionLogging() in
 C:\Development\monocross-net\branches\Alpha\CustomerManagement.Samples
\LoggingSample.cs:line 30
 Data: key:Uri, value:www.monocross.net; key:Object Type Name, value:Product;
```

Sample logging output similar to expected output of logging samples

ACCESSING NETWORK FUNCTIONALITY

No man is an island, nor is an application. Applications often need to access data on a web server to display on a mobile device or even save the user's changes back to a centralized database. The MonoCross Network Utility provides a simple and reliable means of accessing RESTful services via the `Get()` and `Post()` methods.

Understanding the Network Utility

The MonoCross Network Utility supports the interaction with websites and URIs. This utility is used to access RESTful interfaces and return data in XML or JSON format as required by your particular application. It does this in a synchronous or asynchronous method as needed by the relevant platform.

In addition, the `Get()` and `Post()` methods can inject header information into the web requests. This header information is most often used to pass authentication information, such as user ID and password, from your application to the RESTful server being accessed. The server then uses the information to authenticate the user or confirm that a previous authentication is still valid before allowing the transaction to proceed.

You can find the MonoCross Network Utility within the `MonoCross.Utilities.Network` namespace. Table 10-7 describes the available methods.

TABLE 10-7: MonoCross Network Utility

METHOD	DESCRIPTION
`Get`	Returns the payload of a specified URI call as a `string`. Method overloads support injection of request header values to transmit `string` values such as authentication tokens.
`PostBytes`	Posts a `byte[]` to a specified URI. Method overloads support injection of request header values.
`PostObject`	Posts an `object` to a specified URI. The object serializes into a `byte[]` prior to transmission. Method overloads support injection of request header values.
`PostString`	Posts a `string` to a specified URI. The string converts into a `byte[]` prior to transmission. Method overloads support injection of request header values.

Putting the Network Utility to Work

Chapter 8, "Consuming Data Services," covers using the MonoCross Network Utility. Following is a simple demonstration of how to use the methods contained in the Network Interface.

Listing 10-16 demonstrates how to use an `MXDevice.Network.Get()` call to return a string from a website URI.

Available for download on Wrox.com

LISTING 10-16: Performing a Simple Get

```
public static void SimpleGet()
{
  // a fictional RESTful site that will return a product with id of 1
  string uri = "https://www.myproducttest.com/products/1.xml";

  // make the network call and results of the GET will be stored in string.
  string returnValue = MXDevice.Network.Get( uri );
}
```

Found in the CustomerManagement.DataServices/CustomerManagement.Samples/NetworkSample.cs file of the download

If a URI call to a RESTful service returns a known object type (such as `Product`), it's a simple matter to deserialize the object from the returned string for use within the application. You can make any necessary changes and then post them to the server for updates on the server.

Listing 10-17 demonstrates how to use an `MXDevice.Network.Get()` call to return a `string` from a website URI.

LISTING 10-17: Performing a Product Get and Post

Available for download on Wrox.com

```
public static void ProductGetAndPost()
{
  // a fictional RESTful site that will return a product with id of 1
  string uri = "https://www.myproducttest.com/products/1.xml";
  string returnValue = MXDevice.Network.Get( uri );

  // serialize response into a product
  ISerializer<Product> serializer = SerializerFactory.Create<Product>();
  Product prod = serializer.DeserializeObject( returnValue );

  prod.Description = "New Description.";

  // post object to server.
  // MXDevice.Network handles serializing object to bytes for the post
  MXDevice.Network.PostObject( uri, prod );
}
```

Found in the CustomerManagement.DataServices/CustomerManagement.Samples/NetworkSample.cs file of the download

As you can see, the MonoCross Network Utility simplifies getting and posting objects from RESTful interfaces. Situations arise in which additional information needs to be part of the request for the server to fulfill the request. These can include perhaps the user ID and password injected with the headers, or perhaps an authentication token on requests performed after authentication occurs.

You can collect any values that you need to include in the headers into a `Dictionary<string, string>` and pass them into the `Get()` and `Post()` methods. Because these values are strings, you can encrypt them prior to sending using Default Encryption or Specific Encryption, provided both the client application making the request and the server fulfilling it know the key and salt.

Listing 10-18 expands the previous example with injection headers.

LISTING 10-18: Getting and Posting with Header Injection

Available for download on Wrox.com

```
public static void ProductGetAndPostWithInjection()
{
  // a fictional RESTful site that will return a product with id of 1
  string uri = "https://www.myproducttest.com/products/1.xml";

  Dictionary<string, string> headers = new Dictionary<string, string>();
```

```
    // add some header information, such as a username and authentication token
    headers.Add( "UserName", "TestUser1" );
    headers.Add( "AuthToken", "ABC123DEF456asd13234edfadf12334" );

    // assuming the server being called knows the appropriate key and salt
    // we can encrypt the header value, example uses Default Encryption.
    string encryptedInfo = MXDevice.Encryption.EncryptString( "Info to Encrypt" );
    headers.Add( "EncryptedInfo", encryptedInfo );

    // now that the headers have been set up, include them in the Get calls
    // the Network Interface will include them in the request.
    string returnValue = MXDevice.Network.Get( uri, headers );

    // serialize response into a product
    ISerializer<Product> serializer = SerializerFactory.Create<Product>();
    Product prod = serializer.DeserializeObject( returnValue );

    prod.Description = "New Description.";

    // post object to server.
    // MXDevice.Network handles serializing object to bytes for the post
    MXDevice.Network.PostObject( uri, prod, headers );
}
```

Found in the CustomerManagement.DataServices/CustomerManagement.Samples/NetworkSample.cs file of the download

THREADING YOUR APPLICATION

Gone are the days when an application, even a small mobile app, can ignore threading and all that entails. Processes may need to run in the background, but not so many at a time to impact performance. The MonoCross Thread Utility provides a simple and effective means to initiate process threads and execute them directly and in thread pools.

Understanding the Thread Utility

The MonoCross Thread Utility supports background threads and related thread pools. Two thread pools exist: the Worker Pool and the Idle Queue Pool. The Worker Pool abstracts the default thread pool of the platform in question, whereas the Idle Thread Queue executes threads only when the user interface is idle — that is, when the user is not navigating within the application. In addition, the `DiscardIdleThread()` method can remove delegate calls placed on the Idle Thread Queue, if they haven't been processed.

You can find the MonoCross Thread Utility within the `MonoCross.Utilities.Threading` namespace. Table 10-8 describes the available methods.

TABLE 10-8: MonoCross Thread Utility

METHOD	DESCRIPTION
`DiscardIdleThread`	Discards all unprocessed `delegate` methods on the Idle Thread Queue.
`QueueIdle`	Adds a `ParameterizedThreadStart` to the Idle Thread Queue. Method overloads support an `object` parameter.
`QueueWorker`	Adds a `ParameterDelegate` to the Worker Pool. Method overloads support an `object` parameter.
`Start`	Starts background process of a `ThreadDelegate` or `Parameter Delegate`. Method overloads support an `object` parameter.

Putting the Thread Utility to Work

The MonoCross Thread Utility encapsulates a common set of threading methods supported across the platforms. Although documenting all the ins and outs of threading are beyond the scope of this section, all rules of multithreaded development are still valid, so you need to properly apply locking code and handle exceptions.

The following code samples demonstrate the use of static methods for simplicity, but you can just as easily implement them using instance methods.

The MonoCross Thread Utility supports two internal delegates for use in threading, one with an `object` parameter and the other with no parameters. Listing 10-19 displays the signature of the internal threading delegates.

Available for download on Wrox.com

LISTING 10-19: Threading Delegates

```
public delegate void ThreadDelegate();
public delegate void ParameterDelegate( object parameter );
```

Found in the CustomerManagement.DataServices/CustomerManagement.Samples/ThreadingSample.cs file of the download

You can use both of these delegates as parameters for the `MXDevice.Thread.Start()` method overloads; any delegates passed into this method must match one of these two signatures. Use the `Start()` method to immediately execute the delegate on a separate thread. Listing 10-20 displays the use of the `Start()` methods, along with their relevant delegate methods.

Available for download on Wrox.com

LISTING 10-20: Starting Threads

```
// matches ThreadDelegate() signature
public static void DoStartWork()
{
  MXDevice.Log.Info( "Starting work." );
```

```
}

// matches ParameterDelegate() signature
public static void DoStartWorkParam( object parameter )
{
  MXDevice.Log.Info( String.Format( "Starting work with {0}.", parameter ) );
}

public static void StartWork()
{
  Product prod = new Product() { ID = "1", Description = "Description" };

  MXDevice.Log.Info( "StartWork() Output" );

  MXDevice.Thread.Start( ThreadingSample.DoStartWork );
  MXDevice.Thread.Start( ThreadingSample.DoStartWorkParam, "StringParameter" );
  MXDevice.Thread.Start( ThreadingSample.DoStartWorkParam, typeof( String ) );
  MXDevice.Thread.Start( ThreadingSample.DoStartWorkParam, prod );
}

// StartWork() will result in a log file similar to the following
07-05-2011 23:26:30:4494 :9: [Info] StartWork() Output
07-05-2011 23:26:30:4564 :9: [Info] Starting work.
07-05-2011 23:26:30:4584 :9: [Info] Starting work with String Parameter.
07-05-2011 23:26:30:4594 :9: [Info] Starting work with System.String.
07-05-2011 23:26:30:4594 :9: [Info] Starting work with
CustomerManagement.Shared.Model.Product.
```

Found in the CustomerManagement.DataServices/CustomerManagement.Samples/ThreadingSample.cs file of the download

Starting a thread immediately is all well and good, but suppose you have multiple tasks that you need to run in the background. The Worker Pool utility supports the execution of background tasks such as refreshing data, cache file cleanup, and so on. Any method that matches the `MonoCross.Utilities.Threading.ParameterDelegate` signature, which contains a single `object` parameter, can be added to the pool. Listing 10-21 demonstrates how to add a delegate to the Worker Pool.

LISTING 10-21: Pooling Threads

Available for download on Wrox.com

```
public static void DoPoolWorkParam( object parameter )
{
  MXDevice.Log.Info( String.Format( "Pooling work with {0}.", parameter ) );
}

public static void PoolingWork()
{
  Product prod = new Product() { ID = "1", Description = "Description" };

  MXDevice.Log.Info( "PoolingWork() Output" );

  // QueueWorker only supports ParameterDelegate Signature
  MXDevice.Thread.QueueWorker( ThreadingSample.DoPoolWorkParam );
```

continues

LISTING 10-21 *(continued)*

```
    MXDevice.Thread.QueueWorker( ThreadingSample.DoPoolWorkParam, "StringParameter" );
    MXDevice.Thread.QueueWorker( ThreadingSample.DoPoolWorkParam, typeof( String ) );
    MXDevice.Thread.QueueWorker( ThreadingSample.DoPoolWorkParam, prod );
}
```

Found in the CustomerManagement.DataServices/CustomerManagement.Samples/ThreadingSample.cs file of the download

Lastly, there are situations in which your application needs to run background threads, but only when the application is idle so the thread processing doesn't negatively impact the user experience with the application. When this occurs, you can add the delegates to the Idle Queue Pool with the `QueueIdle()` method. Listing 10-22 demonstrates how to add delegates to the Idle Queue Pool.

LISTING 10-22: Queueing Threads

Available for download on Wrox.com

```
public static void DoQueueWorkParam( object parameter )
{
    MXDevice.Log.Info( String.Format( "Queueing work with {0}.", parameter ) );
}

public static void QueueingWork()
{
    Product prod = new Product() { ID = "1", Description = "Description" };

    MXDevice.Log.Info( "QueueingWork() Output" );

    // Add delegates to Idle Queue Thread.
    MXDevice.Thread.QueueIdle( ThreadingSample.DoQueueWorkParam );
    MXDevice.Thread.QueueIdle( ThreadingSample.DoQueueWorkParam, "StringParameter" );
    MXDevice.Thread.QueueIdle( ThreadingSample.DoQueueWorkParam, typeof( String ) );
    MXDevice.Thread.QueueIdle( ThreadingSample.DoQueueWorkParam, prod );

    // The Idle Queue Thread runs when navigation is idle.
    // The DiscardIdleThread removes any unprocessed delegates from the queue.
    MXDevice.Thread.DiscardIdleThread();
}
```

Found in the CustomerManagement.DataServices/CustomerManagement.Samples/ThreadingSample.cs file of the download

SUMMARY

In this chapter, you explored the MonoCross Utilities and how they simplify cross-platform coding for many common tasks. You learned how to encrypt data, interact with the file system, serialize objects, log events, make network GETs and POSTs, and multithread your applications. All this was possible through a collection of simple, abstracted interfaces that enable you to focus on your business logic rather than on cross-platform idiosyncrasies.

In the next chapter, you learn more about hybrid applications. Specifically, you learn what they are and, more important, how to create them.

11

Hybrid Applications

WHAT'S IN THIS CHAPTER?

- Understanding the benefits and drawbacks of hybrid applications
- Understanding the architecture of hybrid applications
- Building hybrid applications for iOS, Android, and Windows Phone

Throughout the book you've learned how to build native applications, but because of existing infrastructure, technology choice, or other reasons, you might want to use a web-based approach. We've discussed uses for web-based browser applications, and you can combine the two approaches when needed. Hybrid mobile applications involve a combination of a web-based application and a native platform application. The popular PhoneGap application framework uses this approach but with native development done in the de-facto standard programming language for the platform it targets. Using .NET you can improve on some aspects of this approach and offer additional options.

THE REASONING BEHIND THE WEB HYBRID APPROACH

First briefly consider the merits and shortfalls of both the completely native approach and the completely web-based approach. Then see if you can extract the best parts of each to make your own decision as to whether you can use the architecture to your advantage.

Native Applications

Native applications are built using the software development stacks provided by the operating system implementer or device manufacturer. Figure 11-1 shows a simple architectural diagram of how a native application interacts with a mobile operating system.

Here are some features of native applications you should be aware of when considering an application development strategy.

- **Written entirely in native code (.NET/C# included):** Native applications are built for the mobile device they are targeted to and have full access to all the hardware and graphic features exposed to application developers. Native applications also have full access to the native API, making the rich native interface, native APIs, and widgets accessible to the developer.
- **Performance:** Native applications are designed and built for a specific mobile operating system in the tools provided by the system vendor, giving native applications the edge on speed.
- **App Store:** Native applications must be packaged and distributed when the application code changes for features or for bug fixes.

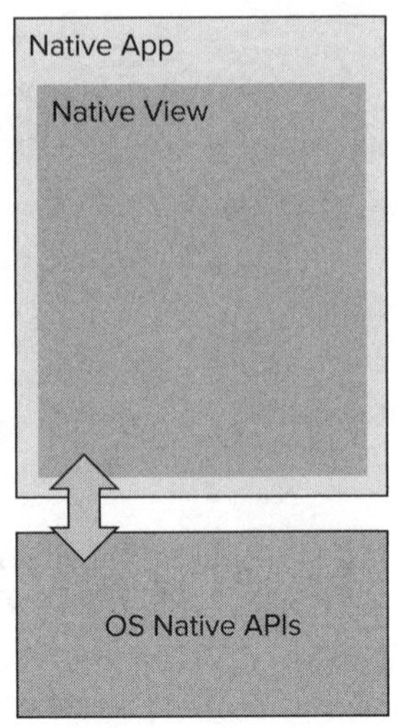

FIGURE 11-1: The native application architecture is fairly simple.

Web Applications

Web applications are built using HTML and are housed on web servers using software designed to generate web pages. Figure 11-2 shows a simple architectural diagram of how a web application interacts with a mobile operating system.

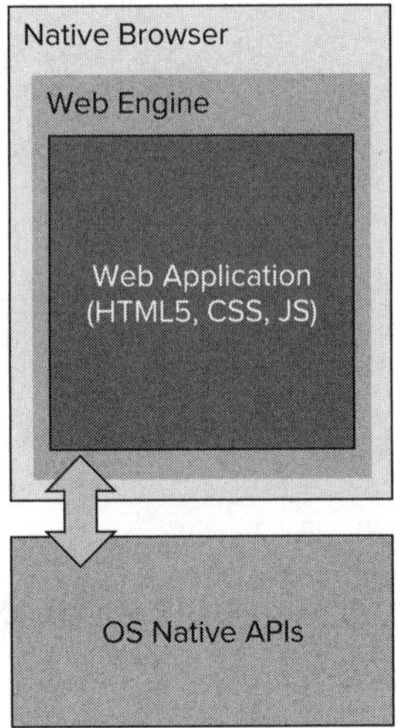

FIGURE 11-2: The web application architecture uses the built-in browser for applications.

Here are some features of mobile web applications you should be aware of when considering an application development strategy.

- **Written entirely in web technologies (HTML5, CSS, and JavaScript):** Web applications are becoming increasingly interactive and capable with the addition of feature-laden JavaScript libraries and the offline capabilities added to HTML5. Web applications can even install themselves into the operating system of the device like a native application. Many believe this is the silver bullet of mobile application development, but HTML5 is not yet standardized to the point of supplying all the foreseen features developers are implementing to the same level for all mobile platforms.

  New features may not be available; you must wait for new hardware support or other device features, for example Near Field Communications isn't even a planned feature for HTML5.
- **All application code interpreted, rendered, and executed by the browser:** Web applications are not as fast as native applications; depending on what your application is intended to do, this might not be a big issue. JavaScript optimization and performance has been a focus of vendors for several years, and the speed of devices has been increasing steadily at the same time. However, applications

with a large object model or complex business requirements get hard to run without server support, and JavaScript wasn't intended for the complexity that can come with some applications.

- **No App Store:** There is currently no significant option for a customer to access your web application other than browser searches. Of course, you can send that customer the URL to find the application. This may or may not be a downside, depending on how you expect your users to find and use your application. For an enterprise application, this might be a benefit. For a consumer application, this may be a tremendous downfall because you must host the application and drive demand for it.

Hybrid Applications

Now that you've rehashed, to varying degrees, completely native mobile applications and web-based HTML5 applications, what about building a combination of the two? What can stop you from building part of your application as a native application? You could build difficult data entry forms — that you just can't get right on a mobile application — using HTML and CSS, either retrieved from the web or downloaded as part of an application installation from a corporate app store. You know how to get your data from the web; why not get content that can change often or can easily be built with static or dynamic HTML pages from the web? All your help documentation could easily be placed online. Such materials are generally a set of non-interactive documents that look more like HTML than native application content, and you can update the documents without making changes to your application.

Figure 11-3 shows a combination of the native and web applications. With a hybrid approach, you can choose which pieces would work well as native views and which would work as web pages, depending the strengths and weaknesses of native and web approaches and how they suit your application.

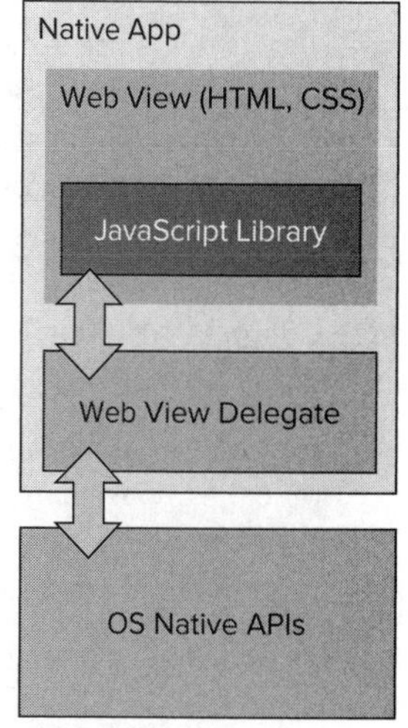

FIGURE 11-3: The hybrid application architecture is more complex.

Even though you might be leaning toward mobile web applications to simplify upgrading and deploying updates, you still might need some of the features available only to native device applications and not to browser-based web applications. For example, if your company needs a complex security process that can't be handled by web applications, for example, access to a fingerprint scanner, barcode scanner, or other device, there would be no way to do that from a standard browser. Hybrid applications can be extended to provide this functionality, whereas pure web applications cannot.

The rest of this chapter shows how to implement a web-hybrid application in C# and provides the HTML, CSS, and JavaScript needed to make it all work together. Our example application shows the basics of implementing and extending the interactions between the web application and the native mobile operating system.

IMPLEMENTING A HYBRID APPROACH

This section implements a hybrid application for iOS, Android, and Windows Phone. All the HTML, CSS, and JavaScript files are identical for each platform, with the exception of a minor difference in the JavaScript for Windows Phone. The C# code is specific to each platform but follows a similar pattern. The principles are largely the same, but the implementations vary from platform to platform because of how each platform exposes its web components and consumes local HTML on the device.

The samples supplied use only local content and do not require either a network connection or a live server to host HTML. There is no limitation on the location of the HTML or any other resource other than the hosting application. If differences are required in the HTML, CSS, or JavaScript, the web server can handle serving up the proper content.

The examples don't use the MonoCross pattern for the implementation of the platform hybrid containers so that you can focus on the implementation of the container. You could still easily use the web containers built here as part of a larger MonoCross application using the approach for parts of a MonoCross application, for example, if you already have a mobile web application and want to use HTML for documentation or a help system. Another example of when you might want to use the web containers as part of a larger application is if you want to build out your mobile applications in stages but give access to your online content while you implement functionality to replace it.

Understanding How Hybrid Applications Work

Before getting into the implementation, consider the technical aspects of how hybrid applications work. The goal is to build a way to allow a web application to interact with features of the device. All platforms use a native web view component to enable the application developer to display web content and interact with the content. The web application is then loaded into the web component by the native application by either loading the local HTML page or directing the web component to an HTML page on a web server via a URL. The HTML page, then, loads a JavaScript framework for accessing the device in addition to whatever CSS and JavaScript libraries it intends to use.

How the Web Application Interacts with the Device

The most important part for the application developer is how the web application accesses the platform-specific functionality, such as playing a sound or accessing the compass. All the JavaScript function calls are asynchronous, meaning you cannot expect an immediate result to be returned. To make calls to functions that need data returned, such as the compass or accelerometer, you specify callback functions for both success and failure so you can deal with either scenario in your web applications.

Because this chapter is intended to show you how this works instead of implementing a full native access API, it defines a basic API that shows enough for you to understand how to build your own. For the sample, you implement a notification component to enable a default sound and vibration to notify the users of an event of some sort, and you implement access to the compass and accelerometer. The compass and accelerometer component must return data to the web application; the notification component does not. Given those requirements, Listing 11-1 shows calls to your components. Additionally it, defines the callback function's success and failure function prototypes.

Available for download on Wrox.com

LISTING 11-1: JavaScript library functions

```
notify.playSound();
notify.vibrate(duration);
compass.watchCompass(compassSuccess, compassFail);
compass.cancelWatch();
accelerometer.watchAccelerometer(accelSuccess, accelFail);
accelerometer.cancelWatch();

// prototypes for the functions passed as parameters in the watchAccelerometer
// and watchCompass methods
function compassSuccess(heading) {
  // application code
}
function compassFail(message) {
  // application code
}
function accelSuccess(x, y, z) {
  // application code
}
function accelFail(message) {
  // application code
}
```

Found in the WebHybrid/WebHybrid.Touch/container.js file of the download

So the accelerometer and compass methods can return your compass heading and acceleration values. What the web application does with the result of the call is up to the application developer; this implementation just shows the results to the user.

How to Implement the Device Interaction

Now that you have defined how the application developer works with your device integration, look at how to implement the interaction between the web application and the native container. To communicate to the native layer, use a URL-based navigation protocol with the following syntax:

```
'hybrid://{component}/{action}/{param1}/{param2}/.../{paramN}'
```

Use this protocol because it gives you the flexibility needed to make requests to the native layer and because all the web components implement navigation events that the native application can intercept, thus giving you a way to pass the request to the native layer. When the browser attempts to load a new page, the URL of that page is given to the application, and the application can inspect it and either allow or disallow the navigation. A web page would normally do this in JavaScript by setting the `document.location` from the HTML DOM to the URL to which you want to navigate, for example:

```
document.location = 'hybrid://notify/vibrate/1000';
```

This works for both the iOS and Android platforms. Windows Phone does not yet enable access to the location in the document or window DOM elements, so instead you can make use of a special JavaScript method exposed in the Windows Phone web component:

```
Window.external.Notify('hybrid://notify/vibrate/1000');
```

To explain further, instead of using the normal `http` prefix, you can instead use `hybrid`; in fact, you could use any other unused URI prefix. Then extend the URI syntax to the component, action, and parameters needed to make the request to the native layer. The use of the separate URI prefix allows the native layer to easily distinguish normal `http` navigation from requests from the web application.

You have a way to make requests to the native layer, but how can you get results back? Making calls into the native layer is an asynchronous operation, look to the web component from the native application. All platforms expose a way to call a JavaScript function; this allows the application to return a status or data to a web application. Using this mechanism, the native layer can make calls back to the components on the success and fail functions defined in the API shown in Listing 11-1.

Building the Web Components

To keep the code and concepts as simple as possible, the example code uses only simple HTML or CSS. The sample code does not use external JavaScript or other web frameworks for the display. Instead, the code highlights providing native device access to custom features not exposed through the browser; specifically, consider the accelerometer, compass, and simple sound and vibrate functionality. This is a limited sample size to keep the code simple enough to digest. Following the patterns implemented here, you can easily extend the code to fit your needs.

Start by looking over the HTML content for the hybrid application in Listing 11-2. For the most part it's just a standard HTML page with a few meta tags plus some simple added formatting that is accepted by standard mobile web browsers to fit the content to the page. The content can consist of four link tags and four div sections; the links are formatted as buttons. You can use them to make calls into the native container so that you can try out the code. The div sections are for output messages. Notice the inclusion of `container.css` and `container.js`. The first, `container.css`, has the defined formatting for the elements in the page; and `container.js` holds the JavaScript library for calling the native container.

Listing 11-2 provides some highlighted script sections. In them, five functions are defined that you need to use: The first, `writeInfo()`, takes a tag ID and sets the inner text of the tag to the message text in the argument. The only reason for this function is to show output from the compass and accelerometer.

LISTING 11-2: HTML implementation of the container

Available for download on Wrox.com

```
<!DOCTYPE HTML PUBLIC "-//W3C//DTD HTML 4.01//EN"
  "http://www.w3.org/TR/html4/strict.dtd">
<html>
  <head>
    <title>Mobile Container Document</title>
```

```
    <meta name="viewport" content=
      "width=device-width; initial-scale=1.0; maximum-scale=1.0; user-scalable=0"/>
    <meta http-equiv="Content-type" content="text/html; charset=utf-8"/>
    <link rel="stylesheet" href="container.css"
          type="text/css" media="screen" title="no title" charset="utf-8"/>
    <script type="text/javascript" charset="utf-8" src="container.js" ></script>
    <script type="text/javascript">
      function writeInfo(location, message) {
        var element = document.getElementById(location);
        element.innerHTML = message + '<br/>';
      }
      function compassSuccess(heading) {
        writeInfo("infoCompass", "heading: " + heading);
      }
      function compassFail(message) {
        writeInfo("infoCompass", message);
      }
      function accelSuccess(x, y, z) {
        writeInfo("infoAccelerometer", "x: " + x + " y: " + y + " z: " + z);
      }
      function accelFail(message) {
        writeInfo("infoAccelerometer", "accelerometer failed!");
      }
    </script>
  </head>
  <body  id="stage" class="theme">
    <a href="#" class="btn large"
       onclick="javascript:compass.watchCompass(compassSuccess, compassFail);">
         Compass
    </a>
    <div id="infoCompass"> </div>
    <a href="#" class="btn large"
    onclick="javascript:accelerometer.watchAccelerometer(accelSuccess, accelFail);">
           Accelerometer
       </a>
       <div id="infoAccelerometer"> </div>
       <a href="#" class="btn large" onclick="javascript:notify.playSound();">
         Play Sound
      </a>
       <div id="info"> </div>

    <a href="#" class="btn large"
       onclick="javascript:notify.vibrate('2000');">
      Vibrate
    </a>
    <div id="info2"> </div>
  </body>
</html>
```

Found in the WebHybrid/WebHybrid.Touch/container.html file of the download

Diving into the JavaScript implementation, Listing 11-3 shows the implementation of the Notify, Accelerometer, and Compass components. All the components implement their method calls to the native layer by calling a helper function `Container.exec()` to abstract the URI formatting and the mechanics of passing on the URI to the native layer. In addition to the method calls for the native layer, the `Accelerometer` and `Compass` classes have success and failure callback methods defined. On calls to the native layer, you can stash away the callback functions into local objects so that the native layer has a known entry point at which to call back into the web application. Note also the creation of instances of each component. Defining the entry points isn't enough because the native layer needs a known object instance in addition to the function and object definitions.

Available for download on Wrox.com

LISTING 11-3: JavaScript implementation of the container

```
function Notification() {
  this.vibrate = function (mills) {
    Container.exec('notify.vibrate', mills);
  }
  this.playSound = function () {
    Container.exec('notify.playSound');
  }
}
var notify = new Notification();

function Accelerometer() {
  Accelerometer.prototype.onAccelerometerSuccess = function (x, y, z) {
  };
  Accelerometer.prototype.onAccelerometerFail = function (message) {
  };
  Accelerometer.prototype.watchAccelerometer = function (onSuccess, onFail) {
    this.onAccelerometerSuccess = onSuccess;
    this.onAccelerometerFail = onFail;
      Container.exec('accelerometer.start');
  }
  Accelerometer.prototype.cancelAccelerometer = function () {
    Container.exec('accelerometer.cancel');
  }
}
var accelerometer = new Accelerometer();

function Compass() {
  Compass.prototype.onCompassSuccess = function (heading) {
  };
  Compass.prototype.onCompassFail = function (message) {
  };
  Compass.prototype.watchCompass = function (onSuccess, onFail) {
    this.onCompassSuccess = onSuccess;
    this.onCompassFail = onFail;
    Container.exec('compass.start');
  }
  Compass.prototype.cancelCompass = function () {
    Container.exec('compass.cancel');
  }
}
var compass = new Compass();
```

Found in the WebHybrid/WebHybrid.Touch/www/container.js file of this download

Listing 11-4 shows the implementation of the call to the native layer, where you can parse the component, action, and parameters into a URI. You can also encode each parameter to allow for special characters in string arguments so that more complex JSON objects can be passed as parameters. You can also call out the differences between the iOS and Android implementations and the Windows Phone implementation.

LISTING 11-4: JavaScript implementation of the container

Available for download on Wrox.com

```
if (typeof (DeviceInfo) != "object") {
  DeviceInfo = {}
}
Container = {
  commands: []
};
Container.exec = function () {
  Container.commands.push(arguments);
  var args = Container.commands.shift();
  var uri = [];
  var dict = null;
  for (var i = 1; i < args.length; i++) {
    var arg = args[i];
    if (arg == undefined || arg == null) {
      arg = ""
    }
    if (typeof (arg) == "object") {
      dict = arg
    } else {
      uri.push(encodeURIComponent(arg))
    }
  }
  var actionUri = args[0].replace(".", "/");
  var url = "hybrid://" + actionUri + "/" + uri.join("/");
  if (dict != null) {
    url += "?" + encodeURIComponent(JSON.stringify(dict))
  }
  // Andriod and iOS implementations
  document.location = url;
  // Windows Phone implementation
  window.external.Notify(url);
};
```

Found in the WebHybrid/WebHybrid.Touch/www/container.js file of the download

Building the Native Containers

Now that you have the common Web components for the solution, dive into building containers for each platform, starting with iOS. First you get a glimpse of the resulting applications. Figure 11-4 shows you the web components running on the emulators of each of the platforms you built containers for.

Building the iOS Container

In addition to the common web application components you have implemented, the main implementation of the native web component is a `UIViewController` that creates a child view in the form of a `UIWebView`, the web component exposed to the application developer in the iOS SDK. Listing 11-5 shows the implementation of the `UIViewController`.

FIGURE 11-4: The web hybrid application runs on the iOS, Android, and Windows Phone platforms.

LISTING 11-5: iOS Web View container

Available for download on Wrox.com

```
namespace WebHybrid.Touch
{
  public class WebViewController : UIViewController
  {
    UIWebView _webView;

    public override void ViewDidLoad ()
    {
      base.ViewDidLoad ();
      SetupView();
    }

    void SetupView()
    {
      _webView = new UIWebView();
```

```
      _webView.Frame = new RectangleF(0f, 0f, 320f, 422f);
      _webView.Delegate = new WebViewDelegate(_webView);

      NSUrl url = NSUrl.FromFilename("www/container.html");
      _webView.LoadRequest(new NSUrlRequest(url));
      this.View.AddSubview(_webView);
    }
  }

  public class WebViewDelegate : UIWebViewDelegate
  {
    UIWebView _webView = null;

    public WebViewDelegate(UIWebView webView)
    {
      _webView = webView;
    }

    public override bool ShouldStartLoad (UIWebView webView, NSUrlRequest request,
                                        UIWebViewNavigationType navigationType)
    {
      string actionUri = string.Empty;
      string uri = request.Url.AbsoluteUrl.ToString();
      if(uri.ToLower().Contains("hybrid://"))
      {
        actionUri = uri.Substring(9);
        CallNativeMethod(actionUri);
        return false;
      }
      return true;
    }

    void CallNativeMethod(string actionUri)
    {
      string[] paramArray = actionUri.Split(new Char[] { '/' });
      string action = paramArray[0].ToString();
      string[] itemArray = paramArray.Skip(1).Take(paramArray.Length-1).ToArray();

      System.Console.WriteLine("WebViewActivity: CallNativeMethod: " + action);

      switch (action) {
      case "compass":
        if (itemArray[0].Equals("start")) {
          CompassStart();
        } else if (itemArray[0].Equals("cancel")) {
          CompassCancel();
        }
        break;

      case "accelerometer":
        if (itemArray[0].Equals("start")) {
          AccelerometerStart();
        } else if (itemArray[0].Equals("cancel")) {
          AccelerometerCancel();
```

continues

LISTING 11-5 *(continued)*

```
        }
        break;

      case "notify":
        if (itemArray.Length >= 1) {
          if (itemArray[0].Equals("vibrate"))
          {
            MonoCross.Utilities.Notification.Notify.Vibrate();
          }
          else if (itemArray[0].Equals("playSound"))
          {
            MonoCross.Utilities.Notification.Notify.PlaySound(itemArray[1]);
          }
        }
        break;
    }
  }

  static CLLocationManager _lm;

  void CompassStart()
  {
    if (_lm != null) {
      _lm = new CLLocationManager();
      _lm.UpdatedHeading += delegate(object s, CLHeadingUpdatedEventArgs e) {
        string javascript = string.Format("compass.onCompassSuccess({0:0.00})",
          _lm.Heading.MagneticHeading);
        _webView.EvaluateJavascript(javascript);
      };
      _lm.StartUpdatingHeading();
    }
  }

  void CompassCancel()
  {
    _lm.StopUpdatingHeading();
  }

  void AccelerometerStart()
  {
    if (UIAccelerometer.SharedAccelerometer != null) {
      UIAccelerometer.SharedAccelerometer.UpdateInterval = 0.05;
      UIAccelerometer.SharedAccelerometer.Acceleration +=
        delegate(object s, UIAccelerometerEventArgs e) {
          string javascript =string.Format(
           "compass.onAccelerometerSuccess({0:0.0}, {1:0.0}, {2:0.0})",
           e.Acceleration.X, e.Acceleration.Y, e.Acceleration.Z);
          _webView.EvaluateJavascript(javascript);
        };
    }
  }
```

```
        void AccelerometerCancel()
        {
          UIAccelerometer.SharedAccelerometer.UpdateInterval = 0.0;
        }
      }
    }
```

Found in the WebHybrid/WebHybrid.Touch/WebViewController.cs file of the download

The two most interesting parts of the code are where you intercept the URI navigation and the callback to the web application. To intercept the call from the web application, you need to define a delegate object to look at the URI to determine if it's a normal navigation URI or your call from the web application. The delegate implements an override of the function `ShouldStartLoad()`, which is responsible for inspecting and optionally processing the URL of the navigation. If you process the call, return `false` and end the navigation; if it's not one of your special URLs, return `true` and forget it ever happened.

If you handle a call from the web application, you must call back the web application if it expects a response; for example, for the compass and accelerometer, you need to pass back either success or failure. To do this in the iOS web component, use the following method call:

```
_webView.EvaluateJavascript("compass.onCompassFail('No Compass');");
```

The remainder of the code takes care of interpreting the call from the web application and making the appropriate native APIs. Now would be a good time to build and run the sample code and become more familiar with the code. Note that it is most effective on a physical device, because the compass, accelerometer, vibrator, and audio do not work in the iOS simulator.

Building the Android Container

Continuing to the Android platform, the main implementation of the native web component is an Android Activity that loads a layout containing a WebView view. Listing 11-6 shows the implementation of the Activity.

LISTING 11-6: Android Web View container

Available for download on Wrox.com

```
namespace WebHybrid.Droid
{
  [Activity(Label = "Web Hybrid", MainLauncher = true)]
  public class WebViewActivity : Activity
  {
    WebView _webView;

    protected class WebViewClientOverride : WebViewClient, ISensorEventListener
    {
      Context _context;
      WebView _webView;

      public WebViewClientOverride(Context parent, WebView webView)
      {
```

continues

LISTING 11-6 *(continued)*

```
    _context = parent;
    _webView = webView;
  }

  public override bool ShouldOverrideUrlLoading(WebView view, string url)
  {
    if (url.ToLower().StartsWith("hybrid://")) {
      string actionUri = url.Substring(9);
      CallNativeMethod(actionUri);
      return true;
    }
    return base.ShouldOverrideUrlLoading(view, url);
  }

  void CallNativeMethod(string actionUri)
  {
    string[] paramArray = actionUri.Split(new Char[] { '/' });
    string action = paramArray[0].ToString();
    string[] itemArray = paramArray.Skip(1).Take(paramArray.Length-1).ToArray();

    Log.Info("WebViewActivity", "CallNativeMethod: " + action);

    switch (action) {
    case "compass":
      if (itemArray[0].Equals("start")) {
        CompassStart();
      } else if (itemArray[0].Equals("cancel")) {
        CompassCancel();
      }
      break;
    case "accelerometer":
      if (itemArray[0].Equals("start")) {
        AccelerometerStart();
      } else if (itemArray[0].Equals("cancel")) {
        AccelerometerCancel();
      }
      break;
    case "notify":
      if (itemArray.Length >= 1) {
        if (itemArray[0].Equals("vibrate")) {
          MonoCross.Utilities.Notification.Notify.Vibrate(_context, 500);
        } else if (itemArray[0].Equals("playSound")) {
          MonoCross.Utilities.Notification.Notify.PlaySound(_context,
            itemArray[1]);
        }
      }
      break;
    }
  }

  protected void CompassStart()
  {
```

```
    SensorManager sm =
      _context.GetSystemService(Context.SensorService) as SensorManager;
    Sensor sensor = sm.GetDefaultSensor(SensorType.Orientation);
    if (sensor != null) {
      sm.RegisterListener(this, sensor, SensorDelay.Ui);
    } else {
      _webView.LoadUrl(
        "javascript:compass.onCompassFail('No Compass Found');");
    }
  }

  static void CompassCancel() {
    SensorManager sm =
      _context.GetSystemService(Context.SensorService) as SensorManager;
    Sensor sensor = sm.GetDefaultSensor(SensorType.Compass);
    sm.RevokeListener(this, sensor);
  }

  protected void AccelerometerStart()
  {
    SensorManager sm =
      _context.GetSystemService(Context.SensorService) as SensorManager;
    Sensor sensor = sm.GetDefaultSensor(SensorType.Accelerometer);
    if (sensor != null) {
      sm.RegisterListener(this, sensor, SensorDelay.Ui);
    } else {
      _webView.LoadUrl(
        "javascript:accelerometer.onAccelerometerFail('No Accelerometer');");
    }
  }

  static void AccelerometerCancel()
  {
    SensorManager sm =
      _context.GetSystemService(Context.SensorService) as SensorManager;
    Sensor sensor = sm.GetDefaultSensor(SensorType.Accelerometer);
    sm.RevokeListener(this);
  }

  public void OnAccuracyChanged (Sensor sensor, int accuracy)
  {
  }

  public void OnSensorChanged (SensorEvent e) {
    string js = "";
    switch (e.Sensor.Type) {
    case SensorType.Orientation:
      js = string.Format(
       "javascript:compass.onCompassSuccess({0:0.00})", e.Values[0]);
      break;
    case SensorType.Accelerometer:
      js  = string.Format(
        "javascript:accelerometer.onAccelerometerSuccess({0:0.00})",
          e.Values[0], e.Values[1], e.Values[2]);
```

continues

LISTING 11-6 *(continued)*

```
                break;
            }
            if (js.Length > 0) {
                _webView.LoadUrl(js);
            }
        }
    }

    protected override void OnCreate(Bundle bundle)
    {
        base.OnCreate(bundle);

        SetContentView(Resource.Layout.Main);

        _webView = FindViewById<WebView>(Resource.Id.WebView);

        _webView.ScrollBarStyle = ScrollbarStyles.InsideOverlay;
        _webView.Settings.JavaScriptEnabled = true;
        _webView.SetWebViewClient(new WebViewClientOverride(this, _webView));
        _webView.LoadUrl(@"file:///android_asset/container.html");
    }
  }
}
```

Found in the WebHybrid/WebHybrid.Droid/WebViewActivity.cs file of the download

The two most interesting parts of the code are, again, the interception of the URI navigation and the call back to the web application. When looking at the code in Listing 11-6, you may notice a lot of similarity between the Android method of URL interception and that of the iOS platform. They are similar because both are built on the open source WebKit web browser client.

To intercept the call from the web application, you need to define a delegate object to look at the URI to determine if it's a normal navigation URI or your call from the web application. The delegate implements an override of the function `ShouldOverrideUrlLoading()`, which is responsible for inspecting and optionally processing the URL of the navigation. If you process the call, return `false` and end navigation, if it's not one of your special URLs, return `true` and forget it.

If you handle a call from the web application, call back the web application if it expects a response; for example, for the compass and accelerometer, you need to pass back either success or failure. To do this in the Android web component, use the following method call:

```
_webView.LoadUrl("javascript:compass.onCompassFail('No Compass');");
```

It might seem a bit strange that you call the `LoadUrl()` method with a JavaScript function call, but this is how the Android SDK implements calls back to the WebView.

Now that you have reviewed the more interesting implementation steps, you can step through the remaining code to become more familiar with the implementation of the device interaction pieces.

Note that the sample code is much more interesting on an actual device. The emulator for Android doesn't support the compass, accelerometer, vibrator, or audio.

Building the Windows Phone Container

Last, but not least, is Windows Phone. The main implementation of the native web component is in a XAML view derived from the `PhoneApplicationPage` class that contains the definition for your WebView control. Listing 11-7 shows the code behind the implementation, where all the magic and pixie dust is located.

LISTING 11-7: Windows Phone Web View container

Available for download on Wrox.com

```
namespace WebHybrid.WindowsPhone
{
  public partial class MainPage : PhoneApplicationPage
  {
    // Constructor
    public MainPage()
    {
      InitializeComponent();
    }

    protected override void OnNavigatedTo(NavigationEventArgs e)
    {
      base.OnNavigatedTo(e);

      this.webBrowser1.IsScriptEnabled = true;
      this.webBrowser1.Base = "www";
      this.webBrowser1.Navigate(new Uri("container.html", UriKind.Relative));
      this.webBrowser1.ScriptNotify +=
        new EventHandler<NotifyEventArgs>(webBrowser1_ScriptNotify);
    }

    void webBrowser1_ScriptNotify(object sender, NotifyEventArgs e)
    {
      if (e.Value.ToLower().StartsWith("hybrid://")) {
        string actionUri = e.Value.Substring(9);
        CallNativeMethod(actionUri);
      }
    }

    void CallNativeMethod(string actionUri)
    {
      string[] paramArray = actionUri.Split(new Char[] { '/' });
      string action = paramArray[0];
      string[] itemArray = paramArray.Skip(1).Take(paramArray.Length-1).ToArray();

      switch (action)
      {
        case "compass":
          if (itemArray[0].Equals("start"))
```

continues

LISTING 11-7 *(continued)*

```
          CompassStart();
        else if (itemArray[0].Equals("cancel"))
          CompassCancel();
        break;

      case "accelerometer":
        if (itemArray[0].Equals("start"))
          AccelerometerStart();
        else if (itemArray[0].Equals("cancel"))
          AccelerometerCancel();
        break;

      case "notify":
        if (itemArray.Length >= 1) {
          if (itemArray[0].Equals("vibrate"))
            MonoCross.Utilities.Notification.Notify.Vibrate();
          else if (itemArray[0].Equals("playSound"))
            MonoCross.Utilities.Notification.Notify.PlaySound(itemArray[1]);
        }
        break;

      default:
        break;
    }
  }

  static Compass _compass;

  void CompassStart()
  {
    if (!Compass.IsSupported) {
      Deployment.Current.Dispatcher.BeginInvoke(() => {
        this.webBrowser1.InvokeScript("eval",
          "compass.onCompassFail('Compass not available.')");
      });
      return;
    }
    if (_compass == null) {
      _compass = new Compass();
      _compass.TimeBetweenUpdates = TimeSpan.FromMilliseconds(100);
      _compass.CurrentValueChanged +=
        new EventHandler<SensorReadingEventArgs<CompassReading>>(
          _compass_CurrentValueChanged);
      try {
        _compass.Start();
      }
      catch (InvalidOperationException) {
        this.webBrowser1.InvokeScript("eval",
          "compass.onCompassFail('Could not start the compass.')");
      }
    }
  }
```

```
void _compass_CurrentValueChanged(object sender,
       SensorReadingEventArgs<CompassReading> e)
{
  string callBack = string.Format(
    "compass.onCompassSuccess({0:0.00})", e.SensorReading.TrueHeading);
  Deployment.Current.Dispatcher.BeginInvoke(() => {
    this.webBrowser1.InvokeScript("eval", callBack);
  });
}

void CompassCancel()
{
  if (_compass != null) {
    _compass.Stop();
    _compass.Dispose();
    _compass = null;
  }
}

Accelerometer _accelerometer = new Accelerometer();

void AccelerometerStart()
{
  if (!Accelerometer.IsSupported) {
    Deployment.Current.Dispatcher.BeginInvoke(() => {
      this.webBrowser1.InvokeScript("eval",
        "compass.onCompassFail('Accelerometer not available.')");
    });
    return;
  }
  try {
    // Start accelerometer for detecting compass axis
    _accelerometer = new Accelerometer();
    _accelerometer.CurrentValueChanged +=
      new EventHandler<SensorReadingEventArgs<AccelerometerReading>>
      (_accelerometer_CurrentValueChanged);
    _accelerometer.Start();
  } catch (InvalidOperationException) {
    Deployment.Current.Dispatcher.BeginInvoke(() => {
      this.webBrowser1.InvokeScript("eval",
        "compass.onCompassFail('Could not start the accelerometer.')");
    });
  }
}

void _accelerometer_CurrentValueChanged(object sender,
       SensorReadingEventArgs<AccelerometerReading> e)
{
  string callBack = string.Format(
    "accelerometer.onAccelerometerSuccess({0:0.00}, {1:0.00}, {2:0.00})",
    e.SensorReading.Acceleration.X, e.SensorReading.Acceleration.Y,
    e.SensorReading.Acceleration.Z);

  Deployment.Current.Dispatcher.BeginInvoke(() => {
```

continues

LISTING 11-7 *(continued)*

```
            this.webBrowser1.InvokeScript("eval", callBack);
          });
        }

        void AccelerometerCancel()
        {
          if (_accelerometer != null) {
            _accelerometer.Stop();
            _accelerometer.Dispose();
            _accelerometer = null;
          }
        }
      }
    }
```

Found in the WebHybrid/WebHybrid .WindowsPhone/MainPage.xaml.cs file of the download

The two most interesting parts of the code are, again, the interception of the URI navigation and the call back to the web application. The implementation of the interception is different from, but similar to, the implementations in iOS and Android.

To intercept the call from the web application, you need to define a delegate object to intercept an override of the `ScriptNotify` event. This is different from both iOS and Android in that it is a call specifically intended for the purpose of the web application notifying the native container. You still use the URI protocol to implement the communication to the native application. This allows you to be consistent with the other platforms and to keep the HTML and JavaScript largely the same.

If you handle a call from the web application, you need to call back the web application if it expects a response; for example, for the compass and accelerometer, you need to pass back either success or failure. To do this in the Windows Phone web component, use the following method call:

```
Deployment.Current.Dispatcher.BeginInvoke(() => {
  webBrowser1.InvokeScript("eval", "compass.onCompassFail('Compass unavailable.')");
});
```

The remainder of the code takes care of interpreting the call from the web application and making the appropriate native APIs. If you take the time now to build and run the Windows Phone sample hybrid application, you will find that the emulator supports the accelerometer, compass, and audio. This allows you to better see the hybrid application in action, even without an actual device.

SUMMARY

This chapter examines some of the important aspects of interactivity between web applications and native applications on iOS, Android, and Windows Phone. You combine them to form a hybrid application that utilizes some of the strengths, and solves some of the shortcomings, of each. These simple examples of hybrid application for iOS, Android, and Windows Phone devices can serve as a starting point for advanced development of richer functionality.

In the next chapter we extend the concepts of cross-platform mobile development. The chapter looks into moving an application onto the desktop and into cloud, allowing for true cross-platform utilization.

12

Bringing Applications to the Enterprise

WHAT'S IN THIS CHAPTER?

- Bringing your application to nonmobile platforms
- Supporting multiple platforms

So at this point, you have learned a lot about MonoCross. You've learned how to design and build mobile applications, and you've learned about the architecture and how it's used in your applications. You've learned how to create and consume RESTful services and about the MonoCross utilities in writing cross-platform code for mobile applications. All of this leads to the question: Is MonoCross just for mobile applications? The answer is most definitely no!

You can develop MonoCross applications for any platform that supports C# and includes web applications and Windows applications with WPF and XAML. In this chapter you see how easy it is to leverage your design and modeling efforts and create a sample application for the desktop. You also learn how to bring your applications to the cloud via Windows Azure.

Lastly, the chapter covers additional concerns and thoughts you should consider as you build MonoCross applications going forward, including architectural considerations and a preview of how to build a single view in MonoCross that you can use for all your application platforms.

EXPANDING YOUR APPLICATION'S DOMAIN

The examples in previous chapters have shown you how to create a MonoCross application for the iPad, iPhone, and Android, as well as for web browsing on the mobile devices via WebKit containers. But the capabilities of MonoCross do not end there. You can bring the same application that you wrote for the iPad to the Windows desktop and web applications for your personal computer's browser — and from there to the cloud.

Bringing Your Application to the Desktop

When you develop MonoCross applications for the Windows desktop, you simply need to create a WPF container to house the custom views that are written in WPF.

The steps to create a Windows Customer Management sample are as follows:

1. Create a new solution named `CustomerManagement.WPF` (or name it something else if you prefer).
2. Add the existing shared projects to the solution. The solution and existing projects are shown in Figure 12-1.

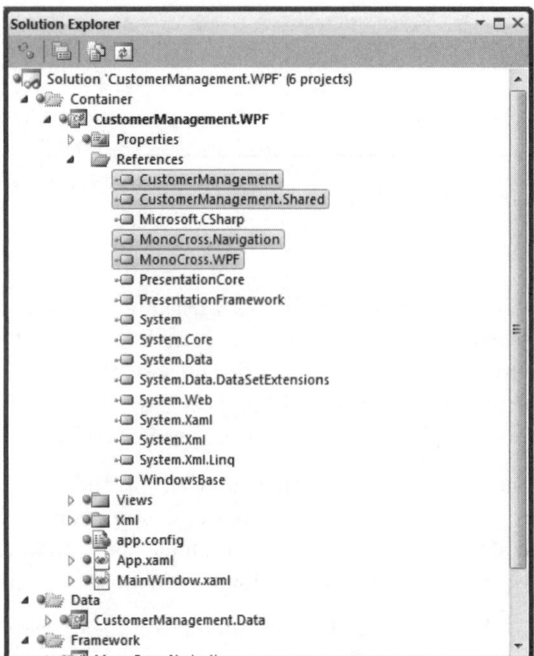

FIGURE 12-1: Your new solution should have a similar appearance.

3. Create a new WPF Application project and add it to the solution. Name the project **CustomerManagement.WPF**.
4. Add Project References to your new project. A complete list of references to include displays along with the project in Figure 12-2.

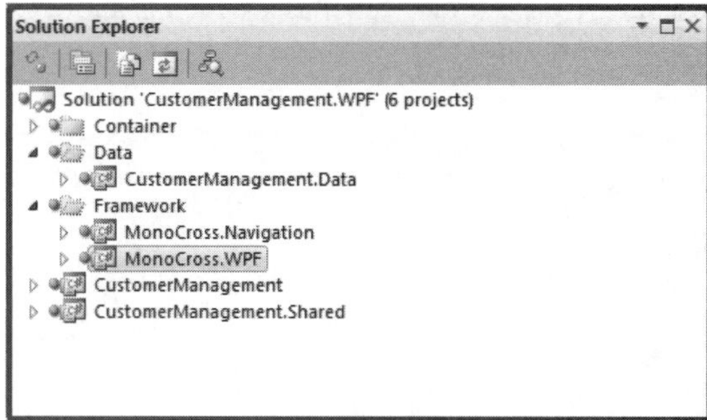

FIGURE 12-2: Add Project References to your project.

Now that you set up the solution and project files, take a closer look at the implementation of the WPF views. The application structure is similar to the other samples. The main difference, of course, is that the WPF views are implemented in XAML, but otherwise they correlate to other views in the other platform examples.

As in the previous examples, three views have been implemented for this sample. They are `CustomerListView`, `CustomerEditView`, and `CustomerView`. Each view provides a simple implementation of the sample to demonstrate that you can run MonoCross on Windows.

Each view is a simple WPF form that contains XAML with the corresponding C# file, known as a code-behind file. Code-behind files are used to create C# methods accessible to the WPF form and also to response to code events. Listing 12-1 shows the XAML for the `CustomerListView`.

LISTING 12-1: Customer List View XAML

Available for download on Wrox.com

```
<src:ListViewGlue
  x:Class="CustomerManagement.WPF.Views.CustomerListView"
  xmlns="http://schemas.microsoft.com/winfx/2006/xaml/presentation"
  xmlns:x="http://schemas.microsoft.com/winfx/2006/xaml"
  xmlns:mc="http://schemas.openxmlformats.org/markup-compatibility/2006"
  xmlns:d="http://schemas.microsoft.com/expression/blend/2008"
  xmlns:src="clr-namespace:CustomerManagement.WPF.Views"
  xmlns:model
    ="clr-namespace:CustomerManagement.Shared.Model;assembly=CustomerManagement.Shared"
  mc:Ignorable="d"
  d:DesignHeight="296" d:DesignWidth="401"
  Title="Customer List">
  <ListBox Name="lbxCustomers">
    <ListBox.ItemTemplate>
      <DataTemplate>
        <TextBlock Text="{Binding Path=Name}" />
      </DataTemplate>
    </ListBox.ItemTemplate>
  </ListBox>
</src:ListViewGlue>
```

Found in the CustomerManagement.WPF/Views/CustomerListView.xaml file of the download

Each XAML code-behind class derives from the MonoCross `MXPageView` class, which is shown in Listing 12-2.

Available for download on Wrox.com

LISTING 12-2: Generic MXPageView class

```
using System;
using System.Windows.Controls;
using MonoCross.Navigation;

namespace MonoCross.WPF
{
  public abstract class MXPageView<T> : Page, IMXView
  {
    public T Model { get; set; }
    public Type ModelType { get { return typeof(T); } }
    public abstract void Render();
    public void SetModel(object model)
    {
      Model = (T)model;
    }
  }
}
```

Found in the MonoCross.WPF/MXPageView.cs file of the download

Your `CustomerListView` actually derives from the `ListViewGlue` class, which is a simple wrapper around the generic `MXPageView<List<Customer>>` class. This wrapper can simplify consumption of the `MXPageView` for lists in XAML for the WPF platform. Listing 12-3 displays the implementation of `ListViewGlue` class.

Available for download on Wrox.com

LISTING 12-3: ListViewGlue implementation

```
using System.Collections.Generic;
using CustomerManagement.Shared.Model;
using MonoCross.WPF;

namespace CustomerManagement.WPF.Views
{
  /// <summary>
  /// This class is used to simplify using a generic class in XAML
  /// </summary>
  public abstract class ListViewGlue : MXPageView<List<Customer>> { }
}
```

Found in the CustomerManagement.WPF/Views/ListViewGlue.xaml.cs file of the download

Finally, the `CustomerListView` C# contains the methods to render the view and respond when a customer is selected from the list. This code simply binds the customer list contained in `Model` to the `ListBox` that actually displays the values and subscribes to the `SelectionChangedEventHandler` to support navigation to the `CustomerView`. Listing 12-4 shows the C# code-behind for the `CustomerListView`.

Available for download on Wrox.com

LISTING 12-4: Customer List View code

```
using System.Windows.Controls;
using MonoCross.WPF;

namespace CustomerManagement.WPF.Views
{
  /// <summary>
  /// Interaction logic for CustomerListView.xaml
  /// </summary>
  public partial class CustomerListView : ListViewGlue
  {
    public override void Render()
    {
      InitializeComponent();
      lbxCustomers.ItemsSource = Model;
      lbxCustomers.SelectionChanged
        += new SelectionChangedEventHandler(lbxCustomers_SelectionChanged);
    }

    void lbxCustomers_SelectionChanged(object sender, SelectionChangedEventArgs e)
    {
      MXWindowsContainer.Navigate(string.Format("Customers/{0}"
                                  , Model[lbxCustomers.SelectedIndex].ID));
    }
  }
}
```

Found in the CustomerManagement.WPF/Views/CustomerListView.xaml.cs file of the download

After you create your views, all you need to do to test your new MonoCross WPF sample is to run the `CustomerManagement.WPF` project. Either make the project the startup project or from the project files context menu, select **Debug ➪ Start New Instance**. Figure 12-3 shows the sample running in Windows.

As you can see, after you create a MonoCross application, it is a relatively easy task to support the application on a new platform. You can reuse the bulk of your application and create as simple or complex a set of views as you like for each new platform. Now, how can you take your MonoCross web application to the cloud using Windows Azure?

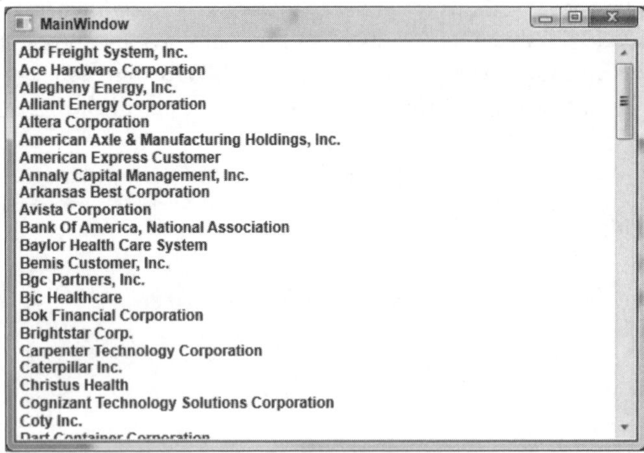

FIGURE 12-3: The Customer List View runs in Windows.

Bringing Your Application to the Cloud

Sometimes you may not have the infrastructure in place to support your websites and RESTful services, or you may not want to use the available infrastructure. The cloud, especially when using Microsoft Azure, can come in handy in these situations.

Azure can scale your application automatically as you need more power. In addition, you can deploy Azure apps as a Windows service extended into the cloud or as a web application.

The basic structure of an Azure application includes two or more projects. One is the main project, which includes the wrappers/configuration that describe the actual applications that are part of the cloud application. The other projects, known as *roles* in Azure parlance, are either a web application (a web role) or a Windows service (a Windows role). Each Azure application can include multiple roles of either type, depending on the needs of your cloud applications.

You can create projects for deployment to the cloud in a couple ways. The first and simplest is to create a cloud deployment project from an existing ASP.NET web project, and the other is to create the cloud projects directly.

But before you can create any cloud projects, you need to install the Microsoft Azure SDK.

Installing the Azure SDK

The first step to create a cloud application is to install the Azure SDK, which you can access at `www.microsoft.com/windowsazure/learn/get-started/?campaign=getstarted`. Simply download the installation executable `WindowsAzureToolsVS2010.exe` and install the Azure SDK. (Incidentally, in addition to the SDK installation executable, many tutorials on creating Azure cloud applications are worth perusing.)

The following sections focus on how to create and deploy cloud applications based on the `CustomerManagement.Webkit` sample.

Creating the Cloud Deployment Project

The first of the two methods you consider to create cloud applications is to create a cloud deployment project associated with an existing web project. This is the easier of the two approaches but, of course, it requires that you already have a web project you intend to deploy to the cloud.

For this example, use the `CustomerManagement.Webkit` sample project to create the cloud deployment project. Follow these two steps:

1. In the Solution Explorer select the **`CustomerManagement.Webkit`** project.
2. Right-click the project, and from the context menu select **Add Windows Azure Deployment Project** to create a new deployment project with a WebRole defined for `CustomerManagement.Webkit`. The name of the new project is `CustomerManagement.Webkit.Azure`, as shown in Figure 12-4.

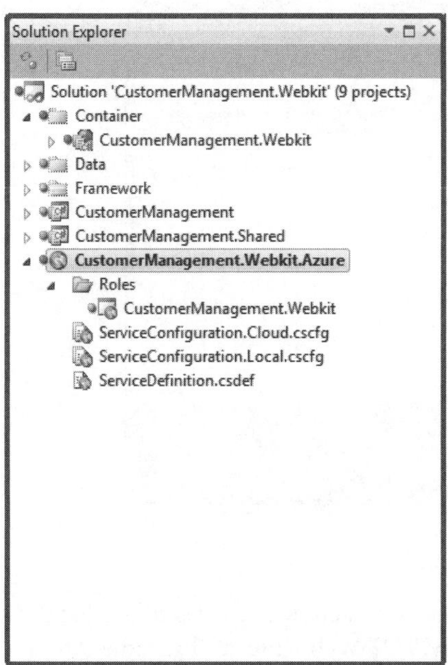

FIGURE 12-4: Create the CustomerManagement.Webkit.Azure deployment project.

Now that you have created the Azure deployment project, you are ready to deploy to the cloud. You learn the deployment steps in the "Preparing for an Azure Project Deployment" section later in this chapter, after you learn how to create a cloud application from scratch (or in your case copying the files from `CustomerManagement.Webkit`).

Creating the Cloud Projects from Scratch

Creating a cloud application in Azure is straightforward. You simply create a cloud project with an associated web role project. Web roles can be ASP.NET applications and ASP.NET MVC2 or

MVC3 applications. After you create the web role project, you can create new web forms for the application, or you can copy the files from another web application.

For this example, reuse the `CustomerManagement.Webkit` sample to create a new cloud-based application. This process adds two new projects to the `CustomerManagement.Webkit` solution. One is for the cloud project, and the other is for a web role project.

Follow these steps:

1. Open up the `Customer.Webkit` sample solution in Visual Studio.
2. Add a new cloud project to the solution by right-clicking the solution and selecting **Add - New Project** from the context menu. Select the cloud template for the new project using the **`Visual C3 Template - Cloud - Windows Azure`** Project, and name it **`CustomerManagement.Cloud`**, as shown in Figure 12-5.

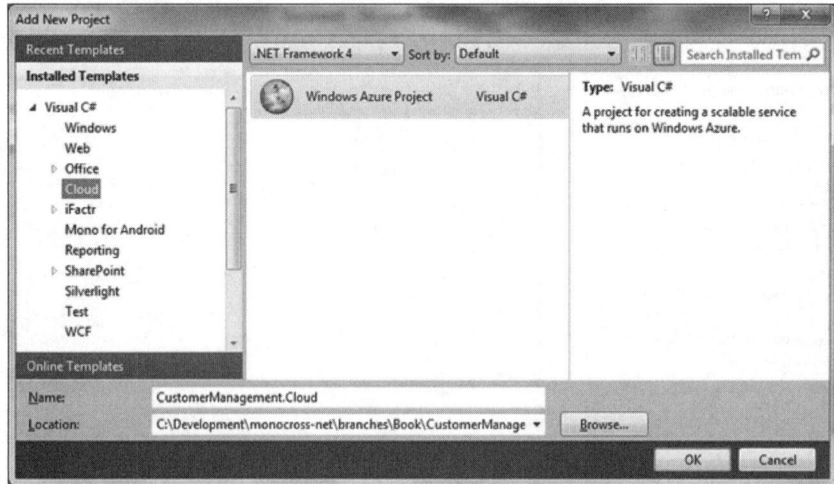

FIGURE 12-5: Create your cloud project.

3. Click **OK**. Another window pops up that shows your initial choice of roles to use for the application. For this example, select the **ASP.NET MVC2 Web Role**, and rename it to `CustomerManagement.Cloud.Webkit`, as shown in Figure 12-6.
4. Click **OK** again, and both the cloud project and the web role project are added to your solution file. The solution file should look like the solution in Figure 12-7.

   The new `CustomerManagement.Cloud.Webkit` project contains many default folders and files that are intended to help you create a web role project from scratch. You do not need all these files because you copy the `CustomerManagement.Webkit` project files and use them for this example.
5. Delete all folders and files in the `CustomerManagement.Cloud.Webkit` project folder except for `WebRole.cs`. Also delete the scripts folder and the project file (`*.csproj`), and then copy all the files from the `CustomerManagement.Webkit` project to the new `CustomerManagement.Cloud.Webkit` project folder.

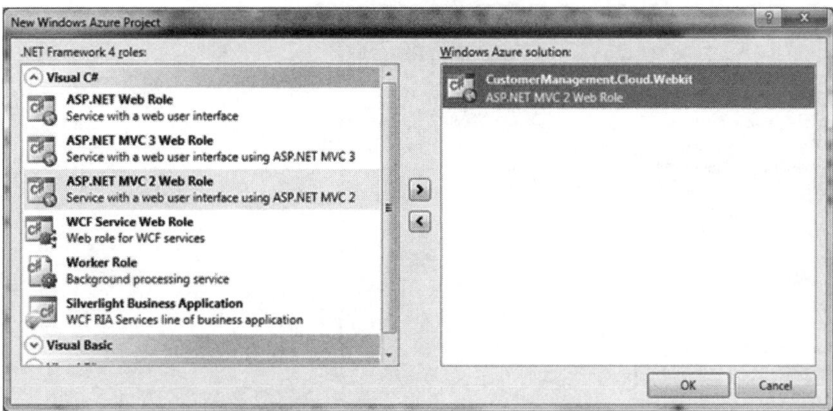

FIGURE 12-6: Create the web role project.

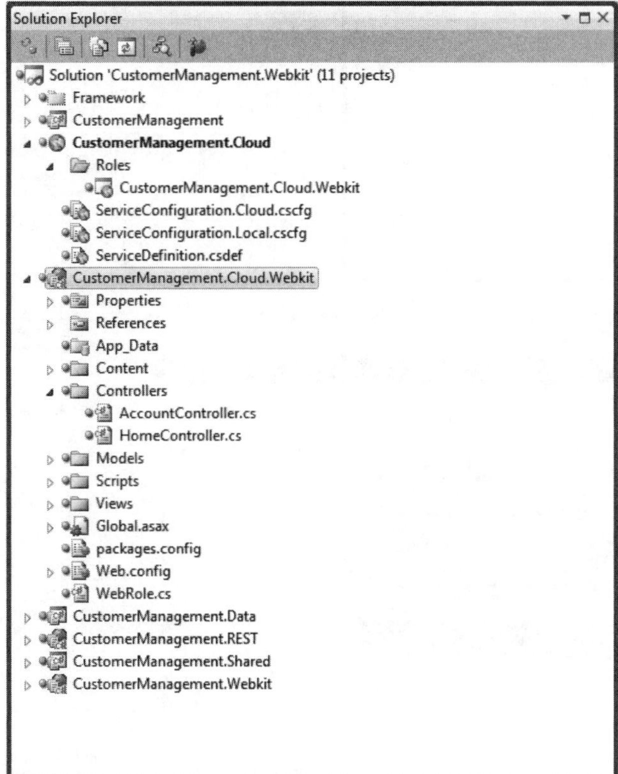

FIGURE 12-7: Your initial solution file should look like this.

Your solution file should look similar to Figure 12-8.

6. Copy the project references that you need to build the project. The project references you need to add to the web role project are the ones highlighted in Figure 12-9.

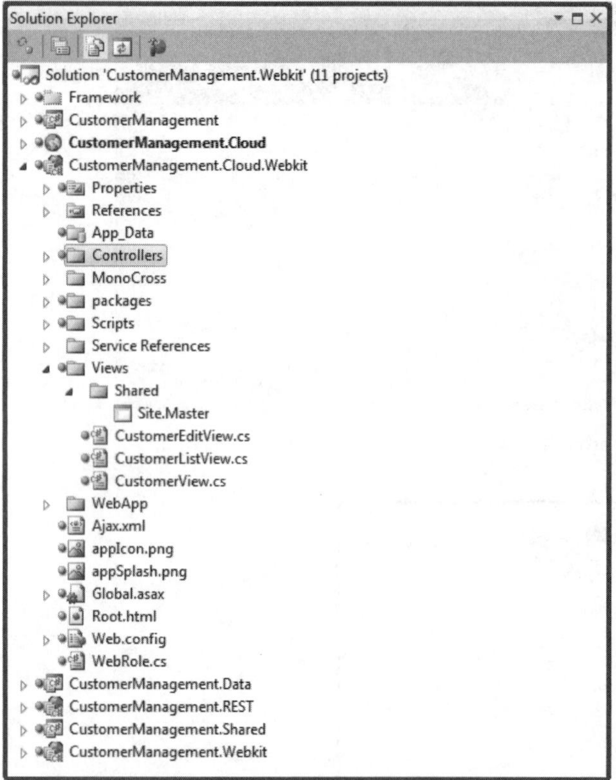

FIGURE 12-8: Copy files from your WebKit project to the cloud Webkit project.

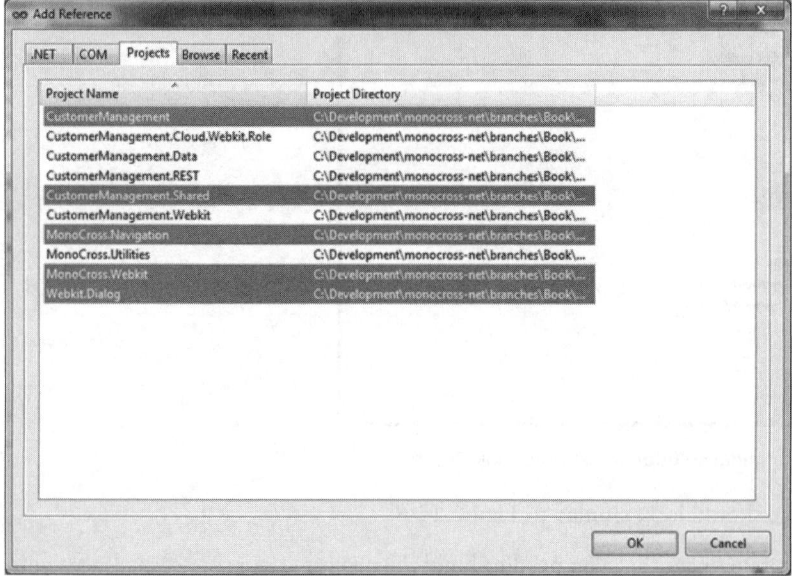

FIGURE 12-9: Select these web role references.

7. Build your application (right-click on the solution file and select **Rebuild Solution** from the context menu) and resolve any errors that may have crept in. Your new cloud-enabled WebKit application will be complete. Similar steps would work for other web and ASP.NET MVC applications.

Testing Your Cloud Application

Now that you have created the `CustomerManagement.Cloud` project, the next step is to test it locally in your development environment to ensure that it works as expected before you try to deploy it to the cloud.

Because the `CustomerManagement.Cloud.Webkit` project makes RESTful calls to the `CustomerManagement.REST` project, that project needs to be running as well. Simply right-click the **`CustomerManagement.REST`** project and from the context menu select **Debug ⇨ Start New Instance**. When the RESTful service is running, the next step is to start the cloud application.

You don't start the `CustomerManagement.Cloud.Webkit` project; instead the `CustomerManagement.Cloud` application in which it is referenced as a role starts it. Start the `CustomerManagement.Cloud` project by right-clicking it; then select **Debug ⇨ Start New Instance** from the context menu. That starts the application in the local Application Fabric (or AppFabric for short), which is the test environment on your development computer that simulates the cloud.

The Windows Azure Debugging Environment becomes available, as shown in Figure 12-10.

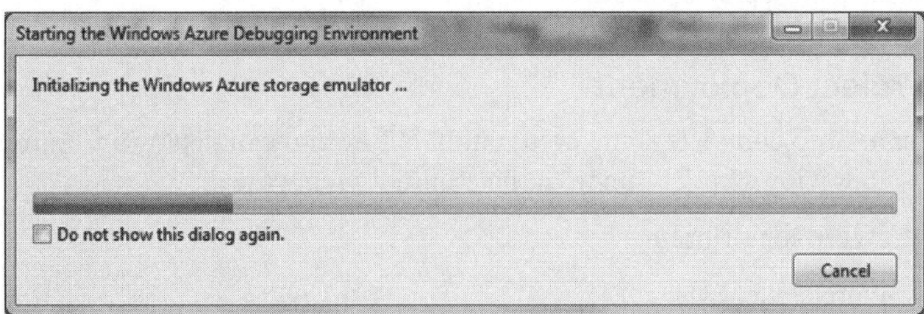

FIGURE 12-10: These steps start the Windows Azure Debugging Environment.

After the debugging environment is initialized, the application starts in your default browser. Figure 12-11 shows the initial view of the `CustomerManagement.Cloud.Webkit` project running in the local application.

The next couple sections cover how to deploy your application to the Microsoft Azure cloud.

Use the `LOCAL_DATA` *attribute on the* `CustomerManagement` *shared project. This allows the service to get the data from the files contained within the local XML folder in the* `CustomerManagement.Webkit` *project. Because you use local XML data for this example, you don't need to create a* `CustomerManagement.REST.Azure` *project to obtain the data via RESTful Services. Although, most production applications need to have both the RESTful services and the web-based projects deployed independently to the cloud.*

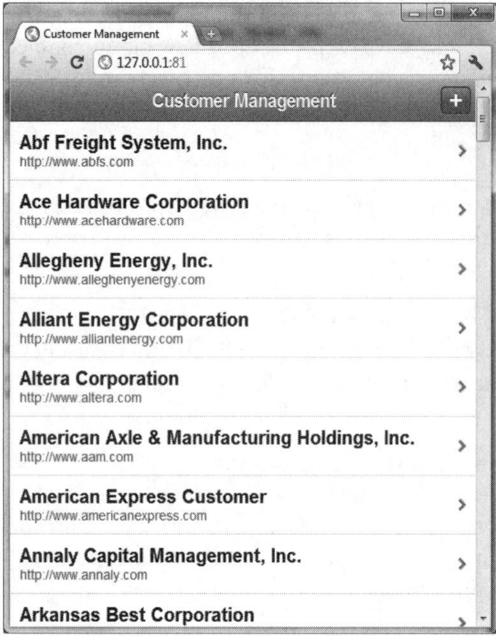

FIGURE 12-11: The Customer Management project runs in the browser.

Preparing for an Azure Project Deployment

As you've likely guessed, you need to complete some preparation before you can deploy an Azure application to the cloud. The following steps summarize the required prep work:

1. Establish a Windows Azure subscription.
2. Set up the Windows Azure credentials.
3. Set up a hosted service in Windows Azure.
4. Set up a storage account in Windows Azure.

Signing Up for a Subscription

You need to sign up for a subscription to the Azure Management Portal, which is the portal that you use for deploying and managing your cloud applications. Currently, temporary trials with limited bandwidth are available free of charge.

Go to `www.microsoft.com/windowsazure/free-trial` and select **Get the Free Trial.** Follow the instructions to create your subscription. Have your credit card ready. You need to enter contact and billing information to establish your trial subscription.

Creating Certificates and Credentials

To deploy applications to the cloud, you need to create a set of certificate-based credentials for your applications to use. You can obtain the certificate from a signing service, or you can create one.

1. Select the `CustomerManagement.Cloud` project, the `CustomerManagement.Webkit.Azure` project, or whatever cloud project you have created and need to deploy from the Solution Explorer. Right-click the project and select **Publish** from the context menu. The Windows Azure Publish Settings window displays, as shown in Figure 12-12.

FIGURE 12-12: The Windows Azure Publish Settings window enables you to add credentials.

2. Select **Add** from the Credentials drop-down list, and the Windows Azure Project Management Authentication window displays, as shown in Figure 12-13. You can use this window to set up your credentials. Windows Azure named the credentials `WindowsAzureAccount1` by default, but we'll change them to `MonoCrossCloudAccount`.

3. From step 1 on the Project Management Authentication window, either indicate you want to create a new certificate or select an existing certificate you may already have prepared for Azure cloud deployments.

   If you decide to create a new certificate, then the Create Certificate window displays. On this window, you simply need to enter a name for the certificate and click **OK**. For the purposes of this exercise, the name of the certificate is `MonoCrossCloudCertificate`, as shown in Figure 12-14.

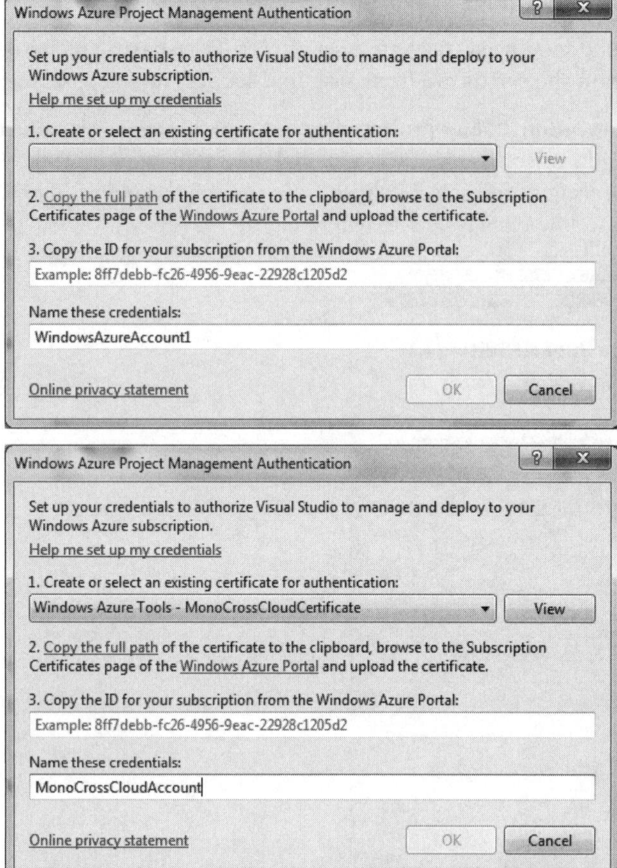

FIGURE 12-13: Set up your credentials through the Project Management Authentication window.

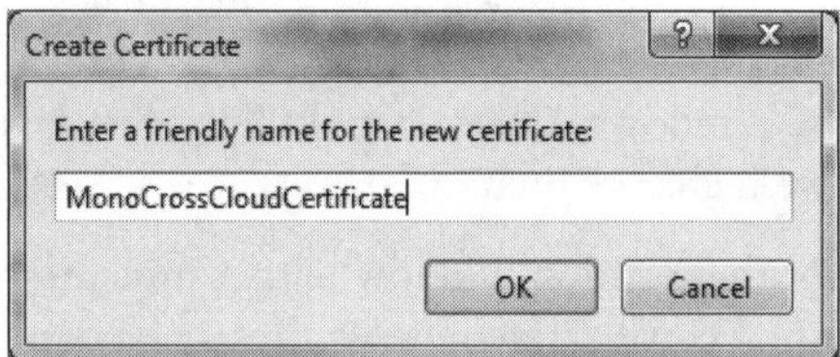

FIGURE 12-14: Name your certificate in the Create Certificate window.

4. Apply the newly created certificate to the Windows Azure Project Management Authentication window. The name of the credentials is `MonoCrossCloudAccount`, as shown in Figure 12-15.

5. Log in to the Windows Azure Management Portal using the subscription credentials that you set up in the previous section. Copy the full path of your newly created certificate, and then follow the instructions on the Windows Azure Portal to upload it. You can find complete instructions for setting up named authentication credentials at `http://msdn.microsoft.com/en-us/library/windowsazure/ff683676.aspx`. Figure 12-16 shows the Management Certificates section on the current Windows Azure Platform, where you can add your certificate.

FIGURE 12-15: Apply the certificates and credentials in the Publish Settings window.

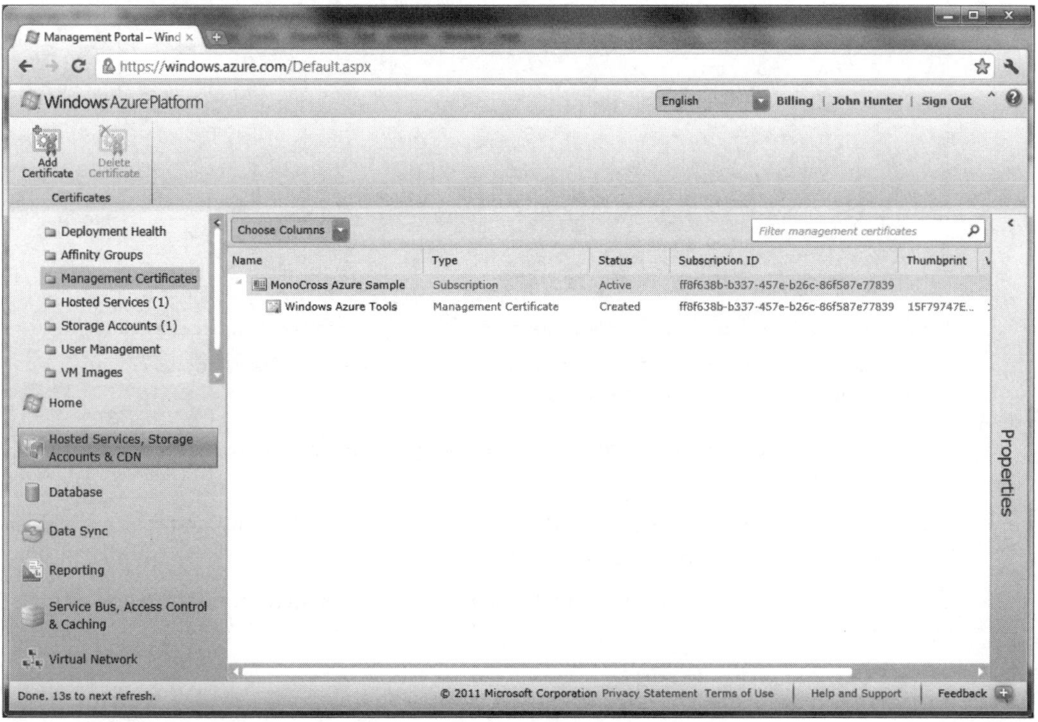

FIGURE 12-16: Add your certificates to the Windows Azure platform.

6. After the certificate is uploaded and saved, the last step is to copy the Subscription ID associated with the certificate, enter it on the Windows Azure Project Management Authentication window, and click **OK**. In this example, the Subscription ID is `ff8f638b-b337-457e-b26c-86f587e77839`.

You have now completed setting a set of certificate-based credentials your applications can use when deploying to the Azure cloud.

Creating a Hosted Service in Windows Azure

A hosted service in Windows Azure is a combination of your cloud application and its associated configuration files that tells Windows Azure how to run your application as a service in the cloud. To create a hosted service you need a deployment package from your cloud application that contains the configuration files needed for deployment:

1. Right-click your cloud application and select **Deploy Package** from the context menu.

   This both creates the configuration files and opens an instance of the Windows Explorer folder that contains them, as shown in Figure 12-17.

   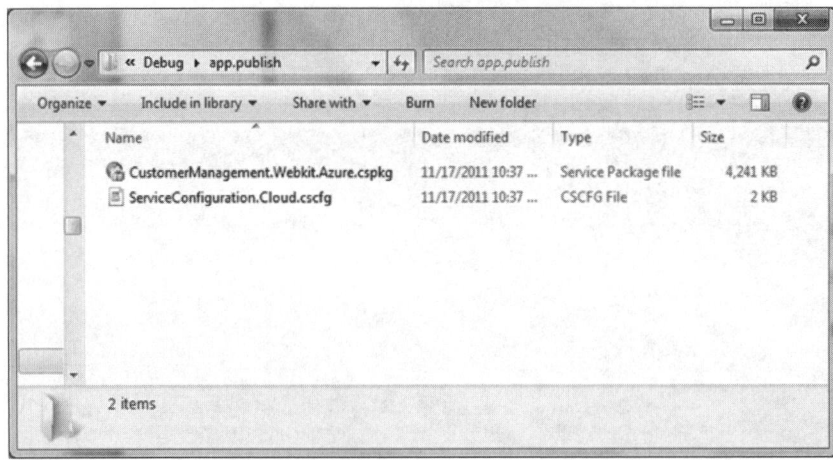

   FIGURE 12-17: The configuration files are created and an instance of the Windows Explorer folder that includes them displays.

   In this example, you create the deployment package from the `CustomerManagement.Webkit.Azure` project.

2. Log in to the Windows Azure Portal (if you have not already done so) and select the **Hosted Services, Storage Accounts & CDN** tab on the left.

   This opens the portal to a page where you can add a new hosted service, as shown in Figure 12-18.

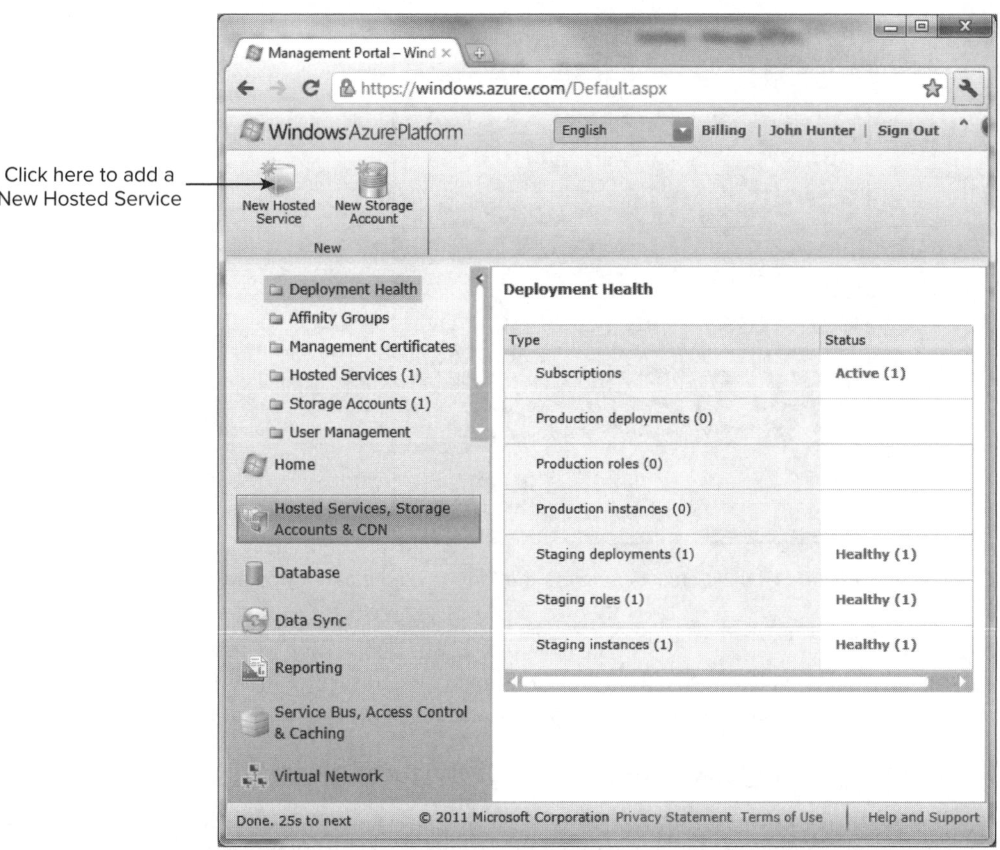

FIGURE 12-18: You can add Windows Azure hosted services.

3. Click the **New Hosted Service** button. A window displays for you to enter the necessary information. Enter a name for the service (such as **MonoCrossHostedService**), and then enter the remaining fields on the New Hosted Service window.

4. Enter the Package location.

   Click the **Browse Locally** button next to Package location, and navigate to the folder that contains the configuration files. If you still have the explorer window open to the configuration, just copy and paste the location. Select the **`CustomerManagement.Webkit.Azure.cspkg`** to place it into the service package location.

   Likewise, for the Configuration file setting, click the **Browse Locally** button; then locate and select the **`ServiceConfiguration.Cloud.cscfg`** file to include it in the Hosted Service settings. Figure 12-19 shows the completed Create a New Hosted Service form.

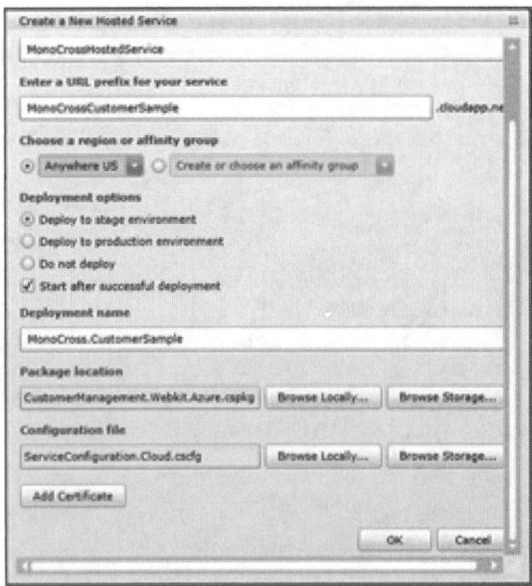

FIGURE 12-19: You must complete the form to create a new hosted service.

5. Click **OK**; then you are done creating a new hosted service.

You can find complete instructions for creating a hosted service in Windows Azure at `http://msdn.microsoft.com/en-us/library/windowsazure/gg432967.aspx`.

Creating a Storage Account in Windows Azure

A storage account in Windows Azure allows the service administrator (that is, you) to access the cloud-based storage available to cloud applications. Here's all you need to do:

1. Log in to the Windows Azure Portal (if you have not already done so) and select the **Hosted Services, Storage Accounts & CDN** tab on the left. This brings the portal to a page where you can add a new Storage Account, as shown in Figure 12-20.
2. Click the **New Storage Account** button. A window displays on which you enter the necessary information.
3. Assign the subscription, and enter a URL to assign to the account (such as **monocrosscustomersample**; yes, it must be lowercase); then enter the remaining fields, as shown in Figure 12-21.
4. Click **OK**; then you are done creating a new hosted service.

You can find complete instructions for creating a storage account in Windows Azure at `http://msdn.microsoft.com/en-us/library/gg433066.aspx`.

After you create the storage account, you can view its properties on the Windows Azure Platform, as shown in Figure 12-22. To modify the properties, simply expand the Properties panel by clicking on the < and make any necessary changes.

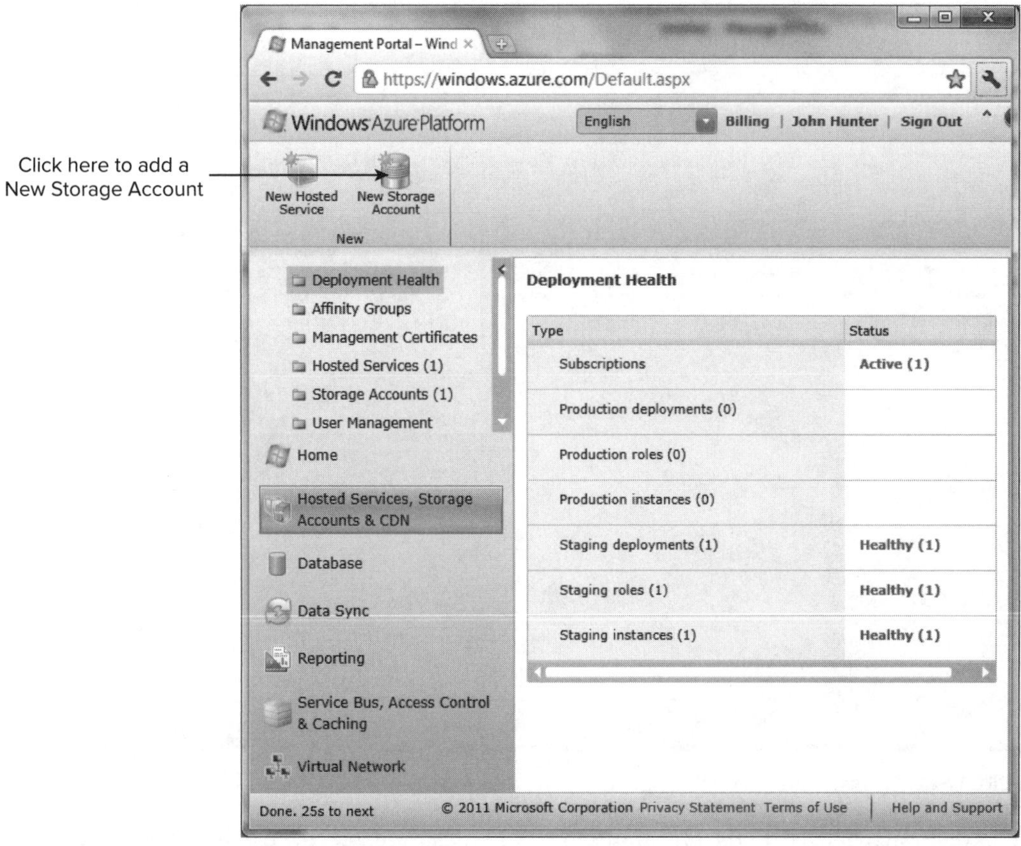

FIGURE 12-20: You can add Windows Azure storage accounts.

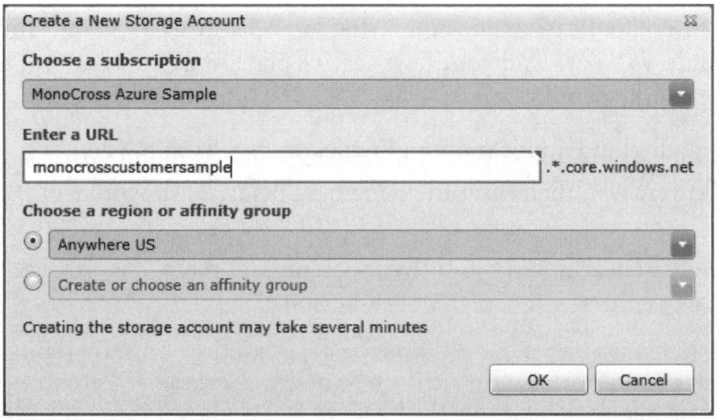

Create a New Storage Account

Choose a subscription

MonoCross Azure Sample

Enter a URL

monocrosscustomersample .*.core.windows.net

Choose a region or affinity group

(•) Anywhere US

( ) Create or choose an affinity group

Creating the storage account may take several minutes

OK Cancel

FIGURE 12-21: Enter the new storage account settings.

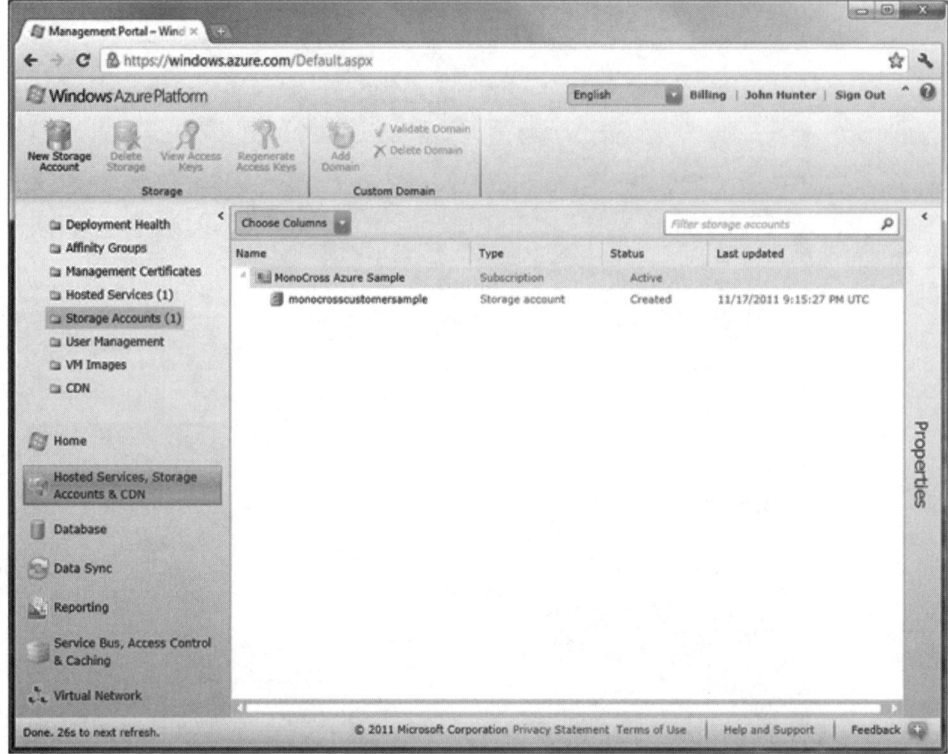

FIGURE 12-22: New storage account settings

You have now completed all the preparatory work needed for deploying cloud applications.

Deploying and Managing Your Cloud Application

At this point, you have created your cloud application and completed your preparatory work: You have created your subscription to Windows Azure and your host service and storage accounts. The next step is to deploy your application to the cloud.

1. In the Solution Explorer find your cloud application, right-click it, and from the context menu select **Publish**. The Publish Windows Azure Application window displays, as shown in Figure 12-23.

2. On this form, specify your credentials, the Windows environment, and the storage account that you created in the previous sections. Click the **Publish** button.

   If the environment is in use (that is, you've deployed previously) a window appears telling you that the environment is in use and offers you a choice to delete the deployed environment and continue or cancel the deployment altogether. Figure 12-24 shows the confirmation window that displays when the deployment environment is in use.

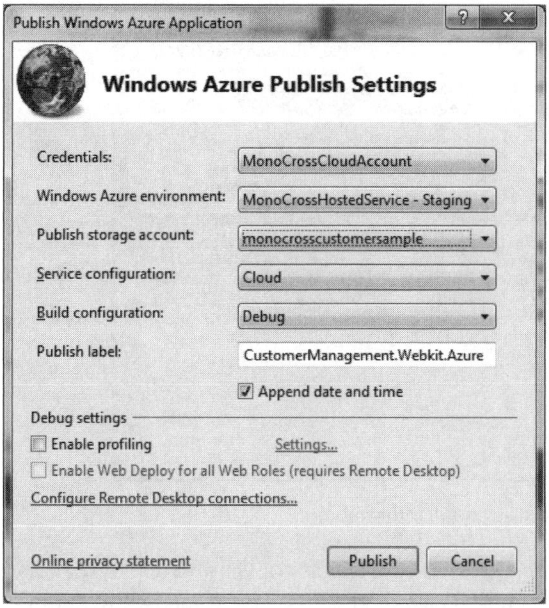

FIGURE 12-23: Set the Windows Azure Publish Settings.

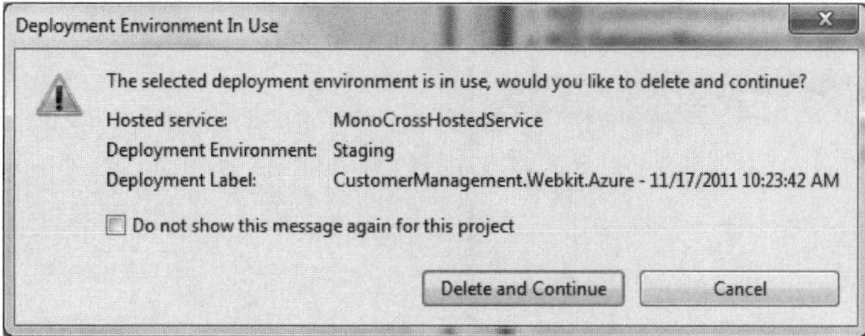

FIGURE 12-24: The Deployment Environment in Use message displays if you have deployed previously.

3. Click **Delete and Continue.**

   This brings up the Windows Azure Activity Log, which contains the list of deployment activity. It displays the deployment list in order of most recent to least recent and shows a status bar or the word *Completed*, depending on the status. In addition, the Azure Activity Log shows details of the deployment, including a convenient website URL you can use to test the deployment, as shown in Figure 12-25.

   The publishing step may take several minutes, so don't be alarmed. Instead, use the time to take a break and refill your soda or coffee cup or something equally as productive....

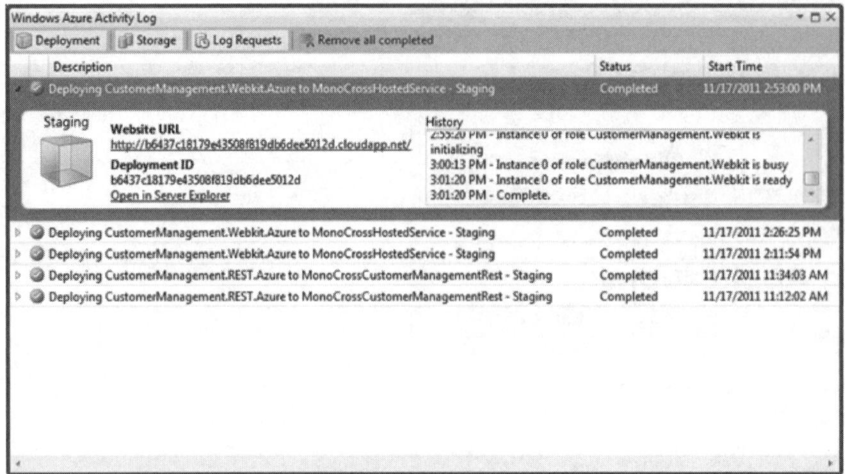

FIGURE 12-25: The Azure Activity Log provides useful information.

When the deployment does complete successfully, your cloud application deploys, and you can test it by clicking the URL link in the Azure Activity Log. The `CustomerManagement.Webkit` sample displays the initial page populated with the customer list, as shown in Figure 12-26.

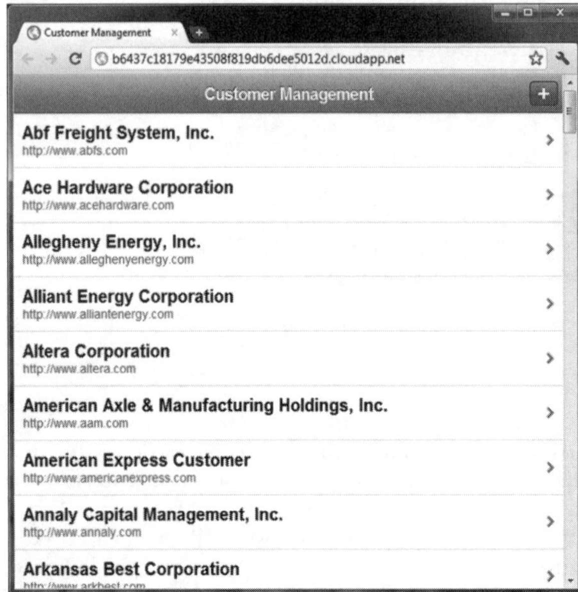

FIGURE 12-26: The Customer Management application as it appears when deployed in the cloud.

There you have it. You have deployed your first MonoCross application to the cloud.

SUPPORTING MULTIPLE PLATFORMS

Throughout this book you've explored techniques for writing cross-platform mobile applications. In this chapter, you've explored ways to take your application from the various mobile platforms to the enterprise, but some key principles can help you stay one step ahead of the competition and the mobile marketplace you should keep in mind as you bring your applications to new platforms across your enterprise.

Future-Proofing Applications

When the iPad was released in the spring 2010, needless to say, it created quite a stir. At the time, we were working on a cross-platform application for one of our biggest enterprise clients. When it came to us to inquire about the possibility of porting the not-yet-finished application over to the iPad, I can't say we were surprised. Luckily for us, we had spent a great deal of time designing and optimizing the user-experience for the iPhone, and Apple's changes to the iOS SDK made it easy for existing iPhone applications to be ported to their new killer device.

What this experience illustrates so clearly is that the only certainty in mobile development is change. The ability to plan for and adapt to that change is essential for enterprises that want to survive in this environment. Mono and MonoCross can be key tools to achieve the goal of future-proofing your applications to enable rapid response to mobile market changes.

Because Mono and MonoCross adhere to both C# and .NET standards and support all the major mobile platforms in the marketplace today, you have great flexibility in both development and deployment of your applications across platforms and across the web/hybrid/native spectrum of architectures. As of this writing, Microsoft Windows Phone is only beginning to make inroads into an enterprise market dominated by iOS and Android devices; however, most industry analysts fully expect Windows Phone to become a major player in the marketplace in the coming years. By standardizing your applications on C#, .NET, and MonoCross, you'll be ahead of your competition when it comes to delivering new and existing applications to Windows Phone as demand increases. You simply can't do that as quickly or efficiently using the proprietary native languages and technologies of each platform vendor.

Building for Reuse

Beyond the future-proofing of your applications, the standardization on a single C#/.NET technology stack provides tremendous flexibility in your application development efforts. In Chapter 1, "Choosing the Right Architecture," you learned about ways to create extendible modules that you could use across your applications. You can apply the same principles, coupled with sound, layered software architecture, to your application code as well to maximize reuse and code portability.

Layering Your Architectures

Beginning in Chapter 4, "The MonoCross Pattern," you learned about the foundational architecture of MonoCross as loosely coupled layers that separate your platform-specific presentation code from your shared business logic and data access code. This separation is a time-tested and proven technique for creating robust, flexible applications that can be re-engineered easily in response to change. When you write your application code, always do so with a mind toward reuse. Continually ask yourself how the logic you write might be packaged in a way to allow other applications to take advantage of your hard work. This practice begins with careful, disciplined adherence to object-oriented principles such as encapsulation and interface abstraction.

Recall that encapsulation is the grouping of application behavior and data into logical pieces that can, optionally, hide the details of their implementation from other pieces that need to interact with them. This is one of the most powerful principles in object-oriented development, and one that is easily overlooked in the get-it-done-yesterday world of enterprise software development. However, with the multiple platforms and development paradigms inherent to mobile development, good encapsulation becomes even more critical.

Take the example of user interface and workflow development. Each mobile platform takes a slightly different approach to constructing and navigating between UI views. As you've learned in your exploration of MonoCross, each targeted platform has a different way to solve the same problem of presentation, consumption, and interaction with application information. To help minimize the impact of this mismatch, MonoCross employs the Model-View-Controller pattern to encourage proper encapsulation and separation of your application logic from the presentation layer. By keeping your presentation logic separated, the interaction between layers is simplified and standardized. Take these examples to the next level as you build out your applications, and refactor your code to provide a simple, logical model upon which to grow your suite of enterprise applications.

Now that you've created logically encapsulated objects that accurately model your application's behavior and data, you can begin to put them together into modules of functionality that can be packaged as components for reuse across your enterprise. Often the best way to do this is by defining public interfaces that expose the module's functionality in a logical manner. MonoCross uses two simple interfaces, `IMXController` and `IMXView`, to transfer control from the shared application to and from the platform container. We've created generic helper classes, `MXController<T>` and `MXView<T>`, which you can use as base implementations, but they are not required for a successful implementation. The contract for a MonoCross application is defined in the interfaces; as long as you adhere to that contract, you are free to implement your views and controllers in any way you want. This technique of public interface abstraction can be powerful when building any number of enterprise application modules. Look for opportunities to provide an interface abstraction for common business and application functions to enable reuse across your business.

Porting Your Code

The whole point to layering, encapsulation, and interface abstraction is to enable code portability. This has been the proverbial Holy Grail of software development for years, and the challenges of cross-platform development make the value of portable code even greater. Organizations that take these techniques seriously have much greater success when bringing new and existing applications to the mobile world. Standardization on C#/.NET technologies adds another dimension to code portability.

It pays to push the complexities of platform and architectural differences into well-encapsulated modules with simple, clearly defined interfaces. Take basic file or storage access as an example. We've created the `MonoCross.Utilities.Storage` namespace using this principle. The .NET `System.IO` namespace contains a much richer, complex implementation that works on some of our targeted platforms, but it is different on others. Full `System.IO` support is not available on all platforms. So we've created a simple, public interface to provide the most frequently used functions, and we provided working implementations for each supported platform. What's more, these implementations work on the device or the server, in a native or web application. Because we use a simple public interface to define the storage contract, we are now free to re-implement the contract when new platforms emerge in the market or business needs require a shift in our implementation approach.

For example, you may decide that a portion of your application would best be implemented on the server. A product catalog is generally a large set of data that would be impractical to put on a mobile device, but you may discover after implementing your server-based product catalog that your field sales personnel may have slow or sporadic connectivity that makes an online catalog unusable. Now you're faced with a problem: You have potentially large portions of your application that rely on the catalog to complete various workflows, and you are faced with re-engineering this important module. It is in this circumstance that a simple, well-defined interface provides the necessary flexibility to accomplish this rework. You can implement an abridged or partial catalog for delivery to the mobile device by using the best techniques for retrieval and caching; and, as long as you keep the interface intact, you can extend and port your catalog logic to the device.

Using View Abstraction

Another powerful technique you can apply to your application is view abstraction. Most enterprise applications focus on delivery and consumption of large sets of business information, as well as on completing transactions using that information. Time has shown that the method for presenting this information is best achieved using a few, well-proven user interface components.

Searchable lists, menus, blocks of text, panels, and forms are all common enterprise presentation components, and they generally translate well across platforms and architectures. A menu is a menu no matter what platform you're on. There may be some slight differences on each platform, but the interface needed to describe these concepts is relatively straightforward. Both menus and lists have a collection of items; menus have an optional header or name to further describe them. Forms have text entry fields, check boxes and date fields, with labels and values across the board. So, defining an abstraction using the techniques we've discussed can be accomplished and translation of these abstractions to platform-specific implementations achieved.

iFactr (`www.ifactr.com`) is a mobile enterprise development framework built on top of MonoCross that employs this view abstraction strategy. iFactr enables you to define your cross-platform views using these abstract concepts for deployment to multiple platforms. You define your abstract views once and deploy them with your shared application. The abstract views are compiled and processed at runtime, with your model data and controller logic rendered by the framework into a user experience that is optimized for each of your targeted platforms. An example of an iFactr abstract view is shown in Listing 12-5.

LISTING 12-5: An iFactr abstract view

```
using System;
using System.Collections.Generic;
using System.Linq;
using System.Text;

using iFactr.Core;
using iFactr.Core.Layers;

using MonoCross.Navigation;

namespace CustomerManagement.Views
{
  public class CustomerListView : iView<List<Customer>>, IView, IMXView
  {
    public override void Render()
    {
      iMenu menu = new iMenu();
      menu.Text = "Customers";
      foreach (Customer customer in Model)
      {
        menu.Items.Add(new iItem(Customer. Name));
      }
      Items.Add(menu);
      iApp.Factory.OutputView(this);
    }
  }
}
```

This example uses the `iFactr iView<T>` generic class to create a list of customers. Inside the `Render()` method it uses the iFactr `iMenu` class, which represents a simple menu of items. The `List<Customer>` model is then enumerated, and the menu built from the information contained there. Finally, the menu is added to the view's items collection, and a call is made to the iFactr `iApp .Factory`, where the view is interpreted and outputted for the appropriate platform target.

iFactr offers a powerful view abstraction mechanism that greatly reduces development and maintenance of cross-platform views that are easily represented in conventional enterprise controls and presentations. iFactr offers a robust suite of abstract view concepts that makes cross-platform development rapid and simple.

Using a Mixed-View Model

Because iFactr views are built on top of MonoCross, they are fully compatible with MonoCross views and you can use them with one another. The code in Listing 12-6 shows an example of this technique.

LISTING 12-6: Using mixed model views

```
using System;
using System.Collections.Generic;
using System.Linq;
```

```
using System.Text;
using System.Text.RegularExpressions;

using MonoCross.Navigation;
using MonoCross.Console;

using iFactr.Console;

namespace CustomerManagement.Console
{
  class Program
  {
    static void Main(string[] args)
    {
      // initialize container
      MXConsoleContainer.Initialize(new CustomerManagement.App());

      // initialize factory
      ConsoleFactory.Initialize();

      // initialize views
      MXConsoleContainer.AddView<List<Customer>>(
                         new CustomerManagement.Views.CustomerListView(),
                         ViewPerspective.Read);
      MXConsoleContainer.AddView<Customer>(
                         new Views.CustomerView(),
                         ViewPerspective.Default);
      MXConsoleContainer.AddView<Book>(
                         new Views.CustomerEdit(),
                         ViewPerspective.Update);

      // navigate to first view
      MXConsoleContainer.Navigate(null, MXApplication.Instance.NavigateOnLoad);
    }
  }
}
```

The highlighted code in Listing 12-6 shows the mixed view usage in a MonoCross application. The first step is to initialize the iFactr factory for the targeted platform. In this case, you deploy to the simple Windows console target, so the call to `ConsoleFactory.Initialize()` loads the components necessary to translate your abstract view to a console implementation. When that completes, you need to register only your abstract view as you would any MonoCross view by calling the `AddView<T>()` method of the container. Listing 12-6 places an instance of your abstract `CustomerListView` from Listing 12-5 into the view map for your initial view, while using the platform specific defined in your MonoCross console container project for the subsequent views.

This mixed-view approach empowers developers to develop cross-platform applications that take advantage of the power of iFactr view abstraction where it can be best applied, while maintaining the flexibility of platform-specific MonoCross views when a richer user experience is needed. In large cross-platform enterprise applications, this can translate into a huge savings in development cost and time to market because abstract views need to be written only once and can be shared across platforms.

SUMMARY

In this chapter, you learned how to deploy your application to the desktop, the enterprise web, and to the cloud. You also learned how to design and build your applications in a cross-platform manner, and you saw how designing in MonoCross can enable you to future-proof your applications. You learned how to code your applications to optimize reuse. By layering your applications through implementing loosely-coupled encapsulation you can increase your code's portability across platforms. Finally you began to explore the power of view abstraction and mixed model views as a technique for sharing even more of your code on multiple devices.

As you move on to new projects and new applications, keep in mind the principles outlined in this book. The mobile landscape is changing every day, and the demand for cross-platform development is continuing to grow. Continue to look for opportunities to apply the knowledge you now possess to change the way your enterprise develops software.

INDEX

B

C

D

E

I

J

K

L

M

N

O

P

Q

R

S

T

U

V

W

X

Y

Z

Try Safari Books Online FREE for 15 days + 15% off for up to 12 Months*

Read this book for free online—along with thousands of others—with this 15-day trial offer.

With Safari Books Online, you can experience searchable, unlimited access to thousands of technology, digital media and professional development books and videos from dozens of leading publishers. With one low monthly or yearly subscription price, you get:

- Access to hundreds of expert-led instructional videos on today's hottest topics.
- Sample code to help accelerate a wide variety of software projects
- Robust organizing features including favorites, highlights, tags, notes, mash-ups and more
- Mobile access using any device with a browser
- Rough Cuts pre-published manuscripts

START YOUR FREE TRIAL TODAY!

Visit **www.safaribooksonline.com/wrox31** to get started.

*Available to new subscribers only. Discount applies to the Safari Library and is valid for first 12 consecutive monthly billing cycles. Safari Library is not available in all countries.

An Imprint of WILEY
Now you know.